"All men's thoughts have been
shaped by Homer from the beginning."

The words of Xenophanes are still applicable.
The *Iliad,* composed around 750 B.C. by the
blind, wandering poet, Homer, has not only
shaped the directions of Western thought,
it has also proven a constant inspiration to
artists who continue to take, in Aeschylus'
phrase, "slices from the great banquet of
Homer."

Here, in a completely new prose translation
by Alston Chase and William Perry, Jr., the
strength, lucidity, and wonder of Homer is
brought to the modern reader. This *Iliad* is, as
Dudley Fitts said in *The New York Times,*
"classical translation at its rare best . . ."

To implement the reader's entry into the
world of Homer, this amplified edition contains
an illuminating essay, "Troy: The Bible of
Ancient Greece," by historian Herbert J. Muller,
a discussion by the translators of the art and
structure of the *Iliad,* and an extensive and
useful glossary of names, places, and epithets.

THE ILIAD
HOMER

Translated by
ALSTON HURD CHASE
and
WILLIAM G. PERRY, JR.

With a selection,
"Troy: The Bible of Greece" by
HERBERT J. MULLER

THE ILIAD

*A Bantam Book / published by arrangement with
Little, Brown & Company, Inc.
in association with The Atlantic Monthly Press*

Bantam Classic edition published September 1960

2nd printing ... November 1961	6th printing .... July 1965
3rd printing .... February 1963	7th printing ... December 1965
4th printing ...... August 1963	8th printing ..... October 1967
5th printing ..... January 1964	9th printing ...... August 1968

*10th printing......December 1969
Bantam edition published February 1972*

12th printing

*Bantam Books are published by Bantam Books, Inc., a National
General company. Its trade-mark, consisting of the words "Bantam
Books" and the portrayal of a bantam, is registered in the United
States Patent Office and in other countries. Marca Registrada.
Bantam Books, Inc., 666 Fifth Avenue, New York, N.Y. 10019.*

PRINTED IN THE UNITED STATES OF AMERICA

TO HELEN

TROY: THE BIBLE OF GREECE

by Herbert J. Muller

"I BEGIN the real history of Greece," said Grote in the Preface to his monumental history, "with their first recorded Olympiad, or 776 B.C." For earlier times, he explained, there was only the testimony of such legends as the Trojan War, and "in the eyes of modern enquiry" it would be "essentially unphilosophical" to confound these legends with real history. He wrote this in 1846, when scholars were generally agreed that Homer's fabled Troy was only a fable. And they had good reason for their distrust of legends. The Trojan War as pictured in the *Iliad* was, after all, a preposterous affair, even apart from the constant intrusion of childish gods—heavenly playboys—and from the great battles in which armies served as a kind of chorus for combats between a few boastful heroes. The Persians pointed out to Herodotus the absurdity of all this fuss over "a single Spartan girl." He himself doubted that Helen could have been in Troy; the Trojans would surely have had the sense to give her up rather than endure all the hardships of a war that lasted for ten years.

Yet the Greeks never doubted the historic actuality of Troy or of this war; and by now scholars have come around to agreeing with them. Today anyone may see the site for himself. A philosophical historian may then appreciate a further irony about the place of legends in "real history." The truth is that the imaginative—or even imaginary—Troy of Homer is historically much more important than the real one.

We owe the real one to the fabulous exploits of Heinrich Schliemann, one of the great pioneers of archaeology in the last century. Schliemann's own story has become a popular legend: how he was inspired by a schoolboy passion for Homer; how when only eight years old he resolved to find the great walls of Troy, or Ilios, which he was sure must still exist; how he devoted his remarkable abilities to making a fortune in business, in the cause of proving Homer's veracity;

1

and how he retired, about 1870, to begin his search for the
"golden city." Scholars who were still inclined to believe
in Troy generally agreed that its probable location was a
place called Bunar Bashi, on a high cliff—the most picturesque
spot in the region. Schliemann, sticking to the clues in the
Iliad, settled on a commonplace hillock by the Turkish village
of Hisarlik, a few miles inland from the entrance to the
Dardanelles. Here, sure enough, he found his golden city.
He found, indeed, a series of Troys in layers—nine of them,
by a later count; but in one near the bottom, a settlement
that had been destroyed by a great conflagration, he was
thrilled to hit upon a hoard of thousands of gold objects
that he identified at King Priam's treasure. Schliemann then
had the same fantastic success when he excavated Mycenae
in Greece, the capital of King Agamemnon. Here again he
was seeking to vindicate Homer, who had described Mycenae
as " a well-built city, abounding in gold"; and again he hit
upon just such a city, with another hoard of golden treasures.

Since then the story has grown more fantastic. We now
know that the golden city Schliemann found at Troy was more
than a thousand years older than Homer's Troy; he unwittingly dug right through the city he was looking for.
Likewise at Mycenae he went through Homer's city, finding
his treasure in a much older settlement. Eventually realizing
his mistake, Schliemann returned to the search for the great
walls of Homer's Troy. He never had the satisfaction of con-
templating them himself, but shortly after his death they were
found by his assistant Dörpfeld, who identified them as Troy
VI (the sixth city up from the bottom). Then, in the 1930's
an American expedition led by Carl Blegen spent seven more
seasons on this mound, excavating systematically in the
modern manner, layer by layer. They broke down the nine
cities into a finer series of sublevels, marking distinct periods
of resettlement or rebuilding within each of the nine major
periods. They made out forty-six successive Troys, going back
to about the year 3000 B.C. Homer's city is now known as
Troy VIIa.

An uninitiated pilgrim will be disappointed by the ruins
of Troy. They are not at all spectacular, consisting of the
usual jumble of foundations and litter of stone, and including
no monuments from Homer's city. Most imposing are the
remains of the fortification wall of Troy II, with a ramp leading to it, and the exceptionally well-built walls of Troy VI,
but it takes a specialist to appreciate these. And none of the

historic Troys was so splendid as the Troy that Homer built. His had broad avenues, temples to Athena and Apollo, and royal palaces with sixty chambers or more; it was defended by a "thousand tribes" of warriors. The actual Troy was a five-acre lot, it had no such temples or great palaces, and it was hardly a real city at all—it was a fortress, which at most could hold a few thousand men. The fabled landscape is on the same small scale, like so much in the classical world. The Scamander River is a mud creek, the Simois a mere trickle of a brook. The "vast Hellespont" under the dominion of King Priam is an ordinary channel some forty miles long.

The Greeks themselves made no effort to unearth the monuments of their revered ancestors. They too were uncertain about the location of Troy; Strabo, among others, rejected the site of Hisarlik where the Romans had rebuilt Novum Ilium (Troy IX). But while they speculated, it apparently never occurred to them to dig up the site, or Mycenae either. Meanwhile they had used the walls and buildings of Troy as stone quarries, just as Turkish peasants were to use their own temples. The still more pious Romans, who believed that the Trojan hero Aeneas was the father of their race, were still more incurious. They neither speculated nor dug; or when they had to dig, to lay the foundations of their buildings, they paid no attention to the ancient walls they ran across. One reason why Schliemann missed Homer's Troy was that he naturally concentrated on the central part of the mound, and this part had been leveled by the Greeks and Romans to build their temples to Athena, the patron goddess of Troy. They unwittingly destroyed most of the city they were commemorating by their temples.

Of the earlier Troys they knew nothing of course, nor did Homer. Although he would scarcely have been interested in most of them, their history was in some respects appropriate. Troy I was a royal stronghold, setting the pattern. Troy II, where Schliemann found his treasures, was by far the strongest and wealthiest of the early settlements; its artisans did astonishingly fine work for their royal master, considering its remoteness from the centers of civilization. After it was destroyed by fire, toward the end of the third millennium, the site was occupied by relatively poor, undistinguished villages. The inhabitants of Troy III in particular were a remarkably dirty, stupid people, who left their refuse and garbage on the floors of their homes until the stench became unbearable, or locomotion difficult; then they covered the filth with a new earth floor, and so in time were forced to raise the roof. But in general life remained much the same in the first five Troys over a period of a thousand years.

With Troy VI, however, came a sharp break. Early in the second millennium a new people moved in, bringing a wholly different culture. Among other things they introduced the horse—the famous horses of Troy that were coveted by Homer's Achaeans. Since there are no signs of devastation in Troy V, and some local artifacts continued in use, Blegen permits the speculation that the simple inhabitants were so overawed by the "terrifying exotic steeds" of the invaders that they submitted tamely, and were allowed to remain as serfs or servants. In any event, the newcomers settled down and soon grew rich. Fine builders, they made over the site into an exceptionally strong, handsome citadel. Troy VI flourished behind its great walls for some five hundred years, until destroyed by an earthquake shortly after 1300 B.C. Its culture persisted through the early phases of Troy VII, the city of Homer's Trojans; they used its walls, which had stood up under the earthquake. Historically, Troy VI was the greatest of them all.

Presumably Homer knew nothing about it either. He may have preserved a dim memory of it in the legend that Heracles had sacked it when refused the horses promised by Laomedon, father of King Priam, but he was certainly not well acquainted with its culture. Although he gave King Priam an Oriental cast by endowing him with a harem, he represented the Trojans as worshiping the same gods and having substantially the same culture as the Greeks, whereas the excavations show that they had different cults and customs. Nevertheless with Troy VI we definitely enter the Greek world. The pottery of its founders indicates that they were related to the early Greeks, who entered Greece at about the same time (possibly by way of the Dardanelles). While the Trojans went on to develop a distinctive culture in Asia Minor, they maintained the local tradition of trading chiefly wth the Aegean area rather than with central Anatolia, now dominated by the Hittites. No unmistakably Hittite artifacts have been found on the site. In particular the Trojans imported a great deal of Mycenaean pottery. And these Mycenaeans were Homer's Achaeans.

The Mycenaeans take us to the brilliant, gay, gracious Minoan civilization of Crete. In the *Odyssey* Homer speaks of King Minos, who ruled from the "great city" of Knossos. This king, who with his sea empire, his labyrinth, and his Minotaur was always a historical figure to the Greeks, was to modern scholars another purely mythical figure—until Sir Arthur Evans paralleled the feats of Schliemann by excavating the magnificent Palace of Knossos, and recovering still another lost civilization. We now know that Homer's Achaeans owed much of their culture to this civilization, and probably were responsible for its fall; the gaiety of the Minoans ceased about 1400, when all their great cities were destroyed. The Achaeans then succeeded to their sea empire, spreading over the Aegean world and developing a far-flung commerce; their mass-produced pottery has been found all over the Near East. They remained warriors, however, living in strongly fortified cities like Mycenae, and given to plundering expeditions. The "Akaiwasha" were among the "Sea Peoples" who raided Egypt shortly before 1200—"fighting to fill their bellies daily," according to the Egyptian scribes. This was just the time that Greek tradition dated the expedition of the Argonauts up the Black Sea and the raids by Heracles on the Amazons and on Troy.

As we approach the Trojan War—still in the realm of conjecture—we come to a more significant puzzle. Whence the wealth and power of Troy? This famous site was only a hillock—it was not a natural stronghold commanding the Troad. Neither was it a port, or a road center, or a natural site for a city. It became an important center just twice in its long history—the periods of Troy II and Troy VI (including the early phase of VII). Why then?

Scholars have answered, unromantically, that Troy was a "robber city" preying on the commerce of the Dardanelles. Ships entering from the Aegean would be forced to tarry here by the strong currents and winds that regularly come down from the Black Sea; the Trojans could then exact tribute from them, as well as payment for water and supplies. Walter Leaf developed an elaborate thesis that Troy also held an annual market fair, where traders from the Aegean met the Black Sea fleet, and that the Trojan War was a commercial war over the domination of the lucrative Black Sea trade; unable to storm or even besiege the stronghold, as other peoples of Asia Minor kept coming to its aid, the Achaeans fought a ten-year guerrilla war, shutting off its trade and gradually bleeding it to death. Other scholars have shot holes in this thesis. But at least it seems clear that Troy VI exploited its command of the entrance to the Dardanelles, whether for plunder or for trade.

In any case, there almost certainly was a Trojan War. We know for a fact that Troy was a rich enough prize, and that it was destroyed at about the time Greek tradition dated the war. If the war was purely mythical, Homer's placing it here would be a strange coincidence, for in his own day Troy was an insignificant village again. And the indulgence of all this conjecture and sentiment may be justified by the historic aftermath. Shortly after the fall of Troy, Mycenaean civilization went into a rapid and apparently ignominious decline as a ruder people, the Dorians, came flooding in from the north. These barbarians were able to sack Mycenae even though it was a much greater natural stronghold than the hillock of Troy. Homer never mentions the Dorians, but his epics presage the end of the Achaeans: few of their heroes returned safely from the Trojan War. It would seem that their victory was a costly one, or possibly no real victory at all. As a result of all this turmoil, however, other Greeks began leaving their homeland and settling along the coast of Asia Minor. The future belonged to these refugees. The supreme historic importance of the Trojan War is the meaning it had for them, and in time for the whole Greek world.

The *Iliad* was not merely a great poem for them. It was a record of their first great national adventure, comparable to the War of Independence in America. While it revealed the internal dissension that was to plague them throughout their history, it symbolized their spiritual unity in an all-Greek crusade. "It is clear," Leaf wrote, "that the Greeks saw in the capture of the Hellespont the critical point of national expansion, the step which brought Greece out of the limits of little local tribes into the atmosphere of the large human world, and opened the career of colonization which made them the creators of modern Europe." By the time of Herodotus they saw in the Trojan War the beginning of the conflict between Asia and Europe, or East and West. Herodotus states that the Persians traced their enmity to the Greeks to this wanton invasion of Asia over the abduction of a mere woman. When Xerxes invaded Greece—with an army that incidentally included contingents of Phrygians, Mysians, Paphlagonians, Lydians (Maeonians), and other peoples listed by Homer as Trojan "allies"—he visited Ilium, before crossing the Hellespont, to pay his respects to the Trojan heroes, and to sacrifice a thousand oxen to the Trojan Athena. Alexander the Great was pleased to agree with the Persians as he toppled their empire, inspired by the belief that he was completing the mission of Homer's Achaeans; he carried with him a copy of the *Iliad*, corrected by Aristotle. He too went straight to the shrine of Ilium after crossing the Hellespont to invade Asia. Plutarch described how he "anointed the pillar on Achilles' tomb with oil and ran around it with his friends, naked, according to the custom, after which he put a crown upon it."

What inspired Alexander was a pure fiction. If we do not know just why the Achaeans attacked Troy, we can be confident that they were not crusaders from the West, carrying the torch for Europe. Homer himself gives no suggestion of a clash of ideals; his Trojans have the same ideals as the Achaeans. Nevertheless he did so inspire Alexander, who was a conscious crusader. He at least had prophetic historical sense when he chose for his scene the Hellespont, to which his Dardanians gave the Dardanelles its name. It became so great a highway between East and West that it has been called the most important channel in the world. Today more monuments along its shores, commemorating the soldiers who died in the Gallipoli campaign during World War I, are a reminder that it was again fought over in our own time.

The fascination of Homer—as of ancient Greece—has its dangers too. In piety let us remember that we are dealing with a man speaking out of a particular culture, not the voice of Nature speaking timeless truth. As traditional poems, full of stock epithets, the epics contain topical materials that we may find trivial or tedious. Gilbert Murray himself once confessed that the *Iliad* has a second-rate subject in "the wrath of Achilles," a "bitter rancor" occasioned by the loss of a captive girl who had been his share of the spoils of war.

It was in some respects a still primitive age. The heroes of the *Iliad* are war lords whose main goals in life are fame and plunder; the chief means to both is killing. One can hardly imagine Achilles living anywhere but on the battlefield. And even a devotee of the comic strips might weary of the endless battles and catalogues of the slain in the *Iliad*.

Yet Homer was unmistakably superior to the world of the *Iliad*, and far from primitive himself. Even in this celebration of the greatest military exploit of the Greeks he does not merely glorify war; at times his heroes express their hatred of this "lamentable war." He reveals his embarrassment over some of their traditional behavior, which was evidently too well known to be suppressed, passing hurriedly over the episodes in which Achilles drags the body of royal Hector around the walls of Troy, and then stretches the body in the dirt to be devoured by dogs. We see Homer himself most clearly in "untraditional" scenes, such as the tender one between Hector and his wife and child, which appear to be the poet's own invention. Hector too—the most sympathetic character in the *Iliad,* even though the champion of the "enemy"—may have been Homer's creation, for he kills no Greek leader except Patroclus, and a traditional hero would normally have a number of eminent victims. In general, the reason why most readers still believe in one Homer is that throughout the *Iliad,* as in the *Odyssey,* is felt the presence of a thoroughly civilized spirit, marked by qualities of humor, compassion, tolerance, breadth, mellowness, and sanity which are rarely found in heroic epics.

The astonishing thing about the first poet to emerge in the Grecian world is his imaginative and intellectual command of his materials. If the *Iliad* is no marvel of artistic form, it will seem marvelous enough to one who has come from the sprawl of the Babylonian Epic of Gilgamesh—a comparable traditional poem, and the product of some thousand years of thought and imagination. We may still echo Aristotle's praise of Homer's skill in mingling narrative and dramatic art, his tact in unifying his poem by concentrating on the wrath of Achilles instead of on the obvious subject of the conquest of Troy. But we can appreciate more than Aristotle could his freedom from Oriental bombast and extravagance. The great hero Gilgamesh proves himself in conflict with monsters in a fabulous world, still primitive in its supernaturalism. Homer's heroes have to contend with the gods but they live and die in a real world, and prove their heroism in facing the sorrows, terrors, and horrors that men actually have to deal with. Essentially there is little nonsense in this celebration of the heroic age of Greece.

The heroic ideal itself is not so naïve and vainglorious as may appear on the surface. In his passion for fame through glorious deeds, the Homeric hero had an ideal of integrity and honor above material comfort or success. If his conception of the good life was not lofty, he was at least "spiritual" in his living faith that the good life mattered more than the long life. In courting death he was more admirable because he had a natural zest for life, and with it nerves. W. H. Auden has said that he "cannot be called brave in our sense because he never feels fear," but actually he often feels it, to the point of panic or despair. Hector was so afraid of Achilles that he ignominiously took to his heels, fleeing three times around the walls of Troy in full sight of his fellow Trojans. Then he met the test of bravery in any sense. He turned to face the dread Achilles, gaining heart as he took his stand; and when his doom was upon him, he stood up to it too.

A more striking proof of Homer's mature artistry is what he was able to make of the traditionally fierce Achilles, and his "second-rate" subject. Achilles is not at all attractive as he sulks while his fellow Greeks are being slaughtered, and he becomes positively repellent in his fury when aroused by the death of his lover-friend Patroclus. We are reminded, however, that he is crazed by grief and long fasting. He knows, too, that he himself is doomed. His goddess-mother had told him that he would live a long, prosperous, comfortable life if he returned to his native land, but was fated to certain death if he stayed to fight at Troy; and he had spurned the life of ease to win his brief glory. Finally he makes amends for his outrages on the body of Hector, in the sublimely simple scene when old King Priam comes to beg him for the body. Still, Achilles remains in character—the scene does not fade out in sweetness and light. He makes no pretense of remorse for the slaying of Hector, instead asking forgiveness of the shade of Patroclus. There is no profit in sorrowing either: man must endure. And meanwhile man must sup.

There is nothing naïve in such simplicity. It is the work of a humane poet who knew and respected his heroes, but also knew and respected much more than they did. For Achilles, Homer provided a tutor, Phoenix, to teach him the arts of speech and try to warn him against the evils of stubbornness, hardheartedness, and violence of temper. Other warriors, such as wise old Nestor, often recall the values of peace and civility, which receive more stress in the mellower *Odyssey*. These naturally include the arts—even Achilles plays a lyre—and in particular poetry, since Homer was a proud minstrel. Altogether, the ideal expressed in the epic as a whole is not simple glory through valor, but *arete*, a word for which there is no equivalent in English but which is usually translated as "excellence." It covers all forms of human excellence—physical, intellectual, artistic, moral; it implies the ideal of wholeness and harmony. Odysseus is the supreme example of *arete:*

a mighty warrior, with the valor and unconquerable soul of
the hero; an athlete who excels at running, boxing, wrestling,
and throwing the discus; a practical man who can skin an ox,
plow a straight furrow, and build his own boats; a civil man,
of fine tact and courtesy; a lover of song, unashamed to be
moved to tears; a ready speaker and a crafty schemer, never at
a loss for words or wiles; a genuinely wise man too, famous
for his understanding mind—in short, a master of all the arts
of peace and war, equal to any civilized occasion.

These values are more convincing because Homer wrested
them from an unflinching pessimism about man's destiny, the
powers beyond his control. The final proof of his sovereign
spirit is his tragic sense of life. As Dio of Prusa noted, he
"praised almost everything" from the fruits of the good earth
to horses and men; his narrative is constantly vivified by his
intense interest in all that man can see, do, and enjoy on
earth; but this very zest for life deepened his sense of mortality,
of the living truth in the commonplaces about the generations
of men that pass like the leaves and forever cease to enjoy. He
offered no easy consolations about a life to come. All the
heroes end in Hades, a ghostly underworld in which there is
nothing to see, do, or enjoy, nothing but shadow, and which to
them was dreadful even though it was not yet lit with hellfire.
On earth meanwhile there was always sorrow, with no clear
justice. The immortal gods dispensed good and evil fortune
with a sovereign unconcern for propriety. It did not help that
they too were subject to Moira, a mysterious, impersonal, in-
exorable Necessity. Morai made Zeus himself forgo his humane impulses. It put the seal of the cosmos on the tragic
reality, that no man can escape his fate.

Greek literature is notorious for such "fatalism." Yet the
upshot in Homer is not fatalistic resignation, much less depair.
While his heroes often talk like fatalists, they seldom act so.
Their talk is conventional piety, or sensible recognition that
men are indeed at the mercy of greater powers. Their action
is a dauntless assertion of their own power, by which they will
win glory and demand full credit for it. When they know they
are doomed, they are still free in spirit. Like Hector, they will
meet death with a final assertion of their unconquerable soul:
Such defiance of death is quite irrational, since fame will do
the hero no good in his grave, and it may still seem unspiritual
to those who look forward to an eternal reward in heaven. In
Homer it nevertheless amounts to a historic declaration of
spiritual independence, from "miracle, mystery, and authority."

Magic, myth, and religion are literally matters of life and death—especially death. Primitive religion generally does not recognize death as natural or normal. Myths often attribute it to some accident, when they do not explain it away or simply deny it. Later religion would more positively deny the reality of death, while philosophy would conjure up elaborate proofs that man is immortal. Homer faced up to the stark reality. He does not explain why men must die: "Do not try to explain death to me," Achilles says to Odysseus in Hades. Homer simply says that death is the law of man's being, that he must learn to accept it—and that he can learn. He teaches the art that is the final lesson of philosophy: how to live well and how to die well.

The heroic personality, not myth or religion, was the inspiration of his work. In a historical view, nothing is more astonishing than the freedom with which Homer treated the myth. Although we cannot be sure how seriously or literally he took the traditional myths, it is at least clear that unlike the Eastern peoples before him and around him he possessed them—he was no longer possessed by them. He took them in his stride, using them unaffectedly for his poetic purposes much as he used the similes he was so fond of.

Freedom is much more than Engels' "consciousness of necessity." The lamentations of Eastern peoples record a keen consciousness of painful necessities. Some end in despair, some in resignation, some in pious acceptance; but all state or imply the utter dependence of man upon the gods. None give dignified expression to a dignified way of life that man can maintain by his own efforts, in defiance of his mortality. Homer was the first to demonstrate the independent power of the human spirit. He alone showed that by facing his inescapable destiny, man might escape his bondage to it.

When Plato grew hostile to poetry, as a mere imitation of mere appearances and an inducement to emotions unbecoming a philosopher, he centered his attack on Homer. Why, he asked rhetorically, had Homer's pupils not handed down to posterity a Homeric way of life? But already he had implied the answer: they had done so. He himself was attacking this way of life. As he went on to say, he wanted to give his own pupils an answer to all the eulogists who declared that Homer was the "educator of Hellas," and that he was "profitable for education." Xenophanes, another who deplored Homer's influence, likewise testified to it. "All men's thoughts have been shaped by Homer from the beginning," he wrote.

Homer himself might well have been surprised, or amused, by his later reputation. It seems safe to assume that his primary aim as a minstrel was entertainment, not education. Yet he would also have been surprised at the idea of pure poetry, composed simply for art's sake or the poet's own sake. As traditional poems composed for traditional purposes, his epics were expressions of national ideals. As a proud minstrel he evidently took for granted that poetry was absolutely good, but also that it was always good for something else. It made life better and men better.

At any rate, Homer unquestionably did become an educator for Hellas. In the classical period his epics were recited by relays of minstrels at the major national festivals. They were a basic course in formal education; we hear of Athenians who knew all of Homer by heart. He was studied more intensively than ever in the later Hellenistic period, when scholars edited his texts and finally, about 150 B.C., gave them their canonical form. Meanwhile his stamp was all over the culture of Hellas. Among his early pupils was Pindar, who consciously sought to educate. Another famous pupil was Herodotus, whose history is a prose epic about the heroic war to preserve Greek independence; he too was fond of praising the deeds of great men, despite his melancholy refrain that the gods seem bent on destroying them merely because they are great. Still other pupils were the tragic poets. Aeschylus described his own plays as "slices from the great banquet of Homer"; Sophocles was called the closest disciple of Homer. Both made tragic drama the heir of the high epic tradition, a means of expressing the national ideals of Athens.

These were somewhat different from Homer's ideals, however, and they bid us pause again over the limitations of his curriculum. His civics was old-fashioned. The heroes are kings and nobles, loosely united in a semifeudal organization under the great King Agamemnon, a feudal overlord. We hear several times that the great king gets his right from the gods; he consults with the lesser chieftains on affairs of state much as Zeus calls a council of the gods on Mt. Olympus. A shadowy popular assembly also makes an appearance on important occasions, but acts merely as a sounding board. As a courtly poet celebrating the great old days, Homer naturally showed little interest in the common people or, for that matter, in political affairs. The Greeks hardly consulted him as they developed their republican *polis* and drew up constitutions. But they never quite outgrew the cult of the hero, the great leader. Later on, Alexander the Great, Homer's star pupil, would restore the kingship that the less cultivated Macedonians had preserved from Homeric times.

At his best Homer had the defects of his virtues, in particular of his distinctive clarity and sureness. As Erich Auerbach pointed out in *Mimesis,* nothing is left unrealized or unexpressed, veiled or shadowed; there are no fleeting glimpses or haunting suggestions. Everything is set in the foreground, bathed in full light, with little sense of perspective either in time or in space. The inner world is as self-contained and free from shadow or lacuna. Character is clearly defined; emotion and motive are simple and completely expressed, with no suggestion of unplumbed depths. Neither does character grow or change; after twenty years of adventure Odysseus returns to Ithaca the same man he left it, just as Helen retains her ageless beauty. In general, the world of Homer is like the beautifully drawn world of Keats' Grecian urn, two-dimensional, unwavering, fixed for all time. It may lead one to brood over why things should be as they are, but what and where and how they are is perfectly clear. No great poet is less hospitable to the hunter of secrets or underlying meanings.

We must therefore qualify the obvious criticism of Homer's politics, or lack of politics. What state, asked Plato in the *Republic,* was ever better governed by his help? The stooge in the dialogue answers truly enough that not even the Homerids pretended that he was a legislator. But at least a people brought up on Homer would not accept the despotism natural to the East, or Plato's own ideal of an anthill state. The epics incidentally contain the seeds of democratic government, as in the popular assembly. The nobles are not aloof from the common life and have no fancy gentility; in war they lead their men in a common action, in peace join them in manual labor. As W. P. Ker observed, Sir Lancelot was horribly distressed when he had to ride in a cart, but in a similar situation Odysseus was not at all embarrassed—he had no doubt built a cart with his own hands. All the leaders owe their prestige to their exploits, not to noble birth or blood. Most important, the kings are not absolute monarchs, nor their subjects slaves. They are expected to govern responsibly, in accordance with "Themis" or law, not by arbitrary command or private whim. Nor are they gods. If in theory they rule by divine right, they do not actually talk or act as if they were divine agents, and are never regarded as themselves divine.

In general, the breadth and sanity of Homer's spirit allowed the Greeks to develop freely, and to continue to revere him as an educator even when they were learning quite different lessons in new schools. Poets and artists were most directly indebted to him, and for much more than specific themes or slices. By his freedom he made the traditional mythology a treasury instead of an intellectual nuisance. For philosophers it became something of a nuisance, while for ordinary Greeks it remained a source of confusion; they were always prone to mistake fable for fact. The great tragic poets wrote as if they knew better. Like Homer, they handled the traditional myths with imaginative independence, to suit their different poetic purposes and express their different religious thought. After denouncing the poets, Plato himself felt free to introduce new myths of his own, in essentially the same spirit as Homer.

Another common name for the Homeric epics is "the Bible of the Greeks." As Herodotus said, Homer was the first to name the Olympian gods and put them in their place, giving them their forms and their functions. Although he did not create them out of nothing, since he was not himself a god, he was in a real sense their author. The glorious inspiration of Greek art, the Olympians were created by it. And also ruined by it, one might add; for we come at once on an anomaly. While the blessed gods became revered all over the Greek world, Homer himself showed less respect for them than he did for his heroes. Often he made fun of them; they are the chief source of comedy in the *Iliad*, and the comedy is sometimes farcical. Hence there is considerable difference of opinion about the glory of Homer's handiwork. Gilbert Murray himself veered between the extremes. In an early work he lamented the incalculable "injury done to the human race" by the invasion of this blasé, mocking spirit into the greatest of poems and highest of concerns. In a later work he concluded that Olympianism was one of the great religious reforms in history, marking the triumph of Hellenism over barbarism.

Homer's Olympians were originally mountain gods of the invaders from the north. As conquerors, they mostly lost what interest in agriculture they may have had, becoming more concerned with fighting and feasting. Zeus, the "Cloud Gatherer," had started as a sky god and was always given to boasting and hurling thunderbolts. The family he collected had more obscure, mixed origins, like the Greeks themselves. Hera, who became his second wife, had been an earth mother; whether she is of Hellenic descent is uncertain. The names of the other goddesses, including the ultra-Greek Athena, are not Greek. That Athena began life as a nature deity may be inferred from the symbols she kept to the end of her life— her owl and her olive branch. Aphrodite and Artemis plainly were sprung from fertility goddesses, and were always especially susceptible to Oriental influences. As for the gods, Poseidon and Apollo are probably Indo-European by name but certainly of mongrel ancestry. Poseidon, the sea god who was somehow the "Earth-shaker," had been a river god and apparently also a horse. Apollo was an earth god, not Greek in origin, who came to have some connection with the sun, though not until after Homer's time did he become the glorious Phoebus Apollo. The chances are that he came from Asia Minor, where he might have picked up the priestesses who delivered his oracles.

Although Homer was probably unfamiliar with most of this, he reflects some of the confusion. The Asiatic connections of Poseidon and Apollo are suggested by the myth that they built the walls of Troy; but whereas Poseidon is bent on destroying the city, Apollo—the chief god of the Ionians—is a champion of the Trojans and the slayer of Achilles. Athena, the most ardent champion of the Achaeans, is nevertheless the patron goddess of Troy. The Scamander is now a river, now a god; when Achilles starts to wade the river he has to fight the raging god. Yet in so doing he expresses his contempt for this god—and here we are led to Homer's handiwork. Homer brought order out of the confusion. He eliminated the fertility daemons, the mother goddesses, and all but the traces of primitive nature worship. He refused admission to Olympus even to Dionysus. He reduced the countless gods to a definite family, with a definite home. Zeus has emerged as the leader of this family, with sovereign powers that the others may resent, but never deny. Apollo and Athena have lost their Asiatic traits and acquired much of the dignity and the radiance that were to make them the most Hellenic of the gods. All the Olympians have clear personalities and clear functions.

Much too clear, indeed; so we are struck at once by their glaring limitations. They are not spiritual gods, but only glorified human beings. Even for mere supermen their behavior is often shockingly undignified, quite apart from all their philandering. They bicker and scold, and then complain that their breakfast has been spoiled; they tell clumsy lies and are caught in them; they fight with men and bawl when they get wounded. They call their father a hard-hearted tyrant; call one another fools and bitches.

Zeus was essentially no more than a feudal overlord, reflecting the aristocratic society of Homer's time. Hence he was both tyrannical and limited in the exercise of his authority over the other gods; like the Greek chieftains, they could disobey or connive against their leader, as well as quarrel among themselves. In their relations with men the Olympians were often as arbitrary as feudal lords dealing with their underlings. While they were generally expected to deal justly, they played favorites and might act on caprice when not out of pique or spite; men were often dismayed but never surprised by their capricious or cruel behavior. They performed little service in return for the attentions they demanded of their worshipers. They assumed no responsibility for the life of nature or the fate of man.

In fact they couldn't. They had not made this world, they could not explain it—they could not answer the first questions put to them by a religious thinker. When the later Greeks groped toward the conception of one god, Zeus might lend his name but could hardly play the role. The pious Aeschylus appealed to "Zeus, whoe'er he be"; the noncommittal Sophocles referred to a "God of many names." Xenophanes gave him up—Zeus would never do for the purely spiritual god he had in mind.

Yet they too represented a clear religious progress. It was something that the gods feasted, laughed, and went to sleep at night, for men did not have to live in constant fear, and might even go abroad in the dark. Homer's world is almost entirely free from black magic, fetish and taboo, demon and monster. The traces of barbarous practice, such as human sacrifice, that survive in his myths only accentuate his emancipation from the heritage of primeval anxiety. His creation of the Olympians in man's own image was actually no degradation of the supernatural, or loss of spirituality. It meant first of all that the gods were no longer brutish or material, no longer identified with snakes or stones. Men could now distinguish between the human and the non-human, and so might realize their humanity—without which there can be no true spirituality. Likewise the shift of the gods from the earth to the heavens meant that men were no longer obsessed with food and phallus, and might cultivate finer possibilities of life.

But the Olympians never had it all their own way in the Greek world, even aside from Moira. Peasants clung to the fertility gods, as well as to prehistoric magic. (Blessed is he, wrote Hesiod, who is "knowing in Birds and not overstepping taboos.") The man in the street honored all the Olympians, but more fervently he worshiped the mystery gods, such as Dionysus, who became increasingly popular even though Homer had banned them from Olympus. Zeus himself was confused with the Cretan Zeus, a mystery god who dwelt in a cave. These earth gods all had a dark, unholy aspect; typically their rites involved the sacrifice of black animals and were celebrated in the evening or the dead of night, whereas the Olympians were honored by the offering of white animals in the morning. Nevertheless the earth gods were more "spiritual" than the heavenly gods in that they enabled communion, an ecstatic transport out of the world and the self.

Jane Harrison accordingly argued that the inadequacy of the Olympians was due not so much to their human shortcomings as to their idealization. Because they were a product of reflection and differentiation, they could not inspire the fervor that comes from a sense of the unity of man, nature, and deity. As they were idealized and transported to their heaven on Olympus they were freed from the woes of mortality —suffering, failure, death—and by the same token were separated from mankind by an impassable gulf. At worst they bred the notion that any effort to bridge this gulf was *hubris,* seeming pitiless in their jealousy of human fame. At best their worshipers could never really commune with them, be at one with them in this life or the next. "It is only a step further," Jane Harrison wrote, "to the conscious philosophy which will deny to God any human frailties, any emotions, any wrath or jealousy, and ultimately any character whatever except dead, unmeaning perfection, incapable of movement or change"—the chill Absolute of Aristotle. But short of this, the Olympians were doomed by the very completeness of their victory over the earthborn daemons, as reflected in the myth of the Gigantomachia; for thereafter they simply lived like lords. "The god like the man who substitutes privilege for function, for duty done, is self-doomed and goes to his own place. 'If any will not work, neither let him eat.'" Although the Olympians were long given enough to eat, out of sentiment or mere habit, real worship went to the hard-working fertility daemons and mystery gods, who did not dwell at ease but kept on the job, serving their people, even dying for them.

The Olympians never authorized a church or a powerful priesthood, a class set above the citizenry. Neither did they authorize scriptures, or any rigid dogmas to impede the advance of thought; "the Bible of the Greeks" was in the Christian sense no Bible at all. Though like all gods the Olympians tended to be conservative in matters of ritual, demanding the proper ceremonial respect, they tolerated critical inquiry and accommodated themselves to new ideals. By such reasonableness they encouraged the effort to live in accordance with reason. Most of all, they encouraged the life of the distinctive Greek *polis*. They were essentially neither earth gods nor sky gods but community gods—champions *against* the forces of nature—who presided over major civic occasions, enjoined civic duties, promoted the civic welfare; instead of private salvation they offered a rich communal life. As gods who were accepted all over the Greek world, the Olympians helped to unite this world in a common consciousness of Hellenism, but they deepened fellow feeling especially by their devotion to the *polis* that every Greek was devoted to.

In this view the subsequent career of the Olympians is neither so incongruous nor so pathetic as may at first appear. On the surface it is simply a matter for irony. After Homer had brought order out of chaos, illustrating the reputed Greek genius for simplicity and harmony, the Greeks reverted to chaos—retaining many ancient deities, adopting many foreign ones, foisting more bastards on the Olympians. The Olympians seem absurdly ineffectual, lost in the crowd—unless we keep in mind that hospitality was one of their chief virtues, and civic patriotism one of their chief concerns. Since this patriotism may be called the living religion of classical Greece, they were of real account while the *polis* was flourishing. When the *polis* lost its independence and self-sufficiency, they lost their vital function. They displayed some resentment at the intrusion of foreign gods, but eventually they retired with becoming dignity, content to dwell at ease again while holding purely honorary positions. The proof of their virtue is that they did not have to be killed.

But the Olympians may also suggest certain disagreeable analogies. Among the masses of Christians, ritual has become as mechanical as the sacrifices once offered to the gods; sacramental communion may give little real sense of union, especially to city men lacking any deep sense of nature. Thoughtful Christians are troubled, as the Greeks were, by traditional practices and beliefs that they wish to honor, in respect for venerable tradition, but cannot really believe in, because of new knowledge and changing ideals. "One reason why it is so hard to please the gods," Jane Harrison noted, "is that it is so hard to know beforehand at what moment they will have outgrown the sort of things which used to please them."

One way of easing this difficulty is by remembering that historically the morality of the gods has seldom been in advance of that of their worshipers. Loftier moral, social ideals have generally been the cause rather than the result of loftier conceptions of deity. So Aeschylus taught Zeus to be just. And so Homer had given the Olympians their first lessons in *arete*.

AN INTRODUCTION TO
THE ILIAD

THE LISTENERS for whom Homer composed the *Iliad* were to hear it over and over again, and those who in later centuries read it at all gained the same familiarity through many readings. For such audiences the *Iliad* was always the greater and the better loved of the two Homeric poems. In modern times, however, since the classics have taken a lesser role in our culture, those who read Homer have time in general to read him only once. At a single reading, the structure and the subtlety that produce the *Iliad's* dramatic power tend to be obscured by its mass, so that readers, and translators with them, have turned away toward the more immediately comprehensible *Odyssey*.

The present revival of interest in the *Iliad* must spring from a variety of causes, perhaps among them our refusal to shun any longer, through romanticism or cynicism, the facts of war. In any case, readers appear to be turning again to this greatest of epics, the earliest and one of the most profound descriptions of the pity and terror, the splendor and the squalor of war and of the nobility and baseness which it calls forth in men and women. But in order to derive from a reading or two something of that profound experience which an understanding of the *Iliad* brought to previous generations, the modern reader needs a translation which should try to interpret it as faithfully as possible in a style appropriate to his own day, and he needs the light which recent criticism has thrown upon the structure and art of the poem.

Of this Translation

Most translations of the *Iliad* have been consciously archaistic—not without good reason, since Homeric Greek was certainly archaic to the ear of Sophocles or Plato, and since attempts to present Homer in modern idiom too easily produce results either comic or flat. But such artificial formality destroys for the modern reader the ease of Homer's tempo. In the present translation we have attempted to find a medium which shall neither lose Homeric rapidity through archaism nor sacrifice Homeric dignity to a slick colloquialism. We have banished the formal "thou" except in addresses to the gods, since it survives today almost solely in the language of ritual; and we have avoided much of the traditional ornateness of epic translation in favor of simpler and more direct transcription of the original, for Homer's heroic epithets and conventional formulae supply quite enough archaic flavor to make the reader aware of the epic style. The real problem has been to convey to the reader through prose the sensation that he is reading a translation of poetry. The mannered prose sentence of traditional translations produces something of this effect, but through embellishment of short cadences it distorts the nature of the original, in which the greatest poetry rises from the sweep of many lines. We have striven to reproduce these longer cadences through the greater rapidity of Homer's peculiar simplicity of speech. We have done this with the hope that when we fail as prose metrists the sense of poetry may still be supported by the vigor of Homer's stride.

We ourselves admire, for the very qualities we have had in mind, George Herbert Palmer's rendering of the *Odyssey*. But imitation has proved impossible, not simply, we believe, because we may lack Palmer's art, but because the *Iliad* is itself markedly different from the *Odyssey* in style. Except for some passages in which it relaxes into the *Odyssey's* more feminine ease and grace, the *Iliad* moves in bone and muscle. Its sentences are passionate rather than romantic, active rather than adventuresome; their dignity is not in the leisure of fiction but in the facing of fact. It has seemed to us that this forcefulness of style is vital not only to the vast action of the *Iliad's* battle setting, but also to the power of the central tragedy, which Homer builds around Achilles' spurning of the supplication of his friends.

Of the Iliad's Art and Structure

One of the striking qualities of Homer's narrative style is that of "simplicity." It is all too easy to suppose that this manner of presentation reflects some sort of primitive naïveté of thought. For example when Homer wishes to begin his story of Achilles' wrath, he says in effect, "To begin at the beginning—it all started when Chryses, a priest, came to the ships to plead for his daughter." But the reader should not be misled by such ingenuousness into supposing that he is listening, in fact, to some childishly simple storyteller. Homer's simplicity is an artistic illusion which conceals his art. The reader will discover in retrospect how effectively this very opening scene of supplication by a minor character strikes the major ethical key of the entire poem. The climactic decision in the *Iliad*, which in Book IX seals the fate of the tragedy, involves Achilles' refusal to accede to the request of his suppliant friends; the dramatic tensions of this terrible refusal are resolved in the final book through Achilles' acceptance of the request of his suppliant enemy. Homer's effect of "simplicity" in his opening scene is therefore more probably the ultimate achievement of a great art than the accidental grace of a childish innocence.

The subtleties of Homer's art have fascinated critics from Aristotle to the present time. During the nineteenth century, to be sure, critical attention was diverted from the art itself by a scholarly debate which failed to determine whether Homer was one person or many, but recent critics have returned with renewed vigor and new methods to the masterpiece itself. For them, "Homer" is simply the creative genius that produced it. Two of these critics, Sheppard and Owen, have produced especially readable and sensitive handbooks * which illuminate the *Iliad's* pattern and dramatic method and provide also a more general insight into the way an artist goes about his work. Sheppard is best read in reminiscence, after one has read the *Iliad* itself; Owen may be read as a companion Book by Book.

We shall not attempt here to duplicate the work of these men. It may be helpful to say something, however, about certain of Homer's conventions and about the scale on which he worked.

1. CONVENTIONS

As the culmination of a great art, the *Iliad* employs the conventions which were traditional in that art. The traditions were developed by "pre-Homeric" bards who sang the various stories of the Trojan legend to petty kings and their people along the eastern coasts of the Aegean Sea centuries after the fall of

* Sheppard, J. T., *The Pattern of the Iliad,* London, Methuen & Co., 1922. Owen, E. T., *The Story of the Iliad,* Toronto, Irwin Clarke & Co., Ltd., 1947.

Troy. They developed a highly conventional style suited to the dactylic hexameter in which they sang.

Much that seems strange or awkward or repetitious to the modern reader arises from these conventions, which were the result partly of the exigencies of meter, partly of long years of purely oral transmission, and partly of religious formalism. They were too firmly established to be given up; indeed, many of them have persisted in epic poetry ever since. Among these conventions are the use of patronymics ("Son of Atreus," etc.) and of genealogies (for which a parallel may be found in the Old Testament); the use of traditional epithets for gods and heroes (ox-eyed, queenly Hera), the exact repetition of messages, the employment of certain fixed narrative phrases ("so he spoke"), and the minute description of certain ceremonies, such as sacrifices.

With all these the poet of the *Iliad* had to work, sometimes more, sometimes less successfully in the eyes of modern readers. But with one convention he proved eminently successful—with the epic simile, in which some action, emotion or scene in the poem is compared with one familiar to his readers. These similes are nearly always apposite, often of great beauty, and always a link between the particular of the action and the universal of human experience. The poet is often so carried away with them that he elaborates his picture far beyond the point of comparison, a liberty which transgresses the conventions of our own day. The reader should even be prepared for Homer to begin a simile with one point of comparison and to emerge with another which has struck his mind as he developed the description. Nor is Homer constrained by disparities which limit our present-day choice of analogies. He can praise a hero by saying that he was inspired "with the courage of a fly," a comparison so jarring to our modern demand for overall sameness that the similarity would never occur to us. From the loftiest to the humblest aspect of human life there is none which he rejects, and he touches all with a profound and exquisite understanding.

Homer exploits another convention with a freedom which jars at first upon our sense of the way stories should be told—the use of external, supernatural intervention in the plot itself. It is not difficult to adjust to Homer's general view of his gods; they perform many functions in the drama, including that of comic relief, which the modern reader can appreciate at sight, and he will feel quickly enough how the irresponsibility and shallowness of the immortals heightens the pathos of the mortal struggle. But when the gods seem to interfere with, and to distort, the outcome of this struggle, the first reaction of the reader will usually be one of intense irritation. The heroes will seem to start nothing without the prompting of the gods and accomplish little without their gratuitous interference. When Aphrodite rescues Paris from his defeat in a fair fight with Menelaus, we are likely to feel disgusted; when in the end Athena frustrates the beloved Hector's defense against Achilles by deceiving him into his death, we are likely to feel furious. In short, this apparently capricious interference by the gods seems in its first impact on the modern reader to detract from the emotional conviction of the tragedy.

It may be helpful to look more closely at the artistic purposes to which Homer puts this curious device. To the audience of his time, ignorant of our psychological jargon, that a god should "put a thought" into somebody's mind was as good and poetic an explanation of the mysteries of motivation as any. In a way, it still is. All we need ask is that the "thought" be in keeping with the character of the person and with the circumstances. To this artistic demand Homer is always loyal. A good example is Agamemnon's dream in Book II. Zeus has promised Thetis that Achilles will be avenged through the defeat of the Achaeans, whom Agamemnon commands, and pursuant of this promise "this seemed to his mind the best plan, to send to Agamemnon a deceitful dream." The point to observe is that the dream is psychologically the very dream which is proper to Agamemnon in the circumstances. He is in a bad position, and the dream offers the solution which his pride would most desire: to defeat the Trojans now, without Achilles' help.

When, however, the gods assist or interfere at the moment of culmination of an act, the artistic purpose goes beyond the metaphorical. When Aphrodite rescues Paris by breaking the strap on his helmet (just the kind of luck irresponsible people like Paris seem to have), the action is of course necessary to the plot. But a *deus ex machina* designed simply to rescue the plot from its difficulties is an ignoble device. The real purpose of the entire sequence is to broaden the personal conflict between Menelaus and Paris so as to involve dramatically all the Trojans through the subsequent breaking of the truce. In other instances Homer has the gods intervene because it was in keeping with the conventional honor of a hero that he should not meet defeat even by a better man, except through outside agency. We see Hector protected by Apollo throughout' the story, and when in the end Zeus weighs the fates of Hector and Achilles, and Hector's fate sinks, we are told: "And Phoebus Apollo left him." There is, in a way, no more poignant line in the *Iliad*. After that we know, and we can accept even the ruthless aid which Athena lends to the already too powerful Achilles as a harmonious part of a deadly destiny.

Homer's conventions, therefore, simply by being different from ours, can obscure on a first reading the direct plainness of style which Matthew Arnold saw in Homer. But they cannot obscure his rapidity and his nobility of manner. Homer moves rapidly largely because he is almost completely free from static description; if he would describe a king's raiment, he pictures the king putting it on. Even the shield of Achilles is described as it is formed beneath Hephaestus' hammer. Homer's ideas are the eternal ideas of all men, arising from their basic emotions of love, hate, fear, and wonder. And he is always noble in manner. He can deal with the humblest activities of men and women with dignity because they are dignified in his eyes by their connection with man in his brief and tragic destiny.

2. LEGEND

The *Iliad* tells a story which begins in the tenth year of the Trojan War with a quarrel between Achilles, the best warrior of the Achaeans (Greeks), and Agamemnon, the chief Achaean leader. The story ends forty-five days later with the funeral of Hector, the mainstay of the Trojan defense. Although Hector's death foreshadows the fall of Troy, the *Iliad* does not complete the history of the Trojan War. Homer, more dramatist than historian, selects from the narrative of the past a single, brief, and tragic sequence.

But the epic is a literary form which can support better than any other the sense of a vast background for its action, and in the *Iliad* Homer exploits the medium fully. In it, as on Achilles' shield, he places the constellations, and the sun, and the earth, and the fates, and all of creation, and he bounds it "by the great might of the Ocean." He reaches out to the outermost limits of time, space, and number and then places the immediate "now" of his action in sharp focus against his vast backdrop.

This effect is lost if, through lack of that familiarity which was common to Homer's listeners, the reader is lost. In a dramatic sense, Homer takes nothing for granted, and a careful study of the poem will reveal that it is dramatically self-contained. Indeed Homer has been accused by the literal-minded of "carelessness" in including in his account of the tenth year of the war events which "should" have occurred in the first. Homer seems to have included whatever events he felt to be dramatically necessary. However he did take for granted in his audience of the eighth century B.C., a familiarity with the setting of his story in the following legend:

Among the many women upon whom Zeus, the ruler of the gods, had once cast his wandering eye was Thetis, one of the fifty daughters of Nereus, a minor sea divinity. But Zeus' passion was quickly extinguished when he learned that it was fated that the son of Thetis should be greater than his father. She was, accordingly, married off to one Peleus, a respectable hero from Thessaly. To their magnificent wedding all the gods were bid, with the single and understandable exception of Eris, goddess of Discord. But Eris came nonetheless, and brought with her a golden apple inscribed TO THE FAIREST, which she cast upon the table at the wedding banquet. Immediately each goddess claimed it for herself, but all other claimants soon retired before the three great divinities, Hera, wife of Zeus and queen of the gods, Athena, goddess of wisdom, and Aphrodite, goddess of love. None of the gods was rash enough to judge between them, so they decided to submit their claims to a handsome, naïve prince, Paris, son of King Priam of Troy, who was tending sheep upon Mount Ida. Before him the goddesses appeared in their naked beauty, but each, not completely confident in her charms, offered Paris a further consideration. Hera promised him power and riches; Athena promised him glory; Aphrodite promised him the most beautiful woman in the world. Paris gave the apple to Aphrodite.

Unhappily, the acknowledged queen of beauty among women, Helen, happened to be already married to Menelaus of Sparta. So furious had been the original rivalry for Helen's hand that her Achaean suitors had taken an oath to abide by her choice and to defend the rights of the man whom she married. So when, with Aphrodite's aid, Paris came to Sparta as guest of Menelaus and ran away to Troy with Helen and all her treasures, Menelaus immediately called upon his former rivals to fulfill their pledge. These, with some reluctance on the part of a few, assembled at Aulis under the leadership of Agamemnon, Menelaus' brother, and set sail for Troy. Besides Agamemnon and Menelaus, the army contained such notable heroes as Achilles, the son of Peleus and Thetis; the huge and valiant Ajax; Diomedes, Tydeus' son, a warrior second only to Achilles; Odysseus, the wiliest of men; and the aged and garrulous Nestor.

Troy, the object of their attack, was immensely rich from the tolls she levied on the Hellespont and was well fortified with beetling walls. Priam, her aged king, was the father of a numerous and valiant progeny. Chief among these was Hector, the leader of the Trojan forces, a man of character and fortitude. Other Trojan heroes were Hector's cousin Aeneas, son of Anchises and Aphrodite, and such warriors as Deiphobus, Glaucus and Sarpedon. From all Asia Minor and Thrace allies poured in to help the Trojan cause.

For nine years the Greeks strove vainly to capture the city. They supported and amused themselves at times by raids upon nearby cities and islands, bringing back booty and women to divide among the various leaders. From one of these raids in the tenth year there fell to Agamemnon's share Chryseis, daughter of Chryses, priest of Apollo. It is at this point that the *Iliad* opens with the attempt of Chryseis' father to ransom her from Agamemnon. The latter's angry refusal causes Apollo to send a plague upon the Greek army, Agamemnon is forced to yield, but in his anger he takes away from Achilles his prize, Briseis. This rouses the wrath of Achilles.

3. DRAMATIC STRUCTURE

The unifying theme of the poem is the story of the Wrath of Achilles. Running in a kind of counterpoint to this theme are two other themes, the war against Troy, and the will of Zeus, who works out his own tragic fulfillment of the "presumptuous prayer" of Thetis that her son be honored by a defeat of the Achaean armies. These three themes are introduced in the first books and continue contrapuntally until they are welded together in the person of Achilles himself as he returns in passion to battle. In this return he works out the destiny to which his wrath led him, settles the fate of Troy, and brings to its close the plan of Zeus. Dramatically, the poem divides into three great acts or movements. The first movement ends with Achilles' refusal to accept either a reasonable apology from Agamemnon or the pleas of his friends (Book IX). The second ends in his grief over the death of his friend Patroclus (Book XVIII) and the last with his restitution of the body of Hector, and its burial (Book XXIV). As a means of keeping clear his position in this vast drama, the reader may wish to refer occasionally to the following outline:

First Movement: Book I * mobilizes both the wrath of Achilles and the intentions of Zeus. In Book II the Achaeans undertake to wage the Trojan War without Achilles, and Homer pauses to list their leaders and to spread upon his spacious backdrop all the lovely names of the lands and cities from which they came. In Book III Homer pits Menelaus against Paris in single combat, pausing again to characterize the major Achaean heroes through Helen's charming conversation with Priam on the walls of Troy. The truce is broken by the Trojans in Book IV and the war becomes general. In Book V the heroic ideal for which Achilles stands is dramatized through the exploits of a warrior named Diomedes, who, though a lesser man, drives back the Trojan host. Threatened by defeat, Hector returns to the city in Book VI to ask that offerings be made to the gods, and as he departs again for battle, he says farewell to his wife Andromache. Hector then, in Book VII, fights a duel with Ajax, the greatest fighter among the Achaeans next to Achilles, and the Achaeans capitalize on a truce to build a defensive wall before their ships. In Book VIII the battle goes against the Achaeans, and the Trojans encamp for the night outside the wall. His hopes at an end, Agamemnon confesses his folly and sends Odysseus, Ajax and Phoenix on the fateful embassy to Achilles in Book IX.

In this first movement Homer presents dramatically all that we need to know; he introduces his themes, characterizes his dramatis personae, illustrates the ethics and the conventions by which they live, involves entire peoples in a tragedy which might otherwise have been a mere "triangle," paints his enormous setting of space and destiny, and allows his central character to become committed to a disastrous choice.

Homer then relaxes his audience with an interlude, Book X.

Second Movement: The second movement, Books XI-XVIII, is slow and premonitory. The battle seesaws as the gods who favor the Achaeans strive to avert Zeus' will and force him to state for the first time clearly just how far he plans to go. Books XI to XV change the defeat of the Achaeans from a fear to a dramatic reality and face Achilles with the results of

* Book I is an *artistic* unit. This is not always true of the other books, for the divisions were not Homer's, being made primarily for the convenience of publishers in a later day. The books have become, however, the *Iliad's* traditional units, and we note them here for ease in reference.

his egocentric insistence upon his honor and his wrath. The great artistic triumph of these books lies in the gradual acceleration of Achilles' involvement, beginning with his mild, spectator's curiosity about the identity of a wounded fighter and ending with his eager participation in the "compromise" which sends his friend Patroclus to battle in his stead. Books XVI through the first half of XVIII bring upon Achilles the calamity which Zeus has foretold: Patroclus is slain by Hector.

Here the poet describes in a second interlude the armor which the gods give to Achilles to clothe him as he goes forth to accomplish his own destiny and that of Troy.

Third Movement: The *Iliad's* three themes, which have so far been contrapuntally arranged, now join in a harmony as Achilles returns to the war. The gods themselves join the battle, and the martial chords rise in a crescendo of slaughter and superhuman strife which ends abruptly in Hector's death (Book XXII). Perhaps the best way to understand the *Iliad* is to consider why Homer did not end the poem here, in the consummation of Achilles' revenge and the evident doom of Troy. Instead of doing so, he pictures Achilles continuing in his wrath, unassuaged, through his futile mutilation of a lifeless corpse and through the lighter diversions of ceremonial (Book XXII), never to find peace until he has accepted an old man's prayer and taken his hand "lest he be fearful in his heart." The Greek poet then ends his epic with the mourning for Hector, the defender of Troy.

We have become accustomed in our time to search in great books for their authors' solutions to the problems of human life and thought. Through the breadth and the intensity of his poetic genius Homer conveys a vivid and poignant realization of certain fundamental problems with which human life is invested. But Homer was an artist rather than a philosopher, and it is perhaps best not to look in his work for "answers." He himself does not appear to have expected them.

The events which followed the *Iliad's* story were familiar to Homer's audience through the legend. The war went on, and soon came the fatal day which Achilles had long foreseen. He was treacherously wounded in the heel with a poisoned arrow by Paris. The city eventually fell through Odysseus' clever devices, and was sacked and burned among scenes of horror. Most of the Trojan men, including Priam, were slain, and the women and children were carried off into slavery. Few of the Greeks returned safely or happily home. Menelaus did take

Helen back to Sparta, where she settled down to a blameless life. But Agamemnon was murdered on his return by his wife Clytemnestra and her lover Aegisthus. Ajax, Oileus' son, was slain by Athena. Odysseus returned to his Penelope only after those ten years of wandering which are the theme of the *Odyssey*.

ACKNOWLEDGMENT

OUR THANKS go to Robert McClay Peet, whose studies of our initial efforts helped to shape and settle the style of the whole work. Among those at Harvard University who aided us, we are especially indebted to Professors James B. Munn and John Huston Finley; among those at Phillips Academy, Andover, to Dudley Fitts, Emory Basford, Walter Gierasch and Ralph Small.

A. H. C.
W. P. G.

THE ILIAD

THE WORLD OF
HOMER'S ILIAD

BOOK I

SING, O GODDESS, of the wrath of Peleus' son Achilles, the deadly wrath that brought upon the Achaeans countless woes and sent many mighty souls of heroes down to the house of Death and made their bodies prey for dogs and all the birds, as the will of Zeus was done, from the day when first the son of Atreus, king of men, and godlike Achilles parted in strife.

Which one of the gods, then, set them to angry quarreling? The son of Leto and Zeus. For in anger at the king he sent a grim plague throughout the army, and the men perished, because the son of Atreus scorned Chryses, the priest, who came to the swift ships of the Achaeans to free his daughter, bearing a boundless ransom and holding in his hands upon a golden staff the garlands of unerring Apollo. He entreated all the Achaeans, but especially the two sons of Atreus, the marshals of the people: "Sons of Atreus, and you other well-greaved Achaeans, may the gods, who have their homes upon Olympus, grant that you sack the city of Priam and go safely home. And may you release my dear child to me and accept these gifts of ransom, reverencing the son of Zeus, unerring Apollo."

Then all the rest of the Achaeans shouted their assent, to honor the priest and take the glorious ransom, but this did not please the heart of Agamemnon, Atreus' son; rather, he sent him rudely off and laid on him a harsh command: "Let me not find you, old man, beside the hollow ships, either lingering now or coming back hereafter, lest the staff and garland of the god avail you not. Her I will not set free. Sooner even shall old age come upon her in my home in Argos, far from her native land, as she paces before the loom and shares my bed. Now go, anger me not, that you may go the safer."

So he spoke, and the old man was afraid and obeyed his command and went in silence by the shore of the resounding sea. When he was far away, the aged man offered many a prayer to lord Apollo, whom fair-haired Leto bore: "Hear me, thou of the silver bow, who dost protect Chryse and hold Cilla and dost rule over Tenedos with might. Sminthian, if ever I roofed for thee a pleasant temple or if ever I burned for thee fat thighs of cattle and of goats, grant me this wish: may the Danaans pay for my tears beneath thy shafts."

So he spoke in prayer, and Phoebus Apollo heard him and came down from the peaks of Olympus angry at heart, his bow and covered quiver on his shoulders. The arrows rattled on the shoulders of the angry god as he sped, and he came like night. Then he sat down far from the ships and sent an arrow toward them; dreadful was the twang of his silver bow. First he shot the mules and the swift dogs, and then he sent a sharp arrow against the men and smote them. And the crowded pyres of the dead burned on, unceasing.

Nine days throughout the camp fell the missiles of the god, and· on the tenth Achilles called the host to an assembly. For the white-armed goddess Hera had put the thought in his heart, since she pitied the Danaans as she saw them dying.

When they were gathered together, Achilles spoke to them: "Son of Atreus, now I think we shall be driven back and shall flee homeward, if indeed we escape from death, if war and plague alike are to destroy the Achaeans. Come, let us ask some prophet or priest or reader of dreams—for a dream, too, comes from Zeus—who might tell why Phoebus Apollo is so angered, whether he finds fault with some vow or offering, if possibly he may be willing to receive the fat of unblemished sheep or goats and ward off from us this plague."

So speaking, he sat down, and before them arose Calchas, Thestor's son, far best of readers of dreams, who knew things present, things to be, and things now past, and had guided the ships of the Achaeans to Ilium through his foresight which Phoebus Apollo gave him. With wise and kindly thought for them he spoke and said: "Achilles, dear to Zeus, you bid me explain the wrath of lord Apollo, the unerring. Therefore I shall speak; but for your part promise and swear to me loyally to protect me both by words and hands, for I expect to anger a man who rules mightily over all the Argives and whom the Achaeans obey. For a king is the mightier when he is angry with a lesser man. If he swallow his wrath on the day itself, still thereafter he nurses a grudge in his heart until he may satisfy it. Tell me if you will protect me."

Swift-footed Achilles answered him and said: "Be of good courage and declare the prophecy you know. For by Apollo, dear to Zeus, to whom you pray, Calchas, when you reveal to the Danaans the oracles of the gods, none of all the Danaans shall lay harsh hands upon you by the hollow ships as long as

I live and look upon the earth, not even though you speak of Agamemnon, who now boasts to be by far the best of the Achaeans."

Then the blameless seer took courage and declared: "He finds no fault with us for vow or offering, but on his priest's account, whom Agamemnon scorned, neither did he free his daughter nor accept the ransom. Because of that the unerring one has sent suffering, and will yet send it until we give back the bright-eyed maiden to her father without price or ransom and take a sacred offering to Chryse. Then might we appease and win him."

So speaking, he sat down. Then before them arose the heroic son of Atreus, wide-ruling Agamemnon, furious; his dark heart was filled with rage and his eyes were like gleaming fire. First he addressed Calchas, with an evil glance: "Prophet of evil, never yet have you spoken a good omen to me. Always your heart loves evil prophecies and never have you spoken one good word, nor ever yet fulfilled one. Now, prophesying among the Danaans, you proclaim that for this cause the unerring one brings woe upon them, namely because I refused to take the splendid ransom for Chryses' maiden daughter, since it is my great desire to keep her in my home. I prefer her, indeed, to Clytemnestra, my wedded wife, since she is inferior to her neither in form nor stature nor in mind nor skill at work. Yet even so I am willing to give her back, if that be better, after all. I had rather the men be safe than that they die. But do you at once prepare for me a prize, that I alone among the Argives be not prizeless, since that is not fitting. For you all see what a prize of mine goes elsewhere."

Then swift-footed, godlike Achilles answered him: "Most noble son of Atreus, greediest of men, how shall the great-hearted Achaeans give you a prize? For we know of no great store of common goods; those things which we took from the sack of cities have been divided, nor is it fitting that the men should gather them again. But do you now surrender her to the god; then we Achaeans shall repay you three and four times over, if ever Zeus grant that we sack the well-walled city of Troy."

Mighty Agamemnon answered him and said: "Seek not thus in your heart to deceive me, brave though you be, godlike Achilles, since you shall not trick nor persuade me. Is it your wish, so that you may keep your prize, that I meanwhile sit tamely lacking mine, and do you bid me give her back? Yet, if the great-hearted Achaeans will give a prize to suit my heart,

one that will serve as well—but if they will not, then I myself
will go and take your prize, or Ajax', or Odysseus', and bear it
off. Angry will he be to whom I come. But we will think of
this hereafter; now let us launch a black ship upon the shining sea, and let us quickly muster in it oarsmen and put in it
an offering, and place on board the fair-cheeked Chryseis herself. Let one counsel-bearing warrior be its captain, Ajax
or Idomeneus or godlike Odysseus or you, son of Peleus, most
terrible of men, that you may offer sacrifice and appease for us
the Warder."

Swift-footed Achilles looked at him scornfully and said:
"Greedy one, clothed in shamelessness, how shall any of the
Achaeans willingly obey your bidding, either to go a journey
or stoutly to fight with men? For I did not come hither to do
battle on account of the Trojan spearmen, since they are by no
means guilty in my eyes. Never have they driven off my cattle
or horses, never wasted the harvest in fertile Phthia, nurse of
men, since in between lie many shadowy mountains and the
resounding sea. No, it was you, utterly shameless, that we
followed hither, to win revenge from the Trojans for Menelaus and for you, dog-face, that you might rejoice. But these
things you neither care for nor consider. You even threaten to
take away my prize yourself, the prize for which I labored
much, and which the sons of the Achaeans gave me. Nor do I
ever receive a prize equal to yours when the Achaeans sack
some fair-lying city of the Trojans. The greater burden of furious war my hands sustain, yet whenever there comes division
of the spoil, your prize is far the greater and I return to the
ships with some small thing, but my own, when I am weary of
war. Now I will go to Phthia, for it is far better to go home
with the curved ships, nor do I intend unhonored to pile up
wealth and riches here for you."

Then Agamemnon, king of men, replied to him: "Flee then,
if your heart so bids you, nor will I beg you to remain for me.
I have others who will honor me; above all, Zeus the counselor.
You are the most hateful to me of Zeus-nurtured kings, for
dear to you always are strife and wars and battles. If you are
very strong, surely it is a god who made you so. Go home with
your ships and your companions and rule over the Myrmidons;
I do not care about you nor am I troubled by your anger. This
warning I will give you: since Phoebus Apollo takes Chryseis
from me, I will send her in my ship with my companions, but
I will go myself and lead to my tent your prize, fair-cheeked
Briseis, that you may know well how much I am your better,

and that any other man may hate to speak as my equal and match himself against me face to face."

So he spoke, and anger arose in Peleus' son. His heart within his shaggy breast pondered two courses—whether, drawing his sharp sword from his thigh, he should disperse the others and slay the son of Atreus, or should quell his wrath and curb his spirit. While he was debating this in heart and mind and was drawing from the sheath his mighty sword, Athena came from heaven. The white-armed Hera sent her, she who loved and cherished in her heart both men alike. She stood behind the son of Peleus and grasped his yellow hair, appearing to him alone, and none of the others saw her. Achilles was amazed and turned about and at once knew Pallas Athena, for her eyes gleamed dreadfully. Addressing her, he spoke winged words: "Why hast thou come here, child of aegis-bearing Zeus? That thou mightest behold the insolence of Agamemnon, Atreus' son? This I will tell thee, and I think it will come to pass. By his overbearing pride he will soon destroy himself."

Then the bright-eyed goddess Athena addressed him: "I came from heaven to check your fury, if possibly you will obey. The white-armed goddess Hera sent me, she who loves and cherishes in her heart both men alike. Come, give up your wrath, draw not your sword in hand, but reproach him with words, even as it shall be hereafter, for thus I prophesy and thus shall it come to pass: some day you shall have thrice as many splendid gifts because of this piece of insolence; restrain yourself and obey us."

Swift-footed Achilles answered her and said: "I must respect your command, O goddess, though very angry at heart. For it is better thus. The gods give ear above all to him who obeys them."

So he spoke, and stayed his heavy hand upon the silver hilt and thrust the great sword back into its sheath, nor did he disobey the command of Athena. And she went toward Olympus to join the other gods in the house of aegis-bearing Zeus.

But the son of Peleus again with harsh words addressed the son of Atreus and still did not abate his wrath: "Sot, dog-eyed, deer-hearted, never has your spirit dared to arm for battle with the host nor to go forth to ambush with the best of the Achaeans. For this seems death to you. No doubt it is far better in the broad camp of the Achaeans to wrest away the prize of him who dares oppose you. A folk-devouring king you are, since you rule over men of no account; otherwise, son of Atreus, this would be your last insolence. But I shall speak out to you and swear a great oath upon it: By this scepter, which shall never put forth leaves and shoots once it has left its stump among the mountains nor shall it bloom again, for the bronze has stripped it of leaves and bark and now the sons of the Achaeans bear it in their hands, the judges, those who guard the laws that come from Zeus—and this shall be for you a mighty oath—truly a longing for Achilles shall some day come to all the sons of the Achaeans, and then, though you be frantic, you shall be able in no way to give aid when many fall in death before man-slaying Hector, and you shall rend your soul in rage within you that you paid no honor to the best of the Achaeans."

So spoke the son of Peleus and hurled the golden-studded scepter to the ground, and he himself sat down; and the son of Atreus faced him raging. Then among them arose Nestor, sweet of speech, the clear-voiced orator of the men of Pylos, from whose tongue the words flowed sweeter than honey. Already two generations of mortal men had passed before him, who were born and reared of old with him in sacred Pylos, and now he ruled among the third. With wise and kindly thought for them, he spoke and said: "Ah, a great sorrow has come upon the land of Achaea. Surely Priam and Priam's sons and the other Trojans would rejoice greatly in heart should they learn the full tale of this strife between you two, who are the leaders of the Danaans in council and in war. Come, listen to me, for you are both younger than I. Long ago I was the comrade of men far better than you and never did they scorn me. Never yet have I seen, nor shall I see, such warriors as Peirithous and Dryas, shepherd of the people, and Caeneus and Exadius and godlike Polyphemus and Theseus, Aegeus' son, like to the immortals. Mightest of men reared on the earth were these, and with the mightiest they fought, the mountain-ranging centaurs, and fiercely they destroyed them. With these men was I companion when I came from Pylos, from a far distant land, for they summoned me themselves. I fought in single combat; with that foe no one of the mortals who are now upon the earth could fight. They listened to my counsels and heeded my word. So do you two heed it, for it is better to heed. Brave though you are, do not deprive him of his maiden, but let her be, as the Achaeans first gave her to him as a prize. Nor do you desire, son of Peleus, to struggle with a king on equal terms, for a sceptered king, to whom Zeus has granted, glory, holds no common honor. Even if you be mighty and a goddess mother bore you, still is he mightier, since he rules over more. You, too, son of Atreus, cease your anger. I beg you, check your rage against Achilles, who for all Achaeans is a mighty bulwark against evil war."

Then mighty Agamemnon answered him and said: "Indeed, old man, you have spoken all these things with justice. But this man would surpass all others; he would rule over all and lord it over all and give orders to all, which I think someone will not obey. Even if the gods who live forever have made him a spearman, do they therefore suffer him to speak reproach?"

Then godlike Achilles interrupted him and answered: "I should be called cowardly and worthless if I yielded to everything you say. Lay these commands on others, give them not to me, for I no longer intend to obey you. I will tell you something else, and do you turn this over in your heart: I will not for the maiden's sake lift a hand in strife with you or any other, since you are taking from me what you gave. But of all the rest that is mine beside my swift, black ship, naught could you seize and take away against my will. Or come and try, so that these men too may know; at once will your dark blood flow about my spear."

So having striven against one another with hostile words, they arose and dismissed the assembly by the ships of the Achaeans. Peleus' son went to his tents and his fair-lined ships with the son of Menoetius and his comrades. But the son of Atreus had a swift ship launched upon the sea and chose twenty oarsmen for it and sent on board an offering for the god and brought the fair-cheeked Chryseis and placed her on the ship. As captain, many-wiled Odysseus went aboard.

These, then, embarked and sailed the watery ways, and the son of Atreus ordered the men to purify themselves. So they purified themselves and cast the defilement into the sea, and they made to Apollo unblemished offerings of bulls and goats by the shore of the barren sea, and the savor, eddying amid the smoke, arose to heaven.

Thus they toiled throughout the camp. But Agamemnon did not cease from the wrath with which he first threatened Achilles. He spoke to Talthybius and Eurybates, who were his heralds and ready servants: "Go to the tent of Achilles, Peleus' son, and take the fair-cheeked Briseis by the hand and bring her here. If he will not give her, then will I myself go with more men and take her, and that shall be the worse for him."

So he spoke, and sent them forth, and he laid on them a harsh command. Unwillingly they went along the shore of the barren sea and came to the tents and ships of the Myrmidons. They found Achilles seated near his tent and his black ship; nor was he glad to see them. The two stood fearful and awe-struck before the king and neither spoke to him nor asked him anything. But he knew their errand in his heart and said: "Wel-come, heralds, messengers of Zeus and men; draw near. For it is not you I blame, but rather Agamemnon, who sent you here for the maiden Briseis. Come, Zeus-born Patroclus, bring out the maid and give her to them to lead away. And do you two be witnesses before the blessed gods and mortal men and be-fore that ruthless king, if ever hereafter there be need of me to ward off shameful ruin from the rest. For indeed he rages in his baneful heart and knows not how to look before and after, that his Achaeans may fight in safety by the ships."

So he spoke, and Patroclus obeyed his dear companion and brought the fair-cheeked Briseis from the tent and gave her to them to lead away. They went back past the ships of the Achaeans and the woman went with them, against her will. Then Achilles went apart from his companions and sat weep-ing upon the shore of the gray sea, looking out across the boundless deep. And stretching out his hands, he offered many a prayer to his dear mother: "Mother, since it was you who bore me, brief though my life may be, honor at least should high-thundering Zeus have granted me. But now he has not honored me in the least. For Atreus' son, wide-ruling Agamem-non, has insulted me. He has taken my prize and holds it, hav-ing wrested it away himself."

So he spoke, weeping, and his queenly mother heard him as she sat in the depths of the sea beside her aged father. Swiftly she rose from the gray sea like a mist and sat down beside him as he wept, and caressed him with her hand and spoke and said to him: "My child, why do you weep? What grief has come upon your heart? Speak, hide nothing in your mind, so that we both may know."

Swift-footed Achilles sighed heavily and said to her: "You know; why should I tell all this to you when you know it al-ready? We went to Thebe, the holy city of Eëtion, and we sacked it and brought all the booty here. The sons of the Achaeans divided the rest fairly among themselves and put aside for Atreus' son fair-cheeked Chryseis. Then Chryses, priest of unerring Apollo, came to the swift ships of the bronze-clad Achaeans to free his daughter, bearing a boundless ransom and holding in his hands upon a golden staff the garlands of unerring Apollo. He entreated all the Achaeans, but especially the two sons of Atreus, the marshals of the people. Then all the rest of the Achaeans shouted their assent, to honor the priest and take the glorious ransom, but this did not please the heart of Agamemnon, Atreus' son; rather, he sent him rudely off and laid on him a harsh command. The old man went away in anger, and Apollo heard him when he prayed, for he was very dear to him, and he sent an evil bolt upon the Argives. Now the people died in swift succession, for the shafts of the god fell everywhere throughout the broad camp of the Achaeans. Then a prophet, well informed, delivered to us the oracle of the unerring one. At once I was the first to urge that we appease the god. Then anger seized the son of Atreus, and straightway he arose and made a threat which has been fulfilled. For the bright-eyed Achaeans are sending the one maiden on a swift ship to Chryse and are bearing gifts to the god, but the heralds have just now departed from my tent taking the other maiden, the daughter of Briseus, whom the sons of the Achaeans gave to me. But do you, if you can, protect your son. Go to Olympus and petition Zeus, if ever you have gladdened his heart by word or deed. For often in my father's hall have I heard you boasting, as you said that alone among the immortals you warded off shameful ruin from the black-clouded son of Cronus when the other Olympians wished to bind him—Hera and Poseidon and Pallas Athena. But you, goddess, went to him and loosed him from his bonds, quickly summoning to high Olympus him of a hundred hands, whom the gods call Briareus but all men Aegaeon—indeed, he was greater in strength than his own father. He sat beside the son of Cronus, exulting in his glory. And the blessed gods took fright and tried no more to fetter Zeus. Reminding him of this, sit by him and clasp his knees, in the hope that he may consent to aid the Trojans and hem the Achaeans about the sterns of their ships along the sea as they are slain, that they may all enjoy their king, and that Atreus' son, wide-ruling Agamemnon, may know his folly in paying no honor to the best of the Achaeans."

Then Thetis, weeping, answered him: "Ah, my child, why did I rear you, accursed in your birth? Would that you might sit tearless and free from sorrow by the ships, since your lot is brief and not for very long. Now you are both swift of doom and wretched beyond all. Therefore, to an evil fate did I bear you in our halls. To speak this word for you to Zeus, who delights in the thunder, I myself will go to snow-capped Olympus, in the hope that he may be persuaded. But do you sit beside the swift ships and nurse your wrath against the Achaeans and withhold entirely from war. For Zeus went yesterday to the Ocean to feast with the blameless Aethiopians, and all the gods went with him. But on the twelfth day he will come again to Olympus and then I will go on your behalf to the bronze-floored house of Zeus, and I will clasp his knees, and I think that I shall persuade him."

So speaking, she departed, and left him there angered at heart because of the fair-girdled woman whom they had taken from him by force, against his will.

Meanwhile, Odysseus was arriving at Chryse with the holy offering. When they had entered the deep harbor, they furled the sail and stowed it in the black ship, and they lowered the mast by the forestays and brought it quickly to its crutch, and rowed her to the anchorage with oars. Out they cast the mooring stones and tied the stern cables, and out they stepped themselves into the surf; out they brought the offering for Apollo, the unerring, and out stepped Chryses' daughter from the ship that fared the sea. Then the many-wiled Odysseus led her to an altar and gave her into the arms of her dear father and addressed him: "Chryses, Agamemnon, king of men, sent me to bring your child to you and to make to Phoebus a holy offering on behalf of the Danaans, that we may appease the lord who but now sent upon the Argives lamentable woes."

So speaking, he gave her into Chryses' arms, and he received his dear child with joy. Quickly they set the sacred offering for the god in due order about the well-built altar. Then they washed their hands and took up the sacred barley, and before them Chryses lifted up his hands and prayed aloud: "Hear me, thou of the silver bow, who dost protect Chryse and holy Cilla and dost rule over Tenedos with might. Truly thou didst hear me when I prayed to thee before, didst honor me, and didst fiercely smite the host of the Achaeans. So now as well grant me this wish. Dispel now from the Danaans the shameful pestilence."

So he spoke in prayer, and Phoebus Apollo heard him. Then, when they had prayed and had sprinkled the sacred barley, they first drew back the heads of the victims and slew and flayed them. The thighs they cut out and wrapped in fat, making two layers, and placed raw meat upon them. The old man burned them on split wood and poured upon them shining wine. And the young men at his side held five-pronged forks in their hands. Then, when the thighs were burned and they had tasted the entrails, they cut up the rest and placed it on spits and roasted it carefully and drew it all off. When they had ceased from their toil and had made the banquet ready, they ate, and no heart lacked due portion of the feast. But when they had put aside desire for food and drink, the youths filled brimming bowls with wine and served to all, having first filled the cups for the libations. So all the day long the sons of the Achaeans appeased the god with song and dance, singing a fair paean in praise of the Warder. And he rejoiced at heart to hear them.

But when the sun set and the twilight came, they lay down by the stern cables of the ship. When the early, rosy-fingered Dawn appeared, they set sail for the broad camp of the Achaeans. The Warder Apollo sent them a following breeze. They set up the mast and spread the white sail; the wind struck squarely upon the sail, and about the stem the blue wave sang aloud as the ship sped on; across the swell she ran, making good her course. When they came to the broad camp of the Achaeans, they drew the black ship out upon the land, high upon the shingle, and placed long props beneath her, and they themselves scattered to their tents and ships.

But the Zeus-born son of Peleus, swift-footed Achilles, sat in anger beside the swift ships. Never did he go to man-ennobling council or to war, but he ate out his heart, abiding there, and longed for the battle cry and war.

When the twelfth dawn after this arose, the gods, who live forever, came all together to Olympus, led by Zeus. Nor did Thetis forget the bidding of her son; she arose from a wave of the sea and early in the morning went up into high heaven and Olympus. She found the far-thundering son of Cronus seated apart from the others on the highest peak of many-ridged Olympus. She sat down beside him and clasped his knees with her left hand, and, touching him beneath the chin with her right, she spoke in supplication to lord Zeus, Cronus' son: "Father, Zeus, if ever by word or deed I have helped you among the immortals, grant me this wish: honor my son, who is brief-fated beyond all others. Yet now Agamemnon, king of men, has insulted him, for he has taken his prize and holds it, having wrested it away himself. But do you avenge him, Olympian Zeus, the counselor. Give might to the Trojans until the Achaeans reverence my son and pay him honor."

Thus she spoke, yet cloud-gathering Zeus did not address

her but sat long in silence. Still Thetis clasped his knees, still clung to him, and once again implored him: "Promise me this in truth and confirm it with your nod, or else deny me, since there is no fear in you, that I may know well how much I am the least in honor among all the gods."

Then, greatly distressed, cloud-gathering Zeus addressed her: "This is a ruinous business, for you would bid me stir up strife with Hera, when she shall taunt me with reproachful words. Even as it is, she always nags at me among the immortal gods and says that in battle I support the Trojans. But do you now go back, lest Hera notice. It shall be my concern to carry out these things. Come now, I will nod to you, that you may trust me. For this is the greatest pledge from me even among the immortals. For I may not take back nor betray nor fail to carry out that pledge to which I nod my confirmation."

So speaking, the son of Cronus nodded with his black brows and the ambrosial locks flowed down from the lord's immortal head, and he made great Olympus tremble.

When they had plotted thus, they parted. She plunged to the deep sea from bright Olympus, and Zeus went to his home. All the gods arose from their seats before their father, nor did any dare abide his coming, but they all stood up to meet him. So he sat down there upon his throne; nor did Hera fail to realize, when she saw him, that silver-footed Thetis, daughter of the old man of the sea, had been taking counsel with him. At once she addressed Zeus, son of Cronus, with reproaches: "Which of the gods was taking counsel with you, deceitful one? Always it is your pleasure to sit apart from me and debate and pass judgment in secret. Never have you dared willingly to tell me what plan you are debating."

The father of gods and men replied to her: "Hera, do not expect to know all my words. For they will be hard for you, even though you be my wife. That which it is suitable for you to hear, no one of gods or men shall learn before you. But that which I wish to consider apart from the gods, of this do you not always ask or question."

Then ox-eyed, queenly Hera answered him: "Most dreadful son of Cronus, what sort of word is this which you have uttered? I have never before asked of you or sought to know too much, but you consider, quite unmolested, what you will. Yet now I fear dreadfully in my heart lest silver-footed Thetis, daughter of the old man of the sea, may have beguiled you. For, early this morning, she sat beside you and clasped your knees. I think you gave her solemn promise by a nod to honor

Achilles and destroy many beside the ships of the Achaeans."

Then cloud-gathering Zeus answered her and said, "Mad one, you are always suspicious, nor do I escape you; yet you shall be unable to do anything; you will be but the further from my heart, and that shall be the worse for you. If it be as you say, such is my pleasure. Sit down in silence and obey my order, lest all the gods who dwell upon Olympus avail you not if I come closer, when once I lay invincible hands upon you."

So he spoke, and ox-eyed, queenly Hera was afraid. She sat down in silence, curbing her heart. The heavenly gods in the house of Zeus were troubled, and Hephaestus, the famed artisan, began to address them, favoring his dear mother, white-armed Hera: "Truly this will be a ruinous business, no longer bearable, if these two strive thus because of mortals and bring wrangling among the gods. There will be no pleasure in our noble banquet, since the worse course prevails. But I advise my mother, who thinks the same herself, to humor my dear father, Zeus, that my father may not again be angry and trouble our feast. If the Olympian lord of lightning wishes to cast us from our seats, for he is mightiest by far—but soothe him yourself with soft words. Then straightway the Olympian will relent toward us."

So he spoke, and, springing up, he placed in his mother's hands the double-handled cup and said to her: "Take heart, Mother, and endure, though grieved, lest dear though you be, I see you struck before my eyes; then, however distressed, I shall be powerless to help you. For the Olympian is hard to counter. Already once before, when I tried to save you, he caught me by the foot and hurled me from his awful threshold. All day I fell, and with the setting sun dropped upon Lemnos, and little was the life still in me. But the Sintians straightway cared for me after my fall."

So he spoke, and the white-armed goddess Hera smiled, and smiling received the cup in her hand from her son. Then going from left to right he poured sweet nectar for the other gods, drawing it from a bowl. And unquenchable laughter arose among the blessed gods as they watched Hephaestus bustling about the hall.

So all the day until the sun had set they feasted, and no heart lacked due portion of the feast, nor of the fair lyre which Apollo held, nor of the Muses, who sang in answer with their lovely voices.

But when the bright light of the sun had set, each of them went home to sleep where lame Hephaestus, the renowned, had by his skillful cunning made for each a house. And Zeus, the Olympian lord of lightning, went to his bed, where of old he used to rest when sweet sleep came upon him. There he went and slept, with Hera of the golden throne beside him

BOOK II

Now THE OTHERS, gods and warrior charioteers, slept all the night, but sweet sleep did not hold Zeus; rather, he was considering in his heart how he might honor Achilles and destroy many men beside the ships of the Achaeans. And to his mind this seemed the best plan to send to Agamemnon, Atreus' son, a deceitful dream. Addressing the dream, he spoke winged words:

"Go forth, deceitful dream, to the swift ships of the Achaeans; enter the tent of Agamemnon, Atreus' son, and tell him everything exactly as I bid you. Tell him to arm the long-haired Achaeans in all haste; for now he might take the wide-wayed city of the Trojans. For the immortals, who have their homes upon Olympus, are no longer of two minds, since Hera has bent them all by her entreaties, and sorrows overhang the Trojans."

So he spoke, and the dream departed when it had heard his bidding. Quickly it came to the swift ships of the Achaeans and went to Agamemnon, Atreus' son. Him it found slumbering in his tent, and ambrosial sleep was shed about him. The dream stood by his head, resembling Nestor, Neleus' son, whom Agamemnon honored most among the elders. In his semblance the divine dream spoke: "You sleep, son of Atreus the warlike tamer of horses. Not all the night should a counsel-bearing hero sleep, one to whom soldiers are committed and upon whom rest so many cares. Now listen to me quickly. I am the messenger of Zeus, who, though far away, yet has great care and pity for you. He bade you arm the long-haired Achaeans in all haste; for now you might take the wide-wayed city of the Trojans. For the immortals, who have their homes upon Olympus, are no longer of two minds, since Hera has bent them all by her entreaties, and from the hands of Zeus sorrows overhang the Trojans. Do you hold this in your heart, and let not forgetfulness overcome you when honeyed sleep shall let you go."

So speaking, it departed, and left him there dreaming in his heart of those things which were not to be. For he thought

49

that he should capture Priam's city that very day, fool that he was, nor did he know what Zeus was scheming. For he was about to lay still further pains and groans on Trojans and on Danaans as well, in mighty battles.

Then Agamemnon awoke from slumber, and the god's voice echoed about him. He sat up and put on a soft tunic, fair and new, and he threw a great cloak about him; upon his shining feet he bound fair sandals and around his shoulders threw his silver-studded sword. Then he grasped his ancestral scepter, indestructible forever, and with it went among the ships of the bronze-clad Achaeans.

Now the divine Dawn went up to high Olympus to tell of day to Zeus and the other immortals. And Agamemnon bade the clear-voiced heralds summon the long-haired Achaeans to assembly. So they gave summons, and the soldiers gathered very quickly.

But first of all he held a council of the great-hearted elders beside the ship of Nestor, the king born in Pylos. When he had called them together, he devised a crafty scheme: "Hear me, my friends. A divine dream came to me in slumber, during the ambrosial night. Most like to noble Nestor was it in appearance, form, and stature. It stood by my head and spoke to me: 'You sleep, son of Atreus the warlike tamer of horses. Not all the night should a counsel-bearing hero sleep, one to whom soldiers are committed and upon whom rest so many cares. Now listen to me quickly. I am the messenger of Zeus, who, though far away, yet has great care and pity for you. He bade you arm the long-haired Achaeans in all haste; for now you might take the wide-wayed city of the Trojans. For the immortals, who have their homes upon Olympus, are no longer of two minds, since Hera has bent them all by her entreaties, and sorrows overhang the Trojans from Zeus. Do you hold this in your heart.' So speaking, it went flying off, and sweet sleep let me go. Come, let us see if we may somehow arm the sons of the Achaeans. But first I will try them with words, as is right, and will bid them flee with the many-oared ships. And do you, from one side and another, restrain them by your words."

So speaking, he sat down, and before them arose Nestor, who was king of sandy Pylos. With wise and kindly thought for them, he spoke and said: "My friends, leaders and counselors of the Argives, if any other of the Achaeans had told of this dream, we could call it false and shun it the more. But now that man has seen it who boasts to be by far the best of the Achaeans. Come, let us see if we may somehow arm the sons of the Achaeans."

So speaking, he began to leave the council. The other scepter-bearing kings arose and obeyed the shepherd of the people, and the men rushed about them. Even as swarms of humming bees pour from some hollow rock in never-ending line and fly in clusters over the flowers of spring, swarming some here, some there, so from the ships and tents along the wide beach marched forth by troops their many tribes to the assembly. Among them flared Rumor, messenger of Zeus, urging them on. So they gathered; the meeting place was in a turmoil, and the earth groaned beneath the men as they sat down, and a din arose. Nine heralds, shouting, strove to silence them, in hope that they might stop their clamor and give ear to the Zeus-nurtured kings. Reluctantly the men sat down and were kept in their seats, their shouting ended. Then up stood mighty Agamemnon, holding his scepter, which Hephaestus toiled to make. Hephaestus gave it to lord Zeus, Cronus' son, then Zeus gave it to the guide, the slayer of Argus, and lord Hermes gave it to Pelops, the driver of horses; then Pelops in turn gave it to Atreus, shepherd of the people, and Atreus, when he died, left it to Thyestes, rich in flocks, and then Thyestes in his turn left it to Agamemnon to carry, that he might rule over many isles and all of Argos. Leaning thereon, he spoke his word among the Argives:

"Friends, Danaan heroes, squires of Ares: great Zeus, Cornus' son, has snared me in ruinous folly, merciless god, for formerly he promised and assured me that I should sack well-walled Ilium and depart, but now he has devised a harsh deception and bids me go inglorious to Argos after losing many men. Such seems to be the pleasure of almighty Zeus, who has humbled the heads of many cities and shall humble more hereafter, for his power is mightiest. This is a shameful story for men to learn, even in times to come, that thus in vain so good and great a host of the Achaeans fought and strove in fruitless war with men less numerous, and the end is not in sight. For if we wished, Achaeans and Trojans both, to swear a solemn oath with sacrifice and both be counted, and the native Trojans were taken one by one and we Achaeans were grouped by tens and chose each squad a man of the Trojans to pour wine, many a squad of ten would lack a servant. So far, I say, do the sons of the Achaeans outnumber the Trojans who live within the city. But there are allies out of many cities, spear-wielding men, who greatly hinder me and will not suffer me to sack the fair-lying citadel of Ilium as I desire. Nine years of great Zeus have passed already, and now the timbers of the ships are rotten and the tackle loose, and our wives and little children sit in our halls and wait. Yet our task is quite unfinished, for the sake of which we came. Come, let us all do as I say: let us flee with our ships to our dear native land; for never shall we capture wide-wayed Troy."

So he spoke, and he stirred the spirit in the breasts of all of them throughout the throng, as many as had not heard his plan. The assembly stirred like the long waves of the deep, of the Icarian Sea, which the East Wind and the South have raised, roaring down upon them from the clouds of Father Zeus. Or as when the West Wind comes and stirs a field of tall grain, swiftly rushing down upon it, and the ears nod before the wind, so stirred their whole assembly. With a shout they rushed for the ships; and from beneath their feet the dust arose and hung above them. They called to each other to seize the ships and drag them to the shining sea, and they cleared the ways for launching. Their shouts went up to heaven as they yearned for home, and they took the props from underneath the ships.

Then to the Argives would have come a return undestined, had not Hera spoken to Athena: "What, Atrytone, child of aegis-bearing Zeus, shall the Argives thus flee homeward across the broad back of the sea to their dear native land? They would leave a boast to Priam and the Trojans, even Argive Helen, for whose sake many of the Achaeans have died at Troy, far from their dear native land. But go now throughout the host of the bronze-clad Achaeans, with your gentle words hold back each man, and do not let them drag their curved ships to the sea."

So she spoke, and the bright-eyed goddess Athena did not disobey her; she went darting down from the peaks of Olympus and quickly came to the swift ships of the Achaeans. Then she found Odysseus, like to Zeus in wisdom, standing there. He had not touched his ship, well-benched and black, for grief had come upon his heart and soul. Standing close by, bright-eyed Athena said: "Zeus-born son of Laertes, Odysseus of many wiles, will you thus throw yourselves into your many-oared ships and take flight homeward to your dear native land? You would leave a boast to Priam and the Trojans, even Argive Helen, for whose sake many Achaeans have died at Troy, far from their dear native land. But go now throughout the host of the Achaeans; with your gentle words hold back each man, and do not let them drag their curved ships to the sea."

So she spoke, and he knew the voice of the goddess as she talked, and he started on the run, throwing aside his cloak—his herald picked it up, Eurybates the Ithacan, who served him. Odysseus went to Agamemnon, Atreus' son, and received from him the ancestral scepter, indestructible forever, and with it went among the ships of the bronze-clad Achaeans.

Any king or noted man he met he held back with soft words, confronting him: "Sir, it is not seemly you should fear like any coward. Come, sit down yourself and make the men as well sit down. For you still have no true knowledge of the mind of Atreus' son. Now he is trying the sons of the Achaeans, but soon he will chastise them. Did we not all hear what he said in council? Let him not in anger harm the sons of the Achaeans. The spirit of Zeus-nurtured kings is proud, and their honor is of Zeus, and Zeus the counselor loves them."

But any man of the people whom he saw or found shouting, him he would beat with the scepter and call out to him: "Fellow, sit still and listen to the words of others who are your betters, whereas you are cowardly and weak and never count for anything in war or council. By no means shall we Achaeans all be kings here, nor is it good to have many rulers. Let there be one ruler, one king, to whom the son of crooked-counseled Cronus has given the scepter and the power to take counsel for his people."

So lording it he went throughout the army. And again they rushed to the assembly from their ships and tents, with such a noise as when a wave of the resounding sea roars on a wide beach and the ocean thunders.

The others sat them down and kept their seats, but Thersites still screamed on alone, the endless talker. His mind was filled with many unruly words with which to strive in rash disorder against kings—words which it seemed to him would raise a laugh among the Argives. He was the ugliest man who came to Ilium. Bandy-legged he was, and lame in one foot, with shoulders bent and rounded over his chest. His head rose to a peak and a sparse down grew upon it. Most hateful was he to Achilles above all, and to Odysseus, for he often nagged them. Now he was shrieking shrill reproaches against noble Agamemnon, with whom, indeed, the Achaeans were utterly disgusted, hating him in their hearts. Now, shouting loudly, he railed at Agamemnon: "Son of Atreus, why are you complaining? What do you lack? Your tents are full of bronze and in your tents are many chosen women whom we Achaeans give you first, whenever we take a city. Do you still want gold, which some one of the horse-taming Trojans shall bring from Ilium as ransom for his son, whom I or another of the Achaeans have bound and led off captive? Or are you seeking some young woman whom you may know in love and keep for yourself apart? It is not right that he who rules should bring the sons of the Achaeans to misfortune. Cowards, wretched fools, women of Achaea, not men, let us sail homeward with our ships and leave him to digest his prizes here in Troy, that he may know whether we are his defense or not. Even now he insulted Achilles, a far better man than he, for he has taken his prize and holds it, having wrested it away himself. But there can be no anger in Achilles' heart; no, he does not care at all. Otherwise, son of Atreus, this would be your last insolence."

So spoke Thersites, railing at Agamemnon, shepherd of the people; Odysseus was quickly at his side, and looking at him grimly, he rebuked him with harsh words: "Thersites, senseless babbler, clear-voiced orator though you be, restrain yourself and desire not alone to strive with kings. For I think no worse man than you exists among all who came to Ilium with the sons of Atreus. Therefore you should not speak with the names of kings upon your lips, nor should you heap reproaches on them nor work for your return. For we do not yet know clearly how these things shall be, whether we sons of the Achaeans shall go home for good or ill. You sit reproaching Agamemnon, Atreus' son, the shepherd of the people, because the Danaan heroes give him very many things, and you speak with railing. But this I tell you—and it shall surely come to pass: if again I find you playing the fool as now, may the head of Odysseus no longer be upon his shoulders, may I no longer be called the father of Telemachus, if I do not take you and strip your very garments off, your cloak and shirt, which hide your nakedness, and send you wailing back to the swift ships, after beating you from the assembly with shameful blows."

So he spoke, and with the scepter beat his back and shoulders. Thesites cringed, and a heavy tear fell from him, and a bloody welt arose upon his back beneath the golden scepter. So he sat down in terror, and in his pain looked foolishly about and wiped away a tear. The rest, though troubled, laughed at him gaily. And glancing at another close beside him, one would say: "Many a good deed has Odysseus done,

offering wise counsel and preparing for war, but now this is by
far the best thing he has done among the Argives when he
checked this impudent slanderer in his talk. Surely not again
will his arrogant spirit urge him to rail reproachfully at
kings."

So spoke the mob; but Odysseus, sacker of cities, stood
holding his scepter. At his side, bright-eyed Athena, in a
herald's shape, bade the men be still, that both the first and
last of the sons of the Achaeans might hear his speech and
give attention to his plan. With wise and kindly thought for
them, he spoke and said: "Son of Atreus, now, my lord, the
Achaeans wish to set you in deepest disgrace before all mortal
men, nor will they fulfill the promise which they made you
while still on their way here from horse-raising Argos—that
you should return only after you had pillaged well-walled
Ilium. For like young boys or widowed women they weep to
one another to go home. And there has been hardship enough
to make a man return discouraged. A man who stays but one
month from his wife with his many-benched ship grows restless, blocked by winter winds and rising seas; but for us this
is the ninth revolving year that we have stayed here. Therefore I do not wonder that the Achaeans fret by the curved
ships. Yet still it is disgraceful to stay long and go back empty.
Endure, my friends, and stay a while, that we may learn if
Calchas prophesies the truth or not. For this we know well
in our hearts, and you can all bear witness, all whom the
fates of death have not borne off. Yesterday, was it, or the
day before, when the ships of the Achaeans were gathering
at Aulis, bearing evil to Priam and the Trojans, and we, beside
a spring, were making unblemished offerings to the immortals
on the sacred altars beneath a fair plane tree, whence the
sparkling water flowed, there appeared a mighty omen. A
serpent, blood-red on the back, a frightful thing, which the
Olympian himself had sent into the light, slipped from beneath the altar and darted toward the plane tree. A sparrow's
young, mere fledglings, were hiding there upon the topmost
bough beneath the leaves. Eight there were, and the mother
who hatched them made the ninth. Then the serpent ate them
as they cheeped piteously, and the mother fluttered about
them, lamenting her dear children. And as she flew shrieking
about, the serpent coiled himself and seized her by the wing.
And when he had eaten the sparrow's young and her as well,
the god who had caused him to appear made him an obvious
omen. For the son of crooked-counseled Cronus turned him

to stone, and we stood and marveled at the wondrous happening. Now when the dread portent broke in upon the offerings to the gods, Calchas spoke at once in prophecy: 'Why are you speechless, long-haired Achaeans? Zeus, the counselor, sent us this great portent, late, late to be fulfilled, the fame of which shall never die. For as this serpent devoured the fledglings and the sparrow herself—eight they were, but the mother who hatched them made the ninth—so many years shall we make war there, but in the tenth we shall take the wide-wayed city.' Thus he spoke. Now all this is being fulfilled. Come now, remain here, all of you, well-greaved Achaeans, until we take the great city of Priam."

So he spoke, and the Argives gave a mighty shout and dreadfully did the ships re-echo round about to the cries of the Achaeans as they cheered the speech of glorious Odysseus. Then to them spoke Nestor, the Gerenian horseman: "Strange it is; you hold assembly like thoughtless children who have no care for deeds of war. What will become of our compacts and our oaths? To the fire with the counsels and the plans of men, their pure libations and the pledges in which we put our trust! Fruitlessly do we contend in words, nor are we able to find any remedy, though we have been here long. Son of Atreus, do you, still holding as before a will unshaken, lead the Argives into mighty combat, and let those perish, the one or two among the Argives who take their own counsel—yet success shall not be theirs—to go first to Argos before learning whether the promise of aegis-bearing Zeus be false or not. For I say that the mighty son of Cronus nodded his assurance on that day when the Argives sailed in the swift ships, bearing death and doom to the Trojans. For he lightened on the right, giving a fair omen. Let no one, therefore, be eager to go home before each has lain with some Trojan's wife and has avenged himself for his cares and groans for Helen's sake. And if any be very eager to go home, let him seize his ship, well-benched and black, that he may meet with death and fate before the rest. Come, my lord, consider well and heed another. For the word I utter shall not be despised. Marshal the men by tribes, by clans, Agamemnon, that clan may help clan, and tribe may help tribe. If you do this and the Achaeans obey you, you will then know which of the leaders and which of the men are cowardly, for they will fight by themselves. And you will know whether you shall not sack the city through the will of heaven or through men's cowardice and ignorance of war."

Mighty Agamemnon answered him and said: "Truly once

more, old man, you have bested the sons of the Achaeans in counsel. Father Zeus and Athena and Apollo, would that I had of the Achaeans ten such counselors! Then the city of lord Priam would soon fall, captured and laid waste beneath our hands. But the son of Cronus, aegis-bearing Zeus, has laid woe upon me, casting me among vain quarrels and contentions. For indeed Achilles and I fought over a woman with hostile words, and I was the first to grow angry. But if ever we can be of one mind, then no longer will there be for the Trojans any putting off of doom, not even for a little. But now go to your meal, that we may join battle. Let every man whet well his spear and well adjust his shield. Let each feed well his swift-footed horses. Let each look carefully to his chariot and take good thought of war, that all the day long we may prove ourselves in hateful strife. For there shall be no break for rest, not even for a little, until night comes and parts the fury of men. A man's belt shall sweat upon his chest, the belt of his covering shield, and his hand shall grow weary upon the spear and his horse shall sweat, dragging the well-polished chariot. But whomsoever I shall see desirous of remaining apart from battle beside the curved ships, there shall be no hope for him then to escape the dogs and birds."

So he spoke, and the Argives gave a mighty shout, as when a wave upon some lofty headland, stirred by the South Wind's coming, roars on a jutting cliff, which the waves never leave, whatever wind may blow, from here or there. The men stood up and rushed in all directions to their ships, and, lighting fires before their tents, they took their meal. And each sacrificed to some one of the eternal gods, praying to escape death and the mill of Ares. But Agamemnon, king of men, made offering of a bull, a fat one, five years old, to Cronus' mighty son. He invited the best of the elders of all the Achaeans, Nestor first, and lord Idomeneus, and then the two Ajaxes and Tydeus' son, and, as the sixth, Odysseus, like to Zeus in wisdom. Menelaus of the mighty war cry came self-invited, for he knew in his heart how his brother was troubled. They stood about the bull and held up the sacred barley, and mighty Agamemnon spoke in prayer on their behalf: "Zeus, most glorious, most great, dark-clouded dweller on high, may the sun not set or the twilight come before I throw headlong the blackened beams of Priam's hall and burn its doors with hostile fire and split on Hector's breast his tunic, ripped by bronze. And prostrate in the dust in crowds about him may his comrades bite the earth."

So he spoke, but not yet did the son of Cronus grant his prayer. Instead, he accepted the sacrifice yet increased their wretched toil. Then, when they had prayed and had sprinkled the sacred barley, they first drew back the head of the victim and slew and flayed him. The thighs they cut out and wrapped in fat, making two layers, and placed raw meat upon them. These they burned upon split, leafless wood, and having spitted the entrails, they held them over the fire. Then, when the thighs were burned and they had tasted of the entrails, they cut up the rest and placed it on spits and roasted it carefully and drew it all off. When they had ceased from their toil and had made the banquet ready, they ate, and no heart lacked due portion of the feast. But when they had put aside desire for food and drink, Nestor, the Gerenian horseman, began to address them:

"Most glorious son of Atreus, Agamemnon, king of men, let us talk here no longer, nor any longer put off the work which god gives to our hand. Come, let the heralds call and gather the host of the bronze-clad Achaeans among the ships, and let us go thus in a body throughout the broad camp of the Achaeans that we may the more quickly rouse sharp war."

So he spoke, and Agamemnon, king of men, did not fail to heed him. Straightway he bade the clear-voiced heralds call the long-haired Achaeans forth to war. They gave the summons, and the men gathered very quickly. The Zeus-nurtured kings, around Atreus' son, hurried to marshal them, and with them went bright-eyed Athena, holding her glorious aegis, which knows not age nor death. A hundred golden tassels flutter from it, each well-plaited, each worth a hundred oxen. Splendid with this, she rushed through the host of the Achaeans, urging them on. In the heart of each she roused unfailing might for war and strife. To them at once war became sweeter than to return in the hollow ships to their dear native land.

As a destructive fire devours a great wood on a mountain's peaks, and from afar the blaze is seen, so, as they marched, the dazzling glare from multitudinous bronze rose through the sky to heaven.

And as the many flocks of winged fowl, of geese or cranes or long-necked swans, fly here and there upon the Asian meadow, about Caÿster's streams, glorying in their flight as they settle down with cries, and the meadow rings with clamor, so the many tribes of men from ships and tents poured forth upon the plain of the Scamander. Under the feet of men and horses rose the earth's dread echo. They stood by tens of thousands on the flowery meadow of Scamander, numerous as the leaves and flowers of spring.

Like the many swarms of buzzing flies that hover about a herder's farm in springtime when the milk drenches the pails, so many stood the long-haired Achaeans facing the Trojans on the plain, eager to destroy them.

As goatherds easily separate broad herds of goats when they mix at pasture, so the leaders separated the men to this side and to that, that they might go to battle. In their midst was mighty Agamemnon, in eyes and head like Zeus who delights in the thunder, in waist like Ares, in chest like Poséidon. Even as a bull in a herd stands forth from all the rest, for he is pre-eminent among the herded cattle, so did Zeus on that day make Atreus' son stand forth among many, pre-eminent among the heroes.

Tell me now, ye Muses, who have your home upon Olympus, for ye are goddesses and are ever present and know all things, while we hear but rumor and know nothing—who were the leaders and rulers of the Danaans? The common throng I shall not name nor mention, not though I should have ten tongues and ten mouths and an unwearying voice and a heart of bronze within me, unless the Olympian Muses, daughters of aegis-bearing Zeus, should call to mind all those that went to Ilium. Now shall I name the captains of the ships and all the ships together:

The Boeotians' leaders were Peneleos and Leitus and Arcesilaus and Prothoenor and Clonius. These were they who dwelt in Hyria and rocky Aulis and Schoenus and Scolus and Eteonus with its many glens, in Thespeia and Graea and spacious Mycalessus. They dwelt also around Harma and Eilesium and Erythrae, and held Eleon and Hyle and Peteon and Ocalea and Medeon, a goodly city, Copae, Eutresis, and Thisbe with its many doves. They held Coroneia and grassy Haliartus and Plataea, and they dwelt in Glisas. They held Hypothebae, a goodly city, and sacred Onchestus with the glorious grove of Poseidon. They held Arne with its many grapes, and Mideia and holy Nisa and Anthedon on the border. Fifty ships of theirs set sail and in each went a hundred and twenty lads of the Boeotians.

As for those who dwelt in Aspledon and Minyaean Orchomenus, they were led by Ascalaphus and Ialmenus, sons of Ares, whom Astyoche bore in the house of Actor, Azeus' son; bashful maiden, she had gone into the upper chamber. To

Ares she bore them, for he had lain with her in secret. Thirty hollow ships of theirs advanced in order.

Schedius and Epistrophus commanded the Phocians; they were the sons of great-hearted Iphitus, son of Naubolus. These were they who held Cyparissus and rocky Pytho and holy Crisa and Daulis and Panopeus, who dwelt around Anemoreia and Hyampolis, and lived by the bright river Cephisus and held Lilaea by the springs of the Cephisus. Forty black ships followed with them. They marshaled and halted the lines of the Phocians and stood under arms close on the left of the Boeotians.

Swift Ajax, Oileus' son, led the Locrians, the lesser Ajax, by no means so great as Telamon's son, but much the less. For he was short, armed with a breastplate of linen, yet with the spear he surpassed all the Hellenes and the Achaeans. The Locrians dwelt in Cynus and Opoeis and Calliarus and Bessa and Scarphe and lovely Augeiae and Tarphe and Thronium and about the streams of Boagrius. Forty black ships followed him of the Locrians who dwelt beyond holy Euboea.

And the Abantes, breathing might, who dwelt in Euboea, in Chalcis and Eretria and Histiaea, with its many grapes, in Cerinthus by the sea and the steep city of Dios, who held Carystus and who dwelt in Styra—these were led by Elephenor, scion of Ares, Chalcodon's son, chief of the great-hearted Abantes. With him followed the swift, long-haired Abantes, spearmen eager to pierce the armor of the enemy upon their breasts with thrusting spears. With him followed forty black ships.

And those who held Athens, the goodly city, the realm of great-hearted Erechtheus, whom long ago Athena, daughter of Zeus, had reared, but the wheat-giving earth had borne him. And Athena set him down in Athens in her own rich temple. There through all the revolving years the sons of the Athenians worship him with bulls and rams. Their leader was Menestheus, Peteos' son. No man on earth was his equal in the marshaling of horses and of shieldmen. Nestor alone could rival him, for he was older. With him followed fifty black ships.

Ajax from Salamis brought twelve ships. He led his men and stationed them where stood the companies of the Athenians.

And those who held Argos and walled Tiryns, Hermione and Asine, which guard the deep vale, and Troezen and Eïonae and Epidaurus with its vineyards, and those sons of the Achaeans who held Aegina and Mases—these were led by

Diomedes of the mighty war cry and by Sthenelus, the dear
son of far-famed Capaneus. A third went with them, Euryalus,
that godlike mortal, the son of lord Mecisteus, Talaus' son.
Diomedes of the mighty war cry led them all. With him followed eighty black ships.

And those who held Mycenae, the goodly city, and rich
Corinth and goodly Cleonae and who dwelt in Orneiae and
lovely Araethyrea and Sicyon, where first Adrastus ruled;
those who held Hyperesia and steep Gonoessa and Pellene and
who dwelt about Aegium and throughout all Aegialus and
around broad Helice—of their hundred ships mighty Agamemnon, son of Atreus, had command. With him followed by
far the best and most numerous soldiers and among them he
himself put on the flashing bronze, exultant, and he stood
out among all the heroes because he was the mightiest and led
by far the largest army.

And those who held hollow Lacedaemon with its ravines,
and Pharis and Sparta and Messe with its doves, and who
dwelt in Bryseiae and lovely Augeiae, and those who held
Amyclae and Helus, the city by the sea, and those who held
Laas and dwelt round Oetylus—over these Agamemnon's
brother, Menelaus of the mighty war cry, had command—
over sixty ships. These armed themselves apart. He himself
went among them, trusting in their eagerness, urging them to
war. Above all, he desired in his heart to avenge his cares and
groans for Helen's sake.

And those who dwelt in Pylos and lovely Arene and
Thryum by the course of the Alpheus, and in goodly Aepy;
and those who dwelt in Cyparisseis and Amphigeneia and
Pteleos and Helus and Dorium, where the Muses met Thamyris the Thracian and made him cease from song as he came
from Oechalia, from the house of Eurytus the Oechalian, for
he boastingly engaged to win, even though the Muses themselves should sing, the daughters of aegis-bearing Zeus. So
they in anger made him blind and took away as well his wondrous song and caused him to forget his harping. These were
led by the Gerenian horseman Nestor; ninety hollow ships of
his advanced in order.

And those who held Arcadia beneath the sharp peak of
Cyllene, by the tomb of Aepytus where men fight hand to
hand; those who dwelt about Pheneos and Orchomenus, rich
in flocks, and Rhipe and Stratia and wind-swept Enispe, and
who held Tegea and lovely Mantinea, and who held Stym-
phalus and who dwelt in Parrhasia—over these the son of

Ancaeus, mighty Agapenor, had command—over sixty ships, and many men of Arcadia went in each ship, well versed in war. For Atreus' son Agamemnon himself, the king of men, gave them well-benched ships to cross the wine-dark seas, since they have no care for the lore of the sea.

And those who dwelt in Buprasium and bright Elis, all the land bounded by Hyrmine and the border town of Myrsinus and the rock of Olen and Alesium—these had four leaders, followed each by ten swift ships, which many Epeians manned. Amphimachus and Thalpius led them, the one the son of Cteatus and the other of Eurytus, who were Actor's sons.[1] Others mighty Diores, son of Amarynceus, led. The fourth division was led by godlike Polyxenus, son of lord Agasthenes, Augeias' son.

And those who came from Dulichium and the holy isles of Echinae, who dwelt across the sea off Elis, these were led by Meges, Phyleus' son, like to Ares. The horseman Phyleus, dear to Zeus, begot him; he once in anger at his father went to Dulichium. With Meges followed forty black ships.

Now Odysseus led the great-hearted Cephallenians, who held Ithaca and Neritum with its dancing leaves, and those who dwelt in Crocyleia and rough Aegilips, and those who held Zacynthus and dwelt on Samos, and those who held the mainland and dwelt in the lands across the sea. These Odysseus ruled, like to Zeus in wisdom. With him followed twelve red-cheeked vessels.

Thoas, son of Andraemon, led the Aetolians, who dwelt in Pleuron and Olenus and Pylene and Chalcis by the sea and rocky Calydon. For no longer were the sons of great-hearted Oeneus alive, for he himself, and the fair-haired Meleager, had perished. Thoas had been bidden to take full command of the Aetolians. With him followed forty black ships.

Idomeneus, the famous spearman, led the Cretans, who held Cnossus and walled Gortys and Lyctus and gleaming Lycastus and Phaestus and Rhytium, fair-lying cities, and the rest who dwell in hundred-citied Crete. Idomeneus, the famous spearman, led them, with Meriones, like to man-slaying Enyalius. With them followed eighty black ships.

And Tlepolemus, the brave and mighty son of Heracles, led from Rhodes nine ships of the lordly Rhodians, who dwelt in Rhodes, being divided into three groups dwelling in Lindos

---

[1] The Greek actually refers to Amphimachus and Thalpius, but the best sense seems to be that given here.

and Ialysus and gleaming Cameirus. These were led by the
famous spearman Tlepolemus, whom Astyocheia bore to
mighty Heracles. He carried her away from Ephyra, from the
river Selleis, after sacking many cities of Zeus-nurtured heroes.
As soon as Tlepolemus had been reared in the well-built hall,
he straightway killed his father's dear uncle Licymnius, scion
of Ares, who was already growing old. And at once he built
ships and, gathering many men, he ran away to sea, for many
other sons and grandsons of mighty Heracles made threats
against him. Then on his wanderings he came in dire suffering to Rhodes. The island was divided among three tribes and
was beloved by Zeus, who rules both gods and men. And the
son of Cronus poured upon them wondrous wealth.

Nireus brought three fair-lined ships from Syme—Nireus,
the son of Aglaea and lord Charops, Nireus, who was, after
Peleus' blameless son, the handsomest man of all the Danaans
who came to Ilium. But he was weak, and few men followed
him.

And those who held Nisyrus and Crapathus and Casus and
Cos, the city of Eurypylus, and the islands of Calydnae, these
were led by Pheidippus and Antiphus, the two sons of lord
Thessalus, son of Heracles. Thirty hollow ships of theirs advanced in order.

Now as for all those who dwelt in Pelasgian Argos, who
lived in Alos and Alope and Trachis, who held Phthia and
Hellas with its fair women, and who were called Myrmidons
and Hellenes and Achaeans—of their fifty ships Achilles was
commander. But they took no thought of tumultuous war, for
there was none to lead them into line. For the swift-footed,
godlike Achilles lay amid the ships, angered over the fair-
haired maiden Briseis, whom he captured with much trouble
from Lyrnessus when he had sacked Lyrnessus and the walls
of Thebe and had slain Mynes and Epistrophus, fighters
with the spear, the sons of lord Evenus, son of Selepus. For
her he lay grieving, yet soon was he to arise.

And those who held Phylace and flowery Pyrasus, shrine of
Demeter, and Iton, the mother of flocks, and Antron by the
sea and meadowy Pteleos—these were led by warlike Protesilaus, while he lived. But then already the black earth held him.
His wife, her cheeks torn with grief, and his half-finished home
had been left behind in Phylace. A Dardanian warrior slew
him as he leapt from his ship, by far the first of the Achaeans.
But his men were not leaderless, though they mourned for
their leader. They were marshaled by Podarces, scion of Ares,

son of Iphiclus, rich in flocks, the son of Phylacus. Podarces was own brother of the great-hearted Protesilaus, younger in birth; the warlike hero Protesilaus was at once older and braver. So the men did not lack a leader but they mourned for him who was so brave. With him followed forty black ships.

And those who dwelt in Pherae beside Lake Boebeis, in Boebe and Glaphyrae and well-built Iolchus, were led by Eumelus, the dear son of Admetus, with eleven ships. Alcestis, goddess among women, bore him to Admetus, she who was fairest of face among Pelias' daughters.

And those who dwelt in Methone and Thaumacia, and held Meliboea and rough Olizon, were led by Philoctetes, well skilled with the bow, in seven ships. In each embarked fifty oarsmen, well skilled to fight mightily with bows. But Philoctetes lay on an island suffering great pain, on sacred Lemnos where the sons of the Achaeans left him suffering from the bitter wound of a deadly snake. There he lay, grieving in anguish; but soon were the Argives beside the ships to remember lord Philoctetes. Yet even so his men were not leaderless, though they mourned for their leader. But Medon marshaled them, Oileus' bastard son, whom Rhene bore to Oileus, sacker of cities.

And those who held Tricca and rocky Ithome, and who held Oechalia, the city of Oechalian Eurytus, were led by the two sons of Asclepius, the two good physicians Podaleirius and Machaon. Thirty hollow ships of theirs advanced in order.

And those who held Ormenius and the spring of Hypereia, and who held Asterium and the white peaks of Titanus, were led by Eurypylus, Euaemon's glorious son. With him followed forty black ships.

And those who held Argissa and dwelt in Gyrtone and Orthe and the city of Elone and white Oloösson were led by the steadfast warrior Polypoetes, son of Peirithous whom immortal Zeus begot. The famous Hippodameia bore Polypoetes to Peirithous on that day when he took revenge upon the shaggy centaurs whom he drove from Pelium and forced toward the Aethices—not alone, for with him was Leonteus, scion of Ares, the son of high-hearted Coronus, Caeneus' son. With them followed forty black ships.

And Gouneus brought from Cyphus two-and-twenty ships. With him came the Enienes and the steadfast Peraebi who made their homes round wintry Dodona and plied their work round lovely Titaresius, which pours its fair-flowing waters into Peneius, yet mixes not with silver-eddying Peneius but runs on top of it like oil, for it is a branch of the water of Styx, the dreadful oath.

Prothous, Tenthredon's son, led the Magnetes, who dwelt round Peneius and Pelion with its dancing leaves. These swift Prothous led, and with him followed forty black ships.

These were the leaders and rulers of the Danaans. Who of them was far the best, do thou tell me, O Muse—of the men and of the horses who followed Atreus' sons.

The best horses by far were the mares of Pheres' son, those which Eumelus drove, as swift as birds, matched in color, matched in age, and matched to the level in height. Apollo of the silver bow had reared them in Pereia, both of them mares, bearing with them Ares' panic. The best of the men by far was Telamonian Ajax, so long as Achilles was angry, for the latter was much the best, and so too were the horses which bore the blameless son of Peleus. But he lay amid the curved, seafaring ships, angry with Agamemnon, Atreus' son, the shepherd of the people. And Achilles' men along the sea's edge played at hurling the discus and the javelin and shot their bows. And the horses stood each by his chariot munching clover and marsh parsley, and the chariots stood well covered in the leaders' tents. But the men, longing for their leader, wandered here and there throughout the camp and took no part in battle.

The Achaeans advanced as though the whole earth blazed with fire. And the earth groaned beneath them as beneath the anger of Zeus, who delights in thunder, when he scourges the earth about Typhoeus at Arimi, where, they say, is Typhoeus' resting place. So did the earth groan loudly beneath their feet as they went, and very swiftly they advanced across the plain.

But to the Trojans went swift wind-footed Iris, a messenger from aegis-bearing Zeus, with grievous tidings. They, all met together, both young men and old, were holding council at the gates of Priam. And swift-footed Iris stood close by and spoke, likening her voice to that of Priam's son Polites, who, sure of his swift feet, sat as the Trojans' sentinel on the very top of old Aesyetes' tomb, watching for the moment when the Achaeans should start from the ships. Likening herself to him, swift-footed Iris spoke: "Sire, even still do you love fruitless words, as of old, in time of peace. But stubborn war has arisen. Often indeed have I entered the battles of heroes, but never yet have I seen a host so mighty or so great. For they are very like the leaves or the sands, as they march across the plain to the city to do battle. Hector, to you chiefly do I give this order—do as I bid: there are, you know, many allies throughout the great city of Priam, and there is a different tongue for every group of men scattered over the earth. Let each man take command of those he rules, and when he has brought his countrymen to order, let him lead them forth."

So she spoke, and Hector did not fail to recognize the goddess's voice. At once he dismissed the council, and they rushed to arms. All the gates were opened, and the men poured out, both infantry and charioteers, and a great din arose.

Now there is a steep hill before the city, far out upon the plain, standing alone; men call it Batieia, but the immortals, the tomb of fleet Myrine. There, then, did the Trojans and their allies muster.

Priam's son, great Hector of the glancing helmet, led the Trojans. With him the most men, and the best by far, armed themselves with eagerness to ply their spears.

Aeneas, the brave son of Anchises, led the Dardanians, he whom divine Aphrodite bore to Anchises, having lain, goddess with mortal, in the vales of Ida. Aeneas was not alone; with him were the two sons of Antenor, Archelochus and Acamas, well skilled in every form of battle.

Those Trojans who dwelt in Zeleia, on the lowest slope of Ida, rich, drinking the black water of Aesepus, were led by Pandarus, Lycaon's glorious son, to whom Apollo himself had given a bow.

And those who held Adrasteia and the realm of Apaesus, and who held Pityeia and the sharp peak of Tereia, were led by Adrastus and Amphius of the linen breastplate, the two sons of Percosian Merops, who was skilled above all in prophecy, nor was he willing to allow his sons to march to man-destroying war. But they disobeyed him, for the fates of dark death led them.

And those who dwelt round Percote and Practius, and held Sestus and Abydus and shining Arisbe, were led by Asius, son of Hyrtacus, chief of men—Asius, son of Hyrtacus, whom his great sorrel horses brought from Arisbe on the river Selleis.

Hippothoüs led the tribes of Pelasgians, fighters with the spear, who dwelt with him in fertile Larisa. They were led by Hippothoüs and Pylaeus, scion of Ares, the two sons of Pelasgian Lethus, son of Teutamus.

Acamas and heroic Peirous led the Thracians, all whom the strong-flowing Hellespont bounds.

The leader of the Ciconian spearmen was Euphemus, son of Troezenus, Ceas' Zeus-nurtured son.

Pyraechmes led the Paeonians with their crooked bows from far Amydon on the broad-flowing Axius, whose water is the fairest that spreads upon the earth.

Pylaemenes of the shaggy chest led the Paphlagonians from the Eneti, whence come the race of wild mules. They held Cytorus and occupied Sesamon and dwelt in glorious homes by the river Parthenius and Cromna and Aegialus and lofty Erythini.

Odius and Epistrophus commanded the Halizones from far Alybe, where is the birthplace of silver.

Chromis and Ennomus, the augur, led the Mysians, but not even by his auguries could he ward off dark fate. He was felled by the hands of the swift-footed son of Aeacus in the river where he slew other Trojans as well.

Phorcys and the godlike Ascanius led the Phrygians from far Ascania. They were eager to fight in the combat.

The Maeonians were led by Talaemenes' sons Mesthles and Antiphus whom Lake Gygaea bore; they led the Maeonians who were born beneath Tmolus.

Nastes led the Carians of foreign tongue, who held Miletus and the leafy mountain of Phthires and the streams of Meander and the sharp peaks of Mycale. Amphimachus and Nastes led them, Nastes and Amphimachus, Nomion's glorious sons. Nastes went to war wearing gold like a maiden, fool that he was, nor did it ward off sad death for him, for he was slain by the hands of the swift-footed son of Aeacus in the river, and warlike Achilles took the gold.

Sarpedon and blameless Glaucus led the Lycians from far Lycia on the eddying Xanthus.

BOOK III

THEN, WHEN ALL were marshaled with their captains, the Trojans came on like birds, with a clamor and cry like the clamor of cranes that goes across the sky when they flee from winter and endless rain and with clamor fly over the Ocean's stream bearing death and doom to the Pygmies, and with the dawn they make their fierce attack. But the Achaeans came on in silence, breathing might, eager in heart to aid each other.

As when the South Wind has shed mist upon the mountain peaks, a mist unwelcome to shepherds but better than night to the thief, and a man can see only as far as he can throw a stone, so did the cloud of dust arise from their feet as they came on. And very swiftly they advanced across the plain.

And when they came close to one another in their onset, the godlike Alexander stood forth as champion for the Trojans, with a leopard skin upon his shoulders and with his curved bow and his sword. Then, brandishing two bronze-tipped javelins, he challenged all the bravest of the Argives to fight in deadly combat hand to hand.

When, therefore, Menelaus, dear to Ares, caught sight of him advancing with long strides before the host, then, as a lion is glad when he chances on some great carcass, finding in his hunger a horned stag or a wild goat, for he greedily devours it all though swift dogs and lusty huntsmen drive upon him, so was Menelaus glad when his eyes beheld the godlike Alexander, for he thought that he should punish the wrongdoer. Promptly he jumped with his weapons from his chariot to the ground.

When the godlike Alexander saw him appear among the front ranks, he was dismayed at heart and shrank back into the throng of his companions, avoiding his fate. As when in some mountain glen a man sees a serpent and starts back and a trembling takes his knees, and he draws back and pallor fills his cheeks, so did the godlike Alexander in fear of Atreus' son draw back into the host of valiant Trojans.

And Hector, seeing him, reproached him with taunting words: "Vile Paris, fairest in face, woman-mad, seducer, would that you were never born, or else had died unwed. Even thus would I wish it, and it would be far better than so to be a byword, looked at askance by others. Surely the long-haired Achaeans will laugh aloud, for they thought some chief our champion because you have a handsome face, but there is neither force nor courage in your heart. Were you like this when you sailed the deep in the seafaring ships, gathering your trusty comrades, and having met with strangers led off a fair woman from a distant land, the sister-in-law of spearmen, a great woe to your father, to your city, and to all your people, a joy to your enemies but a hanging of the head to you yourself? Could you not then face Menelaus, dear to Ares? You would learn what sort of man he is whose lovely wife you hold. You would find no help in the lyre and the gifts of Aphrodite, in your hair and your beauty, when you lay in the dust. Surely the Trojans are utter cowards, or you would by now have worn a cloak of stone because of all the evil you have done."

And the godlike Alexander said to him: "Hector, since you have reproached me after my deserts and not beyond—for your heart is ever unyielding as an axe which cuts through a beam in the hands of a man who is hewing out a ship's timber skillfully, and it increases the man's power, so fearless is your heart within your breast—do not reproach me with the lovely gifts of golden Aphrodite, for the glorious gifts of the gods may not be cast away, whatever they give of themselves, for of his own will could no man obtain them. But now, if you wish me to fight and do battle, make the rest of the Trojans and all the Achaeans sit down; there between them match me with Menelaus, dear to Ares, to fight for Helen and all the treasure. And whoever wins and proves the better man, let him take all the treasure and the woman and bear them safely home. And may the rest, swearing true oaths of friendship, live on in fertile Troy, and let the Argives sail to horse-rearing Argos and Achaeis with its lovely women."

So he spoke, and Hector rejoiced greatly when he heard his words, and stepping between the lines, he checked the Trojans' companies, grasping the middle of his spear; and they all sat down. But the long-haired Achaeans bent their bows at him and aimed their arrows and showered him with stones. Then Agamemnon, king of men, cried loudly: "Hold, Argives; do not shoot, sons of the Achaeans, for it seems that Hector of the glancing helmet is about to speak."

So he spoke, and they refrained from battle and were

quickly silent. And Hector spoke between the armies: "Hear
from me, Trojans and well-greaved Achaeans, the word of
Alexander, because of whom this strife arose. He proposes that
the other Trojans and all the Achaeans lay down their bright
weapons upon the fertile earth, and that he and Menelaus,
dear to Ares, fight alone, between the lines, for Helen and all
the treasure. And whoever wins and proves the better man, let
him take all the treasure and the woman and bear them safely
home. But let the rest of us swear true oaths of friendship."

So he spoke, and they were all hushed in silence. Then spoke
Menelaus of the mighty war cry: "Now listen to me also, for
to my heart beyond all others sorrow comes. I desire that Argives and Trojans part now in peace, since you have suffered
many ills because of my quarrel and because of what Alexander began. For whichever of us death and fate is appointed,
let him die, and may the rest of you go your ways at once.
Bring two lambs, a white ram and a black ewe, for Earth and
Sun; and we shall bring another for Zeus. And lead hither
mighty Priam, that he may himself take oath since his sons are
insolent and faithless, lest anyone in violence transgress the
oaths of Zeus. For ever are the hearts of the young unstable;
but when an old man is present, he looks before and after, that
the best may be for either side."

So he spoke, and the Achaeans and Trojans alike rejoiced in
the hope that they might cease from wretched war. Their
horses they drew up in ordered ranks, and they themselves
dismounted from the chariots and stripped off their arms.
These they placed in close piles upon the earth and there was
little clear ground left between. Hector sent two heralds to
the city quickly to fetch the lambs and summon Priam. Then
mighty Agamemnon sent Talthybius the herald to the hollow
ships and bade him bring a lamb, nor did he disobey the godlike Agamemnon.

Then Iris went as messenger to white-armed Helen, in the
likeness of her husband's sister, the wife of Antenor's son, her
whom mighty Helicaon, Antenor's son, had married, Laodice,
the loveliest of Priam's daughters. She found Helen in the hall;
she was weaving a great web, purple, of double fold, and in
it she was picturing the many combats of horse-taming Trojans and bronze-clad Achaeans, which they had endured for
her sake at the hands of Ares. Swift-footed Iris stood close to
her and said: "Come here, my dear, that you may see the wondrous deeds of horse-taming Trojans and bronze-clad Achae-

ans, who formerly waged lamentable war against each other on the plain, eager for deadly battle, but who now sit in silence, and war has ceased. They lean upon their shields, and their long spears stand upright beside them. But Alexander and Menelaus, dear to Ares, will fight for you with long spears, and you shall be called the wife of him who conquers."

So speaking, the goddess cast into her heart sweet longing for her former husband and her city and her parents. At once she veiled herself in fair white linen and left her chamber, shedding soft tears—not alone, for with her went two handmaids, Aethra, the daughter of Pittheus, and ox-eyed Clymene. And quickly they came to the place where were the Scaean gates.

There beside Priam and Panthous and Thymoetes and Lampus and Clytius and Hicetaon, scion of Ares, sat Ucalegon and Antenor at the Scaean gates, prudent men both, as elders of the people. Because of age they had now ceased from battle, but they were goodly speakers, like the locusts, which perch on a woodland tree and pour forth their delicate voices. Such were the leaders of the Trojans as they sat upon the wall. When they saw Helen coming toward the wall, they softly spoke among themselves winged words: "There is no cause for anger that the Trojans and well-greaved Achaeans suffer hardship a long time for such a woman. Wonderfully like the immortal goddesses is she in face. But even so, such though she be, let her depart in the ships; let her not be left as a curse to us and our children hereafter."

So they spoke, and Priam called to Helen: "Come here, dear child, and sit beside me, that you may see your former husband, his brothers, and your friends—for it is not you who are to blame in my eyes; indeed, I hold the gods to blame, who brought upon me this lamentable war with the Achaeans—and that you may name for me this huge warrior, whoever this Achaean hero is, so brave and mighty; others, indeed, are taller by a head, but never yet have my eyes beheld one so fair, nor yet so noble, for he is like a king."

And Helen, goddess among women, answered him with these words: "You are revered and respected in my eyes, dear father-in-law. Oh, would that evil death had pleased me when I followed your son hither, leaving my chamber and my brothers and my little child and the lovely band of my companions. But that did not happen, so I have wasted away with weeping. I will tell you what you ask and inquire of me. That is Atreus' son, wide-ruling Agamemnon, both a good king and a mighty spearman. He was my brother-in-law, shameless that I am—if, indeed, he ever was."

So she spoke, and the old man admired him and said: "Happy son of Atreus, child of fortune, blessed by heaven, now are many of the sons of the Achaeans subject to you. Once I went to vine-clad Phrygia, where I saw many Phrygians with their quick-moving horses, the men of Otreus and godlike Mygdon, encamped upon the banks of the Sangarius. I was mustered with them as an ally on the day when the manlike Amazons came. But even they were not so many as are the bright-eyed Achaeans."

Then the old man, seeing Odysseus, asked a second time: "Come, dear child, tell me who is this man also. He looks shorter by a head than Agamemnon, Atreus' son, but broader in shoulders and chest. His armor lies upon the fertile earth, and he himself wanders like a ram among the ranks of men. Like a ram with a thick fleece he seems to me, that wanders through a great flock of white sheep."

Then Helen, daughter of Zeus, replied to him: "That is Laertes' son, Odysseus of many wiles, who was reared in the realm of Ithaca, rocky though it be, and is skilled in all kinds of tricks and clever counsels."

Then the wise Antenor answered her: "Lady, true indeed is the word that you have spoken. For the noble Odysseus came here once upon a mission concerning you, with Menelaus, dear to Ares; I entertained them and received them in my home. I learned the looks and subtle thoughts of both. When they came into the midst of the assembled Trojans, Menelaus, with his broad shoulders, towered above others when they were standing, but Odysseus was the more stately of the two when seated. Yet when they began to weave the web of speech and counsel before all, then indeed Menelaus spoke fluently, few words, but very clearly, for he was not a man of many words nor one to miss his point, even though he was younger in years. But when the many-wiled Odysseus arose, he stood there and looked down, fixing his eyes upon the ground, and he moved his staff neither this way nor that, but held it rigid like a stupid fellow. You would have thought him a boor and a plain fool. But when he sent his great voice from his chest and words like flakes of snow in winter, then could no other mortal rival Odysseus. Then we did not wonder so, beholding his appearance."

And thirdly the old man looked at Ajax and asked: "Who is this other Achaean, brave and mighty, towering above the Argives with his head and his broad shoulders?"

Then Helen of the trailing robe, goddess among women, answered him: "That is huge Ajax, bulwark of the Achaeans; and beyond, among the Cretans, stands like a god Idomeneus, with the captains of the Cretans gathered round him. Often Menelaus, dear to Ares, entertained him in our home when he would come from Crete. And now I see all the rest of the bright-eyed Achaeans, whom I could well recognize and name. But two marshals of the host I cannot see, Castor the tamer of horses and the great boxer Polydeuces, own brothers of mine, whom my own mother bore. Either they did not come along from lovely Lacedaemon, or they came hither with their seafaring ships but now they are unwilling to enter the battle of heroes, fearing the disgrace and the many reproaches that are mine."

So she spoke, but them already the life-giving earth embraced there in Lacedaemon, in their dear native land.

The heralds brought through the city the oath-offerings for the gods, two lambs and, in a goatskin, cheering wine, fruit of the earth. And the herald Idaeus brought a shining mixing bowl and golden cups, and standing beside the old man he urged him with these words: "Rise, son of Laomedon, the leaders of the horse-taming Trojans and the bronze-clad Achaeans bid you come down into the plain that you may swear true oaths. Alexander and Menelaus, dear to Ares, shall fight with long spears for the woman, and to the victor shall fall the woman and the treasure. May we others, swearing true oaths of friendship, live on in fertile Troy, and they will sail to horse-raising Argos and Achaeis with its lovely women."

So he spoke, and the old man shuddered and bade his companions harness the horses, and they quickly obeyed. Then Priam mounted his chariot and drew back the reins, and Antenor mounted the fair chariot beside him, and they drove the swift horses through the Scaean gates onto the plain.

But when they came to the Trojans and Achaeans, they dismounted from the chariot upon the all-nourishing earth and strode between the Trojans and Achaeans. Then Agamemnon, king of men, and many-wiled Odysseus, arose at once. The noble heralds brought together the oath-offerings for the gods and mixed wine in the bowl and poured water upon the hands of the kings. And the son of Atreus, drawing forth in his hands the knife which always hung beside the great sheath of his sword, cut wool from the heads of the lambs. This the heralds then divided among the leaders of the Trojans and Achaeans, on whose behalf the son of Atreus uttered a solemn prayer, holding his hands aloft: "Father Zeus, who dost rule from Ida, most glorious, most great, and thou, O Sun, who dost see all and hear all, and ye Rivers, and thou, O Earth, and ye who below work vengeance upon those dead who have sworn falsely, be ye our witnesses and watch over our true oaths. If Alexander slay Menelaus, let him then keep Helen and all the treasure and let us depart in the seafaring ships. But if the fair-haired Menelaus kill Alexander, then shall the Trojans return Helen and all the treasure and pay to the Argives proper recompense, that shall live among men yet to be. And if Priam and Priam's sons will pay me no reparation when Alexander falls, then will I fight on for the sake of the penalty, remaining here until I reach the end of war."

So he spoke, and he cut the throats of the lambs with the pitiless bronze and laid them gasping on the ground, bereft of life, for the bronze had taken away their strength. And drawing wine from the bowl in cups, they poured it forth upon the ground and prayed to the gods who live forever. And so would one of the Achaeans or Trojans speak: "Zeus, most glorious, most great, and ye other immortal gods, whoever shall be the first to do a wrong contrary to these oaths, may their brains run out like this wine upon the ground, both theirs and their children's, and may their wives be subject to others."

So they spoke, but not yet would Cronus' son grant them their prayers. Then before them spoke Priam, son of Dardanus: "Hear me, Trojans and well-greaved Achaeans. I shall return at once to wind-swept Ilium, for I truly cannot bear to watch my dear son fighting with Menelaus, dear to Ares. Surely Zeus and the other immortal gods know to which the doom of death is appointed."

So spoke the godlike man, and he put the lambs in the chariot and mounted it himself and drew back the reins. Antenor mounted the beautiful chariot beside him, and the two went back again to Ilium. But Hector, Priam's son, and the godlike Odysseus first measured a space and then took lots and shook them in a bronze-bound helmet to see who first should hurl his brazen spear. And the men prayed and lifted up their hands to the gods, and so some one of the Achaeans or Trojans would say: "Father Zeus, who dost rule from Ida, most glorious, most great, whichever brought these things upon both sides, grant that he may perish and go down into the house of Death, and that between us there may be friendship and true oaths."

So they spoke, and great Hector of the glancing helmet shook the lots, turning away his eyes, and the lot of Paris quickly leapt forth. Then the men sat down in ranks, where stood the high-stepping horses and glittering arms of each. The godlike Alexander, husband of fair-haired Helen, put his splendid armor on his shoulders. First he fastened upon his shins the handsome greaves, fitted with silver ankle-clasps. Next, he put about his chest the breastplate of his brother Lycaon, for it fitted him. Then, over his shoulders he threw his silver-studded sword of bronze, and then his great stout shield. Upon his mighty head he set the well-wrought helmet with its horsehair plume, and the plume nodded dreadfully above it. And he took a sturdy spear which fitted his hand. So, too, did the warlike Menelaus put on his armor.

Now when each had armed himself on his own side of the throng, glaring fiercely they strode out between the Trojans and Achaeans, and amazement fell upon the horse-taming Trojans and well-greaved Achaeans as they beheld them. They stood close in the measured space and shook their spears in hate at one another. First, Alexander hurled his long-shadowed spear and struck the balanced shield of Atreus' son. But the bronze did not break through, for the point was turned in the stout shield. Then, next, Atreus' son Menelaus attacked with his spear, praying to Father Zeus: "Lord Zeus, grant that I may avenge myself upon the godlike Alexander for the wrongs he first did me. Destroy him beneath my hands, so that even among men born hereafter one may shudder to wrong a host who offers him his friendship."

So speaking, he drew back his long-shadowed spear and cast it. He struck the balanced shield of Priam's son. Through the bright shield went the heavy spear and pierced the richly wrought breastplate. Straight through the tunic cut the spear and grazed his flank, but he bent aside and avoided black fate. Then the son of Atreus drew his silver-studded sword, reached high, and struck the crest of Alexander's helmet, but the sword broke into three or four pieces and fell from his hand. Then the son of Atreus groaned and looked up to the broad heaven: "Father Zeus, no other god is more baneful than thou. Truly I thought to avenge myself upon Alexander for his wickedness. But now my sword is broken in my hands and my spear has flown from my grasp in vain, nor have I struck him."

He spoke, and rushing at Paris he seized the horsehair crest upon his helmet and turned to drag him toward the well-greaved Achaeans. The richly embroidered thong beneath Paris' tender throat choked him, for it was drawn beneath his chin as a strap of his helmet. Then Menelaus would have dragged him off and would have won fame beyond telling had not Aphrodite, daughter of Zeus, taken sharp notice and broken the thong made from the hide of a slaughtered ox. The empty helmet came away in his stout hand, and at once the hero whirled about and cast it into the midst of the well-greaved Achaeans, and his trusty comrades picked it up. Then he rushed back, eager to slay with his brazen spear. But Aphrodite snatched Paris away with utmost ease, since she was a goddess, and hid him in thick mist and set him in his fragrant, vaulted chamber. Then she herself went to call Helen; she found her on the high wall and women of Troy in crowds around her. The goddess plucked her by her fragrant robe and drew her back, addressing her in the likeness of an old woman, a carder of wool, who used to comb the fair wool for her when she lived in Lacedaemon, and she loved her much. Likening herself to her, the divine Aphrodite spoke: "Come hither; Alexander calls you home. He is there in the chamber on his rounded bed, radiant with beauty and fair garments. You would not think that he had come from battle with a man, but that he was going to a dance, or sat there having just ceased dancing."

So she spoke, and aroused Helen's heart within her breast, and when she saw the lovely neck of the goddess and her seductive bosom and shining eyes, she was amazed and spoke and said to her, "Strange one, why do you so desire to beguile me? I suppose you will lead me on to some one of the fair-lying cities in Phrygia or in lovely Maeonia, if you have there also some favorite among mortal men. Since Menelaus now has vanquished godlike Alexander and wishes to lead me, hated, to his home, is it for this that you now stand beside me with wily thoughts? Go and sit beside him; depart from the way of the gods and never turn your feet back to Olympus but snivel forever at his side and keep him until he make you either his wife or his slave. Thither I will not go to approach his bed—it would be shameful. The Trojan women will all blame me hereafter, and I have already infinite grief at heart."

But divine Aphrodite answered her in anger: "Cross me not, wretched woman, lest in my anger I desert you and come to hate you as much as I have loved you beyond measure up to now, and lest I contrive bitter hatred for you among Trojans and Danaans alike, and you die an evil death."

So she spoke, and Zeus-born Helen was afraid and went in silence, wrapped in her white and shining robe, unseen by all the Trojan women, for the goddess led the way.

When they came to the fair house of Alexander, the maids turned quickly to their tasks but she, goddess among women, went to her vaulted chamber. There for her the laughter-loving goddess Aphrodite took a chair and carried it and set it down by Alexander. Then Helen, daughter of aegis-bearing Zeus, sat down, turning away her eyes, but she scolded her husband with these words: "You have come back from war. Would that you had died there, overcome by the mighty man who was my former husband. Surely you used to boast you were a better man than Menelaus, dear to Ares, in strength and hand and spear. Go now and challenge Menelaus, dear to Ares, to fight again in single combat. No, I bid you pause and not make war, neither do battle rashly against the fair-haired Menelaus, lest you be quickly worsted by his spear."

But Paris answered her and said: "Do not trouble my heart with harsh words, woman. For this time Menelaus has won with Athena's help, but another time I shall vanquish him. For there are gods on our side, too. Come, let us take pleasure in the bed in love. For desire has never yet so filled my heart as now, not even when first I stole you from lovely Lacedaemon and sailed away in the seafaring ships and lay with you in the bed of love on Cranaë. Now even more I love you and sweet desire seizes me."

So he spoke, and led the way to bed, and his wife followed him.

So they lay down upon the corded bed, but the son of Atreus ranged throughout the throng like a wild beast, in the hope that somewhere he might catch sight of godlike Alexander. But none of the Trojans or their famed allies could then point out Alexander to Menelaus, dear to Ares. Not out of love would they have hidden him, could they have found him, for he was hated like black death by all. Then Agamemnon, king of men, said to them: "Hear me, Trojans and Dardanians and allies, the victory appears to belong to Menelaus, dear to Ares. Do you surrender Argive Helen and the treasure with her and pay such reparation as is proper, which shall live among men yet to be."

So spoke the son of Atreus, and the rest of the Achaeans cheered.

BOOK IV

THE GODS, seated by the side of Zeus, were holding council on the golden floor, and among them queenly Hebe was pouring nectar. They toasted one another in golden cups, looking forth upon the city of the Trojans. Then the son of Cronus strove to provoke Hera with taunting words, speaking with sly malice: "Two of the goddesses are Menelaus' helpers, Hera of Argos and Athena of Alalcomenae. They take their pleasure in watching, while seated far away; but laughter-loving Aphrodite goes ever to her favorite's side with help and shields him from his fate. Even now she has saved him when he thought he was to die. Yet surely the victory belongs to Menelaus, dear to Ares. Let us consider how these things shall be, whether we shall once more stir up evil war and the dread din of battle or whether we shall send peace between both sides. If this could perhaps be pleasing and agreeable to all, then might King Priam's city still be inhabited and Menelaus lead back Argive Helen."

So he spoke, and Athena and Hera murmured; they were sitting close together, plotting evil for the Trojans. Now Athena was silent and said nothing, though she was angry at Father Zeus and wild wrath gripped her. But Hera's breast could not contain her anger, and she spoke: "Most dreadful son of Cronus, what sort of word is this that you have uttered? How can you wish to make my toil vain and fruitless and the sweat which I have sweated in my striving and the labor of my horses as I aroused the host to be a plague to Priam and his sons? Go on, but by no means shall all we other gods approve."

Then in great anger Zeus the cloud-gatherer addressed her: "Strange one, now what great evils do Priam and Priam's sons to you that you are fiercely eager to sack the well-built city of Ilium? If you were to enter the gates and high walls and were to devour Priam raw, and the sons of Priam, and the other Trojans, then you might appease your anger. Do as you wish; let not this quarrel become hereafter the cause of great strife between us. Another thing I will tell you, and do you turn it over in your heart: whenever I eagerly desire to sack that city in which there dwell men dear to you, do not try to thwart my anger, but let me be. For I have freely yielded this to you, though with unwilling heart, for of all the cities in which dwell earthly men beneath the sun and starry heaven, of them, holy Ilium was most honored in my heart, and Priam and the people of Priam of the good ashen spear. For never has my altar lacked due portion of libations or of fat, which is our appointed honor."

Then ox-eyed, queenly Hera answered him: "Indeed, three cities are dearest by far to me—Argos and Sparta and wide-wayed Mycenae. Sack them, whenever they are hateful to your heart. I do not protect them from you nor begrudge them. Yet even if I do begrudge them and strive to forbid you to sack them, I accomplish nothing by my grudging, since you are mightier by far. But you must not make my labor fruitless; for I too am a god and my birth is from the selfsame stock as yours. Cronus of crooked counsel begat me to be most honored both for my birth and also because I am called your wife and you rule over all the immortals. But let us yield this to one another, I to you and you to me, and the other immortal gods will follow. Do you quickly command Athena to go into the dread strife of Trojans and Achaeans, to seek to make the Trojans take the lead in violating their oaths and working harm to the Achaeans of wide renown."

So she spoke, and the father of gods and men did not refuse. At once he addressed Athena with winged words: "Go straight to the army, among Trojans and Achaeans, and seek to make the Trojans take the lead in violating their oaths and working harm to the Achaeans of wide renown."

So speaking, he urged Athena, already eager herself, and she went darting down from the peaks of Olympus; as when the son of crooked-counseled Cronus sends a star to be a portent to sailors or to a broad host of warriors, a shining star, and many sparks fly from it, like such a star did Pallas Athena dart to the earth and leap into their midst, and wonder fell upon them as they watched, upon the horse-taming Trojans and the well-greaved Achaeans, and so one would speak, glancing at his neighbor: "Either there will once more be bitter war and dread strife or Zeus is sending peace between both sides, he who is men's steward of war."

So one of the Achaeans or Trojans would say. But Athena went down among the ranks of the Trojans in the likeness of a warrior, Antenor's son Laodocus, a mighty spearman. She was searching for the godlike Pandarus, if she might find him. She found Lycaon's strong and blameless son standing there, and about him were mighty ranks of shieldmen who had followed him from the streams of Aesepus. Standing close to him, she spoke winged words: "Would you now obey me, prudent son of Lycaon? Then would you dare to shoot a swift arrow at Menelaus and would win thanks and glory from all the Trojans, above all from king Alexander. From him before all others would you receive glorious gifts if he should see the warlike Menelaus, Atreus' son, felled by your shaft and laid upon the grievous pyre. Come, shoot glorious Menelaus and vow to Lycian-born Apollo, the famed archer, to sacrifice a noble offering of first-born lambs when you return home to the city of sacred Zeleia."

Thus spoke Athena, and she persuaded the heart of the fool. Straightway he took from its case his polished bow, made of the horn of a wild mountain goat which he himself, waiting in hiding, had shot in the breast as it leapt from a rock, and had hit in the chest, and it fell upon its back on the rock. Its horn grew sixteen palms from its head. Fashioning it with care, a worker in horn had fitted it and smoothing it well had placed upon it a golden tip. So now he set it firmly, bending it and bracing it upon the ground. Before him his noble comrades held a shield, lest the warlike sons of the Achaeans start up before he hit Menelaus, Atreus' warlike son. Then he took the cap off his quiver and took out a winged arrow which had never been shot, fraught with dark pains, and promptly he fitted the bitter arrow to the string and vowed to Lycian-born Apollo, the famed archer, that he would sacrifice to him a famous offering of first-born lambs when he returned home to the city of holy Zeleia. Then, grasping the arrow's notches and the oxhide string, he drew the bow; he brought the string close to his breast, the iron to the bow. Then, when he had drawn the great bow into an arc, the bow twanged, the string sang aloud, and the sharp arrow leaped, eager to fly amid the throng.

Nor did the blessed, immortal gods forget you, Menelaus, especially not Zeus' daughter, driver of spoil, for she stood before you and warded off the piercing shaft. So far she brushed it from your flesh as a mother keeps a fly from her child when it lies in sweet sleep. The goddess guided it to the spot where the golden clasps of the belt were fastened and the double breastplate was joined. The bitter arrow struck the closely fitted belt, it passed through the cleverly fashioned belt and pierced the richly wrought breastplate and the band which he wore as a protection for his flesh, a bulwark against darts, which gave him most protection. Even through this it passed. Then the arrow grazed the surface of the man's flesh, and at once the dark blood flowed from the wound.

As when some woman of Maeonia or Caria stains ivory with scarlet to be a cheek-piece for horses, and it lies in her chamber and many horsemen have prayed to use it, but it is kept as an offering for a king, both an ornament for the horse and a glory for the charioteer, even so, Menelaus, were your goodly thighs stained with blood, and your shins and your fair ankles below.

Then Agamemnon, king of men, shuddered as he saw the black blood flow from the wound. And Menelaus himself, dear to Ares, shuddered too. But as he saw that the binding and the barbs had not entered, his spirit rose again within his breast. But with a heavy groan, mighty Agamemnon spoke among them, holding Menelaus by the hand, while his comrades groaned about him: "Dear brother, the oaths I swore were death to you, as I sent you forth alone before the Achaeans to fight with the Trojans, since the Trojans shot you and trampled on their sacred oaths. Yet an oath is never vain, the blood of lambs, the libations of unmixed wine, and the handclasps, in which we trusted. Even though the Olympian has not at once fulfilled them, yet does he in the end fulfill them, and men indeed pay dearly, with their own heads and their wives and children. For this I know well in heart and soul; the day shall be when holy Ilium shall fall, and Priam and the people of Priam of the good ashen spear, and Zeus the high-throned, Cronus' son, who dwells in heaven, shall shake his dark aegis against them all in wrath for this deceit. These things shall not fail to be fulfilled. But I shall suffer dreadful grief for you, Menelaus, if you die, your lot in life fulfilled. Then most despised would I return to thirsty Argos. For the Achaeans will quickly remember their native land, and then we would leave to Priam and the Trojans their boast, even Argive Helen. Your bones the earth shall rot as you lie in Troy with your task unfinished. And thus shall a boastful Trojan say, as he leaps upon the funeral mound of glorious Menelaus: 'May Agamemnon in all things fulfill his wrath as vainly as now he led hither the army of Achaeans and has returned home to his dear native land with empty ships, leaving behind brave Menelaus.' So someone will say, and then may the broad earth open at my feet."

But encouraging him, the fair-haired Menelaus said: "Take

heart and do not yet alarm the host of the Achaeans, for the sharp arrow did not strike a vital spot, but the shining belt turned it aside, and the kilt beneath, and the band which the blacksmiths wrought."

Then mighty Agamemnon answered him and said: "May that be true, dear Menelaus; a physician shall probe the wound and spread drugs upon it which shall stop the dark pangs."

He spoke, and addressed Talthybius, the godlike herald: "Talthybius, call here with all speed Machaon, the mortal son of Asclepius the blameless physician, that he may look at Menelaus, Atreus' warlike son, whom someone has shot with an arrow, someone well skilled with the bow, one of the Trojans or Lycians—his glory, but our grief."

So he spoke, nor did the hero fail to obey him when he heard. He set off through the throng of the bronze-clad Achaeans, looking for the hero Machaon. He spied him standing in the midst of the stout ranks of shieldmen who had followed him from horse-racing Tricca. He stood close to him and spoke winged words: "Come, son of Asclepius; the mighty Agamemnon calls, that you may look at warlike Menelaus, leader of the Achaeans, whom someone has shot with an arrow, someone well skilled with the bow, one of the Trojans or Lycians—his glory, but our grief."

So he spoke and aroused his heart within his breast. They set out through the throng, across the wide host of the Achaeans. But when they came to the place where fair-haired Menelaus lay wounded, and all who were chieftains were gathered round him in a circle, Machaon stood by his side in their midst, a godlike mortal, and straightway drew the arrow from the closely fitting belt. As he drew it forth, the barbs broke off. He loosed the gleaming belt and the kilt beneath and the band which the blacksmiths wrought. But when he saw the wound where the bitter arrow had entered, he sucked out the blood and skillfully spread on soothing drugs, which Cheiron once with kindly thought had given his father.

While they were busy about Menelaus of the mighty war cry, the lines of Trojan shieldmen were advancing. So they once more put on their arms and remembered the joy of battle.

Then you would not see the godlike Agamemnon drowsing or skulking or unwilling to fight, but very eager for man-ennobling battle. He left his horses and his chariot, bright with bronze, and Eurymedon, his squire, the son of Ptolemaeus, Peireus' son, held the snorting steeds far off. Agamemnon gave him many instructions to bring them to him whenever weariness should seize his limbs as he did the duties of his wide command. Then on foot he passed among the ranks of men. Whomsoever he saw eager among the Danaans, with their swift steeds, he would approach and encourage greatly: "Argives, do not let up in your furious valor. For Father Zeus will be no helper of liars. But truly vultures shall eat the tender flesh of those who first broke their oaths, and we shall carry off their dear wives and little children in our ships when we have sacked their city."

But whomsoever he saw shirking hateful war, these he roughly reproached with angry words: "Cowardly Argives, men of dishonor, have you now no shame? Why do you stand so dazed, like fawns, which stand still when they are weary of running over a broad plain, nor is there any valor in their hearts. So you too stand dazed and will not fight. Are you waiting for the Trojans to come to close quarters, where the high-sterned ships are drawn up on the shore of the gray sea, that you may see if the son of Cronus will stretch out his hand above you?"

So lording it, he passed among the ranks of the men; and he came to the Cretans as he went through the throng. They were arming themselves around prudent Idomeneus. Idomeneus stood among the foremost, like a boar in valor, and Meriones marshaled the rearmost companies. When he saw them, Agamemnon, king of men, was glad and at once spoke to Idomeneus with kindly words: "Idomeneus, I honor you above the other Danaans with their swift steeds, whether in war or in any other sort of work or at the feast, when the best of the Argives mix in the bowl the gleaming wine of counselors. Even though the other long-haired Achaeans drink but their portion, your cup stands ever full, like mine, to drink whenever the spirit bids. Come, off to battle, brave as you boast to have been before."

Then Idomeneus, leader of the Cretans, answered him: "Son of Atreus, I shall be your trusty comrade, as at first I promised and assured you. But now urge on the other long-haired Achaeans, that we may quickly fight, since the Trojans have broken their oaths. For them there shall be death and grief hereafter, since they were the first to violate the oaths."

So he spoke, and the son of Atreus moved onward, glad at heart. And going through the throng of men, he came to the Ajaxes. Both were arming, followed by a cloud of infantry. As when a goatherd from a lookout has seen a cloud coming across the deep beneath the roaring West Wind—from afar it seems to him blacker than pitch, as it passes over the deep, and it brings a heavy shower and he shudders when he sees it and drives his flocks into a cave—even so, around the two Ajaxes, did the close companies of Zeus-nurtured heroes move into blazing war, dark companies, bristling with shields and spears. The mighty Agamemnon was glad when he saw them and he spoke and addressed to them winged words: "Ajaxes, leaders of the bronze-clad Argives, to you I give no orders, for it is not seemly to urge you on. For of yourselves you urge your soldiers to make war with might. Would to Father Zeus and Athena and Apollo that your spirit were in every breast. Then would the city of King Priam soon bow down, captured and laid waste beneath our hands."

So speaking, he left them there and went among the others. There he found Nestor, the clear-voiced orator of the men of Pylos, urging his comrades to fight and marshaling them around great Pelagon and Alastor and Chromius and mighty Haemon, and Bias, the shepherd of the people. First he placed the charioteers with horses and chariots, then, behind them, the infantry, many and brave, to be a bulwark of war. The cowardly he drove into the center, so that even though unwilling each must fight perforce.

First to the charioteers he gave his orders, for he bade them check their horses and not drive headlong through the fray: "Let no one trusting in his skill at driving or his valor be eager to fight the Trojans alone before the rest. And let no one draw back; for you will be the weaker. Whatever man reaches another chariot with his own should thrust with his spear, for thus it is much better. Even so the men of old took cities and walls, with such a mind and spirit in their breasts."

So the old man, well skilled in former wars, aroused them. Mighty Agamemnon was glad as he beheld him and he spoke and addressed to him winged words: "Old man, would that your knees could follow the spirit in your breast and that your might were unshaken. But old age, which comes to all, bears hard upon you. Would that it were some other man's and that you were among the younger."

Then Nestor, the Gerenian horseman, answered him: "Son of Atreus, greatly would I myself like to be as I was when I slew godlike Ereuthalion. Yet the gods give not to men all things at once. As I was then a youth, so now old age besets me. Yet even so will I join the horsemen and will command them with my words of counsel, for that is the old man's role. The younger shall hurl their spears, they who are younger than I and trust their strength."

So he spoke, and the son of Atreus passed on, glad at heart. He found Menestheus, Peteos' son, the driver of horses, standing in the midst of the Athenians, raisers of the battle cry. Close by, moreover, stood the many-wiled Odysseus, and around him stood the ranks of the Cephallenians—not through weakness, for not yet had their men heard the battle cry; indeed, the companies of the horse-taming Trojans and the Achaeans had just been stirred to action, and they stood waiting until some other column of the Achaeans should advance to attack the Trojans and begin the battle. When he saw them, Agamemnon, king of men, reproached them and spoke and addressed to them winged words: "Son of Peteos the Zeus-nurtured king, and you, expert in evil wiles, crafty one, why do you stand cowering aside and await the rest? It would be right for you to stand among the first and meet the raging battle. For you are the first to hear my summons to the banquet, whenever we Achaeans give a banquet for the elders. Then it is pleasant to eat roast meat and to drink the cups of honey-sweet wine, while you will. But now you would gladly look on even though ten columns of the Achaeans should do battle before you with the pitiless bronze."

Looking at him scornfully, the many-wiled Odysseus said: "Son of Atreus, what word has escaped the barrier of your teeth? How can you say that we withhold from battle when we Achaeans raise sharp Ares against the horse-taming Trojans? You shall, if such be your desire and concern, see Telemachus' dear father mingling with the first line of the horse-taming Trojans. These words of yours are senseless."

Then mighty Agamemnon answered smiling, when he saw that he was angry, and he took back his words. "Zeus-born son of Laertes, Odysseus of many wiles, I do not reproach you nor command you beyond measure, for I know that your spirit in your breast is skilled in pliant counsels; indeed, your purposes are one with mine. But go, we shall make amends for this hereafter, if any wrong has been spoken. And may the gods make it all of no account."

So speaking, he left them there and went among the rest. He found Tydeus' son, high-hearted Diomedes, standing in the midst of the horses and well-joined chariots, and at his side stood Sthenelus, Capaneus' son. When mighty Agamemnon saw him he spoke and addressed to him winged words: "Son of the prudent, horse-taming Tydeus, why do you cower here? Why do you gaze at the dykes of war? Tydeus did not love to cower thus, but rather to battle with the foe far ahead of his dear comrades, as those said who saw him at work, for I myself never met nor saw him. But they say he surpassed the rest. Indeed, he entered Mycenae not as an enemy but as a guest with godlike Polyneices, to raise an army. For they were then marching against the holy walls of Thebes, and much they begged men to give them glorious allies. And men were willing to give them and agreed as they desired, but Zeus changed their minds by showing adverse omens. Then, when they had departed and were well upon their way, and had come to Asopus, in his bed of grass and deep rushes, the Achaeans sent out Tydeus as a messenger. And he went and found the many sons of Cadmus feasting in the house of mighty Eteocles. There, even though a stranger and alone among many Cadmeians, horse-driving Tydeus was not afraid. He challenged them to a contest and easily beat them all, such a helper was Athena to him. And the Cadmeians, goaders of horses, were angry, and they led out fifty young men and laid a clever ambush for him as he journeyed back. There were two leaders, Haemon's son, Maeon, like to the immortals, and the son of Autophonus, steadfast Polyphontes. Now Tydeus brought a shameful doom upon them. He slew them all, save that he let one alone go home. It was Maeon whom he sent, obeying the portents of the gods. Such was Tydeus the Aetolian, but he begot a son inferior to him in battle, though better in council."

So he spoke, but mighty Diomedes answered him not at all, respecting the honored king's reproof. But the son of glorious Capaneus answered him: "Son of Atreus, do not lie when you know how to speak the truth. We boast ourselves far better than our fathers. For we took the seat of seven-gated Thebes, though we led a smaller host against a stronger wall, trusting in the omens of the gods and in the help of Zeus; but they perished by their own blind folly. Therefore never put our fathers on a par with us in honor."

Mighty Diomedes looked at him scornfully and said: "Comrade, sit down in silence and obey my word. I do not blame Agamemnon, shepherd of the people, for urging the well-greaved Achaeans to battle. For glory will come to him if the Achaeans destroy the Trojans and take holy Ilium, but great grief will be his if the Achaeans are destroyed. Come, let us too set our minds upon furious valor."

So he spoke, and leaped in his armor from his chariot to the ground. And terribly rang the bronze upon the chest of the king as he rushed forward, and fear would have seized even the stout-hearted.

As when upon some sounding beach the waves of the sea rush in ever-quickening succession before the urge of the West Wind—first in the deep a wave raises its head, then, breaking on the land, it roars loudly and rises with arching crest around the promontories and spews forth the salt spray—so then in ever-quickening succession the companies of the Danaans rolled unceasingly to war. Each leader commanded his own men, and the rest moved on in silence, fearing their captains; nor would you say that such a host could mutely follow, who had voices in their breasts. Upon them all blazed the well-wrought armor which they wore as they advanced in order. But from the Trojans, as from sheep which in the barnyard of some very wealthy man stand in their thousands giving their white milk and bleat continually as they hear the voice of their lambs, the war cry arose throughout the broad host. For they had not all a like speech nor language, but their tongues were mingled and they were warriors called from many lands. These were urged on by Ares, the Achaeans by bright-eyed Athena and Terror and Rout, and by Strife, endlessly raging, the sister and comrade of man-slaying Ares. Small is she of stature at first, yet soon she rests her head in the heavens and walks upon the earth. She then entered the throng and cast a common strife among them, multiplying the groans of men.

So, then, they met and came together, and clashed shield on shield and spear on spear and might on might of warriors with their brazen arms. The bossed shields pressed each to each and a great din arose. Then there were groans and cheers of men, of the slayers and the slain, and the earth ran with blood. As when winter torrents flowing down the mountains from their great springs to a valley basin join their mighty waters in a deep gorge and afar off among the hills a shepherd hears their thunder, so from these armies' conflict came the shouting and the pain.

First Antilochus slew a helmeted Trojan, a noble in the front rank, Echepolus, Thalysius' son. He struck him first upon the ridge of his helmet with its thick horsehair crest, and he smote his forehead and the brazen spear pierced the bone. Darkness veiled his eyes and he fell, as falls a tower, in the mighty conflict. Stalwart Elephenor, Chalcodon's son, the great-hearted leader of the Abantes, seized him by the feet when he fell and dragged him from under the rain of weapons, eager to strip him quickly of his arms. But his effort was short-lived, for when the great-hearted Agenor saw him dragging away the body, he thrust his bronze spear into his flank, where it was bared beside the shield as he bent over, and he loosed his limbs. Then his life left him and over his body there was grim work by Trojans and Achaeans; like wolves they leaped on one another, and man grappled with man.

Then Telamonian Ajax struck Anthemion's son, the sturdy youth Simoeisius, whom his mother bore upon the banks of Simois as she came down from Ida, for she had gone with her parents to see the flocks. Therefore they called him Simoeisius. But he did not repay his dear parents for his nurture, for short was his life, since he was overcome by the spear of the great-hearted Ajax. For first, as he advanced, Ajax smote him on the right breast beside the nipple and the bronze spear went straight through his shoulder. He fell to the earth in the dust, like a poplar which has grown up in a hollow in a great meadow, smooth of trunk, but with branches at its top. Some wainwright has felled it with gleaming iron, to bend him a felloe for a fair chariot, and it lies to season on a river's bank. Such was Anthemion's son Simoeisius as Zeus-born Ajax stripped him of his armor. Then Priam's son Antiphus of the gleaming breastplate hurled his sharp javelin across the throng at Ajax. He missed him but struck Leucus, Odysseus' noble companion, in the groin, as he was dragging a body away. He fell upon the body, and it slipped from his hands. Then Odysseus was greatly angered at heart for his slaying, and he strode through the foremost fighters armed in gleaming bronze, and standing very close and glaring about him, he hurled his shining spear. The Trojans gave way as the hero hurled his spear, but he did not cast the shaft in vain, for he struck Priam's bastard son Democoon, who had come to him from tending his swift mares in Abydus. Odysseus, angered because of his comrade, struck him with the spear in one temple, and the brazen point passed through to the other. Darkness veiled his eyes and he fell with a crash, and his armor clanged upon him. Then the foremost fighters and glorious Hector gave ground, and the Argives raised a mighty shout, dragged off the bodies, and pressed on further.

Apollo was indignant as he looked down from Pergamus, and he called with a shout to the Trojans: "Arise, horse-taming Trojans and do not yield in the fray before the Argives, for not of stone or iron is their flesh to resist the flesh-biting bronze when they are struck. Nor is Achilles fighting, fair-haired Thetis' son, but beside the ships he broods upon his wrath with aching heart."

So spoke the dread god from the city. But most glorious Tritogeneia, daughter of Zeus, urged the Achaeans on, passing throughout the host wherever she saw them slacking. Next was Diores, son of Amarynceus, caught in the snare of fate, for he was struck by a jagged stone on the right leg near the ankle. A leader of the Thracians threw it, Peirus, son of Imbrasus, who had come from Aenus. The pitiless stone utterly crushed the two tendons and the bones, and he fell back in the dust and stretched out both hands to his dear comrades, gasping out his life. And Peirus, who had wounded him, ran up and thrust him near the navel with a spear, and all his bowels poured out upon the ground and darkness veiled his eyes.

But as Peirus sprang back, Thoas, the Aetolian, struck his chest above the nipple with his spear, and the bronze stuck in the lung. Then Thoas closed in on him and drew the stout spear from his chest and unsheathed his sharp sword. He struck him full in the belly and took away his life. But he did not strip Peirus of his armor, for his comrades, the long-haired Thracians, stood about him with long spears in their hands, and great and brave and noble though Thoas was, they drove him from them so that he yielded and gave ground. So the two lay stretched in the dust by one another, the leaders, one of the Thracians, the other of the bronze-clad Epeians. And many more were slain about them.

Then could no man enter the battle and make light of it, whoever still unstricken and unwounded by sharp bronze might move through the midst, even though Pallas Athena led him by the hand and guarded him from the rain of darts. For many of the Trojans and Achaeans were that day stretched side by side, their faces in the dust.

BOOK V

THEN TO Diomedes, Tydeus' son, Pallas Athena gave strength and valor, that he might become pre-eminent among all the Argives and win glorious renown. From his helmet and shield she kindled an unresting fire, like the harvest star, which shines most brightly when it has bathed in Ocean. Such was the fire she kindled from his head and shoulders, and she urged him into the center, where the close ranks thrust and gave.

There was among the Trojans one Dares, rich and blameless, a priest of Hephaestus, and he had two sons, Phegeus and Idaeus, both well skilled in every form of battle. These two stood forth from the throng and hastened against Diomedes. They were in a chariot, but he advanced on foot upon the ground. And when they came close to one another in their onset, Phegeus first cast his long-shadowed spear. The point passed over the left shoulder of Tydeus' son and did not strike him. Next, Tydeus' son rushed forward with the bronze, and not in vain did the weapon fly from his hand, for it hit Phegeus squarely in the chest and thrust him from his chariot. Idaeus rushed away, leaving the fair chariot, nor dared he to defend his brother who was slain. Yet not even he would have escaped black fate had not Hephaestus guarded him and saved him, hiding him in darkness, that his old priest might not be wholly overcome by grief. Then the son of great-hearted Tydeus drove off the horses and gave them to his comrades to lead to the hollow ships. When the great-hearted Trojans saw the sons of Dares, one retreating and one slain beside his chariot, the hearts of all were troubled. Then bright-eyed Athena took impetuous Ares by the hand and said: "Ares, Ares, bane of mortals, you blood-stained stormer of walls, should we not leave Trojans and Achaeans to fight, to whomsoever Father Zeus shall grant the glory? Let us both withdraw and avoid the wrath of Zeus."

So speaking, she led impetuous Ares from the battle. And then she made him sit down by the Scamander with its changing banks, and the Danaans drove back the Trojans. Each of the leaders slew his man. First Agamemnon, king of men,

hurled great Odius from his chariot, the leader of the Halizones. He struck him in the back between his shoulders as he
turned, the first to flee, and he drove the spear through his
chest. He fell with a crash, and his armor clanged upon him.

Idomeneus slew Phaestus, son of Maeonian Borus, who had
come from fertile Tarne. Idomeneus, famed with the spear,
struck him with his long spear in the right shoulder as he went
to mount his chariot. He fell from the chariot and hateful
darkness seized him.

Him the squires of Idomeneus stripped; Menelaus, Atreus'
son, slew with his sharp spear Strophius' son Scamandrius, a
noble huntsman, cunning in the chase, whom Artemis herself
had taught to shoot all the wild beasts that the forest breeds
upon the mountains. But Artemis the huntress could not avail
him then, nor the long shots in which he had before excelled,
for Menelaus, Atreus' son, famed with the spear, thrust him in
the back between the shoulders as he fled before him and
drove the spear through his chest. He fell on his face, and his
armor clanged upon him.

Meriones slew Phereclus, the son of the carpenter Hapmonides, who knew how to do with his hands all works of
skill, for Pallas Athena loved him above all. He had made for
Alexander the fair-lined ships which were the beginning of
woe and which became a curse to all the Trojans and to himself, for he did not know the purpose of the gods. Meriones
pursued and overtook him and smote him in the right buttock
and the point went straight through the bladder beneath the
bone. He fell groaning to his knees and death enwrapped him.

Meges slew Pedaeus, Antenor's son, who was a bastard, but
the noble Theano reared him as carefully as her own children
as a favor to her husband. Phyleus' son, famed with the spear,
came close to him and smote him in the back of the head with
his sharp spear. The bronze cut straight through beneath his
tongue to the teeth. He fell in the dust, grinding his teeth on
the chill bronze.

And Eurypylus, Euaemon's son, slew godlike Hypsenor, son
of high-hearted Dolopion, who had been the priest of Scamander, and was revered by the people as a god—him did
Eurypylus, Euaemon's glorious son, strike on the shoulder
with his sword as he fled before him, and he cut off his heavy
arm. The bleeding arm fell to the ground, and dark death and
mighty doom descended on his eyes.

So they strove in the mighty conflict, but you could not tell
on which side was the son of Tydeus, whether he was with the

Trojans or the Achaeans, for he rushed across the plain like a winter torrent at the full, which in its swift course bursts the dykes. The restraining levees do not hold it, nor do the walls of the fruitful vineyards stop its sudden coming when the rain of Zeus falls heavily; before it many fair works of men are swept away. So the dense companies of the Trojans strove confusedly before the son of Tydeus, nor did they stand before him, numerous though they were.

When the glorious son of Lycaon noticed him rushing along the plain and driving the shattered companies before him, he straightway drew his curved bow against Tydeus' son and shot him as he dashed forward, hitting him on the right shoulder, in the hollow of his breastplate. Through this the bitter arrow sped and kept its course, and the breastplate was spattered with blood. Then the glorious son of Lycaon shouted loudly: "Arise, great-hearted Trojans, goaders of horses, for the best of the Achaeans has been hit, nor do I think that he can long endure the mighty shaft, as surely as the lordly son of Zeus urged me on my way when I set out from Lycia."

So he bragged, but Diomedes was not subdued by the swift arrow; rather, he drew back and stood beside his chariot and his horses and spoke to Sthenelus, Capaneus' son: "Come, dear Sthenelus, get down from your chariot and draw the bitter arrow from my shoulder."

So he spoke, and Sthenelus leaped from the chariot to the ground and stood beside him and drew the swift arrow straight through his shoulder and the blood shot up through his ringed coat of mail. Then, indeed, Diomedes of the mighty war cry prayed: "Hear me, Atrytone, child of aegis-bearing Zeus, if ever in friendship thou stoodest by me or my father in blazing war, now again be my friend, Athena. Grant that I may take this man and come within spear's reach of him who shot me before I was aware and boastingly says I shall not gaze for long upon the bright light of the sun."

So he spoke in prayer, and Pallas Athena heard him, and she made his limbs swift, his feet and his hands above, and standing close to him she spoke winged words: "Take courage now, Diomedes, to fight against the Trojans, for I have put your father's might within your breast, the fearless might which Tydeus used to have, the horseman and the wielder of the shield. I have taken from before your eyes the mist that formerly was there, so that now you may know well both god and man. So now if any god come here to try you, by no means fight as man to man with any other of the immortal gods, but if Zeus' daughter Aphrodite come to battle, wound her with sharp bronze."

So speaking, bright-eyed Athena went away, and Tydeus' son went forth again and mingled with the foremost fighters. And though before he had been eager at heart to battle the Trojans, now a threefold valor seized him, as it does a lion which a shepherd, guarding his fleecy sheep in the field, has slightly wounded as it leaped the sheepfold wall, yet has not vanquished. He has roused the lion's might, yet now makes no defense but shrinks among the pens. The deserted sheep are terror-stricken and are strewn in heaps beside each other, but the lion, raging, leaps from the deep fold. So raging, mighty Diomedes rushed among the Trojans.

Then he slew Astynous and Hypeiron, shepherd of the people, striking one above the nipple with the bronze-tipped spear and the other he struck with his great sword in the collarbone, next the shoulder, and severed the shoulder from the neck and back. He left them there and went after Abas and Polyidus, the sons of Eurydamas, the aged reader of dreams. The old man read no dreams for them on their departure— rather, mighty Diomedes slew them. And he went after Xanthus and Thoön, Phaenops' sons, mere children both. Their father was worn by wretched age and he begot no other son to leave as heir of his possessions. Then Diomedes stripped them and took away the life of both and left mourning and wretched grief to their father, since he did not welcome them returning home from battle, and heirs of another line divided his possessions.

Then he caught Echemmon and Chromius, two sons of Dardania Priam, in one chariot. As a lion leaping among cattle breaks the neck of a heifer or cow as they graze in a woodland pasture, so the son of Tydeus fiercely made the two dismount from their chariot against their will, and then he stripped off their armor and gave their horses to his friends to drive to the ships.

But Aeneas saw him working havoc on the ranks of the heroes and he set out through the battle and the din of spears, searching for the godlike Pandarus, if he might find him anywhere. He found Lycaon's strong and blameless son and stood before him and spoke to him directly: "Pandarus, where are now your bow and your winged arrows and your fame, in which no man here disputes you, nor does any in Lycia boast to be your better? Come, raise your hands to Zeus and shoot an arrow at this man, whoever this is that lords it there and has worked much ill upon the Trojans, for he has loosed the knees of many valiant men—if indeed he be not some god who is angry with the Trojans, slighted in some sacrifice. The anger of a god weighs heavy."

Then the glorious son of Lycaon addressed him: "Aeneas, counselor of the bronze-clad Trojans, I liken him in all things to Tydeus' warlike son, knowing him by his shield and his crested helmet and by the appearance of his horses. But I am not certain if it be a god. Yet if it be the man I say, the warlike son of Tydeus, not without some god does he so rage, but one of the immortals stands beside him, his shoulders wrapped in cloud, someone who turned away my swift bolt from this man when it had found him. For I have shot an arrow at him and hit him on the right shoulder, straight through the hollow of the breastplate, and I thought I should send him to the house of Death, but none the less, I did not overcome him. Surely he is some angry god. Horses and chariot are not here for me to mount, yet in the halls of Lycaon are eleven fair chariots, new-made, fresh-fashioned, with coverings spread upon them. By each stand two horses champing white barley and wheat. And as I left, the aged spearman Lycaon in his well-built house gave me many a command. He bade me mount a chariot with its horses and lead the Trojans in the mighty fray, but I would not heed—it would have been far better—for I desired to spare the horses, lest where men thronged together they lack fodder, having been ever wont to eat their fill. So I left them there and came on foot to Ilium, trusting in my bow; yet it was not to help me. For already I have shot at two of the best, the son of Tydeus and Atreus' son, and indeed I drew blood from both with my shafts, but only aroused them the more. It was, then, with ill fortune that I took my curved bow from its peg on that day when I led my Trojans to lovely Ilium for noble Hector's sake. If I return and look with my eyes upon my native land and my wife and my great high-roofed house, then may some stranger cut off my head if I do not break this bow in pieces with my hands and put it in the blazing fire, for it goes with me worthless as the wind."

Then Aeneas, leader of the Trojans, answered him: "Do not speak thus; it will be no better until we go with horses and chariots against this man and try him out with arms. Come, mount my chariot, that you may see of what sort are the horses of Tros, skilled to run swiftly hither and yon across the plain in flight or in pursuit. These will take us safely to the

city if Zeus shall again grant glory to Diomedes, Tydeus' son.
Come, now, take the whip and the shining reins and I will
dismount from the chariot to fight; or else do you oppose him
and I will tend the horses."

Then Lycaon's glorious son replied to him: "Aeneas, you
hold the reins and horses, since they will draw the curved
chariot better for their accustomed driver if we must flee from
Tydeus' son—lest they delay in fear and refuse to bear us out
of war for want of your voice, and lest the son of Tydeus,
rushing upon us, slay us both and drive away the single-hoofed
horses. Drive your horses and your chariot yourself, and I will
meet his onset with the pointed spear."

So speaking, they mounted the skillfully wrought chariot
and drove the swift horses eagerly against the son of Tydeus.
Sthenelus, Capaneus' glorious son, caught sight of them and
quickly spoke winged words to Tydeus' son: "Diomedes, son
of Tydeus, dear to my heart, I see two mighty warriors eager
to fight against you, measureless in strength. One is well skilled
with the bow, Pandarus, who boasts to be Lycaon's son, and
Aeneas boasts that he was born the son of blameless Anchises
and that his mother is Aphrodite. Come, let us retreat with the
horses and do you not rage thus among the foremost fighters,
lest you lose your life."

Diomedes looked at him scornfully and said: "Speak not of
flight, because I know that you will not persuade me. For I
was not born to fight a cringing fight or to cower. My strength
is steadfast still. I will not mount the chariot but will go
against them as I am. Pallas Athena will not let me flee. The
swift horses shall not bear them both away from us again, even
if one escapes. Another thing I will tell you and do you turn it
over in your heart: If Athena of many counsels grants me the
glory of slaying both, then hold here these swift horses, binding the reins to the chariot rim, and be ready to rush upon the
horses of Aeneas and drive them from the Trojans into the
midst of the well-greaved Achaeans. For they are of that breed
which far-thundering Zeus gave Tros as pay for Ganymede,
his son, because they are the best steeds of all that are beneath
the dawn and sun. Anchises, king of men, stole the breed,
mating his mares with them without the knowledge of
Laomedon. Six of their stock were born to him in his halls;
four of them he kept himself and reared them at the manger,
but these two he gave Aeneas, two masters of swift coursing,
and could we but capture them we would win glorious
renown."

So they spoke to one another, and the other two came quickly on, driving the swift horses. First the glorious son of Lycaon addressed Diomedes: "Son of noble Tydeus, stout-hearted and wise, the swift bolt, the bitter arrow, did not slay you. But I will try now with my spear if I can hit you."

So speaking, he drew back the long-shadowed spear and hurled it and struck the shield of Tydeus' son. The speeding point of bronze drove right through to his breastplate. And over him Lycaon's glorious son cried loudly: "You are hit clean through the belly, and not for long, I think, will you survive; you have given me great glory."

But fearlessly the mighty Diomedes answered him: "You missed and did not hit me; I do not think you two will stop until the one has fallen and sated with his blood the warrior Ares with the bull's-hide shield."

So he spoke, and hurled his spear, and Athena guided it to his nose beside the eye, and it passed his gleaming teeth. The stubborn bronze cut his tongue off at the root, and the point protruded from beneath his jawbone. He fell from the chariot and his splendid, gleaming armor clanged upon him, and the swift horses shied away. Then his soul and strength were loosed.

Aeneas sprang down with his shield and lengthy spear, fearing lest the Achaeans drag the dead man from him. Over him he strode like a lion, trusting in his might, and before him held his spear and balanced shield, eager to slay whoever should come to face him, and shouting dreadfully. But the son of Tydeus grasped in his hand a stone, a weighty mass which two men, as men now are, could never carry, but even alone he handled it with ease. With it he smote Aeneas on the hip joint —the cup men call it—shattering the joint and crushing both sinews too, and the jagged stone tore through the skin. The hero fell to his knees and with his stout hand leaned upon the earth, and black night veiled his eyes.

Now would Aeneas, king of men, have perished, had not Aphrodite, daughter of Zeus, been quick to see, his mother, who bore him to Anchises as he tended cattle. She threw her white arms about her dear son and spread a fold of her bright robe before him, as a shelter against weapons, lest any of the Danaans with their swift steeds should thrust bronze into his breast and take away his life.

So she was bearing her dear son out of the battle. But Capaneus' son did not forget the orders given him by Diomedes of the mighty war cry. He halted his own single-hoofed horses apart from the conflict, binding the reins to the chariot rim, and then rushed upon the fair-maned horses of Aeneas and drove them away from the Trojans into the midst of the well-greaved Achaeans. He gave them to Deipylus to drive to the hollow ships—his dear companion whom he honored above all others of his age because he was like-minded. Then the warrior mounted his own chariot and took the gleaming reins and in haste drove his strong-hoofed horses hotly after Tydeus' son. The latter was pursuing Cypris with the pitiless bronze, knowing that she was a weakling goddess, not one of those who rule the wars of men, neither Athena nor Enyo, the sacker of cities. But when he had pursued her through a great throng and had come upon her, then great-hearted Tydeus' son reached out his spear and wounded the hollow of her hand, springing upon her with his sharp spear in her weakness. At once the spear passed through her ambrosial robe, which the Graces themselves had woven for her, and pierced her skin at the base of the fingers, above the palm. The ambrosial blood of the goddess poured out, ichor, which flows in the blessed gods, for they eat no bread and drink no gleaming wine; therefore they are bloodless and are called immortal. With a great shriek she cast her son from her and Phoebus Apollo rescued him in his arms, in a dark cloud, lest any of the Danaans with their swift steeds thrust bronze into his breast and take away his life. Over Aphrodite Diomedes of the mighty war cry shouted loudly: "Keep away, daughter of Zeus, from war and combat. Is it not enough that you seduce weak women? If you will enter battle, then truly I think you will come to shudder when you hear tell of war, even though from afar."

So he spoke, and she, beside herself, departed sore distressed. Then wind-footed Iris took her and led her out of the throng in anguish from her pain, and her fair skin was darkened. She found impetuous Ares seated to the left of the battle; his spear and his swift horses rested upon a cloud. She fell upon her knees and with many an entreaty begged for her dear brother's horses with their golden frontlets. "Dear brother, give me your horses to carry me that I may go to Olympus, where is the home of the immortals. I am sorely pained by the wound a mortal man has given me, Tydeus' son, who would now battle even with Father Zeus."

So she spoke, and Ares gave her the horses with the golden frontlets. She mounted the chariot, grieved at heart, and Iris mounted beside her and took the reins in her hands. She lashed the horses and not unwillingly the pair flew off. Staightway they came to steep Olympus, to the dwellings of the gods. There wind-footed swift Iris stopped the horses and loosed them from the chariot and cast ambrosial food before them. But divine Aphrodite threw herself into the lap of her mother Dione, who took her daughter in her arms and caressed her with her hand and spoke and said to her: "Who now of the sons of heaven has done this thing to you, dear child, so wantonly, as though you had done wrong before the face of all?"

Then laughter-loving Aphrodite answered her: "The son of Tydeus wounded me, high-hearted Diomedes, because I was carrying my dear son out of battle, Aeneas, who is far dearest to me of all. For the dread battle is no longer between Trojans and Achaeans; now the Danaans fight even with the immortals."

Then Dione, goddess of goddesses, answered her: "Take courage, my child, and endure, though you be suffering. For many of us who have our home upon Olympus have suffered at the hands of men, while causing one another grievous woes. So suffered Ares when Otus and mighty Ephialtes, sons of Aloeus, bound him in stout fetters. In a brazen jar he lay confined for thirteen months. Then would Ares, insatiate of war, have perished, had not their stepmother, the passing lovely Eëriboea, reported it to Hermes, who stole Ares away in sore affliction, for the grievous bond was wasting him. So suffered Hera when Amphitryon's mighty son struck her in the right breast with a three-barbed arrow and unassuageable pain seized even her. So awful Hades, like the rest, suffered a swift arrow when that man, the son of aegis-bearing Zeus, shot him among the dead in Pylos and gave him over to pain. But Hades went to the house of Zeus and high Olympus, grieved at heart and pierced with anguish. For the shaft was driven into his mighty shoulder and it grieved his soul. Paeon spread pain-assuaging drugs upon the wound and healed him, for he was by no means mortal. He is a headstrong man and violent, caring not for his evil deeds, who wounds with his bow the gods who hold Olympus. It was the goddess, bright-eyed Athena, who set this man upon you; the son of Tydeus is a fool and knows not in his heart that he who fights with the immortals surely will not live long, nor have children at his knees to call him papa when he comes home from war and dreadful strife. So now let Tydeus' son, for all he is so mighty, beware lest one better than you do battle with him, lest Aegialeia, wise daughter of Adrastus, wake her household from its sleep with lamentation, weeping for her wedded husband, the best of the Achaeans—she, the comely wife of horse-taming Diomedes."

So she spoke and with both hands she wiped the ichor from her hand. The hand healed and the heavy pains abated. Athena and Hera, as they watched, taunted Zeus with mocking words. The goddess bright-eyed Athena was the first to speak: "Father Zeus, will you be angry with me for what I shall say? It seems that Cypris, urging one of the Achaean women to go with the Trojans, whom now she loves extremely, and striking one of the fair-gowned Achaean women, has scratched her delicate hand upon a golden brooch."

So she spoke, and the father of gods and men smiled and summoning golden Aphrodite said to her: "Not to you, my child, were the works of war assigned, but do you attend to the lovely works of marriage, and all these things shall be the care of swift Ares and Athena."

So they spoke to one another, but Diomedes of the mighty war cry rushed upon Aeneas, though he knew that Apollo himself held forth his arms above him. But he had no reverence for the great god and still was eager to slay Aeneas and strip off his glorious armor. Thrice then he rushed upon him, eager for the kill, and thrice Apollo struck back his gleaming shield. But when for the fourth time he rushed upon him like a god, then with a dreadful cry Apollo the warder said to him: "Beware, son of Tydeus, and give way, nor seek to match your spirit with the gods, for in no way alike are the race of immortal gods and that of men who walk the earth."

So he spoke and Tydeus' son drew back a little, avoiding the wrath of unerring Apollo. And Apollo laid down Aeneas far from the throng in holy Pergamus, where his temple had been built. Then Leto and Artemis the huntress healed him in the great shrine and gave him glory. But Apollo of the silver bow had made a wraith in appearance and armor like Aeneas, and about the wraith the Trojans and godlike Achaeans smote the curved ox-hide shields and fluttering targets on one another's breasts. Then Phoebus Apollo spoke to impetuous Ares: "Ares, Ares, bane of mortals, you bloodstained stormer of walls, could you not set upon that man and drag him from the battle, the son of Tydeus, who now would fight even with Father Zeus? First he wounded Cypris upon the hollow of the hand in close combat, and then he sprang against me also like a god."

So he spoke, and he himself sat down upon the height of Pergamus, and murderous Ares went among the lines of Trojans and urged them on, likening himself to Acamas, the swift leader of the Thracians. He shouted to the Zeus-nurtured sons of Priam: "Sons of Priam, the Zeus-nurtured king, how long will you suffer your men to be slain by the Achaeans? Until they fight about the well-built gates? Low lies the man whom we honored as much as godlike Hector, Aeneas, son of great-hearted Anchises. Come, let us save our noble comrade from the strife."

So speaking, he aroused the might and spirit of each. But Sarpedon then berated godlike Hector: "Hector, where now is the might which once you had? You used to say that you would hold the city without her men or allies, with your brothers-in-law and kinsmen. Now I cannot see or discover any of them; they skulk like dogs about a lion. But we are the ones who fight, we who are only allies. Indeed, I am an ally and come from very far. For far away is Lycia, upon the eddying Xanthus, where I left my dear wife and my young son and many possessions, which he who lacks, desires. Yet even so I urge the Lycians on and am myself eager to fight my man, though there is nothing here of mine which the Achaeans might bear or drive away. But you stand still, nor do you command the men to hold their ground and defend their wives. Beware lest, like those caught in the meshes of an all-gathering net, you become the prey and sport of your enemies, who will soon sack your fair-lying city. All these things must be your care both night and day, and you must beseech the rulers of your far-famed allies to hold firm; you must ward off harsh reproof."

So spoke Sarpedon, and his words stung Hector to the heart. Promptly he jumped with his weapons from his chariot to the ground, and brandishing his sharp spear he went everywhere throughout the army, urging them to fight, and he aroused dread conflict. So they rallied and stood to face the Achaeans, but the Argives awaited them in close ranks and fled not. Then, even as the wind bears chaff across a sacred threshing floor when men are winnowing, and fair-haired Demeter in the gusts of wind separates grain and chaff, and the heaps of chaff grow white, so now did the Achaeans grow white beneath the clouds of dust which the feet of the horses in their midst raised to the brazen sky as the fight was joined again and the charioteers wheeled round. The might of their hands they bore straight forward, and impetuous Ares threw a veil of night about the battle to aid the Trojans, ranging everywhere. So he did the bidding of Phoebus Apollo of the golden sword, who urged him to rouse the spirit of the Trojans when he saw Pallas Athena depart, for she was the Danaans' helper. Apollo himself sent Aeneas forth from the rich sanctuary and put might into the breast of the shepherd of the people. Aeneas took his place among his comrades, and they rejoiced to see him return alive and well and filled with noble might. But they did not question him at all, for another task prevented, a task that he of the silver bow was stirring, he and Ares, bane of mortals, and ever-raging Strife.

The two Ajaxes and Odysseus and Diomedes were urging on the Danaans to fight, nor did the men themselves fear the Trojan's mighty onset, but they stood firm like mists which Cronus' son holds motionless upon the mountain tops during a windless calm when the might of Boreas sleeps and that of the other raging winds which scatter the shadowy clouds with their shrill blasts. So the Danaans calmly awaited the Trojans and fled not. The son of Atreus went through the ranks with many orders: "My friends, be men and take courage at heart, and think of your repute with one another in the mighty strife. For of men who value honor, more are saved than slain, whereas to them that flee comes neither fame nor rescue."

So he spoke and swiftly cast his spear and hit a foremost fighter, a comrade of great-hearted Aeneas, Deicoön, son of Pergasus, whom the Trojans honored as much as Priam's sons, since he was quick to fight among the foremost. Mighty Agamemnon hit his shield with his spear and the shield did not stop the point, but the bronze passed clean through and drove through the belt into his lower belly. He fell with a crash and his armor clanged upon him.

Then Aeneas slew two of the best men of the Danaans, the sons of Diocles, Crethon and Orsilochus, whose father dwelt in well-built Pherae; he was rich in substance and his line was that of the river Alpheus which runs in a broad stream through the Pylians' land. Alpheus begot Orsilochus, the ruler over many men, and Orsilochus begot great-hearted Diocles, and from Diocles sprang twin sons, Crethon and Orsilochus, well skilled in every form of battle. They, in their youth, came with the Argives on the black ships to Ilium, land of horses, to gain honor for the sons of Atreus, Agamemnon and Menelaus, and now the end of death enwrapped them both. As two lions upon the mountain peaks are reared by their mother in the thickets of a deep wood and, seizing cattle and fat sheep, ravage the folds of men until they themselves are slain by the sharp bronze in men's hands, so these two, slain by the hands of Aeneas, fell like lofty pines.

Menelaus, dear to Ares, was filled with pity for them as they fell, and he went through the front ranks, armed in gleaming bronze, shaking his spear. Ares aroused his might, with the hope that he might be slain by the hands of Aeneas. But Antilochus, son of great-hearted Nestor, saw him, and himself went through the front ranks, since he feared for the shepherd of the people, lest something befall him and he cheat them of the fruit of their labor. Aeneas and Menelaus were lifting their arms and their sharp spears against each other, eager to fight, when Antilochus took his stand beside the shepherd of the people. But Aeneas did not stay, swift warrior though he was, when he saw the two men standing side by side. When, therefore, they had dragged back the bodies into the midst of the host of the Achaeans, they placed the luckless pair in the hands of their companions and themselves returned to fight among the foremost.

Then they slew Pylaemenes, like to Ares, the leader of the great-hearted Paphlagonian shieldmen. The son of Atreus, Menelaus, famed with the spear, struck him as he stood, hitting him in the collarbone with the bronze. Antilochus struck Mydon, his driver and servant, the noble son of Atymnius, just as he was turning the single-hoofed horses, hitting him squarely on the elbow with a stone. The reins, white with ivory, fell from his hands to the dust upon the ground. Antilochus rushed up and thrust his sword into his temple. Then, gasping, he toppled from the well-wrought chariot onto his head and shoulders. A long time he stuck there, for he landed in deep sand, until the horses kicked him and threw him to the dust upon the ground. Then Antilochus lashed them and drove them into the host of the Achaeans.

Hector spied Menelaus and Antilochus in the ranks and rushed upon them with a shout, and with him followed the strong battalions of the Trojans. Ares and awesome Enyo led them; she brought with her Uproar, shameless in slaughter, and Ares plied his dread spear in his hands and raged now before Hector and now behind him.

When Diomedes of the mighty war cry saw him he shuddered. As when a man, passing over a great plain, stops helpless on the bank of a swift river running seaward, and sees it boil with foam, and runs back, so Tydeus' son drew back and said to the army: "Friends, why then do we wonder at godlike

Hector as a spearman and bold warrior? One of the gods is
ever beside him, to ward off destruction. There is Ares now
beside him, looking like a mortal man. So keep your faces
toward the Trojans and draw ever back; let us not be eager to
match our strength against the gods."

So he spoke, and the Trojans came close upon them. Then
Hector slew two men well skilled in battle who were in one
chariot, Menesthes and Anchialus. And as they fell, great
Telamonian Ajax pitied them. He went and stood close by and
threw his shining spear and hit Amphius, son of Selagus, who
dwelt in Paesus and was rich in possessions and in crops, but
fate led him to go as an ally to Priam and his sons. Telamonian
Ajax hit him in the belt and the long-shadowed spear was
fixed in his lower belly and he fell with a crash. Glorious Ajax
ran up to strip him of his armor and the Trojans rained their
sharp and gleaming spears upon him, but his shield caught
many of them. Then he set his heel upon the corpse and drew
out the brazen spear. But he was not able further to strip the
fair armor from his shoulders, for he was pressed by the missiles. Indeed, he feared the mighty resistance of the lordly Trojans, who in numbers and with bravery attacked him, spears in
hand. Great and mighty and noble though he was, they thrust
him from them and he gave ground, reeling.

So they toiled in the mighty conflict. And resistless fate
aroused Tlepolemus, son of Heracles, a brave and mighty man,
against divine Sarpedon. And when they came close to one
another in their onset, the son and the grandson of cloud-
gathering Zeus, Tlepolemus was the first to speak: "Sarpedon,
counselor of the Lycians, why must you be skulking here, a
man unskilled in battle? They lie who say that you are sprung
from aegis-bearing Zeus, for you are far inferior to those who
sprang from Zeus among the men of old—such a one as they
say the mighty Heracles was, my father, bravely steadfast,
lion-hearted. He once came hither for Laomedon's mares and
with only six ships and a smaller host he sacked the city of
Ilium and made desolate its streets. But yours is a cowardly
heart and your men are perishing. In no way, I think, will your
coming from Lycia prove a defense for the Trojans, not even
though you are very strong, but rather you will be slain by me
and pass through the gates of Hades."

Then Sarpedon, leader of the Lycians, answered him:
"Tlepolemus, your father did indeed destroy holy Ilium
through the folly of that proud man Laomedon, who rewarded
his good service with harsh words and would not pay him

the mares for which he had come from afar. But I say that death and black fate shall befall you here at my hand and that slain by my spear you shall give glory to me, and your soul to Hades of the famous steeds."

So spoke Sarpedon, and Tlepolemus raised his ashen spear and the long spears sped from their hands together. Sarpedon hit him full in the neck and the grievous point passed straight through and black night enwrapped his eyes. Tlepolemus had hit Sarpedon with his long spear on the left thigh and the eager point had sped straight through, grazing the bone, but his father still kept off death.

Then his noble comrades bore godlike Sarpedon from the battle. The long spear was heavy upon him as it dragged, but none heeded, nor did they think, in their haste, to pull the ashen spear from his thigh that he might stand, such toil had they to save him.

On the other side, the well-greaved Achaeans bore Tlepolemus from battle, and godlike Odysseus, sturdy of spirit, saw him, and his heart raged within him. He pondered in heart and mind whether he should first pursue the son of loud-thundering Zeus or should take away the lives of more Lycians. But it was not fated for great-hearted Odysseus to slay with sharp bronze the mighty son of Zeus. Therefore Athena turned his fury against the multitude of Lycians. Then he slew Coeranus and Alastor and Chromius and Alcandrus and Halius and Noëmon and Prytanis. And now godlike Odysseus would have slain still more of the Lycians had not great Hector of the glancing helmet been quick to see him. He strode among the foremost fighters, armed in gleaming bronze, bearing terror to the Danaans. Then Sarpedon, son of Zeus, was glad at his coming and spoke a pitiful word: "Son of Priam, do not let me lie a prey to the Danaans but protect me and then may life leave me in your city, since I was not destined to return to my dear native land and give joy to my dear wife and infant son."

So he spoke, but Hector of the glancing helmet answered him no word, but rushed past in haste, eager with all speed to drive the Argives back and to take away the lives of many. Sarpedon's godlike companions set him beneath the fair oak of aegis-bearing Zeus, and mighty Pelagon, who was his dear comrade, pulled the ashen spear from his thigh. His spirit left him and a mist fell upon his eyes, but he breathed again and the blast of Boreas blowing upon him revived him as he was gasping out his life.

The Argives, before Ares and brazen-armored Hector,

neither turned in flight to the black ships nor stood firm in the battle, but yielded ever backwards as they learned that Ares was among the Trojans.

Whom first and whom last did Hector, Priam's son, and brazen Ares slay? The godlike Teuthras, then Orestes, the driver of horses, and Trechus, the Aetolian spearman, and Oenomaus and Helenus, son of Oenops, and Oresbius of the gleaming belt, who dwelt in Hyle hard by Lake Cephisis and cared much for his riches, and near him dwelt other Boeotians, possessors of a right fertile land.

When the white-armed goddess Hera saw them making havoc of the Argives in the mighty conflict, she forthwith spoke winged words to Athena: "Well, child of aegis-bearing Zeus, Atrytone, in vain did we give our word to Menelaus, that he should sack well-walled Ilium and sail home, if we shall allow murderous Ares thus to rage. But come, let us as well remember furious valor."

So she spoke, and the bright-eyed goddess Athena did not fail to heed. Hera, august goddess, daughter of great Cronus, harnessed the horses with their golden frontlets and Hebe quickly put upon the chariot the round wheels, brazen, eight-spoked, on either side of the iron axle. Their golden felloes are imperishable and on them are fitted brazen tires, a wonder to behold; hubs of silver turn on either side. The car is plaited with gold and silver thongs and two rims run around it. A silver pole projected from it, and at the end she bound a fair yoke of gold and threw upon it golden collars. Hera, hungry for strife and the battle cry, led the swift-footed horses underneath the yoke.

But Athena, daughter of aegis-bearing Zeus, let fall upon her father's threshold her soft and many-colored robe which she herself had woven and fashioned with her hands, and putting on the tunic of cloud-gathering Zeus, she armed herself for tearful war. Around her shoulders she cast the dread tasseled aegis, which is wholly fringed with Fear. On it is Strife, on it is Valor, on it is blood-chilling Attack and the head of the dread and monstrous Gorgon, horrible and grim, the portent of aegis-bearing Zeus. Upon her head she put the helmet with double plume and fourfold crest, golden, blazoned with the armed men of a hundred cities. She stepped into the gleaming chariot and grasped her heavy spear, huge and strong, with which she vanquishes the ranks of heroes at whom she, the daughter of the mighty sire, is angry. Hera quickly lashed the horses with the whip and the gates of heaven groaned, self-moving. These the Hours keep, to whose charge great heaven and Olympus are committed, either to throw open a thick cloud or draw it to. Straight through the gates they drove the goaded horses. They found the son of Cronus seated apart from the other gods on the highest peak of many-ridged Olympus. There the white-armed goddess Hera stopped the horses and questioned most high Zeus, the son of Cronus, saying: "Father Zeus, are you not angry with Ares for these violent deeds, destroying as he has so great and brave a host of the Achaeans ruthlessly and wantonly, to my sorrow; whereas Cypris and Apollo of the silver bow rejoice untroubled, having set this madman on, who knows not right from wrong? Father Zeus, will you be angry with me if I smite Ares shamefully and drive him out of battle?"

Then Zeus the cloud-gatherer answered her and said: "Come, then, send against him Athena, driver of spoil, who is most wont to bring sore pain upon him."

So he spoke, and the white-armed goddess Hera did not fail to heed. She lashed the horses and not unwillingly the pair flew off between the earth and starry sky. As far as a man sees with his eyes into the haze, as he sits on a lookout gazing out upon the wine-dark sea, so far leap the loud-neighing horses of the gods. But when they came to Troy and the two flowing rivers, where Simoïs and Scamander join their streams, there the white-armed goddess Hera stopped the horses and released them from the chariot and shed thick mist about them. And Simoïs made ambrosia spring up for them to eat.

The goddesses made their way with steps like timid doves, eager to aid the men of Argos. But when they came to the place where stood the largest number and the best, in close array about the mighty Diomedes, tamer of horses, like lions who eat raw meat, or wild boars of unfailing strength, there the white-armed goddess Hera stopped and shouted, likening herself to great-hearted Stentor of the brazen voice, who could shout as loud as fifty others: "Shame, Argives, wretched cowards, brave only in appearance. As long as noble Achilles went to battle, the Trojans never came forth before the Dardanian gates, for they feared his mighty spear. But now they fight far from the city by the hollow ships."

So speaking, she aroused the might and spirit of every man. And to the side of Tydeus' son sprang the bright-eyed goddess Athena. She found that chieftain beside his horses and his chariot, cooling the wound which Pandarus gave him with his arrow, for the sweat chafed him beneath the broad strap of his rounded shield. By this was he chafed, and his arm grew weary, and, lifting up the strap, he was wiping away the dark blood. Then the goddess laid her hand upon his horses' yoke and said: "Tydeus indeed begot a son but little like himself. Tydeus was small of stature but a fighter. Even when I would not let him fight or rush madly to the fray, when he went from the Achaeans as a messenger to Thebes among many Cadmeians—I bade him dine in peace within their halls—he, with his spirit mighty as of old, challenged the sons of the Cadmeians and easily won victory in all things; such a helper was I to him. But as for you, though I stand by your side and guard you and bid you battle gladly with the Trojans, either the weariness of much fighting has fallen upon your limbs or now, perhaps, a spiritless fear possesses you. No offspring, then, are you of Tydeus, Oeneus' prudent son."

The mighty Diomedes answered her and said: "I know you, goddess, daughter of aegis-bearing Zeus. Therefore I will gladly speak my mind to you and shall not hide it. No cowardly fear possesses me, nor any shrinking, but I remember still the commands you laid upon me. You would not let me fight against any other of the blessed gods, but told me that if Zeus' daughter Aphrodite should come into battle I should wound her with sharp bronze. So now I myself draw back and have ordered the other Argives all to gather here, for I discern Ares lording it upon the battlefield."

Then the bright-eyed goddess Athena answered him: "Son of Tydeus, Diomedes, dear to my heart, fear neither Ares, in this case, nor any other of the immortals, such a helper am I to you. Come, drive your single-hoofed horses against Ares first and strike him in close combat and do not dread impetuous Ares, that madman, a born plague, that renegade, who lately spoke to Hera and to me and promised to fight against the Trojans and aid the Achaeans, and who now joins with the Trojans and forgets the others."

So speaking, she drew back Sthenelus with her hand and thrust him from the chariot to the ground, and he instantly sprang away. The goddess eagerly mounted the chariot beside godlike Diomedes and loudly did the oaken axle groan beneath its burden, for it carried a dread goddess and the bravest of men. Then Pallas Athena grasped the whip and reins and quickly drove the single-hoofed horses against Ares first. Now he was despoiling of his armor huge Periphas, by far the best of the Aetolians, Ochesius' glorious son; him was bloodstained

Ares stripping. Then Athena put on the helmet of Hades, lest mighty Ares see her.

When Ares, bane of mortals, saw godlike Diomedes, he left huge Periphas to lie where first he had slain him and taken away his life, and he went straight toward Diomedes, tamer of horses. When they came close to one another in their onset, Ares thrust forward his brazen spear over the yoke and reins of the horses, eager to take away his life. But the bright-eyed goddess Athena caught the spear in her hand and thrust it up over the chariot to fly uselessly away. Then Diomedes of the mighty war cry attacked with his brazen spear. And Pallas Athena guided it to the nethermost part of Ares' belly, where he was girt by a belt. There Diomedes hit and wounded him and pierced the fair skin and drew forth the spear again. Brazen Ares bellowed as loud as nine thousand warriors, or ten thousand, shout in battle as they join in Ares' strife. A trembling fell alike upon Achaeans and Trojans, in their fear, so loudly bellowed Ares, insatiate of war.

As a black gloom appears in the clouds, when after burning heat a storm wind rises, so to Diomedes, Tydeus' son, did brazen Ares seem as he passed through the clouds to the broad heaven. Swiftly he came to the dwelling of the gods, to steep Olympus, and he sat down, grieved at heart, near Zeus, the son of Cronus. He pointed to the ambrosial blood pouring from his wounds and spoke winged words in lamentation: "Father Zeus, are you not angry to behold these violent deeds? Ever indeed do we gods suffer most cruelly through one another's will, when we show favor to men. We are all aroused against you, for you gave birth to a heedless maiden, accursed, whose mind is ever set on violent deeds. All we other gods, as many as are in Olympus, obey you and are each subject to you. But her you reprove neither by word nor deed; rather, you set her on, since you yourself bore this insolent child. She has now stirred up Tydeus' son, the mighty Diomedes, madly to attack the immortal gods. First he wounded Cypris upon the hand's edge in close combat, and next he rushed upon me like a god. But my swift feet bore me away, else I would have endured long anguish there among the grim heaps of the dead or lived on strengthless from the woundings of the bronze."

Looking at him scornfully, cloud-gathering Zeus replied: "Do not sit beside me, fickle one, and whimper. You are to me the most hateful of the gods who dwell upon Olympus. For dear to you always are strife and wars and battles. You have your mother Hera's intolerable, unyielding spirit. Hardly can

I restrain her with words. Therefore I think that it is at her promptings that you suffer thus. But still I will not long endure that you suffer pain, for you are my offspring and your mother bore you to me. If you had been born so insolent of any other of the gods, long ago would you have been lower than the sons of heaven."

So he spoke, and he ordered Paeon to restore him. And Paeon spread pain-easing drugs upon the wound and healed him, for he was not made like a mortal. As when fig sap quickly curdles white liquid milk and very quickly it thickens round it as it is stirred in, so swiftly did he heal impetuous Ares. Hebe bathed him and put fair garments upon him and he sat near Zeus, the son of Cronus, exulting in his glory.

But Argive Hera and Athena of Alalcomenae returned to the house of great Zeus, having stopped Ares, bane of mortals, from his slaying of men.

BOOK VI

So THEY LEFT the dread strife of Trojans and Achaeans. Often to this side and to that the battle surged across the plain as men aimed their brazen spears at one another between Simoïs and the streams of Xanthus.

First, Telamonian Ajax, bulwark of the Achaeans, burst through the phalanx of the Trojans and brought light to his companions, smiting the man who was chief among the Thracians, Eussorus' son, Acamas, the brave and mighty. Him first he smote upon the horn of his helmet with its thick horsehair crest, and he drove the spear into his forehead; the bronze blade pierced the bone, and darkness veiled his eyes.

Then Diomedes of the mighty war cry slew Axylus, Teuthras' son, who dwelt in well-built Arisbe; rich in wealth was he, and dear to men, for he dwelt in a house by the side of the road and entertained them all. Yet none of those then stood before him to ward off sad death, but Diomedes robbed him of his life, both him and his servant Calesius, who was then his charioteer. So both passed beneath the earth.

Euryalus stripped Dresus and Opheltius, and went after Aesepus and Pedasus, whom once the naiad Abarbarea bore to blameless Bucolion. Bucolion was the son of noble Laomedon, his eldest born, whom his mother bore in secret. And when Bucolion was keeping the sheep he lay with the nymph in love and she conceived and bore twin sons. The son of Mecisteus loosed their might and glorious limbs and stripped the armor from their shoulders.

Steadfast Polypoetes slew Astyalus. Odysseus with his brazen spear layed low Pidytes the Percosian, and Teucer slew godlike Aretaon. Antilochus, Nestor's son, slew Ablerus with his shining spear, and Agamemnon, king of men, slew Elatus, who dwelt in steep Pedasus on the banks of the fair-flowing Satnioeis. The hero Leitus took Phylacus as he fled, and Eurypylus stripped Melanthius.

Then Menelaus of the mighty war cry captured Adrastus alive, for his horses, as they bolted across the plain, stumbling on a tamarisk shoot, broke the end of the pole of the curved chariot and by themselves made for the city, whither the rest were fleeing in terror. But Adrastus was thrown out over the chariot's wheel, headlong upon his face in the dust. Beside him stood Atreus' son, Menelaus, with his long-shadowed spear. Then Adrastus clasped his knees and begged him: "Take me alive, son of Atreus, and accept a fitting ransom. Many treasures lie in my rich father's house, bronze and gold and iron, wrought with much labor. From these my father would give you boundless ransom if he should learn that I was alive beside the ships of the Achaeans."

So he spoke, and he persuaded the heart within the other's breast. And Menelaus was about to give him to his servant to lead to the swift ships of the Achaeans, but Agamemnon came running toward him and shouting cried: "You weakling, Menelaus, why thus do you spear warriors? Have you been so well treated by the Trojans in your home? Let no one of them escape utter destruction at our hands, not even the infant whom the mother bears within her womb, let not even him escape, but may all perish together out of Ilium, unlamented and unmarked."

So speaking, the hero changed his brother's mind, for he counseled wisely. With his hand, Menelaus thrust Adrastus from him and mighty Agamemnon struck him in the side; he fell backward and the son of Atreus put his heel upon his chest and drew out his ashen spear.

Then Nestor cried with a great shout to the Argives: "Friends, Danaan heroes, squires of Ares, let none now fall upon the spoil and stay behind, so that he may carry back most booty to the ships, but let us slay the men. Then at your will you may strip the dead that lie upon the plain."

So speaking, he roused the might and spirit of each. Then again the Trojans, overcome by fear, would have gone up into Ilium before the Achaeans, dear to Ares, had not Helenus, son of Priam, far best of the readers of dreams, stood beside Aeneas and Hector and said to them: "Aeneas and Hector, since upon you above all the Trojans and Lycians rests the task, because you are the best to fight or plan in every undertaking, stop here and hold the men before the gates, approaching them from all sides, before they fall in flight into the women's arms and become a source of gladness to the foe. Then, when you two rouse all our companies, we shall stay here and fight against the Danaans, even though much wearied, for necessity compels us. Then, Hector, do you go to the city and speak to your mother and mine; she shall gather the old women to the temple of bright-eyed Athena on the city's heights and shall open with a key the doors of the holy house and shall place upon the knees of the fair-haired Athena the robe which seems to her the fairest and largest in her chamber and which is far dearest to herself, and she shall promise to sacrifice to her in the temple twelve yearling heifers which have never felt the goad, in hope that the goddess may have mercy upon the city and the wives and little children of the Trojans, so as to ward off from holy Ilium the son of Tydeus, that savage spearman and mighty deviser of rout, whom I declare to be the mightiest of the Achaeans. Not even Achilles did we ever fear so much, the chief of men, who, they say, was born of a goddess. But this man rages beyond measure and no one can match his strength against him."

So he spoke, and Hector did not fail to heed his brother. Promptly he jumped with his weapons from his chariot to the ground, and brandishing his sharp spear he went everywhere throughout the army, urging them to fight, and he aroused dread conflict. So they rallied and stood to face the Achaeans, and the Argives gave ground and ceased their slaying, thinking one of the immortals had come from starry heaven to help the Trojans as they rallied. Hector, with a great shout, called to the Trojans: "High-hearted Trojans and far-famed allies, be men, my friends, and remember furious valor, while I go back to Ilium and bid the aged counselors and their wives to pray to the gods and promise offerings."

So speaking, Hector of the glancing helmet departed, and against his ankles and his neck beat the black rawhide, the rim that ran around his studded shield.

But Glaucus, son of Hippolochus, and Tydeus' son met between the two armies, eager to fight. When they came close to one another in their onset, Diomedes of the mighty war cry first addressed him: "Who among mortal men are you, good warrior? For I have never before seen you in man-ennobling battle. But now in your valor you have advanced far before all the rest, braving my long-shadowed spear. Wretched are they whose children face my might. But if you be one of the immortals come down from heaven, I would not fight with the heavenly gods. Even the son of Dryas, mighty Lycurgus, did not long endure after fighting with the heavenly gods. He drove the nurses of Dionysus over sacred Nyseium and they all dropped their wands upon the ground, struck with an ox-goad by man-slaying Lycurgus. Dionysus, in terror, dived beneath the waves of the sea and Thetis received him in her arms in his fear, for a mighty trembling seized him at the warrior's shout. Then the gods, who live in ease, were angered with Lycurgus, and the son of Cronus made him blind, nor did he live long thereafter, for he was hated by all the immortal gods. Therefore, against the blessed gods I would not wish to fight. But if you are of mortals, who eat the fruit of the field, draw near, that you may the sooner reach the snares of doom."

Then the glorious son of Hippolochus answered him: "Great-hearted son of Tydeus, why do you ask my birth? Even as the generation of leaves, such also is that of men. The leaves the wind scatters upon the earth, but the forest, as it buds, puts others forth again when the season of spring comes around. So also one generation of men blooms and another passes away. But if you wish to learn this too, that you may know well my birth—and many men do know it—there is a city Ephyra, in a corner of horse-raising Argos, and there Sisyphus dwelt, who was the craftiest of men, Sisyphus, Aeolus' son. And he begot a son, Glaucus, and Glaucus begot blameless Bellerophon. To him the gods gave beauty and lovely manhood. But Proetus plotted evil against him in his heart and drove him from the Argives' land, since he was mightier far, for Zeus had made Bellerophon subject to Proetus' scepter. For Proetus' wife, divine Anteia, was mad for him and longed to lie with him in secret love. But she could not persuade the wise Bellerophon, because he was upright of heart. So she spoke falsely to King Proetus: 'Die, Proetus, or else slay Bellerophon, since he wished to lie with me in love against my will!' So she spoke, and anger seized the king at what he heard. But he forbore to slay him, for he feared it in his heart, and he sent him to Lycia and gave him fatal tokens, writing in a folded tablet many soul-destroying things, and bade him show these to Anteia's father, that he might be slain. So he went to Lycia under the blameless escort of the gods. Now when he came to Lycia and to flowing Xanthus, the king of broad Lycia was eager to do him honor. For nine days he entertained him and slew nine oxen. But when the tenth rosy-fingered dawn appeared, then he questioned him and asked to see the token he bore from his daughter's husband, Proetus. Then, when he had received the evil token from his son-in-law, he first bade Bellerophon to slay the raging Chimaera. Now she was of immortal race and not of men, in front a lion, in back a serpent, in the middle a goat, and she breathed forth a dreadful might of gleaming fire. But he slew her, trusting in the portents of the gods. Next he fought against the glorious Solymi, and this, he said, was the mightiest battle of warriors that he ever entered. Thirdly, he slew the Amazons, who were a match for men. And when he returned, the king wove another subtle plot against him. Choosing the best men from broad Lycia, he set an ambush, but they never returned home, for blameless Bellerophon slew them all. But when the king saw that he was a brave offspring of the gods, he kept him there and gave him his daughter and half of all the honor of his kingdom. And the Lycians carved out for him a property superior to all the rest, fair with fruit and plowland, bearing wheat, that he might own it. And his wife bore three children to wise Bellerophon— Isander and Hippolochus and Laodameia. Zeus the counselor lay with Laodameia and she bore him godlike Sarpedon of the brazen armor. But when even Bellerophon became hated of all the gods, he wandered alone over the Aleian plain, eating out his heart and shunning the paths of men. His son Isander was slain by Ares, insatiate of war, as he fought against the glorious Solymi, and Artemis of the golden reins slew his daughter in anger. Hippolochus begot me, and I say that I am sprung from him. He sent me to Troy and he told me many times ever to excel and be pre-eminent above the rest, and not to bring shame upon my father's race, who were by far the bravest in Ephyra and in broad Lycia. Of that race and blood I boast to be."

So he spoke, and Diomedes of the mighty war cry rejoiced. He thrust his spear into the fertile earth and then with gentle words addressed the shepherd of the people: "Indeed, now, you are an old family friend of mine. For godlike Oeneus once entertained blameless Bellerophon and kept him in his halls for twenty days, and they gave one another fair gifts of friendship. Oeneus gave a belt bright with scarlet and Bellerophon a two-handled cup of gold, which I left in my palace when I came away. I do not remember Tydeus, for he left me when I was still small, when the army of the Achaeans fell at Thebes. Therefore am I your host in the midst of Argos and you mine in Lycia, when I journey to that land. So let us avoid each other's spears even amid the throng; for there are many Trojans and famed allies for me to slay, whomsoever a god shall grant me and my feet overtake, and many Achaeans for you to slay, whomever you can. Let us now exchange arms with one another, so that these men also may know that we declare ourselves to be friends through our fathers."

So they spoke, and leaped down from their chariots, clasped each other's hand and pledged their faith. Then Zeus, Cronus' son, took Glaucus' wits away, for he exchanged with Diomedes, Tydeus' son, golden arms for bronze, the worth of a hundred oxen for the worth of nine.

When Hector came to the Scaean gates and the oak tree, the wives and daughters of the Trojans ran about him, asking for their sons and brothers, for their kinsmen and their husbands. He bade them all in turn pray to the gods. But over many sorrow hung.

But when he came to the fair house of Priam, with its polished colonnade—in it there were fifty chambers of polished stone, built close beside each other, wherein the sons of Priam slept beside their wedded wives; and over against them on the other side within the court were twelve roofed chambers of polished stone, built close by one another, for his daughters, where slept the sons-in-law of Priam beside their wedded wives—there his bountiful mother came to meet him, bringing with her Laodice, fairest in face among her daughters. She put her hand upon him and spoke and said to him: "My child, why have you left the violent battle and come hither? I suppose the accursed sons of the Achaeans are pressing hard in their fight about the city, and your spirit bade you come hither and raise your hands to Zeus from the citadel. But wait while I bring you honey-sweet wine, that you may pour a libation to Father Zeus and the other immortals first, and then may be refreshed yourself, if you will drink. Wine greatly increases the strength of a man wearied even as you have grown weary bearing succor to your friends."

Then great Hector of the glancing helmet answered her: "Bring me no honey-hearted wine, queenly Mother, lest you deprive me of my might and I forget my valor. I fear to pour a libation of sparkling wine to Zeus with unwashed hands. Nor is it right to pray to the dark-clouded son of Cronus when fouled with blood and gore. But do you go with burnt offerings to the temple of Athena, driver of spoil, gathering together the older women, and place upon the knees of fair-haired Athena the robe which is the fairest and largest in your chamber and which is far dearest to you yourself, and promise to sacrifice to her in her temple twelve yearling heifers which have never felt the goad, in hope that she may have mercy upon the city and the Trojans' wives and little children and that she may ward off from holy Ilium the son of Tydeus, the wild spearman, the mighty deviser of rout. Do you then go to the temple of Athena, the driver of spoil, and I will go after

Paris, that I may summon him, if he will listen to what I say. Would that the earth would open beneath him on the spot, for the Olympian reared him to be a woe to the Trojans and to great-hearted Priam and his sons. If I should see him going down into the house of Death, then would I say that my heart had forgotten its sorrow."

So he spoke, and she went into the hall and gave orders to her handmaids, and they gathered the old women throughout the city. But she went into the fragrant, vaulted storeroom where were her richly embroidered robes, the work of Sidonian women whom godlike Alexander himself brought from Sidon, sailing the broad deep, on the same voyage on which he carried away high-born Helen. Taking one of these robes, Hecuba bore it as a gift to Athena, that one which was the fairest with embroidery and the largest, and shone like a star, and lay beneath the others. Then she set out, and many aged women followed her.

When they came to the temple of Athena on the heights of the city, fair-cheeked Theano, Cisses' daughter, the wife of horse-taming Antenor, opened the doors for them, for the Trojans had made her priestess of Athena. Then all with lamentations lifted up their hands to Athena, and fair-cheeked Theano took the robe and laid it on fair-haired Athena's knees and prayed in supplication to the daughter of great Zeus: "Revered Athena, protectress of the city, goddess of goddesses, break now Diomedes' spear, and grant that he may fall headlong before the Scaean gates, so that we may now straightway sacrifice to thee in thy temple twelve yearling heifers which have never felt the goad, in the hope that thou mayest have mercy upon the city and upon the wives and little children of the Trojans."

So she spoke in prayer, but Pallas Athena refused her. Thus were they praying to the daughter of great Zeus, but Hector went to the fair palace of Alexander, which Paris himself had built, with the men who were then the best builders in fertile Troy. They had built him a chamber and hall and court close to Priam and Hector, on the heights of the city. There entered Hector, dear to Zeus, and in his hand he held a spear of eleven cubits; at the end of the shaft gleamed the brazen tip and around ran a golden ferrule. He found Paris in his chamber, busy with his beautiful armor, his shield and breastplate, and handling his curved bow. Argive Helen sat with the women of her household and appointed to her maids their glorious work. When Hector saw Paris, he reproached him with scornful words: "Accursed one, you have no right to nurse this anger in your heart. The people perish in battle about the city and the steep wall, and it is for your sake that the battle cry and war have flamed about this city. And you would rage against any other whom you might see shirking hateful war. Up then, lest soon the city burn with hostile fire."

Then the godlike Alexander answered him: "Hector, since you have reproached me after my deserts and not beyond, I will explain to you. Do you give heed and hear me. It was not so much because of anger and indignation at the Trojans that I remained sitting in my chamber, but I desired to give myself up to grief. And just now my wife, persuading me with soft words, urged me to war. And it seems to me also that it will be better thus. Victory visits various men in turn. Come now, remain; let me put on the arms of Ares; or go, and I will follow —I think that I shall overtake you."

So he spoke, but Hector of the glancing helmet did not answer him at all. And Helen addressed Hector with humble words: "Brother of mine, horrible, malicious vixen that I am, would that on the day when first my mother bore me, some evil blast of a storm had come to bear me away to the mountain or to the billow of the resounding sea where the waves would have swept me away before these things came to pass. But since the gods so decreed these things, would that I had been the wife of a better man, who knew the meaning of disgrace and men's numerous reproaches. But this man's heart is not firm now nor shall it ever be hereafter. Therefore I think that he shall reap its fruits. Come now, enter and sit down upon this chair, my brother, since weariness has fallen most upon your heart because of my shamelessness and Alexander's folly. Upon us both Zeus sent an evil fate, that we should make matter for song for men who shall be hereafter."

Then great Hector of the glancing helmet answered her: "Ask me not to sit down, Helen, though it be from love, for you shall not persuade me. For already my spirit is eager to help the Trojans, who greatly miss me in my absence. But do you arouse this man and let him make haste himself, so that he may overtake me while I am still within the city. I shall go home that I may see my household and my dear wife and infant son, for I do not know if I shall ever come back to them again, or whether the gods will now destroy me at the hands of the Achaeans."

So speaking, Hector of the glancing helmet departed and quickly came to his comfortable house, but he did not find white-armed Andromache within its walls, for she, with her child and fair-robed servant, had taken her stand upon the wall, with lamentation and tears. When, therefore, Hector did not find his blameless wife within, he went and stood upon the threshold and called to the serving women: "Come now, serving women, tell me truly, where went white-armed Andromache forth from the hall? Has she gone to the home of one of my sisters or of my brothers' fair-robed wives, or to Athena's temple, where the other fair-tressed Trojan women propitiate the dreadful goddess?"

Then the busy housekeeper addressed him: "Hector, since you bid us answer truly, she has gone neither to the house of one of your sisters nor of your brothers' fair-robed wives, nor to Athena's temple, where the other fair-tressed Trojan women propitiate the dreadful goddess, but she has gone to the great wall of Ilium because she heard that the Trojans were hard-pressed and the might of the Achaeans great. So she has gone to the wall in haste, like one distraught. And the nurse went with her, carrying the child."

So spoke the housekeeper, and Hector hastened from his home back the same way through the well-built streets. When in his passage through the great city he came to the Scaean gates, where he was about to pass through onto the plain, there his richly dowered wife came running to meet him, Andromache, the daughter of great-hearted Eëtion—Eëtion, who dwelt under wooded Placus in Thebe-under-Placus, ruling over the men of Cilicia. His daughter was the wife of brazen-armored Hector. So then she met him, and the nurse came with her, holding in her arms the tender child, a mere infant, the beloved son of Hector, like to a fair star, whom Hector called Scamandrius, but the rest Astyanax, for Hector alone watched over Ilium. So Hector smiled and gazed upon his child in silence. But Andromache stood close beside him weeping, and she put her hand upon him and spoke and said to him: "What can possess you? Your own might will destroy you, nor have you any pity on your infant son or hapless me, who soon shall be your widow. For soon will the Achaeans all set upon you and slay you. When I am bereft of you, it would be better for me to pass beneath the earth. There will be no more warm comfort for me when you have met your doom, but only grief. No father have I nor queenly mother; godlike Achilles slew my father and utterly laid waste the comfortable city of the Cilicians, Thebe of the lofty gates. He slew Eëtion, but he did not despoil him of his arms, for he feared in his heart to do so. Rather, he burned him in his well-wrought armor and raised a mound above him. Around it the mountain nymphs, daughters of aegis-bearing Zeus, planted elms. And the seven brothers who were mine within those halls all in one day passed into the house of Death; for swift-footed, godlike Achilles slew them all among their shambling cattle and white sheep. And my mother, who ruled as queen under wooded Placus, he brought here with the rest of the spoil, but set her free when he had taken a boundless ransom; and Artemis the huntress, slew her in her father's halls. Now, Hector, you to me are father and queenly mother and brother as well, and you are my stalwart husband. Come now, have pity; remain here upon the wall, lest you make your son an orphan and a widow of your wife. Station your army here by the wild fig tree, where the city may best be assaulted and the wall be scaled. For three times the best of them have come here to try the wall with the two Ajaxes and glorious Idomeneus and the sons of Atreus and Tydeus' valiant son; whether someone well skilled in soothsaying told them or now even their own spirit urges and drives them on."

Then great Hector of the glancing helmet said to her: "I, too, take thought of these things, dear wife. But I feel great shame before the Trojans and their long-robed wives if like a coward I skulk from war. Nor does my own heart permit it; for I have learned to be valiant always and to fight among the foremost Trojans, striving greatly for my father's glory and my own. For well I know this in my heart and soul: there will come a day when holy Ilium shall fall, and Priam and the people of Priam of the good ashen spear. But not so much does the anguish of the Trojans of aftertime move me, nor Hecuba's own nor King Priam's nor that of my brothers, many and brave, who may fall in the dust at the hands of their foemen, as your anguish, when some bronze-clad Achaeans shall lead you forth weeping and rob you of your day of freedom. And then, perhaps, dwelling in Argos, you shall weave at another's bidding or carry water from Messeïs or Hypereia, much against your will, and harsh necessity shall lie upon you. Then some man shall say as he sees you weeping, 'This was Hector's wife, he who was the best in battle of the horse-taming Trojans when they fought around Ilium.' So someone will say. And upon you then shall come fresh grief for want of such a man to ward off the day of bondage. But may the heaped earth cover me in death before I hear your cry or the sound of your captivity."

So spoke glorious Hector, and reached out for his son, but the child shrank back with a cry into the arms of his fair-girdled nurse, frightened at the sight of his dear father, afraid of the bronze and the horsehair crest as he saw it nodding dreadfully from the helmet's peak. His dear father and queenly mother laughed, and glorious Hector quickly took his helmet from his head and laid it all gleaming on the ground. Then, when he had kissed his dear son and dandled him in his arms, he spoke in prayer to Zeus and the other gods: "Zeus, and ye other gods, grant that this child of mine also may become, even as I am, pre-eminent among the Trojans, as great in strength, and that he may rule with might over Ilium. And may someone say of him one day, as he returns from war, 'This man is much better than his father.' May he slay his enemy and bear away the bloodstained spoils, and may his mother's heart rejoice."

So speaking, he put the child in the hands of his dear wife, and she took him in her fragrant arms, smiling through her tears. When her husband saw it, he pitied her, and he caressed her with his hand and spoke and said to her: "Foolish one, do not grieve too much at heart. For no man shall send me down to the house of Death contrary to my fate. No man, I say, has escaped his doom, be he cowardly or brave, when once he has been born. But do you go home and busy yourself with your own tasks, the loom and distaff, and bid your handmaids ply their work. And war shall be for all men, for all who live in Ilium, but especially for me."

So spoke glorious Hector, and took up his crested helmet. His dear wife went homeward, turning often to look back, and shedding great tears. Quickly then she came to man-slaying Hector's comfortable house. Within she found her many handmaids, and she set them all to weeping. So they wept for Hector in his house while still he lived, for they thought he never would return again from war, escaped from the might and hands of the Achaeans.

Nor did Paris linger in his lofty house, but as soon as he had put on his glorious armor, all fairly wrought of bronze, he rushed out through the city, confident in his swift feet, like a horse from his stall, well fed at the manger, who breaks his tether and runs galloping over the plain, accustomed to bathe in a fair-flowing river. Proud he is; he holds his head high and the mane flows about his shoulders. His knees quickly bear him, trusting in his beauty, to the haunts and pastures of the mares. So Paris, Priam's son, strode down

from the heights of Pergamus, gleaming in his armor like the
shining sun, and laughing; and his swift feet bore him on.
Quickly then he met his brother Hector, just as he was about
to turn from the place where he had lingered with his wife.
The godlike Alexander addressed him first: "Brother, surely
I have delayed you in your haste by tarrying too long and I
have not come quickly as you bade."

   Then Hector of the glancing helmet answered him: "Fool,
no man is just who would make light of your work in battle,
when you are valiant. But you willingly grow slack and careless, and my heart is grieved within me when I hear reproaches against you from the Trojans, who suffer much
hardship for your sake. But let us go; we shall make amends
for this hereafter, if Zeus ever grants us to set for the heavenly
gods, who lived forever, a bowl to toast deliverance in our
halls, when we have driven the well-greaved Achaeans out of
Troy."

BOOK VII

So speaking, glorious Hector rushed forth from the gates, and with him went his brother Alexander. Both of them were eager at heart for war and battle. And as a god gives a fair wind to sailors in their longing, when they are weary of driving across the sea with their well-polished oars of pine, and their limbs are loosed with weariness, so these two appeared to the Trojans in their longing.

Then Paris slew the son of lord Areithous, Menestheus, who dwelt at Arne, who was born of Areithous the mace-bearer and of the ox-eyed Phylomedousa. Hector with his sharp spear struck Eioneus on the neck beneath his helmet's rim of bronze and loosed his limbs. And Glaucus, son of Hippolochus, leader of the men of Lycia, hurled his spear through the mighty conflict at Iphinous, son of Dexius, as he sprang up behind his swift mares, and struck his shoulder; he fell from the chariot to the ground, and his limbs were loosed.

Now when the bright-eyed goddess Athena saw them slaying the Argives in the mighty conflict, she came rushing down from the peaks of Olympus to holy Ilium. But Apollo, looking out from Pergamus, hurried to meet her, for he desired victory for the Trojans. The two met beside the oak tree, and lord Apollo, son of Zeus, first addressed her: "Daughter of great Zeus, why have you now come so eagerly from Olympus? Why has your great heart so moved you? So that you may change the course of victory in battle and give it to the Danaans? For you have no pity on the Trojans as they perish. But if you would only heed me, it would be far better. Let us stop war and slaughter for today. Hereafter they will fight again until they win the goal of Ilium, since you goddesses are pleased at heart to overthrow this city."

Then the bright-eyed goddess Athena said to him: "So be it, Warder, for with this in mind I myself came from Olympus to the Trojans and Achaeans. But come, how do you wish us to stop the warriors' battle?"

Then lord Apollo, son of Zeus, addressed her: "Let us rouse the valiant spirit of horse-taming Hector, that he may perhaps

challenge some one of the Danaans to fight against him hand
to hand in deadly combat; the bronze-greaved Achaeans in
surprise would send someone to fight alone with godlike Hector."

So he spoke, and the bright-eyed goddess Athena did not
fail to heed him. Helenus, dear son of Priam, perceived in his
mind the plan which pleased the gods in council, and he went
and stood near Hector and addressed him: "Hector, son
of Priam, like to Zeus in counsel, you might listen to me
now, since I am your brother. Cause the rest of the Trojans
and all the Achaeans to sit down, and you yourself challenge
whoever is best of the Achaeans to fight you hand to hand
in deadly combat. For it is not yet your fate to die and meet
your doom, for so I heard the word of the gods who live
forever."

So he spoke, and Hector rejoiced greatly when he heard his
words, and stepping between the lines he checked the Trojans'
companies, grasping the middle of his spear, and they all sat
down. And Agamemnon caused the well-greaved Achaeans to
sit down, and Athena and Apollo of the silver bow sat like
vultures upon the lofty oak of Father Zeus, the aegis-bearer,
rejoicing in the warriors. Their ranks sat close, bristling with
shields and helmets and spears. As a ripple spreads upon the
deep when the West Wind rises fresh and the sea grows dark
beneath it, so sat the ranks of Achaeans and Trojans on the
plain. And Hector spoke to both: "Hear me, Trojans and well-
greaved Achaeans, that I may tell you what the spirit within
my breast commands. High-throned Zeus has not yet fulfilled
our oaths, but with evil purpose sets the lot for both until the
time when either you take well-walled Troy or yourselves are
slain beside the seafaring ships. Among you are the best of all
the Achaeans. Now whomsoever of these his spirit bids do
battle with me, let him come hither before all to be your
champion against godlike Hector. So say I, and may Zeus be
my witness: if that man slay me with the long-edged bronze,
let him strip off my armor and bear it to the hollow ships, but
give back my body home, that the Trojans and the Trojans'
wives may give to me in death the meed of fire. But if I slay
him and Apollo grant me glory, I shall strip off his armor
and bear it to holy Ilium and shall hang it in the temple of
unerring Apollo, but I shall give back his body to the well-
benched ships, that the long-haired Achaeans may bury it with
honor and raise a funeral mound for him by the wide Hellespont. And some day someone even of men who are born long

after, sailing with his many-oared ship upon the wine-dark sea, shall say: 'That is the tomb of a man who died of old, a champion whom glorious Hector slew.' So someone shall some day say, and my glory shall never die."

So he spoke, and they all were hushed in silence. They were ashamed to deny him, but they feared to meet him. But at last Menelaus arose and reproached them with scornful words and gave a deep groan from his heart. "Alas, you braggarts, you women of Achaea, men no longer, this shall be a reproach dreadful beyond dread, if no one of the Danaans will go now to face Hector. May you all turn to earth and water as you sit here, each man disheartened, utterly inglorious. I myself will arm against this man. But the cords of victory are held above, in the hands of the immortal gods."

So speaking, he put on his fair armor. Then, Menelaus, would the end of life have appeared for you at the hands of Hector, since he was mightier far, had not the kings of the Achaeans rushed up and seized you, and Atreus' son himself, wide-ruling Agamemnon, caught you by the right hand and spoken and said to you: "You are mad, Zeus-nurtured Menelaus, and there is no need for this madness. Hold back, however troubled, and be not determined in your wrath to fight a better man than you, Hector, Priam's son, whom the others also dread. Even Achilles shuddered to meet him in man-ennobling battle, though he is far better than you. But join the company of your comrades and sit down; against this man the Achaeans will raise some other champion. Even though Hector be shameless and insatiate of the din of battle, I say that he shall gladly bend his knee, if he escape from blazing war and dreadful slaughter."

So speaking, the hero won over his brother's heart by his just dissuasion, and he obeyed. Then his squires joyfully removed the armor from his shoulders, and Nestor arose and spoke to the Argives: "Ah, truly a great woe has come upon the land of Achaea. Greatly would old Peleus groan, the driver of horses, the noble counselor and orator of the Myrmidons, who once took great pleasure at his house in asking and inquiring of me the race and birth of all the Argives. If now he should hear that they all cower before Hector, he would raise his hands to heaven and utter many a prayer to the immortals to send his spirit from his limbs into the house of Death. Father Zeus and Athena and Apollo, would that I were young as when by the swift-flowing Celadon the angry Pylians and the Arcadian spearmen did battle before the walls of Pheia round the streams of Iardanus. Ereuthalion stood forth as champion of the Arcadians, a godlike mortal, bearing on his shoulders the arms of King Areithous, godlike Areithous, whom the men and the fair-girdled women called by the name of mace-bearer, because he fought not with the bow nor with the long spear but crushed the ranks with a mace of iron. Him Lycurgus slew by guile, not by might, in a narrow road where his iron mace could not ward off destruction from him. For Lycurgus came upon him unawares and pierced his middle with a spear, and he fell backward to the ground. He stripped him of the armor which brazen Ares gave him. This, then, he wore himself amid the mill of Ares. But when Lycurgus grew old in his halls, he gave it to his dear squire Ereuthalion to wear, and he, bearing his armor, challenged all the bravest. And they trembled greatly and were afraid, nor did any of them dare, but my much-enduring spirit sent me forth to fight against his valor, though in years I was youngest of all. So I fought with him, and Athena gave me glory. He was the tallest and the mightiest man I ever slew. A great hulk, he lay sprawled this way and that. Would I were young as then and my might were still unshaken. Then would Hector of the glancing helmet soon meet with battle. But even those of you who are the best of all the Achaeans do not eagerly desire to meet Hector face to face."

So the old man taunted them, and up stood nine in all. But by far the first rose Agamemnon, king of men; then after him rose Tydeus' son, mighty Diomedes, and after them the Ajaxes, clothed in furious valor, and after them Idomeneus and Idomeneus' squire Meriones, like man-slaying Enyalius, and after these Eurypylus, Euaemon's glorious son. Up too stood Thoas, Andraemon's son, and godlike Odysseus. So all these were ready to fight with godlike Hector, and among them Nestor, the Gerenian horseman, spoke again: "Cast lots now in turn among you, whoever shall be chosen, for he shall aid the well-greaved Achaeans and shall himself profit his own spirit if he escape from war and dreadful slaughter."

So he spoke, and they each marked a lot and cast it into the helmet of Agamemnon, Atreus' son. And the people prayed and raised their hands to the gods, and thus one would cry, looking up to broad heaven: "Father Zeus, may the lot fall either to Ajax or to the son of Tydeus, or to the king himself of Mycenae, rich in gold."

So they spoke, and the Gerenian horseman, Nestor, shook the lots, and from the helmet leaped forth the lot that they themselves desired, that of Ajax, and a herald carried it every-where throughout the throng, and passing it from left to right showed it to all the noblest of the Achaeans. But they did not recognize it, and each disowned it. But when, as he carried it everywhere throughout the throng, he came to him who marked it and cast it into the helmet, glorious Ajax, then Ajax held out his hand and the herald stood close by him and dropped the lot into it; and when Ajax saw the mark on the lot, he recognized it and rejoiced in heart. He threw the lot to the ground at his feet and said: "See, friends, the lot is mine, and even I rejoice in heart since I expect to conquer godlike Hector. Come now, while I put on my battle gear, pray to lord Zeus, Cronus' son, silently to yourselves, so that the Trojans may not hear it—or even do it openly, since, after all, we fear no one. For no one with his will against mine shall put me to flight by force, nor yet by skill, since I hope that I was not born and reared so great a fool in Salamis."

So he spoke, and they prayed to lord Zeus, Cronus' son, and thus one would say, looking up to broad heaven: "Father Zeus, who dost rule from Ida, most glorious, most great, grant victory to Ajax and that he may win glorious renown, and even if thou lovest Hector and dost cherish him, grant to both equal might and glory."

So they spoke, and Ajax armed himself in flashing bronze. Then, when he had put all his armor on his body, he rushed out just as huge Ares advances when he goes to war amid the heroes whom the son of Cronus has set on to battle, with the might of soul-devouring strife. Like him sprang forth huge Ajax, bulwark of the Achaeans, with a grim smile upon his face; and his feet beneath took giant strides, and he shook his long-shadowed spear. The Argives rejoiced when they beheld him, and a dread trembling came upon each Trojan's limbs. The heart of Hector himself beat fast in his breast, but in no way could he flee or shrink back into the host of men, since he had challenged to battle. Ajax drew near, bearing a shield like a city wall, seven ox hides bound in bronze, which Tychius had wrought with toil, by far the best of the workers in hide, who lived in Hyle. He it was who made for him the gleaming shield from the hides of seven slick oxen, and on them fastened an eighth layer of bronze. Bearing this before his breast, Telamonian Ajax stood close to Hector and, threatening, said: "Hector, now shall you know well, alone and by yourself, the mettle of the best among the Danaans after Achilles, the lion-hearted breaker of men. He sits by the curved, seafaring ships in anger at Agamemnon, the shepherd of the people, but we are such as to stand against you, and numerous as well. Come, start the war and battle."

Then great Hector of the glancing helmet said to him: "Zeus-born Ajax, son of Telamon, leader of men, try me not as you would a feeble child or woman who knows not the works of war. Indeed, I am well skilled in battles and the slaying of men. I know how to swing to the right or the left my shield of seasoned hide, which is my manner of tough battle. I know how to charge into the tumult of swift horses, and I know how in close combat to tread a measure to furious Ares. Yet I would not strike you, since you are such a man, by catching you unaware, but openly, if I may hit you."

So speaking, he drew back his long-shadowed spear and cast it. He struck the dreadful shield of Ajax with its seven ox hides on the outermost bronze, which was the eighth layer upon it. Through six folds tore the stubborn bronze but was stopped by the seventh. Then in turn Zeus-born Ajax hurled his long-shadowed spear and struck the balanced shield of Priam's son. Through the bright shield went the heavy spear and pierced the richly wrought breastplate. Straight through the tunic cut the spear and grazed his flank, but he bent aside and avoided black fate. Then both at once drew out the long spears with their hands and fell upon one another like ravening lions or like boars, who have no feeble strength. Priam's son struck the center of Ajax' shield with his spear but the bronze did not break through, for its point was turned. Then Ajax leaped forward and pierced Hector's shield. Straight through went the spear and staggered him in his attack. It came so as to graze his neck, and the dark blood gushed forth. But not even so did Hector of the glancing helmet cease from battle, but drawing back he picked up in his stout hand a stone which lay upon the plain, black and jagged and great. With this he smote the dreadful shield of Ajax with its seven ox hides, full upon the boss, and the bronze rang about it. Next Ajax picked up a far greater stone, and swinging hurled it, putting into it immeasurable strength. And he crushed the shield with a cast of the millstone, and he bent down Hector's knees. So Hector was stretched upon his back, crushed beneath his shield, but Apollo raised him up at once. And now with swords they would have wounded one another in close combat, had not heralds come, the messengers of Zeus and men, one from the Trojans and one from the bronze-clad Achaeans, Talthybius and Idaeus, both prudent men. They held their staves between the two, and the herald Idaeus, skilled in wise counsels, spoke: "Fight and do battle no longer, dear sons. For cloud-gathering Zeus loves you both and you are both spearmen, as indeed we are all aware. Already night is here, and it is well to obey the night."

Then Telamonian Ajax answered him and said: "Idaeus, bid Hector say that, for he himself challenged all the best to battle. Let him begin, then I will surely obey, even as he shall say."

Then great Hector of the glancing helmet said to him: "Ajax, seeing that God gave you stature and strength and wisdom too, and you are far best of the Achaeans with the spear, let us now cease from strife and battle for this day. Later we shall fight again, until God judge between us and give one side the victory. Already night is here, and it is well to obey the night, that you may gladden all the Achaeans beside the ships and especially the kinsmen and companions who are yours, and I at the same time in the great city of Lord Priam shall gladden the Trojans and the Trojan women with their trailing robes, who shall enter the precinct of the gods to offer prayer for me. Come, let us each give glorious gifts to one another, that some one of the Achaeans and Trojans may speak thus, 'They fought, indeed, out of soul-devouring hate, but then they made a compact and parted in friendship.' "

So speaking, he gave him his silver-studded sword, which he bore with its sheath and well-cut sword belt. And Ajax gave a belt bright with scarlet. So the two parted, the one went among the men of the Achaeans and the other passed into the throng of Trojans. The latter rejoiced when they saw him approaching safe and sound, escaped from the fury of Ajax and his invincible hands. They led him toward the city scarce believing he was safe. Meanwhile, upon the other side, the well-greaved Achaeans led to godlike Agamemnon Ajax, filled with the joy of victory.

When they were in the tent of Atreus' son, then Agamemnon, king of men, slew a bull for them, a five-year-old bullock, in honor of the mighty son of Cronus. They flayed and dressed it and cut it all up, and divided the pieces expertly and placed them on spits and roasted them carefully and drew them all off. Then, when they had ceased from their toil and had made the banquet ready, they ate, and no heart lacked due portion of the feast. But the warrior son of Atreus, wide-ruling Agamemnon, gave the long chine to Ajax as an honor. Then, when they had put aside desire for food and drink, old Nestor first of all began to weave counsel for them, he whose advice had seemed the best in former times as well. He, with wise and kindly thought for them, spoke and said: "Son of Atreus and you others who are best of all the Achaeans, many long-haired Achaeans have died whose dark blood bitter Ares has now shed beside fair-flowing Scamander, and their souls have gone down into the house of Death. Therefore you must stop the war of the Achaeans at dawn, and we ourselves shall assemble and shall wheel the bodies hither with oxen and mules. Then let us burn them a little way from the ships, so that each of us may carry the bones home to their children when we return to our native land. And let us raise a common tomb about the pyre, building it upon the plain, and close by it let us quickly build a lofty wall, a protection for the ships and for ourselves. And in it we shall set close-fitting gates, that through them there may be way for driving chariots, and close outside let us dig a deep ditch, which with its circuit may hold back horses and men, lest ever the battle of the lordly Trojans fall heavily upon us."

So he spoke, and all the kings assented. And there was also an assembly of the Trojans, dreadfully troubled, on the heights of the city of Ilium, at Priam's very gates. Among them wise Antenor was the first to speak: "Hear me, Trojans and Dardanians and allies, that I may say what the spirit within my breast commands. Come now, let us give Argive Helen and the treasures with her to the sons of Atreus to take away. For now we fight after violating faithful oaths. Therefore I think that no good shall now befall us to deter us from so doing."

So speaking, he sat down, and before them arose the godlike Alexander, husband of fair-haired Helen, and answering him he spoke winged words: "Antenor, these things you say no longer please me. You know how to think of some other, better proposal than this. If you really say this in earnest, then indeed the gods themselves have taken away your senses. Now I shall speak to the horse-taming Trojans. I tell you outright: I will not give back the woman; but all the treasures which I brought home from Argos I am willing to give back and to add still others from our house."

So speaking, he sat down, and before them arose Priam, son of Dardanus, a counselor equal to the gods, and he with wise and kindly thought for them spoke and said: "Hear me, Trojans and Dardanians and allies, that I may say what the spirit within my breast commands. Eat your supper now throughout the city as before, and keep watch and be each of you awake. But at dawn let Idaeus go to the hollow ships to tell to the sons of Atreus, Agamemnon and Menelaus, the proposal of Alexander, for whose sake strife arose. And let him make this sage proposal also, that they may perhaps be willing to cease from tumultuous war until we burn the dead. Then later we shall fight again until God judge between us and give to one side victory."

So he spoke, and they readily listened and obeyed him, and then they ate supper throughout the host by companies. But at dawn Idaeus went to the hollow ships and found the Danaans, the squires of Ares, in council by the stern of Agamemnon's ship. Then the loud-voiced herald stood in their midst and addressed them: "Son of Atreus and you other noblest of all the Achaeans, Priam and the other noble Trojans bade me report the proposal of Alexander, for whose sake strife arose, in the hope that it might prove pleasing and acceptable to you. All the treasures which Alexander brought in the hollow ships to Troy—and would that he had perished before that—all these he is willing to give and to add still others from his house. But the wedded wife of glorious Menelaus he says he will not give back, though indeed the Trojans bid him. And this proposal also they bade me make, that you may perhaps be willing to cease from tumultuous war until we burn the dead. Then later we shall fight again until God judge between us and give to one side victory."

So he spoke, and they all were hushed in silence. Then at last Diomedes of the mighty war cry spoke: "Let no one now accept the treasures of Alexander nor Helen. It is known even to him who is utterly a fool that already the snares of doom have closed upon the Trojans."

So he spoke, and all the sons of the Achaeans cheered, admiring the speech of horse-taming Diomedes. Then mighty Agamemnon addressed Idaeus: "Idaeus, you yourself have heard the speech of the Achaeans, how they answer you. And I too am pleased that it should be thus. But I do not at all begrudge the burning of the bodies. For there can be no failure quickly to appease the bodies of the dead with fire when they have died. And let Zeus, Hera's loud-thundering husband, be witness to the oaths."

So speaking, he raised his scepter to all the gods, and Idaeus went back to holy Ilium. The Trojans and Dardanians were seated, all gathered in the assembly, waiting for the moment when Idaeus should return. So he came and reported his message, standing in their midst, and they made ready very swiftly, some to bring in the dead, others to go after wood. And the Argives on the other side started from the well-benched ships, some to bring in the dead, others to go after wood.

Then the sun was striking the fields afresh, mounting the heavens from smooth-flowing, deep-running Ocean, and the two sides met each other. It was difficult now to recognize each man; but they washed away the bloody gore with water, and shedding warm tears, loaded them upon the wagons. Nor would Priam suffer the Trojans to offer lamentation, so with heavy hearts they silently heaped up the corpses on the pyre, and having burned them with fire departed to holy Ilium. So likewise on the other side the well-greaved Achaeans with heavy hearts heaped up the corpses on the pyre, and having burned them with fire departed to the hollow ships.

And while it was not yet dawn and the night was still turning to gray, a chosen group of the Achaeans arose about the pyre and they raised one common tomb about it, building it upon the plain, and close by it they built a wall and lofty towers, a protection for the ships and for themselves. And in them they set close-fitting gates, that through them there might be way for driving chariots, and outside they dug a deep ditch by the wall, broad and great, and planted stakes therein.

So the long-haired Achaeans toiled; but the gods, seated beside Zeus the lord of lightning, watched the great work of the bronze-clad Achaeans. And Poseidon the earth-shaker began to address them: "Father Zeus, is there any mortal upon the boundless earth who will still reveal his mind and counsel to the gods? Do you not see that the long-haired Achaeans have now built a wall for their ships and driven a ditch around it, but have not given glorious offerings to the gods? The fame of this wall shall reach as far as spreads the dawn, and they will forget that wall which Phoebus Apollo and I built with toil for the hero Laomedon."

Then in great anger cloud-gathering Zeus addressed him: "Strange is this that you say, wide-ruling shaker of the earth. Some other god might fear this thought, one who was much feebler than you in hands and strength. Indeed your fame shall reach as far as spreads the dawn. Come now, when at last the long-haired Achaeans have departed in their ships for their dear native land, you shall break down the wall and sweep it all into the sea and shall cover the great beach again with sand, so that your great wall of the Achaeans may be destroyed."

So they spoke to one another, and the sun set, and the work of the Achaeans was ended; and they slew cattle among their tents and took dinner. And many ships came in from Lemnos, bearing wine, which Jason's son Euneus sent, he whom Hypsipyle bore to Jason, shepherd of the people. To the sons of Atreus separately, to Agamemnon and Menelaus, Jason's son had sent the wine, a thousand measures. So then the long-haired Achaeans bought wine, some with bronze, some with gleaming iron, others with skins, some with the cattle themselves, and some with slaves, and they held an abundant feast. Then all the night the long-haired Achaeans feasted, and the Trojans too and their allies throughout the city; and all the night Zeus the counselor plotted evil against them, thundering dreadfully. Pale fear fell upon them, and they poured wine from the cups upon the ground, nor did any dare to drink before pouring a libation to the almighty son of Cronus. Then they lay down and took the gift of sleep.

BOOK VIII

Now SAFFRON-MANTLED DAWN spread over the whole earth, and Zeus, who delights in thunder, held an assembly of the gods on the highest peak of many-ridged Olympus. He himself addressed them, and all the gods gave ear: "Hear me, all you gods and goddesses, that I may say what the spirit within my breast commands. So let no goddess nor any god attempt to frustrate my word, but do you all at once approve it, that I may with all speed accomplish these things. Whomsoever I shall see eager to depart from the gods and to give aid either to Trojans or Danaans shall return to Olympus struck down in disgrace, or else I shall seize him and hurl him into dark Tartarus, far, far away, where is the deepest gulf beneath the earth, where there are gates of iron and a brazen threshold, as far beneath Death's house as heaven is from the earth. Then he shall know how much I am the mightiest of all the gods. Come now, make trial, gods, that you may all know. Hang a golden rope from heaven and grasp it, all you gods and all you goddesses; but you could not drag from heaven to earth Zeus, the loftiest counselor, not though you should labor with utmost might. But when I should desire to drag you with a ready heart, I could drag you and the very earth and sea itself. Then I should bind the cord about Olympus' peak and these things would all hang in mid-air. So much am I superior to gods and superior to men."

So he spoke, and they were all hushed in silence, struck by his speech, for powerfully did he address their gathering. Then at last bright-eyed Athena spoke: "Our father, son of Cronus, mightiest of rulers, well now do we too know that your strength is unyielding. Yet still do we sorrow for the Danaan spearmen, who fulfill an evil doom and perish. We will indeed refrain from war as you command, but we shall offer counsel to the Argives for their profit, so that not all may perish by reason of your anger."

Smiling, Zeus the cloud-gatherer addressed her: "Take courage, Tritogeneia, dear child. I speak not now with serious purpose and I wish to be gentle with you."

So speaking, he harnessed to his chariot his bronze-hoofed horses, swiftly flying, golden-maned, and he put gold upon his body and grasped the well-wrought golden whip and mounted his chariot and lashed the horses. Not unwillingly the pair flew off between the earth and starry heaven. And they came to many-fountained Ida, mother of beasts, to Gargarus, where he has a sacred precinct and an incense-burning altar. There the father of gods and men checked his horses and loosed them from the chariot and poured a thick mist about them. And he himself sat upon the summit, exulting in his glory, gazing at the Trojans' city and the ships of the Achaeans.

Now the long-haired Achaeans took their meal in haste among the tents, and afterward put on their armor. And the Trojans also on the other side were arming in the city, fewer, but eager even so to fight in conflict, out of stern necessity, for their wives' and children's sake. All the gates were opened and the host rushed out, infantry and horsemen too, and a great din arose.

So then they met and came together, and clashed shield on shield and spear on spear and might on might of warriors with their brazen arms. The bossed shields pressed each to each and a great din arose. Then there were groans and cheers of men, of the slayers and the slain, and the earth ran with blood.

While it was morning and the sacred day still waxed, the darts of both flew quickly and the soldiers fell. But when the sun had reached the middle of the sky, then the Father poised his golden scales. In them he placed two fates of death which brings long woe, one of the horse-taming Trojans and one of the bronze-clad Achaeans, and he grasped the middle and held them up. And down sank the day of doom of the Achaeans. The dooms of the Achaeans lay upon the fertile earth and the Trojans' rose to the broad heaven. And Zeus himself thundered loudly from Ida and sent a gleaming flash into the host of the Achaeans, and when they saw it they were astounded, and pale fear seized them.

Then did neither Idomeneus dare remain, nor Agamemnon; nor did the Ajaxes stay, the squires of Ares. Gerenian Nestor alone remained, the bulwark of the Achaeans, not at all of his own acord, but his horse was wounded, which the godlike Alexander, husband of fair-haired Helen, had shot with an arrow on the top of the head, where the hairs of horses' manes begin upon the skull, at the spot most easily fatal. He leaped up in pain, and the arrow entered his brain, and he threw his mates into confusion as he writhed upon the bronze. While the old man was rushing up with a sword and cutting free the traces, Hector's swift horses came bearing their bold driver, Hector, through the tumult. And now the old man would have lost his life had not Diomedes of the mighty war cry been quick to see. He gave a dreadful yell, to rouse Odysseus: "Zeus-born son of Laertes, Odysseus of many wiles, where are you fleeing, turning tail like a coward in the fray? Look out, lest someone plant his spear in your back as you flee. Come, stay, that we may ward off from the old man this furious warrior."

So he spoke, yet the much enduring, godlike Odysseus did not hear him, but rushed past toward the hollow ships of the Achaeans. The son of Tydeus, though alone, joined with the foremost of the fighters and stood before the horses of the aged son of Neleus and addressing him spoke winged words: "Father, the young warriors press you hard and your strength is failing, and grievous age is at your side; now your squire is weakened and your steeds are slow. Come now, mount my chariot, that you may see of what sort are the horses of Tros, which know how to run swiftly hither and yon across the plain, in flight or in pursuit. From Aeneas I took them, devisers of rout. Let the squires tend those horses, and let us drive these against the horse-taming Trojans so that even Hector may know whether my spear too rages in my hand."

So he spoke, and Nestor, the Gerenian horseman, did not fail to heed him. So then the mighty squires Sthenelus and manly Eurymedon took Nestor's horses, and the two great heroes stepped into the chariot of Diomedes, and Nestor took in his hands the gleaming reins and lashed the horses. Quickly they drew near to Hector. Against him as he rushed straight at them Tydeus' son hurled his spear. He missed him, but he hit his squire and charioteer, Eniopeus, son of high-hearted Thebaeus, in the breast by the nipple, as he held the reins. He slipped from the chariot, and the swift-footed horses started back. And at once his soul and might were loosed. A dreadful grief for his charioteer shadowed the heart of Hector. For the moment he let him lie there, though distressed for his companion, and he sought for a stout charioteer. Nor did the horses long lack a driver, for at once he found Iphis' son, the sturdy Archeptolemus, whom he then made mount his swift chariot and gave the reins into his hands.

Then would ruin have come and deeds been done beyond repair, and now they would have been penned up in Ilium like rams, had not the father of gods and men been quick to notice. He thundered and hurled a dreadful, dazzling bolt, and cast it down upon the ground before Diomedes' horses. Dreadful was the blaze which rose from the burning sulphur. The horses, in fear, crouched beneath the chariot. The gleaming reins dropped from Nestor's hands, and he feared in his heart and said to Diomedes: "Son of Tydeus, come now, drive the single-hoofed horses in flight. Do you not see that no might comes to you from Zeus? For now on this day Zeus, the son of Cronus, gives to that man the glory, but later he will give it again to us. And a man could not turn aside the will of Zeus, were he ever so strong, since Zeus is much the mightier."

Then Diomedes of the mighty war cry answered him: "All this you are right in saying, Father, but this is a dreadful woe which falls upon my heart and soul. For some day shall Hector say, as he speaks among the Trojans: 'The son of Tydeus fled before me and went to the ships.' So shall he some day boast, and then may the broad earth open at my feet."

Then Nestor, the Gerenian horseman, answered him: "Ah, son of prudent Tydeus, what have you said! For even though Hector call you cowardly and spiritless, still the Trojans and Dardanians and the wives of the great-hearted Trojan shield-men will not believe it, they whose stalwart husbands you have hurled into the dust."

So speaking, he turned the single-hoofed horses in flight, back through the din of battle. And the Trojans and Hector, with a dreadful roar, poured after them their grief-laden missiles. And after him great Hector of the glancing helmet shouted: "Son of Tydeus, the Danaans with their swift steeds paid you special honors in place and meat and cups brim-full. But now they shall scorn you; you have grown like a woman. Away, poor coward; not because of my retreating shall you ever scale our towers nor take away our women in your ships; sooner shall I give to you your doom."

So he spoke, and the son of Tydeus had half a mind to turn the horses and fight face to face. Thrice he debated in his heart and mind, and thrice Zeus the counselor thundered from Mount Ida, giving a sign to the Trojans of the shifting victory of battle. And Hector with a great shout called to the Trojans: "Trojans, and Lycians and close-fighting Dardanians, be men, my friends, and remember furious valor. For I know that the son of Cronus has favored me and granted victory and great glory, but to the Danaans, woe. Fools, who have built these feeble walls not worth our notice. These shall not stay our might, and our horses shall lightly leap across the ditch that they have dug. But when I stand upon the hollow ships, then let someone remember consuming fire, that I may kindle the ships with fire and slay the Argives themselves beside the ships, blinded with smoke."

So speaking, he called to his horses and cried: "Xanthus, and you, Podargus, and Aethon and divine Lampus, now repay me for the abundant care which Andromache, daughter of great-hearted Eëtion, gave to you. Wheat, pleasant to your hearts, she put before you, and mixed wine for you to drink when your spirit bade—even before she gave it to me, who boast to be her stalwart husband. Come, press on and hasten, that we may take Nestor's shield, the fame of which reaches heaven, that it is all of gold, both the handles and the shield itself, and that we may take from the shoulders of horse-taming Diomedes the intricately fashioned breastplate which Hephaestus himself fashioned with toil. If we should take these two, I think that the Achaeans would this very night man their swift ships."

So he spoke, boasting, and queenly Hera was angry and trembled upon her throne and shook long-ridged Olympus. And she spoke to the great god Poseidon: "Ah, wide-ruling shaker of the earth, not even your heart now grieves within your breast for the Danaans who perish. Yet they bring many pleasing gifts to you in Helice and Aegae, and you wish them victory. If all of us who favor the Danaans should resolve to push back the Trojans and restrain far-thundering Zeus, then he would be sorry that he sits alone on Ida."

But the mighty earth-shaker replied to her in anger: "Hera, rash of speech, what have you said? I, for one, have no desire that the rest of us should strive with Zeus the son of Cronus, for he is far the mightier."

So they spoke with one another. As for the Achaeans, the whole space between the ditch and the wall in front of the ships was filled with horses and shield-bearing warriors hemmed in close together. Hector, Priam's son, like swift Ares, hemmed them in, since Zeus gave him glory. And now he would have kindled the fair-lined ships with flaming fire if queenly Hera had not put it into Agamemnon's mind to busy himself in swiftly rousing the Achaeans. He set out along the tents and ships of the Achaeans, carrying a great purple cloak in his stout hand, and he stood by the great-bellied black ship of Odysseus, which was in the middle, so that one could make oneself heard on either side, both to the ships of Ajax, Telamon's son, and to those of Achilles, for these two guarded the ends of the row of fair-lined ships, trusting in their valor and the strength of their hands. He called out to the Danaans in a piercing voice: "Shame, Argives, wretched cowards, brave though you seem in show. What has become of our boasting, when we called ourselves the bravest, the boasts you vainly made in Lemnos, devouring much flesh of straight-horned cattle and drinking bowls brimming with wine and vowing each to face in war a hundred or two hundred Trojans? But now we are no match for even one, Hector, who will soon burn the ships with flaming fire. Father Zeus, have you before this ever maddened any other mighty king with such destruction and robbed him of great glory? Never, I believe, have I passed by any fair altar of yours with my many-oared ship as I toiled hither, but on them all I burned the fat and thighs of cattle in my eagerness to lay waste well-buttressed Troy. But, Zeus, grant me at least this wish: grant that we ourselves may flee and escape and do not allow the Achaeans to be so worsted by the Trojans."

So he spoke, and the father pitied him as he shed tears, and granted him that his men should be safe and should not perish. Straightway he sent an eagle, surest omen of winged creatures, holding a fawn in its talons, the young of a swift doe, and it cast down the fawn beside the fair altar of Zeus, where the Achaeans were wont to sacrifice to Zeus the sender of omens. When, therefore, they saw that the bird had come from Zeus, they rushed more eagerly upon the Trojans and remembered the joy of battle.

Then none among the Danaans, though they were many, could boast that he was quicker than Tydeus' son to drive his swift horses out of the ditch to fight hand to hand. He was by far the first to pick out a crested hero of the Trojans, Agelaus, Phradmon's son. Agelaus turned his steeds in flight, but as he turned, Diomedes planted his spear in his back between the shoulders and drove it through his chest. He fell from the chariot and his armor clanged upon him.

After Diomedes came the sons of Atreus, Agamemnon and Menelaus, and after them the Ajaxes, clothed in furious valor, and after them Idomeneus and Idomeneus's squire Meriones, like to Enyalius the man-slayer, and after them Eurypylus, Euaemon's glorious son. Teucer came ninth, bending his supple bow, and took his stand behind the shield of Ajax, Telamon's son. Ajax would move his shield aside and then the hero would look about him and when he had shot the bow and

struck someone in the throng, then would he dodge back to
Ajax like a child behind its mother, and Ajax would hide him
with the shining shield.

Whom first then of the Trojans did blameless Teucer slay?
Orsilochus first, and Ormenus and Ophelestes and Daetor
and Chromius and godlike Lycophontes and Polyaemon's son
Amopaon and Melanippus. All these he brought down in quick
succession to the fertile earth. And seeing him as he slew
companies of the Trojans with his mighty bow, Agamemnon,
king of men, rejoiced and stood beside him and addressed
him: "Teucer, dear heart, son of Telamon, ruler of the people,
shoot thus in the hope that you may become a light to
the Danaans and to your father Telamon, who reared you
when you were little and took you into his home, even though
you were a bastard. Even though he be far away, make him
share your glory. And I will promise you, as indeed it shall be
fulfilled, that if aegis-bearing Zeus and Athena grant me to
sack the well-built city of Ilium, in your hand first after my
own will I place a prize, either a tripod or two horses with
their chariot or a woman who shall share your bed."

And the blameless Teucer replied to him: "Most glorious
son of Atreus, why urge me on when I am myself so eager?
For I shall not stop so long as my strength holds, but from the
moment when we began to push them back toward Ilium I
have been awaiting my chance and slaying men with my bow.
Eight long-pointed arrows have I shot and all were planted in
the flesh of warriors swift in battle. But that mad dog I cannot
hit."

So he spoke, and he shot another arrow from the string at
Hector, and his heart longed to hit him. But he missed him
and with his arrow hit blameless Gorgythion in the chest,
Priam's brave son, whom a mother taken in marriage from
Aesyme bore, fair Castianeira, like the goddesses in beauty.
And as a poppy in a garden bows its head to one side, laden
with bloom and showers of spring, so he bowed his head to
one side, heavy with his helmet.

And Teucer shot another arrow from the string at Hector
and his heart longed to hit him, but yet again he missed, for
Apollo made it glance away. But it struck Archeptolemus,
Hector's brave charioteer, in the chest beside the nipple as he
rushed to battle. He slipped from the chariot and his swift-
footed horses started back, and at once his soul and might
were loosed. Dire grief for his charioteer shadowed Hector's
heart, but he left him for the time, though grieved for his

companion. He bade his own brother Cebriones, who was nearby, to take the reins, and when the latter heard this he obeyed. But Hector himself leapt from the gleaming chariot to the ground shouting fearfully, and he seized in his hand a stone and made straight for Teucer, and his heart bade him attack. Then Teucer from his quiver took a bitter arrow and set it to the string, but even as he drew it back and took eager aim, Hector of the glancing helmet hit him with the jagged stone beside the shoulder where the collarbone parts neck from chest and where man is most vulnerable. He broke the bowstring and Teucer's hand was numbed at the wrist and he fell upon his knees and the bow dropped from his hand. But Ajax did not overlook his brother's fall; he ran and stood above him and spread his shield before him. Then two faithful comrades, Mecisteus, Echius' son, and godlike Alastor stooped down and bore him, groaning heavily, to the hollow ships.

Then the Olympian again roused might in the Trojans and they pushed the Achaeans straight back toward the deep ditch, and Hector moved among the foremost, exulting in his strength. As when with swift feet a hound pursues a wild boar or a lion and grips it from behind by the flank or rump, watching for its turning at bay, so Hector pressed hard upon the long-haired Achaeans, slaying ever the rearmost, and they fled. But when in their flight they had passed the stockade and the ditch, and many had fallen beneath the Trojans' hands, they halted and rallied by the ships, and calling to one another and raising their hands to all the gods, they prayed aloud, each one. But Hector swung his fair-maned horses from side to side, his eyes like those of the Gorgon or man-destroying Ares.

And when the white-armed goddess Hera saw them she had pity and at once addressed Athena with winged words: "Ah, daughter of aegis-bearing Zeus, shall we two no longer think of the Danaans, even in the last moment of their destruction? For in fulfillment of an evil doom they will perish before the onslaught of a single man; Hector, Priam's son, rages beyond endurance and has done much evil."

Then the bright-eyed goddess Athena answered her: "Would indeed that this fellow might lose his life and limb, perishing at the Argives' hands in his native land; but my wretched father raves in a mind perverted, ever at fault, the thwarter of my will, nor does he remember at all that I often saved his son when he was hard-pressed by Eurystheus' labors. He would cry out to heaven, and Zeus would send me from heaven to aid him. If I had known this in my prudent mind when he was sent to the realm of Hades the Warder to bring back from Erebus the dog of horrid Hades, he would not have escaped the sheer-falling stream of Styx's water. But now Zeus hates me and has done the will of Thetis, who kissed his knees and took his chin in her hand, beseeching him to honor Achilles, the sacker of cities. But the day will be when he again will call me his bright-eyed darling. But do you now harness for us the single-hoofed horses while I enter the house of aegis-bearing Zeus and arm me with weapons of war, that I may see whether Priam's son, Hector of the glancing helmet, shall rejoice when we appear upon the dykes of war. Surely some one of the Trojans shall sate the dogs and birds with fat and flesh when he falls by the ships of the Achaeans."

So she spoke, and the white-armed goddess Hera did not fail to heed her. Hera, queenly goddess, daughter of mighty Cronus, went and harnessed the horses with their golden frontlets. But Athena, daughter of aegis-bearing Zeus, let fall upon her father's threshold her soft and many-colored robe which she herself had woven and fashioned with her hands, and putting on the tunic of cloud-gathering Zeus, she armed herself for lamentable war. She stepped into the gleaming chariot and grasped her heavy spear, huge and strong, with which she vanquishes the ranks of men—the heroes with whom she, the daughter of the mighty sire, is angry. Hera quickly lashed the horses with the whip and the gates of heaven groaned, self-moving; these the Hours keep, to whose charge great heaven and Olympus are committed, either to throw open a thick cloud or draw it to. Straight through the gates they drove the goaded horses.

When Father Zeus saw them from Ida, he was extremely angry, and he sent golden-winged Iris to bear a message: "Go forth, swift Iris, turn them back, and suffer them not to meet me, for we shall not be well met in battle. For thus I prophesy and thus it shall come to pass: I will lame their swift horses in the chariot and will hurl them from the car and shatter the chariot. Not for ten revolving years shall they be healed of the wounds the thunderbolt shall wreak upon them, so that the bright-eyed one may learn what it means to battle with her father. With Hera I am not so provoked or angry, for she always frustrates what I say."

So he spoke, and storm-swift Iris set off with his message, and she went from Mount Ida to high Olympus. At the very gates of many-valed Olympus she met and stopped them and gave them Zeus' message. "Whither are you hastening? Why is your heart mad within your breast? The son of Cronus will not suffer you to aid the Argives. For this threat has the son of Cronus uttered, and so will he fulfill it: to lame your swift horses in the chariot and hurl you from the car and shatter the chariot. Not for ten revolving years will you be healed of the wounds the thunderbolt shall wreak upon you, that you may learn, bright-eyed one, what it means to battle with your father. With Hera he is not so provoked or angry, for she always frustrates what he says. But you are utterly abhorrent, a shameless vixen, if you shall really dare to raise your huge spear against Zeus."

So spoke swift-footed Iris and departed, but Hera addressed Athena: "Ah, child of aegis-bearing Zeus, I will no longer suffer us to fight against Zeus for the sake of mortals. Let one perish and the other live as it may chance, and as for him, let him mete out whatever judgment he ponders in his heart for Trojans and Danaans, as is seemly."

So speaking, she turned back the single-hoofed horses. The Hours unyoked the fair-maned horses for the goddesses and tied them at the ambrosial mangers and leaned the chariot against the shining wall, and the goddesses sat down upon golden chairs and joined with the other gods, though grieved at heart.

But Father Zeus drove his fair-wheeled chariot and horses from Ida to Olympus and came to the assembly of the gods. The famed Earth-shaker unyoked the horses for him and placed the chariot in its stand and spread a covering over it. Far-thundering Zeus himself sat down upon his golden throne and beneath his feet lofty Olympus trembled. Athena and Hera alone sat apart from Zeus, and neither spoke nor questioned him. And he was aware of this in his heart and said: "Why are you thus vexed, Athena and Hera? Surely now you have not grown weary of slaying in man-ennobling battle the Trojans, whom you hate so bitterly. Whatever you say, such are my power and my invincible hands that all the gods on Olympus could not turn me. And as for you, a trembling seized your mighty limbs before you looked on war and war's dread works. For this I say, and so it would have come to pass: not in your chariots would you have returned to the home of the immortals on Olympus once you were struck by the thunderbolt."

So he spoke, and Athena and Hera murmured and sat close together, devising evil for the Trojans. Now Athena was silent and said nothing, angry as she was at Father Zeus, and wild wrath seized her. But Hera's breast could not contain her anger, and she spoke: "Most dreadful son of Cronus, what sort of word is this that you have uttered? Well now do we too know that your strength is unyielding. Yet still do we sorrow for the Danaan spearmen who fulfill an evil doom and perish. We will indeed refrain from war as you command, but we shall offer counsel to the Argives for their profit, so that not all may perish by reason of your anger."

Cloud-gathering Zeus replied to her and said: "With the dawn, ox-eyed, queenly Hera, you shall, if you will, behold the almighty son of Cronus destroying yet more of the great army of the Argive spearmen. For mighty Hector shall not cease from war until the swift-footed son of Peleus shall rise beside the ships on that day when they fight beside the sterns, in dreadful straits about the dead Patroclus. For thus it is fated. I care not for your anger, not even if you go to the farthest ends of earth and sea, where Iapetus and Cronus sit and have no delight in the rays of Hyperion the sun, nor in the winds, but deep Tartarus surrounds them. Even though you go thither in your wanderings, I would not care for your anger, for there is nothing more shameless than you."

So he spoke, and white-armed Hera did not answer him. The bright light of the sun sank in Ocean and drew black night over the wheat-giving earth. The Trojans were unwilling for the light to set, but to the Achaeans black night came welcome and thrice prayed for.

Then glorious Hector held a council of the Trojans, leading them far from the ships, beside the eddying river, in the clear where a space showed through the corpses. They dismounted from their chariots and heard the speech made by Hector, dear to Zeus. In his hand he held his spear of eleven cubits; at the end of the shaft gleamed the brazen tip and around it ran a golden ferrule. Leaning upon it, he addressed the Trojans: "Hear me, Trojans and Dardanians and allies. Now I had thought to destroy the ships and all the Achaeans and return to wind-swept Troy, but dusk came on too soon, and that above all has saved the Argives and their ships upon the beach. Let us now heed black night and prepare food. Loose then the fair-maned horses from the chariots and cast fodder before them. From the city quickly bring cattle and fat sheep;

fetch honey-sweet wine and grain from your halls and gather much wood, so that all the night until the early rising dawn we may burn many fires and their gleam may rise to heaven, lest, in the night, the long-haired Achaeans start to flee over the broad back of the sea. May they not embark upon their ships without combat, at their ease, but may many a one of them still nurse some weapon's scar at home, wounded either by an arrow or a sharp spear as he leaps upon his ship, so that any other may abhor the thought of bringing lamentable war upon the horse-training Trojans. Let heralds, dear to Zeus, proclaim throughout the city that boys in their first youth and gray-headed old men shall gather about the city on the towers built by the gods. And let the women each kindle a great fire in her hall. Let there be continual guard, lest an ambush enter the city while the army is away. Let it be, great-hearted Trojans, as I say. May my words now spoken be propitious, and so too those which with the dawn I shall speak among the horse-taming Trojans. I hope and pray to Zeus and to the other gods to drive from here these dogs urged on by evil fates, which the fates brought on the black ships. So let us guard ourselves this night, and early, with the dawn, let us arm ourselves with our weapons and rouse sharp Ares by the hollow ships. I shall know whether Tydeus' son, mighty Diomedes, will drive me from the ships back to the wall, or whether I shall slay him with the bronze and bear away the bloodstained spoils. Tomorrow he will show his valor, if he abide the onslaught of my spear. I think he will lie wounded among the first, and many comrades about him as the sun rises for the morrow. Would I were as surely ageless and immortal all my days and were reverenced as Athena and Apollo are, as surely as this day brings evil to the Argives."

So Hector spoke, and the Trojans cheered. They loosed the sweating horses from the yoke and tethered them with thongs, each by his chariot. They quickly brought cattle and fat sheep from the city and fetched honey-sweet wine and grain from their halls, and they gathered much wood. And the winds bore the smell of roasting meat to heaven.

High-hearted all the night they lay upon the dykes of war, and many fires burned by them. As when in heaven the stars about the gleaming moon shine glorious, when the air is windless and all the lookouts and high headlands and the dells stand out, and the boundless ether opens to the depths of heaven, when every star is seen and the shepherd's heart rejoices, so many, between the ships and the streams of Xanthus, shone the fires the Trojans kindled before Ilium. A thousand fires burned upon the plain, and by each lay fifty men in the light of the gleaming fire. The horses, champing white barley and oats, stood beside their chariots and awaited fair-throned Dawn.

BOOK IX

SO THE TROJANS KEPT THEIR WATCH, but dire Panic, comrade of chill Rout, filled the Achaeans, and all their leaders were struck with grief unbearable. As when the deep which teems with fish is stirred by two winds, Boreas and Zephyr which blow from Thrace, rising suddenly, and the black wave swells quickly and casts much seaweed out along the shore, so was the spirit torn in the breasts of the Achaeans.

The son of Atreus, his heart stricken with great sorrow, went and bade the clear-voiced heralds summon each man by name to the assembly, but not to shout; and he himself toiled among the first. So they sat grief-stricken in the council, and Agamemnon stood up shedding tears like some dark-watered spring which pours its dusky waters down from a sheer rock. So, groaning heavily, he addressed the Argives: "My friends, leaders and counselors of the Argives, great Zeus, Cronus' son, has snared me in ruinous folly, merciless god, for formerly he promised and assured me that I should sack well-buttressed Ilium and depart, but now he has devised a harsh deception and bids me go inglorious to Argos after losing many men. Such seems to be the pleasure of almighty Zeus, who has humbled the heads of many cities and shall humble more hereafter, for his power is mightiest. Come, let us all do as I say: let us flee with our ships to our dear native land. For never shall we capture wide-wayed Troy."

So he spoke, and they all became hushed in silence. Long sat the sons of the Achaeans in speechless sadness, but at last Diomedes of the mighty war cry spoke to them: "Son of Atreus, you first will I oppose in your folly, as is right, my lord, in council. Be not angry. For, first of all, you reproached my valor among the Danaans, calling me unwarlike and cowardly. All this both young and old among the Danaans know. But the son of crooked-counseled Cronus has endowed you by halves: he has given you to be honored above all for your scepter, but valor he has not given you, which is the greatest power. Blind that you are, do you believe the sons of the Achaeans to be so unwarlike and cowardly as you declare? If your own heart is hastening to be gone, depart. Your way lies open; your ships stand close by the sea, the ships which in great number followed you from Mycenae. But the other long-haired Achaeans will remain until we overthrow Troy. And if they also wish, let them flee with their ships to their dear native land, but we two, Sthenelus and I, shall fight until we win the goal of Ilium, for we have come with the god's protection."

So he spoke, and all the sons of the Achaeans cheered, admiring the words of Diomedes, tamer of horses. Then the horseman Nestor arose and addressed them: "Son of Tydeus, you are surpassing strong in war and in council best among all your comrades. None of all the Achaeans will find fault with your speech, much less refute it. But you have not come to the matter's end. You are young and might be my son, the latest born, but you give wise counsel to the kings of the Argives, since you speak in good order. Now I, who boast myself your senior, will speak out and expound everything, nor could anyone fail to honor my words, not even lordly Agamemnon. Clanless, lawless, homeless is he who loves dread civil war. But let us now obey black night and prepare food, and let all the sentinels gather by the sunken ditch outside the wall. So I command the young. But then, son of Atreus, do you take the lead, for you are the most kingly. Prepare a banquet for the elders; it is right for you and not unseemly. Your tents are full of wine which ships of the Achaeans bring daily from Thrace across the broad sea. All means of hospitality are yours, for you are king of many men. Then when many have been assembled, obey him who shall give best counsel. All the Achaeans have great need that it be good and wise, because the foe burns many fires close by the ships. Who could rejoice at this? This night will either destroy the army or preserve it."

So he spoke, and they readily listened and obeyed him. The armed sentinels rushed forth around Nestor's son Thrasymedes, shepherd of the people, and around Ascalaphus and Ialmenus, sons of Ares, and around Meriones and Aphareus and Deipyrus, and around Creon's son, the godlike Lycomedes. Seven were the leaders of the guards, and a hundred young men marched with each, holding their long spears in their hands. They went and sat down between the ditch and the wall, and there they kindled fires and each prepared his meal.

But the son of Atreus led all the elders of the Achaeans to his tent and laid before them a satisfying meal. They stretched their hands out to the food that lay prepared before them. But when they had put aside the desire for food and drink, old Nestor first began to weave counsel for them, he whose advice had seemed the best in former times as well. With wise and kindly thought for them, he spoke and said: "Most glorious son of Atreus, Agamemnon, king of men, with you I shall end and with you I shall begin, because you are lord of many peoples and Zeus has given you the scepter and the power to take counsel for your people. Therefore it is above all your duty both to speak your mind and to listen and to carry out another's wish whenever his spirit moves him to speak to good purpose, for upon you will depend whatever he begins. Now I will say what seems best to me. For no one will conceive a better counsel than this, which I hold now as I have long held it since the time when you went, Zeus-nurtured king, and seized the maiden Briseis from the tent of the angry Achilles, wholly against our will, for often I tried to dissuade you; but you, yielding to your strong-willed desire, heaped insult on a man most excellent, whom even the immortals honored. For you took, and keep, his prize But even now let us consider how we may persuade him, appeasing him with pleasant gifts and gentle words."

Then Agamemnon, king of men, addressed him: "Father, it is no lie that you tell of my accursed folly. I was a blind fool, nor do I myself deny it. Worth many soldiers is the man whom Zeus loves in his heart, as he has honored this man and reduced the host of the Achaeans. But since I have been a blind fool in obeying miserable passion, I wish to make it good and give a recompense past counting. Before you all I name the glorious gifts—seven tripods untouched by fire, ten talents' weight of gold and twenty gleaming caldrons, twelve strong, prize-winning horses who take prizes with their swift feet. Not without wealth, not lacking in his share of precious gold would be the man who had all the prizes that these single-hoofed steeds have won me. And I will give seven women skilled in faultless work, women of Lesbos, whom I chose as my share when he himself took goodly Lesbos, for they surpassed throngs of women in their beauty. These will I give him, and with them will be she whom then I took away, the daughter of Briseus. And I will swear a great oath that I have never entered her bed nor lain with her, as is the way of men and women. All this shall be his at once; and if thereafter the gods grant that we sack the great city of Priam, let him fill his ship with abundant gold and bronze, after he has entered the town, when we Achaéans divide the booty. Let him choose twenty Trojan women, who are the fairest after Argive Helen. And if we should return to Achaean Argos, the fat plowland, he might be my son-in-law, and I will honor him equally with Orestes, who as my young son is being reared in much abundance. Three daughters have I in my well-built hall—Chrysothemis, Laodice, and Iphianassa; let him take whom he will of these to the house of Peleus as his dear wife, yet give no wedding gifts. But I will give very many soothing gifts, so many as no man yet has given with his daughter. Seven fair-lying cities will I give him—Cardamyle, Enope, and grassy Hira, most holy Pherae, deep-meadowed Antheia, fair Aepeia, and Pedasus, rich in vines—all near the sea, neighbors to sandy Pylos. In them dwell men rich in sheep and cattle, who will honor him like a god with gifts and who will pay him splendid tribute under his scepter. These things would I give him if he would cease from his wrath. Let him yield—Hades, it is true, is relentless and implacable, and thus is the hatefulest of all the gods to mortals—and let him submit to me, in so far as I am the more kingly and boast myself by birth his senior."

Then Nestor, the Gerenian horseman, answered him: "Most glorious son of Atreus, Agamemnon, king of men, by no means contemptible are the gifts you offer lord Achilles. But come, let us send chosen men to go immediately to the tent of Peleus' son, Achilles. Let those whom I now fix with my eye obey. First, let Phoenix, dear to Zeus, be the leader, then great Ajax and godlike Odysseus. Of the heralds, let Odius and Eurybates follow, too. Bring water for our hands and call for pious silence, that we may pray to Zeus, the son of Cronus, in the hope that he may take pity on us."

So he spoke, and his words pleased all. Heralds at once poured water on their hands and young men filled brimming bowls with drink, and having performed the rites of dedication, they passed the wine in cups to all. When they had poured a libation and had drunk as their hearts desired, they started from the tent of Agamemnon, Atreus' son. And Nestor, the Gerenian horseman, glancing at each in turn, urged them all, but especially Odysseus, to try to persuade Peleus' blameless son.

So they went along the shore of the resounding sea, offering many prayers to him who encircles the earth and makes it tremble, that they might easily persuade the great heart of the son of Aeacus. And they came to the tents and

ships of the Myrmidons and found him rejoicing his heart with
a clear lyre, fair and well-wrought, upon which was a silver
crossbar. He had taken it from the spoil when he destroyed the
city of Eëtion, and with it he rejoiced his heart and sang the
glorious deeds of heroes. Patroclus alone sat facing him in
silence, waiting for the son of Aeacus to cease his singing.
They stepped forward, led by godlike Odysseus, and stood
before the hero. Amazed, Achilles started up, still with the
lyre, leaving the seat in which he sat; and Patroclus too, when
he saw the men, arose. Then swift-footed Achilles said to them
in welcome: "Greetings; you come as friends. And so you
should, for even in my wrath you are to me dearest of the
Achaeans."

So speaking, the godlike Achilles led them in and seated
them on chairs and purple rugs, and quickly said to Patroclus,
who stood close by: "Set up a larger mixing bowl, son of
Menoetius, and make the mixture stronger, for these men who
are within my halls are very dear to me."

So he spoke, and Patroclus obeyed his dear comrade. He
set a great meat tray in the light of the fire and placed on it
the back of a sheep and of a fat goat and the chine of a fat
hog, rich with fat. Automedon held them while the godlike
Achilles carved them. He cut them up skillfully and speared
them on spits, and Menoetius' son, the godlike man, kindled
a great fire. Then when the fire had burned down and the
flames had died away, he raked the coals into a bed and
stretched the spits above them and sprinkled on them excellent
salt as he lifted the spits from the headstones. When he had
roasted the meat and placed it on the dressers, Patroclus took
bread and placed it on a table in fair baskets, but Achilles
served the meat. He himself sat facing godlike Odysseus by
the opposite wall, and bade Patroclus, his companion, make
offering to the gods; and Patroclus cast the sacrificial parts
into the fire. Then they stretched their hands out to the food
that lay prepared before them. And when they had put aside
the desire for food and drink, Ajax nodded to Phoenix, but
godlike Odysseus noticed it, and filling a cup with wine he
pledged Achilles:

"Your health, Achilles. We do not lack proper banquets,
either in the tent of Agamemnon, Atreus' son, or here and
now, for many satisfying viands are at hand. But the details of
a pleasing feast do not concern us; instead, O beloved of Zeus,
we look on utter ruin and are afraid. We doubt whether we
shall save or lose the well-benched ships, unless you clothe

yourself in your valor, for the high-hearted Trojans and their far-famed allies have made camp near the ships and wall, kindling many fires throughout their army. And they say they will not halt again but will fall upon the black ships. Zeus, Cronus' son, sends them fair omens in his lightning, and Hector, exulting greatly in his strength, rages dreadfully, trusting in Zeus, and fears neither men nor gods. A mighty madness has possessed him. He prays for the shining dawn to come quickly, for he threatens to cut off the ships' high sterns and burn their hulls with devouring fire, and as for the Achaeans, to slay them as they wander frightened through the smoke beside the ships. I fear dreadfully in my heart lest the gods fulfill his threats and it be our doom to die in Troy, far from horse-raising Argos. Up then, if you wish even late to save the sons of the Achaeans, who are overwhelmed beneath the roaring press of Trojans. Your sorrow, too, it will be hereafter, nor is there any way to find a remedy for evil once it is done. Rather, long before that, think how you may ward off the evil day from the Danaans. Dear friend, surely your father Peleus thus advised you on that day when he sent you from Phthia to Agamemnon: 'My son, Athena and Hera will give you strength, if they so wish, but for yourself keep a great-hearted spirit in your breast, for it is better to be friendly. Refrain from anger and its evil schemings, that both young and old among the Argives may revere you more.' So the old man advised, but you forget. Cease even now, give up your anger with its heartache. Agamemnon offers you becoming gifts if you will put your wrath aside. And if you will hear me, I will tell you what gifts now in his tents Agamemnon promised you—seven tripods untouched by fire, ten talents' weight of gold, and twenty gleaming caldrons, twelve strong, prize-winning horses who take prizes with their swift feet. Not without wealth, not lacking in his share of precious gold would be the man who had all the prizes Agamemnon's horses won him with their feet. And he will give seven women skilled in faultless work, women of Lesbos, whom he chose as his share when you yourself took goodly Lesbos, for they then surpassed throngs of women in their beauty. Them will he give you, and with them will be she whom then he took away, the daughter of Briseus. And he will swear a great oath that he has never entered her bed nor lain with her, as is the wont, my lord, of men and women. All this shall be yours at once, and if thereafter the gods grant that we sack the great city of Priam, you may fill your ship with abundant gold and bronze, after you

have entered the town, when we Achaeans divide the booty.
You yourself may choose twenty Trojan women who are the
fairest after Argive Helen. And if we should return to Achaean
Argos, the fat plowland, you might be his son-in-law, and he
will honor you equally with Orestes, who, as his young son,
is being reared in much abundance. Three daughters has he
in his well-built halls, Chrysothemis, Laodice, and Iphianassa.
You may take whom you will of these to the house of Peleus
as your dear wife, yet give no wedding gifts. But he will give
you very many soothing gifts—so many as no man yet has
given with his daughters. Seven fair-lying cities will he give
you—Cardamyle, Enope, and grassy Hira, most holy Pherae,
deep-meadowed Antheia, fair Aepeia, and Pedasus rich in
vines—all near the sea, neighbors to sandy Pylos. In them
dwell men rich in sheep and cattle, who will honor you like a
god with gifts and who will pay you splendid tribute under
your scepter. This would he pay you if you would give up your
wrath. But if the son of Atreus is too hated in your heart, he
and his gifts, yet have pity on all the rest of the Achaeans,
hard-pressed throughout the camp, who will revere you as a
god. For you could surely win great glory in their eyes. For
now you might take Hector, since he would come right up to
you in his dire rage, for he thinks no Danaan his match, of all
that the ships brought hither."

Swift-footed Achilles answered him and said: "Zeus-born
son of Laertes, Odysseus of many wiles, I must refuse his
offer without scruple, as I feel, and as it shall come to pass, so
that you may not sit by me and din it in my ears from this
side and from that. For hateful to me as the gates of Hades is
the man who hides one thing in his heart and speaks another.
So I will speak as seems best to me. I do not think that Atreus'
son Agamemnon or the other Danaans shall persuade me,
since there was never any thanks for always striving bitterly
against the foe. The share was the same for him who stayed
behind and for whoever battled hard. Coward and hero were
honored equally; the idler and the man of many deeds alike
must die. It is no gain for me when my heart must suffer woe
by always staking life in battle. As a bird brings food in
mouthfuls to her young, when she can find it, yet she herself
fares ill, so I watched through many sleepless nights and
fought through many bloody days, striving with heroes for
their wives. Twelve cities of men I sacked from off my ships;
on foot, eleven, I claim, in fertile Troyland. From all these I
took much glorious treasure, and all I brought and gave to

Agamemnon, Atreus' son. And he, staying behind by the swift
ships, divided up a little, but kept much for himself. The other
prizes that he gave to kings and nobles are theirs securely;
from me alone of the Achaeans he snatched my pleasing
mistress and retains her. Let him lie with her and rejoice. Why
need the Argives war against the Trojans? Why did the son of
Atreus gather the men and lead them hither? Was it not for
fair-haired Helen's sake? Are the sons of Atreus the only mortal men who love their wives? Surely whatever man is good
and prudent loves and cherishes his own, even as I loved her
with all my heart, though I won her by my spear. Now, since
he has seized her from my arms and deceived me, let him not
try me out, for I know him well; nor shall he win me. Rather,
Odysseus, let him with you and the other kings think how to
ward the blazing fire from off the ships. He has done very
much without me—indeed, he built a dike and ran a ditch
beside it, wide and deep, and set a stockade there. Yet not
even so can he check the might of man-slaying Hector. While
I fought with the Achaeans, Hector dared not offer battle at
any distance from the wall but came only to the Scaean gates
and the oak tree. There he once awaited me alone and barely
escaped from my attack. But now that I will not fight with
godlike Hector, tomorrow, when I have made sacrifice to Zeus
and all the gods, when I have loaded my ships well and when
I put to sea, you shall, if you wish and care, see my ships very
early sailing on the Hellespont, which teems with fish, and in
the ships men eager to row. And if the famed Earth-shaker
would give fair sailing, on the third day I might come to
fertile Phthia. I have many things I left when I came hither,
and I shall take hence homeward other gold and ruddy
bronze and fair-girdled women and gray iron, which have been
my share. But the man who gave my prize has taken it away
in insolence, the mighty Agamemnon, Atreus' son. Say to him
all, just as I bid you, openly, so that the other Achaeans too
may be indignant if he hopes still to deceive any of the
Danaans, as he is ever clothed in impudence. Yet shameless
as he is, he would not dare to look me in the face. I will not
share in council or in deeds with him, for he deceived and
sinned against me, nor could he again deceive me by his
words. Enough for him; let him go his way for all of me, for
Zeus the counselor has robbed him of his senses. His gifts are
hateful to me and I set no value on them. Not even if he
should give me ten or twenty times what he now has, and if
he should get more from elsewhere, so much as comes into

Orchomenus or Thebes in Egypt, where riches lie in greatest plenty in the houses—the city of a hundred gates; two hundred men can ride through each with chariots and horses—not even if he should give me gifts as many as the sand or dust, not even thus could Agamemnon persuade my heart before he has atoned to me for all this grievous outrage. I will not wed the daughter of Agamemnon Atreus' son, not though she should rival golden Aphrodite in her beauty and should be the peer of bright-eyed Athena in her work; not even then will I marry her. Let him choose some other of the Achaeans, whoever befits him and is kinglier than I. For if the gods preserve me and I reach my home, Peleus himself will then seek out a wife for me. There are many daughters of Achaea in Greece and Phthia, daughters of nobles who guard their cities. Often there my noble heart urged me to wed a wife, a proper helpmate, to rejoice in the wealth that ancient Peleus had won. Not all they say that Ilium, that fair-lying town, possessed in former days of peace before the coming of the sons of the Achaeans, not all that the stone threshold of the archer, Phoebus Apollo, guards within in rocky Pytho, is worth my life to me. For plunder may win cattle and fat sheep, and purchase may gain tripods and the sacred heads of horses, but a man's soul cannot be seized or caught so that it will return once it has passed the barrier of his teeth. For my mother, the silver-footed goddess Thetis, says that two fates bear me to the goal of death. If I remain here and fight around the Trojans' city, then my homecoming is lost to me but my glory shall be undying; but if I come home to my dear native land, my glorious fame is lost to me but my life shall last long, nor will the end of death soon overtake me. The others too I would advise to sail for home, since never, now, will you attain the goal of lofty Ilium, for surely far-thundering Zeus holds his hand above it and its men have plucked up courage. Go then, and give this message to the chiefs of the Achaeans—this is the honorable task of elders—that they may devise a better counsel in their hearts that shall save their ships and the host of the Achaeans on the hollow ships, since this plan which they have now devised cannot be realized, because I shall continue in my wrath. But let Phoenix remain here and sleep with us, that he may go with me in the ships to our dear native land tomorrow, if he wish; for I will not take him by constraint."

So he spoke, and they were all hushed in silence, wondering at his speech, for vehemently did he refuse them. At length the aged horseman Phoenix spoke to him in tears, for he feared greatly for the ships of the Achaeans: "If you do indeed consider in your heart returning, glorious Achilles, and are quite unwilling to ward off devouring fire from the ships, since wrath has fallen into your heart, how then, dear child, could I be left here alone without you? The aged horseman Peleus sent me with you on the day when he sent you, a mere child, from Phthia to Agamemnon, when you as yet knew nothing of war, which deals with all alike, nor of councils, where men come to fame. Therefore he sent me to teach you all these things—to be both a speaker of words and a doer of deeds. Therefore I would not desire to be abandoned by you, dear child, not even though the god himself should promise to smooth away my age and make me young again, as when first I left Hellas with its fair women, fleeing the wrath of my father Amyntor, son of Ormenus, who was angry with me because of his fair-haired concubine, whom he himself loved, and so did dishonor to his wife, my mother. My mother continually clasped my knees, beseeching me to lie with the concubine so that she might come to hate the old man. I heeded her and did it, but my father, as soon as he discovered it, uttered many curses and called upon the hateful Furies, that never upon his knees should sit a dear son begot by me. And the gods fulfilled his curses, Zeus of the Underworld and dread Persephone. Then the spirit in my breast could no longer be restrained to dwell within my angry father's halls. Many friends and kinsmen around me then pleaded with me and tried to keep me in the halls, and they slew many fat sheep and crook-horned cattle of shambling gait, and many swine rich with fat were singed and stretched in the flames of Hephaestus, and much wine was drunk from the jars of that old man. Nine nights long they stayed beside me all the night. They stood guard in turn, and the fires never went out, one in the porch of the well-fenced courtyard and the other in the vestibule, before my chamber doors. But when the tenth black night descended, then I broke my room's close-fitting doors and escaped and easily leaped the courtyard fence, unseen by guards or women of the household. Then I fled far through Hellas, with its wide dancing floors, and came to fertile Phthia, mother of flocks, to King Peleus. He received me with kindness and loved me as a father loves his cherished only son amid rich possessions, and he made me rich and gave me many men to rule. I dwelt in Phthia's borders, ruling the Dolopians. To your present greatness I have reared you, godlike Achilles, loving you from my heart, for with no other would you go to dine nor eat within the halls, until I set you on my knee and cut and fed to you your meat and held your wine cup to your lips. Many a time you wet the shirt upon my chest, spirting out wine in naughty childishness. Much have I toiled and suffered over you, thinking the gods would never give me child of my own; but I made you my child, godlike Achilles, that some day you might ward off unseemly ruin from me. Now Achilles, master your great spirit, nor should you have a heart that knows no pity, for even the gods themselves are placable, although their excellence and honor and might are greater still. With sacrifice and gentle prayers, with libations and the smoke of offerings, men turn them by their supplications when someone has transgressed and erred. For there are Prayers, daughters of great Zeus, lame and wrinkled, with sideward-glancing eyes, who follow troubled behind blind Folly. Blind Folly is mighty and swift of foot, wherefore she runs far ahead of all and is first to reach all parts of the earth and do men harm, and the Prayers heal the hurt thereafter. Whoever reverences the daughters of Zeus as they draw near, him they help greatly and to his prayers they listen. But whoever repels them and harshly says them nay, they go to Zeus, the son of Cronus, and pray that Ruin may follow him so that he may atone in suffering. Come, Achilles, do you too grant that honor may follow Zeus' daughters, honor which bends the will of other noble creatures too. For if the son of Atreus were not bringing gifts and telling of more hereafter, but were persisting in furious anger, I would not bid you put aside your wrath and give protection to the Argives, however they might need it. But now he gives you much and has promised more hereafter and has chosen the best throughout the Achaean army and sent them to entreat you, even those who are dearest to you yourself among the Argives. Do not despise their words or their journey hither. Your earlier anger none can blame. Such, we have heard, were the glorious deeds of the heroic men of old when any furious anger seized them—with gifts they could not be moved, they could be influenced by words. I remember this affair of old, no recent one, and how it happened. I will tell it to all of you, my friends. The Curetes and the Aetolians, stanch in battle, were fighting about the city of Calydon and were despoiling one another; the Aetolians were defending lovely Calydon, the Curetes were eager to sack it in war. For Artemis of the golden throne had brought evil upon the

Aetolians in her anger that Oeneus had not offered the harvest
sacrifice to her upon his orchard hill: the other gods dined
upon sacrifices, and only to the daughter of great Zeus he
made no offering. Either he forgot or thought not of it; in any
case, he made a great fool of himself in his own heart. But
the Huntress in her anger sent a wild boar with gleaming tusks,
a mighty creature, which after its way did much damage to
Oeneus' orchard. Many tall trees it tore up, roots and all,
and threw upon the ground with the blossoms of their fruit.
Oeneus' son Meleager slew it, gathering huntsmen and hounds
from many cities, for it could not have been slain by men in
meager numbers, so great it was, and many it brought to the
grievous pyre. Artemis raised a great hue and cry about the
boar's head and bristly hide, between the Curetes and
the great-hearted Aetolians. Now so long as Meleager, dear to
Ares, fought it went ill with the Curetes and they could not
stay outside their wall, numerous though they were, but when
Meleager was seized by wrath, which swells the hearts of
others too within their breasts, for all their wisdom, he, angered
at heart with his mother Althaea, lay idle at the side of his
wedded wife, fair Cleopatra, daughter of Evenus' daughter,
Marpessa of the lovely ankles, and of Ides, who was mightiest
of men upon the earth in those days—indeed, he drew his bow
against lord Phoebus Apollo for the sake of his fair-ankled
bride. At that time Marpessa's father and queenly mother
called her by the name Alcyone within their halls, because
her mother, bearing the doom of the mournful halcyon, wept
because the Warder, Phoebus Apollo, had carried Marpessa
away—by Cleopatra Meleager lay, nursing his wrathful heartache, angered at his mother's curses, for in her grief at her
brother's murder she had called upon the gods with many a
curse and many a time upon her knees, her bosom wet with
tears, smote with her hand the bountiful earth, calling on
Hades and dread Persephone that they would send death
upon her son, and the Fury who walks in darkness heard
her in Erebus, implacable of heart. Soon the warriors' crash
and roar arose above the gates as the towers were hit, and
the best of the Aetolians sent the gods' noblest priests and
besought Meleager to come out and fight for them, prom-
ising a great gift. At the spot where the plain of lovely Calydon is richest they bade him choose a lot exceedingly fair,
of fifty acres, half of it in wine-producing earth, and to set
aside half of the lot in unwooded plowland. The aged horseman Oeneus often besought him, standing on the threshold

of the high-roofed chamber, shaking the close-fitting doors, begging his son. And his brothers and his queenly mother besought him, but he refused all the more. And often his comrades begged him, they who were his best and dearest friends of all, but not even thus could they persuade his heart within his breast, until his very chamber was often struck and the Curetes mounted the towers and set the great town on fire. Then Meleager's fair-girdled wife begged him with lamentations and told him all the woes that befall men whose citadel is taken. The men they slay, and fire destroys the city, and others carry off the children and the deep-girdled women. His heart was stirred as he heard of these evil things, and he set out and girded on his flesh his shining armor. So he warded off the evil day from the Aetolians, heeding his heart, but they would no more give him many lovely gifts, yet even so he warded off the evil. But for my sake, hold no such plans in mind, and let not an evil spirit turn you toward that path, for it would be worse to protect the ships when they begin to burn. Come on terms of the gifts, for the Achaeans will honor you as a god, but if you enter man-destroying war without the gifts you will not have such honor even though you ward off war."

Swift-footed Achilles answered him and said: "Phoenix, aged father, Zeus-nurtured, I have no need of this honor. I think I am already honored by decree of Zeus, which will abide with me beside the curved ships as long as breath remains in my breast and my knees can move. Another thing I will tell you, and do you turn it over in your heart: do not trouble my soul with grief and lamentation for the sake of Atreus' heroic son; you must not love him, lest you win my hate, who love you. It is but fair that with me you should cherish him who cherishes me. Rule as my peer, share half my honor. These men shall bear my answer, but remain here yourself and lie down on a soft bed, and when the dawn appears we shall consider whether to return to our own or to remain."

He spoke, and to Patroclus he signaled with his brows in silence to make ready a thick bed for Phoenix, that the others might quickly consider their departure from his tent. And the godlike Ajax, Telamon's son, spoke out among them: "Zeus-born son of Laertes, Odysseus of many wiles, let us go. For it seems to me that the goal of our words cannot be reached by this road. We must with all speed report his reply to the Danaans, even though it be not good, for no doubt they now sit awaiting it. But Achilles has made his great-hearted spirit savage in his breast, unhappy man, nor does he care for the love with which his comrades honored him above others beside the ships, pitiless that he is. Men accept quit money from the slayer of their brother or dead son, and the slayer remains there among the people when he has paid a large forfeit, and the kinsman's heart and bold spirit are restrained when he has received the fine. But the gods have made the anger in your breast unceasing and bitter, for the maid's sake alone. Now we offer you seven of the best, and much else besides. Be gentle-hearted and revere your home; we from the Danaan host sit underneath your roof; we desire to be your closest, dearest friends, beyond all others among the Achaeans."

Swift-footed Achilles answered him and said: "Ajax, Zeus-born son of Telamon, leader of men, all you have said is spoken after my own heart, up to a point, but my heart is swollen with anger when I remember the insults heaped on me among the Argives by the son of Atreus, as if on some unregarded wanderer. Now go and tell your tidings. For I shall not think of bloody war until wise Priam's son, the godlike Hector, comes to the tents and ships of the Myrmidons, slaying Argives as he goes, and burns our ships with fire. At my own tent and black ships I expect to put a halt to Hector, eager though he be for battle."

So he spoke, and each of them took a double cup and poured a libation and then went back beside the ships, and Odysseus led the way. But Patroclus bade his comrades and handmaids make ready a thick bed for Phoenix, with all speed. They obeyed and made a bed as he commanded—a fleece, a blanket, and fine nap of linen. There the old man lay down and awaited bright Dawn. But Achilles slept in the inmost corner of his well-built tent. Beside him slept a woman whom he had brought from Lesbos, Phorbas' daughter, fair-cheeked Diomede. And Patroclus lay across from him, the fair-girdled Iphis at his side, whom godlike Achilles gave him when he took steep Scyros, Enyeus' city.

When the others entered the tent of Atreus' son, the sons of the Achaeans stood and pledged them from all sides out of golden cups, and asked their tidings. Agamemnon, king of men, was first to ask them: "Say now, much praised Odysseus, great glory of the Achaeans, is he willing to ward off blazing fire from the ships or did he refuse; does wrath still possess his great-hearted spirit?"

Then much-enduring, godlike Odysseus said to him: "Most glorious son of Atreus, Agamemnon, king of men, he will not quench his anger; he is filled the more with wrath, and he rejects you and your gifts. He bids you contrive among the Argives how to save the ships and men of the Achaeans. He himself threatened at the light of dawn to drag his well-benched, curved ships to the sea. And he said he would advise the others to sail for home, since never, now, will they attain the goal of lofty Ilium, for surely far-thundering Zeus holds his hand above it and its folk have plucked up courage. So he spoke; these who went with me are also here to tell these things, Ajax and the two heralds, both wise men, but old Phoenix sleeps out there, as Achilles ordered, so that he may go with him in the ships to their dear native land, tomorrow, if he wish, for he will not take him by constraint."

So he spoke, and they all were hushed in silence, wondering at his words, for vehemently did he address them. Long sat the Achaeans in troubled silence, but at last Diomedes of the mighty war cry spoke: "Most glorious son of Atreus, Agamemnon, king of men, would that you had not begged the blameless son of Peleus, offering countless gifts, for he is proud enough without that. Now you have confirmed him in his pride the more. But let us forget him, whether he go or stay. He will fight whenever the spirit in his breast compels him and the god arouses him. But now let us all do as I say. So now to bed, when you have had your fill of food and wine, for thence come strength and valor. But when the fair, rosy-fingered Dawn appears, quickly rouse the host and horses and marshal them before the ships, and you yourself fight among the first."

So he spoke, and all the kings applauded, admiring the speech of Diomedes, tamer of horses. Then they poured libations and went each to his tent. There they lay down and took the gift of sleep.

BOOK X

THE OTHER CHIEFS of the Achaeans slept all the night beside the ships, overcome with soft sleep. But sweet sleep did not hold Atreus' son Agamemnon, shepherd of the people, for he pondered many things in his heart. As when the husband of fair-haired Hera lightens, sending much rain or boundless hail or a blizzard, when snow strews the fields, or as when he opens the jaws of ravening war, so thick were the groans in the breast of Agamemnon, rising from the bottom of his heart, and his heartstrings trembled within him. Whenever he gazed out on the Trojan plain he marveled at the many fires that burned before Ilium and at the noise of flutes and pipes and the din of men. But when he looked toward the ships and host of the Achaeans, he tore much hair from his head by the roots and held it up to Zeus, who dwells on high, and he groaned loudly in his noble heart. And this plan seemed to him to be the best—to go to Nestor, Neleus' son, first of all men, in the hope that Nestor with him might form some faultless plan which would ward off evil from all the Danaans. He arose and slipped his shirt upon his chest, and bound fair sandals on his shining feet, and girt about him the tawny skin of a great tawny lion, which hung down to his feet, and then he grasped his spear.

On Menelaus too fell a trembling—for on his eyelids too sleep would not sit—lest some ill befall the Argives, who for his sake had come to Troy across much water, planning bold war. First, with a spotted leopard skin he covered his broad back, and next he lifted a brazen helmet and set it on his head and grasped his spear in his stout hand. Then he set out to arouse his brother, who ruled with might over all the Argives and was honored like a god among people. He found him putting his fair armor upon his shoulders by the stern of his ship, and a welcome sight was Menelaus to him when he arrived. Menelaus of the mighty war cry first addressed him: "Brother, why are you arming thus? Are you about to send one of our comrades as a spy upon the Trojans? I am dreadfully afraid that no one will undertake this work for you, of going alone through the divine night to spy upon our enemies. He will be very bold of heart who does."

Mighty Agamemnon answered him and said: "Zeus-nurtured Menelaus, both you and I have need of helpful counsel that will protect and save the Argives and the ships, since the heart of Zeus has changed. He has been more pleased with Hector's offerings. For I have never seen or heard tell of one man in a day devising so much harm as Hector, dear to Zeus, has done the sons of the Achaeans quite by himself, being son neither of goddess nor of god. Deeds he has done which will, I say, trouble the Argives for a long time to come, so many evils has he wrought upon the Achaeans. Come now, run swiftly by the ships and summon Ajax and Idomeneus, and I will go to godlike Nestor and bid him arise, if he is willing to come to our brave company of guards and give instructions. Him they would best obey, for his son and Idomeneus' squire Meriones command the guards, since to them chiefly we gave that duty."

Then Menelaus of the mighty war cry answered him: "What order or command have you for me? Shall I stay here with these men, waiting till you return, or shall I run after you when I have given them the proper orders?"

Agamemnon, king of men, said to him: "Stay here, lest we miss one another on our way, for there are many pathways through the camp. Wherever you go, call out and command them to arise, calling each man by his name and his father's, according to his birth, honoring all; and be not proud of heart, but let us also labor. For surely Zeus sent this grievous woe upon us from our birth."

So speaking, he sent away his brother, when he had given him clear orders. He himself set out to visit Nestor, shepherd of the people. He found him beside his tent and his black ship in a soft bed. Beside him were his skillfully wrought arms —a shield, two spears, and a shining helmet. Near them lay his gleaming belt, which the old man bound about him when he armed himself and led his men to man-destroying war, for he would not give in to wretched age. He raised himself upon his elbow, lifted his head, and spoke to Atreus' son and asked: "Who are you there that pass alone by the ships through the camp in the murky night, when other mortals are asleep? Are you looking for one of the mules or one of your comrades? Speak; do not come up to me in silence. What do you want?"

Then Agamemnon, king of men, answered him: "Nestor, Neleus' son, great glory of the Achaeans, you will recognize Atreus' son Agamemnon, whom Zeus visits with trouble above all men, continually, so long as there is breath in my lungs and my knees can move. I am wandering thus because sweet sleep sits not upon my eyes but I am troubled by the war and the woes of the Achaeans. For I am dreadfully afraid for the Danaans; my heart is troubled and I am sore distressed; my heart leaps from my breast and my shining limbs are trembling. Come, if you are ready to do something, since sleep will not come even to you: let us go down to the guards to see that they have not fallen asleep, overwhelmed by weariness and slumber, their guard duty all forgotten. The foe are encamped close by; for all we know, they may intend to offer battle in the night."

Then the Gerenian horseman Nestor answered him: "Most glorious son of Atreus, Agamemnon, king of men, Zeus the counselor will not fulfill all Hector's schemes, all that he now hopes. I think that he will suffer further woes if Achilles turn his heart from violent wrath. I will certainly go with you, and let us arouse others too—Tydeus' son, the famous spearman, and Odysseus and swift Ajax[1] and the valiant son of Phyleus. Someone might go and summon them and the godlike Ajax[2] and lord Idomeneus, for their ships are farthest away and not very near. I shall reproach Menelaus, though he is my honored friend and though you take it ill, nor shall I conceal my wrath that he is sleeping and leaving to you alone the labor. For now he should be at work beseeching all the nobles, for a crisis has come upon us which can no longer be endured."

Agamemnon, king of men, addressed him: "Father, another time I would even urge you to arouse him, for often he is remiss and will not toil; not that he yields to sloth or folly, but that he looks to me and awaits my lead. But now he awoke before me and came to my side. I have sent him on to summon those for whom you ask. But let us go; we shall find them before the gates among the guards, where I bade them gather."

Then the Gerenian horseman, Nestor, answered him:

[1] Ajax, Oileus' son.
[2] Ajax, Telamon's son.

"Then none of the Argives will be angry with him or refuse to heed him when he urges or commands."

So speaking, he slipped his shirt upon his chest and bound fair sandals on his shining feet and fastened about him a double scarlet cloak in ample folds, with a thick nap upon it. He took a stout spear, tipped with sharp bronze, and set out beside the ships of the bronze-clad Achaeans. Then the Gerenian horseman, Nestor, first called to Odysseus, like to Zeus in wisdom, and roused him from his sleep, and at once the sound rang round his heart and he came from his tent and said to them: "Why do you wander thus alone beside the ships through the camp in the divine night? What great crisis has arisen?"

Then the Gerenian horseman, Nestor, answered him: "Zeus-born son of Laertes, Odysseus of many wiles, be not angry, so great a woe has overwhelmed the Achaeans. But come with us to arouse still another who should debate with us whether to flee or to give battle."

So he spoke, and crafty Odysseus went to his tent and hung upon his shoulders his well-wrought shield. He followed them, and they went to Tydeus' son, Diomedes. Him they found outside his tent with his weapons; around him slept his comrades, their shields beneath their heads and their spears fixed upright on the spikes; the bronze gleamed from afar like the lightning of Father Zeus. The hero slept, and under him was spread the hide of an ox of the field, but beneath his head was laid a shining rug. The Gerenian horseman, Nestor, stood beside him and awoke him, stirring him with his heel, arousing him and openly reproving him: "Awake, son of Tydeus; why do you sleep all the night? Do you not hear that the Trojans lie upon the rise of the plain, close by the ships, and small is the space that lies between us still?"

So he spoke, and Diomedes sprang at once from his sleep and to him spoke winged words: "Wretched old man, you never rest from toil. Are there not other, younger sons of the Achaeans who could go everywhere and awake each of the kings? You are impossible, old man."

The Gerenian horseman, Nestor, said to him: "You are right in all you say, my friend. I have blameless sons and I have men, many of them, any one of whom might come and call you; but a very great crisis has come upon the Achaeans. The fate of all the Achaeans now stands upon the razor's edge—either wretched destruction or life. Go now and rouse swift Ajax and Phyleus' son—for you are younger—if you pity me."

So he spoke, and Diomedes threw about his shoulders the skin of a great tawny lion, which reached to his feet, and he seized his spear, and he set out and aroused the others from their tents and brought them in.

When they had joined the assembled guards, they did not find the leaders of the guards asleep; they all sat wakeful with their armor. As dogs keep weary watch about flocks in a courtyard, hearing a dauntless beast which prowls through mountain forests—there is much din of men and dogs about him—and sleep flees from them, so sweet sleep had fled from their eyelids as they watched through the bitter night, for they turned ever toward the plain when they heard the Trojans drawing near. The old man rejoiced on seeing them and cheered them with his speech, addressing them with winged words: "So keep your watch, my sons. Let none be overcome by sleep lest we become a source of joy to those who hate us."

So speaking, he hastened from the ditch, and the kings of the Argives followed him, all who had been called to the council. With them went Meriones and Nestor's glorious son, for the nobles bade them join their council. They crossed the ditch and sat down in the open where a spot was clear of the bodies of the fallen, the spot whence mighty Hector turned back from his slaughter of the Argives when night fell about him. There they sat and said their say to one another; the Gerenian horseman, Nestor, opened their debate: "My friends, could not some warrior obey his own bold heart, and go among the high-hearted Trojans, on the chance that he might find some foeman straggling, or might hear some rumor among the Trojans as to what plans they are devising, whether they desire to stay here by the ships, far from the town, or will draw back toward the city, now that they have overcome the Achaeans? All this he might discover and come back to us unharmed, and great would be his glory under heaven among all men, and he shall have a noble gift, for each of all the nobles who command the ships shall give him a black ewe with her lamb beneath her—no gift is like to that; and he shall always sit at every feast and banquet."

So he spoke, and they all became hushed in silence. Then Diomedes of the mighty war cry said to them: "Nestor, my heart and kingly spirit stir me to go in to the camp of our foes the Trojans, who are close at hand. But if some other warrior would go with me, then the greater the comfort and the more the daring. When two set out together one thinks before the other to their profit, whereas even though one alone may think the thought, yet is his mind the slower and his counsel weak."

So he spoke, and many wished to follow Diomedes. So wished the two Ajaxes, squires of Ares, so wished Meriones, and much wished the son of Nestor; so wished the son of Atreus, Menelaus, the famous spearman; and Odysseus the enduring wished to go among the throng of Trojans, for his spirit in his breast was ever daring. Agamemnon, king of men, said to them: "Diomedes, Tydeus' son, dear to my heart, choose that companion you prefer, the best of those who offer, since there are many eager. Do not, through modesty of heart, leave behind the better and choose the worse, from modesty, looking to birth, not even though he be the kinglier."

So he spoke, fearing for fair-haired Menelaus. But Diomedes of the mighty war cry said to them: "If you bid me myself to choose my comrade, how then could I forget god-like Odysseus, whose heart and kingly spirit are exceeding prompt in all our labors, and Pallas Athena loves him? If he went with me, we should return even out of blazing fire, for he is skilled beyond all in counsel."

Much enduring, godlike Odysseus said to him: "Son of Tydeus, neither praise me over much nor blame me; for you say these things among the Argives, who know them well. Come, let us go, for night draws quickly to its close, and dawn is near. The stars have advanced, the greater two parts of the night are past, and only a third remains."

So they spoke, and donned their dreadful arms. Steadfast Thrasymedes gave to Tydeus' son a two-edged sword—for he had left his at the ship—and a shield. Upon his head he set an ox-hide helmet with neither crest nor plume, which is called a skullcap and protects the heads of sturdy youths. Meriones gave Odysseus a bow and quiver and sword and set upon his head a helmet made of hide; it was strengthened by many thongs within, and without, on either side, were many white teeth of a boar of gleaming tusks, set well and skillfully, and the interior was lined with felt. Autolycus had stolen it long ago at Eleon from Amyntor, Ormenus' son, when he broke into his well-built house, and he had given it to Cytherian Amphidamas in Scandeia. Amphidamas gave it to Molus, to be a gift of friendship, and he gave it to his son Meriones to wear. And now it fitted well Odysseus' head when placed upon it.

So when the two had donned their dreadful arms, they set out and left all the nobles there. Pallas Athena sent a heron to them on the right, close by the road. They could not see it with their eyes through the dark night, but they heard it calling. Odysseus rejoiced to hear the bird and prayed to Athena: "Hear me, child of aegis-bearing Zeus, thou who art ever at my side in all my trials, nor can I stir without thy knowledge: cherish me now, once more, especially, Athena, and grant that we return with glory to the ships having done some great deed which shall disturb the Trojans."

Diomedes of the mighty war cry made a prayer in turn: "And now give ear to me, Atrytone, child of Zeus. Go with me as thou wentest once with godlike Tydeus, my father, to Thebes, when he went as messenger for the Achaeans. He left the bronze-clad Achaeans at the Asopus, and bore a gentle message to the Cadmeians there. But when he came back, he devised great deeds with thy help, goddess of goddesses, because thou wast at his side in earnest. So deign now to stand at my side and protect me. I will offer to thee a yearling heifer, with broad forehead, unbroken, which no man has yet led beneath the yoke. Her will I offer to thee, pouring gold upon her horns."

So they spoke in prayer, and Pallas Athena heard them. And when they had prayed to the daughter of great Zeus, they set out like two lions through the black night, among the slain, among the corpses, through the weapons and the dark blood.

Nor did Hector allow the bold Trojans to sleep, but he called all the nobles together, all who were leaders and counselors of the Trojans. When he had summoned them, he devised a well-knit scheme: "Who now would promise this task for me and carry it out in return for a great gift? His reward shall be sufficient. For I will give a chariot and two proud-necked horses, the best there are by the swift ships of the Achaeans, to him who would dare—and would win himself glory for it—to go close to the swift-faring ships and learn whether the swift ships are guarded as before, or whether, already worsted at our hands, the Achaeans are planning flight among themselves and are unwilling to keep guard by night, overwhelmed by dreadful weariness."

So he spoke, and they all were hushed in silence. There was among the Trojans a certain Dolon, son of Eumedes the godlike herald, rich in gold and rich in bronze, ugly of face but swift of foot. He was the only son amid five sisters. He it was who now addressed the Trojans and Hector: "Hector, my heart and valiant spirit bid me go close to the swift-faring ships and play the spy. Come now, hold up to me your scepter and swear to me to give me the horses and the chariot wrought cunningly of bronze which bear the blameless son of Peleus, and I shall be for you no fruitless spy, nor disappointing. Straight through the camp I will go until I come to Agamemnon's ship, where surely the nobles will be debating whether to flee or fight."

So he spoke, and Hector took the scepter in his hand and swore to him: "Be Zeus himself my witness, Hera's loud-thundering husband, no other man among the Trojans shall drive that team; you, I say, shall glory in them always."

So he spoke, and swore an oath upon it and urged him on. Promptly Dolon threw a curved bow across his shoulders and clothed himself in the skin of a gray wolf. On his head he placed a cap of weasel skin, and he grasped a sharp javelin and set out from the camp toward the ships; nor was he destined to return from the ships and bring word back to Hector. Now when he had left behind the throng of men and horses, he set out eagerly along the road, but Zeus-born Odysseus noticed him approaching and said to Diomedes: "Some warrior is coming yonder from the camp, I know not whether to spy upon our ships or to rifle one of the bodies of the slain. Let us allow him to pass us a little on the plain; then, rushing upon him, we might quickly seize him, or, if he should slip by us on swift feet, drive him always towards the ships, away from the camp, rushing upon him with the sword, lest he escape us toward the city."

So speaking, they veered from the road among the corpses, and Dolon ran swiftly by them in his folly. But when he was about a mule's furrow's length away—they are better than cattle to draw a well-joined plow through deep fallow land—the pair ran toward him and he stopped when he heard their noise. For he hoped in his heart that comrades were coming from the Trojans to turn him back because Hector had recalled him. But when they were a spear's length or less away, he knew them to be foes, and he plied swift knees in flight, and they at once gave chase. As when two sharp-toothed dogs, skilled in the hunt, press a deer or hare relentlessly through wooded country, and it runs from them screaming, so Tydeus' son and the sacker of cities, Odysseus, cut him off from his people and pursued him relentlessly. But when he was about to reach the guards in his flight toward the ships, then Athena gave strength to Tydeus' son, that none of the bronze-clad Achaeans might be before him with the boast of hitting Dolon and he be second best. Mighty Diomedes rushed upon him with his spear and said: "Stop, or I will thrust you with this spear, nor do I think you shall long avoid sheer destruction at my hand."

So he spoke, and cast the spear, but missed him on purpose. The point of the polished spear flew over his right shoulder and was fixed in the ground. He stopped, quivering with fright; his teeth chattered in his mouth, and he was pale with fear. Panting, they seized him and grasped his arms. And bursting into tears he said to them: "Take me alive, and I will ransom myself, for I have at home bronze and gold and iron wrought with much labor, from which my father would give you a boundless ransom, if he should learn that I am alive beside the ships of the Achaeans."

Odysseus of many wiles answered him and said: "Courage, think not of death. Tell me this and report it truthfully. Where are you going thus alone from the camp toward the ships through the dark night, when other mortals sleep? Is it to rifle one of the bodies of the slain? Or did Hector send you to spy on all things by the hollow ships? Or did your own heart send you?"

Then Dolon answered him, his limbs a-tremble: "Hector misled my mind with fatal fancies, for he promised to give me the swift-hoofed horses of Peleus' glorious son and his chariot, wrought cunningly of bronze. He bade me go through the swift, black night and draw near to the foe and learn whether the swift ships are guarded as before, or whether, already worsted at our hands, the Achaeans are debating flight among themselves and are unwilling to keep guard by night, overwhelmed by dreadful weariness."

Odysseus of many wiles smiled at him and said: "Great indeed were the gifts on which you set your heart, the horses of the skillful son of Aeacus. But they are hard for mortal men to master and to drive, for any other than Achilles, whom an immortal mother bore. But tell me this, and report it truthfully: Where did you leave Hector, shepherd of the people, when you came hither? Where are his weapons of war, where his horses? How are the guard posts and the beds of the other Trojans? What plans are they devising? Do they desire to stay here by the ships, far from their town, or will they draw back toward their city, now that they have overcome the Achaeans?"

Dolon, Eumedes' son, said to him: "I will answer you this quite truthfully. Hector, with all who are counselors, is deliberating by the tomb of the divine Ilus, far from the roar of battle; as for the guards of which you ask, brave sir, there is none chosen to protect or guard the camp, but by each Trojan campfire, those whose task it is sit wakeful and bid one another keep their watch. But our allies, called from many a land, are sleeping, for they entrust guard duty to the Trojans, since their own children lie not close at hand, nor do their wives."

Many-wiled Odysseus answered him and said: "How then do they sleep? Among the horse-taming Trojans or apart? Tell me, that I may know."

Then Dolon, Eumedes' son, replied to him: "I will answer you this quite truthfully. Near the sea are the Carians, and the Paeonians with their crooked bows, and the Leleges, and the Caucones, and the godlike Pelasgians. Toward Thymbra fell the lot of the Lycians and the impetuous Mysians and the horse-taming Phrygians and the Maeonian charioteers. But why do you ask me all these details? For if you wish to go amid the Trojan host, these Thracians on the edge are newly come and are the furthest from the others. Among them is King Rhesus, Eioneus' son. His horses are the fairest and the largest I have seen, whiter than snow and like the winds for speed. His chariot is well wrought of gold and silver, and he came bearing huge golden armor, a wonder to see, such as mortal men should never wear, but the immortal gods. Now take me to the swift-faring ships, or bind me and leave me here in cruel bonds while you go and test me, whether I spoke the truth or not."

Then mighty Diomedes looked scornfully on him and said: "Cherish no thought of escape within your heart, Dolon, even though you have given a good report, now that you have fallen into our hands. For if we now release you or let you go, you will come later to the swift ships of the Achaeans either to spy or to wage war against us. But if you perish, struck down by my hand, then you can never again be a trouble to the Argives."

So he spoke, and Dolon started to reach for Diomedes' chin with his strong hand in supplication. But Diomedes quickly struck him full in the neck with his sharp sword and cut through both the muscles. Even as Dolon spoke, his head rolled in the dust. They took the cap of weasel skin from off his head, and the wolf skin and the backward-bending bow and the long spear. Godlike Odysseus raised them up in his hand to Athena, divider of spoil, and said in prayer: "Accept these, goddess, and rejoice. To thee first of all immortals on Olympus we will offer gifts. Now bring us to the horses and beds of the Thracian warriors."

So he spoke, and lifting the spoils high over him, he hung them on a tamarisk and he made a sign near by, plain to be seen, weaving together reeds and luxuriant tamarisk shoots, lest they miss the spot as they returned through the swift, black night. The two went forward through the weapons and the dark blood, and as they went they soon came to the company of Thracian warriors. These slept, overwhelmed by weariness, and their fair weapons rested beside them on the earth, well ordered in three rows, and by each man was a pair of horses. Rhesus slept in their midst, and beside him his swift horses were tied by their reins to the edge of the chariot rim. Odysseus saw him first and pointed him out to Diomedes. "There is your man, Diomedes, and there the horses of which we were told by Dolon, whom we slew. Come now, put forth your mighty strength. You must not stand with your weapons useless: loose the horses, or you slay the men, and the horses shall be my concern."

So he spoke, and bright-eyed Athena breathed might into Diomedes, and he slew in all directions. A ghastly groan arose from them as they were struck by the sword, and the earth grew red with blood. As a lion falls on flocks without a shepherd, upon goats or sheep, and rushes in on them with deadly purpose, so the son of Tydeus moved upon the Thracian warriors until he had killed twelve. But many-wiled Odysseus would stop by each whom the son of Tydeus struck with his sword and would seize the body by the foot and drag it aside, with this in mind, that the fair-maned horses might pass through easily and not be frightened at heart by treading on the corpses, for they were as yet unaccustomed to them. But when the son of Tydeus came upon the king, his was the thirteenth sweet spirit he let gasping forth, for an evil dream stood by his head that night, the son of Oeneus' son,[1] through Athena's wisdom. Meanwhile much-enduring Odysseus loosed

---

[1] I.e., Diomedes.

the single-hoofed horses, tied them together with the reins, and drove them from the host, striking them with his bow, since he did not think to seize the shining whip from the cleverly wrought chariot. He whistled as a signal to godlike Diomedes.

But Diomedes lingered, debating what was the most daring deed he could perform, whether he should seize the chariot where lay the cleverly wrought arms and drag it away by the pole, or lift it aloft and carry it away, or whether he should deprive still more Thracians of their lives. While he was debating this in heart and mind, Athena stood close by godlike Diomedes and said: "Think now of your return to the hollow ships, son of great-hearted Tydeus, lest you return in flight and some other god arouse the Trojans."

So she said, and he knew the voice of the goddess as she spoke, and he quickly mounted the horses and Odysseus struck them with the bow and they flew to the swift ships of the Achaeans.

But Apollo of the silver bow kept no blind watch, as he saw Athena following after Tydeus' son. Angry at her he entered the great host of the Trojans and aroused the Thracians' counselor Hippocoön, Rhesus' noble cousin. Starting from sleep, when he saw the post empty where the swift horses had stood and saw the men gasping in cruel slaughter, he lamented and called his dear comrade by name. There was a clamor and continual uproar of the Trojans as they came rushing all at once. And they looked upon the dreadful deeds the warriors had done before returning to the hollow ships.

When the two came to the spot where they had slain Hector's spy, Odysseus, dear to Zeus, checked the swift horses, and the son of Tydeus leaped to the ground and put the bloodstained armor in Odysseus' hands, and remounted the horses. He lashed the horses and they flew, not unwilling, to the hollow ships, for so it pleased their hearts. Nestor first heard the hoof beats and cried: "Friends, leaders and counselors of the Argives, shall I speak falsely or disclose the truth as my heart bids me? The din of swift-footed horses beats upon by ear. Would that Odysseus and mighty Diomedes might be so quickly driving single-hoofed horses from the Trojans. But I fear dreadfully in my heart lest the bravest of the Argives have come to harm amid the Trojans' roaring press."

He had not finished speaking when they came. They dropped to the ground, and their happy comrades greeted them with handclasps and warm words. First the Gerenian horseman, Nestor, asked: "Come, tell me, much-praised Odysseus, great glory of the Achaeans, how you took these horses, entering the Trojans' host, or did some god meet you and give you them? They are wonderfully like the rays of the sun. For I am ever meeting with the Trojans, nor do I stay beside the ships though I am an aged warrior, yet never have I seen or noticed horses such as these. I think some god met you and gave you them, for cloud-gathering Zeus loves both of you, as does the child of aegis-bearing Zeus, bright-eyed Athena."

Odysseus of many wiles answered him and said: "Nestor, Neleus' son, great glory of the Achaeans, a god, if he wished, could easily give us horses better even than these, since gods are mightier far. But these horses about which you ask, father, are Thracians, newly come. Their master, brave Diomedes slew, and with him all his twelve best comrades. A thirteenth man, a spy, we caught close by the ships, sent out by Hector and other noble Trojans to be observer of our camp."

So speaking, he drove the single-hoofed horses across the ditch exultantly, and the rest of the Achaeans went with him rejoicing. When they came to the well-built tent of Tydeus' son, they tied the horses with well-cut thongs beside the manger, where Diomedes' swift-footed horses stood eating wheat as sweet as honey. Odysseus set down by the ship's stern the bloodstained spoils of Dolon until they should prepare an offering to Athena. Then they went into the sea and washed away in it much sweat from shins and neck and thighs. But when the sea waves had washed away much sweat from their skin and refreshed their hearts, they sat in polished tubs and bathed. Then when they had bathed and anointed themselves with shining oil, they sat down to dinner, and drawing honey-sweet wine from a full bowl, they poured it in libation to Athena.

BOOK XI

Dawn from her bed by lord Tithonus rose to bring light to immortals and to men, and Zeus sent violent Strife to the swift ships of the Achaeans with war's dread omen in her hands. She stood by the great-bellied black ship of Odysseus, which was in the center so that one could shout to either side, either to the tents of Ajax, Telamon's son, or to those of Achilles; for these two guarded the rows of fair-lined ships at either end, trusting in their bravery and the might of their hands. Standing there, the goddess gave a great and dreadful cry in a shrill voice, and in the heart of each Achaean she roused unfailing might for war and strife. At once war became sweeter to them than sailing home in hollow ships to their dear native land.

The son of Atreus shouted and bade the Argives gird themselves, and he himself put on the flashing bronze. First he placed upon his shins fair greaves, fitted with silver ankle-pieces; next he strapped upon his chest a breastplate which Cinyras once gave him as a present, for he heard in Cyprus the great news that the Achaeans were about to set sail in their ships for Troy. Therefore he gave the breastplate as a mark of favor to the king. It had ten bands of dark blue enamel, and twelve of gold, and twenty of tin. Three serpents of blue enamel reached up to the neck on either side, like rainbows that the son of Cronus sets upon the cloud as an omen to mortal men. Then he hung his sword about his shoulders. It had studs of gleaming gold, while the sheath was silver, set with rings of gold. He picked up his valorous shield, of body length, well wrought; around it were ten circles of bronze, and there were twenty white bosses of tin upon it and in their midst one of dark blue enamel. The Gorgon's awful face, with dreadful glance, was worked upon it, with Terror and Rout beside her. Its strap was silver, and on the strap there writhed a blue enamel serpent that had three twisting heads sprung from one neck. Upon his head he placed a helmet with double horsehair plume and fourfold crest, and the plume nodded dreadfully above it. He took two stout spears, sharp-tipped with bronze, and the bronze upon them gleamed afar to heaven. Thereupon Athena and Hera thundered, to honor the king of Mycenae, rich in gold.

Then each hero bade his charioteer to check the horses in good order at the ditch's edge. But they themselves marched out on foot under arms, and an unceasing shout arose before the dawn. They were drawn up by the ditch long before the charioteers who took their place a short space behind them. The son of Cronus raised an evil din among them and sent down from the high ether a bloody dew, because he was about to hurl down many mighty heads into the house of Death.

The Trojans mustered on the other side of the plain's rising ground, about great Hector and blameless Polydamas and Aeneas, who was reverenced by the Trojan people as a god, and Antenor's three sons, Polybus and godlike Agenor and young Acamas, like to the immortals. And Hector, in the front ranks, bore a balanced shield. As a baneful star shines radiant from the clouds and then recedes again behind the shadowing clouds, so Hector appeared now among the front ranks and now among the rear, giving his orders. He was all agleam with bronze, like the lightning of the Father, aegis-bearing Zeus.

As reapers facing one another lay a swath of wheat or barley along the field of some rich man, and the sheaves fall thick, so Trojans and Achaeans leaped on one another and slew, and neither thought of ruinous flight. The conflict had equal heads, and the men rushed on like wolves. Strife, who causes many groans, rejoiced as she beheld it, for she alone among the gods happened to stand beside the fighters; the other gods were not with them, but sat at ease within their halls where for each a home was built among the valleys of Olympus. They all blamed the black-clouded son of Cronus for wishing to give glory to the Trojans. But the Father cared naught for them; withdrawn afar, he sat apart from the rest, exulting in his glory, gazing on the Trojans' city and the ships of the Achaeans, the gleam of bronze, the slayers and the slain.

While it was morning and the sacred day still waxed, the weapons of both sides flew quickly and the people fell. But at the hour when a woodcutter makes his dinner in the mountain dells, when his hands have had enough of cutting the tall trees and weariness has filled his heart and desire for sweet food assails his soul, then the Danaans broke the line of battle by their valor, calling to their comrades through the ranks.

Among them Agamemnon was the first to rush ahead; he slew Bienor, shepherd of the people—the man himself and then his comrade Oileus, driver of horses. Oileus leaped from the chariot and faced him, but as he rushed forward Agamemnon pierced his forehead with the sharp spear, nor did his visor, for all its heavy bronze, hold back the spear, but it passed straight through it and the bone, and all his brains were scattered about within, and he slew him despite his bold attack. Agamemnon, king of men, left them there, their chests shining, since he had stripped off their shirts. Then he went to slay Isus and Antiphus, two sons of Priam, bastard and lawful, both in one chariot. The bastard held the reins and far-famed Antiphus stood beside him. Once Achilles had caught them herding sheep in Ida's glens and bound them with pliant willow withes, then loosed them for a ransom. But now wide-ruling Agamemnon, Atreus' son, smote Isus on the chest above the nipple with his spear and struck Antiphus beside the ear with his sword, and hurled him from the chariot. Quickly he stripped them of their fair armor, knowing them well, for he had seen them formerly beside the swift ships when swift-footed Achilles brought them from Ida. As a lion easily crushes the helpless fawns of a swift deer, seizing them in his mighty teeth when he comes upon their bed, and takes away their tender life; and the mother, even though she chance to be very near, cannot help them, for a fearful trembling falls upon her and she rushes quickly through the dense oak copse and the wood, hastening and sweating before the onrush of the mighty beast—so no one could ward off destruction from the Trojans, but they too fled before the Argives.

Then mighty Agamemnon caught in one chariot Pisander and steadfast Hippolochus, sons of that prudent Antimachus who, in hope of gold and gleaming gifts from Alexander, had led in refusing to give Helen back to fair-haired Menelaus. They were both trying to hold the swift horses, for the shining reins were slipping from their hands and the steeds were in a panic. The son of Atreus rose before them like a lion, and from the chariot they begged him: "Take us alive, son of Atreus, and accept a fitting ransom. Many treasures lie in the house of Antimachus—bronze and gold and iron wrought with much labor. From these our father would give you boundless ransom, if he should learn that we are alive beside the ships of the Achaeans."

So, weeping, they addressed the king with humble words,

but they heard a relentless answer: "If indeed you are the sons of prudent Antimachus, who once in the Trojans' council bade them forthwith slay Menelaus, who had come as a messenger with the godlike Odysseus, and not send him back to the Achaeans, now shall you pay for the unseemly outrage of your father."

So speaking, he thrust Pisander in the chest with his spear and threw him from the chariot to the ground. Hippolochus rushed away, but Agamemnon slew him on the ground, cutting off his hands with the sword and severing his neck. He threw the body to roll like a column among the throng. These then he left, and where the thickest battle raged, there he rushed in, while the other well-greaved Achaeans wreaked slaughter with the bronze, foot soldiers slaying foot soldiers as they fled perforce, and horsemen horsemen, and beneath them a dust arose from the plain, stirred by the loud-thundering feet of horses. Mighty Agamemnon, forever slaying, followed, shouting orders to the Argives. As when destructive fire falls on a virgin forest, and a wind, whirling in all directions, carries it, and the bushes fall, torn up by the roots before the onrush of the fire, so fell the heads of the fleeing Trojans before Agamemnon, Atreus' son, and many proud-necked horses rattled their empty chariots along the dykes of war, missing their blameless drivers. But these lay on the earth, far dearer to the vultures than to their wives.

Now Zeus led Hector from the weapons and the dust and the slaughter and the blood and the uproar, but the son of Atreus followed, calling impatiently to the Danaans. Past the tomb of ancient Ilus, son of Dardanus, through the midst of the plain, past the wild fig tree, rushed the Trojans, heading for the city. The son of Atreus followed, ever shouting, and his invincible hands were smeared with gore. But when the Trojans reached the Scaean gates and the oak tree, they stopped and waited for one another. For some were still fleeing in mid-plain, like cattle, all of which a lion coming in the darkness of the night has scattered; and for one of them sharp death appears as first the lion seizes her and breaks her neck with his mighty teeth, and then he gulps down her blood and all her entrails. So Atreus' son, mighty Agamemnon, followed the Trojans, slaying ever the rearmost, and they fled in rout. Many fell from their chariots on face or back at the hands of Atreus' son, for he raged around and before him with his spear. But when he was about to reach the city and its lofty wall, then the father of gods and men came down from heaven and sat down on the peaks of many-fountained Ida, holding the lightning in his hand. He bade golden-winged Iris go as messenger: "Go, swift Iris, and give this command to Hector. As long as he sees Agamemnon, shepherd of the folk, raging in the foremost ranks, slaying the lines of warriors, so long let him retreat and let him order the rest of the men to strive in mighty conflict with the foe. But when Agamemnon leaps to his chariot, smitten by spear or struck by arrow, then I will grant Hector strength to slay until he reach the well-benched ships and the sun set and the holy twilight fall."

So he spoke, and wing-footed, swift Iris failed not to obey, and she went down from Mount Ida to holy Ilium. She found the son of prudent Priam, godlike Hector, standing amid the horses and the well-joined chariots. Then standing close by him, swift-footed Iris said: "Hector, son of Priam, like to Zeus in wisdom, Father Zeus sent me to say this to you. As long as you see Agamemnon, shepherd of the people, raging in the foremost ranks, slaying the lines of warriors, so long draw back from battle and order the rest of the men to strive in mighty conflict with the foe. But when Agamemnon leaps to his chariot, smitten by spear or struck by arrow, then Zeus will give you strength to slay until you reach the well-benched ships and the sun set and the holy twilight fall."

So spoke swift-footed Iris and departed. And Hector leaped in his armor from his chariot to the ground and went throughout the army brandishing sharp spears, bidding men to fight, and he aroused dread conflict. So they rallied and faced the Achaeans, and the Argives on the other side strengthened their lines. Then the battle was joined, and men stood face to face, and among them Agamemnon rushed out first and yearned to fight far out in front of all.

Tell me, now, ye Muses, who have your home upon Olympus, who first of the Trojans themselves or of their famous allies faced Agamemnon—Iphidamas, Antenor's brave and mighty son, who was reared in fertile Thrace, mother of flocks. Cisses, his mother's father, who begot fair-cheeked Theano, raised him in his house when he was but a child. And when he reached the milestone of glorious youth, he kept him there and gave him his daughter. Straight from the marriage chamber he followed the tidings of the Achaeans with twelve curved ships which went with him. Then he left the fair-lined ships in Percote and came on foot to Ilium. He it was who now came to face Atreus' son, Agamemnon. When they came close to one another in their onset, the son of

Atreus missed, and his spear turned aside, but Iphidamas struck him in the belt, below the breastplate, and pressed the blow home, trusting in his heavy hand. Yet he did not pierce the gleaming belt; long before that the point met the silver and bent like lead. Wide-ruling Agamemnon seized the spear with his hand and pulled it toward him as eagerly as a lion, and dragged it from Iphidamas' hand. Then he struck him in the neck with his sword and loosed his limbs. So he fell there, and slept a sleep of bronze, a thing of pity, defending his townsfolk, far from his wedded wife, of whom he had no joy, though he had given much for her; he gave first a hundred cattle, and promised then a thousand head of goats and sheep, which were herded for him in boundless numbers. Then Atreus' son, Agamemnon, stripped him, and carrying his fair armor departed through the throng of the Achaeans.

When Antenor's eldest son Coön, illustrious among men, beheld Iphidamas, his eyes were veiled by overwhelming sorrow for his fallen brother. Standing to one side with his spear, unseen by godlike Agamemnon, he smote him in the center of the arm below the elbow, and the point of the shining spear pierced through and showed on the other side. Then Agamemnon, king of men, shuddered, but even so he did not cease from war and battle, but rushed upon Coön, holding his spear with its wind-toughened shaft. Coön was quickly dragging Iphidamas, his brother, by the foot and was calling to all the nobles. As he dragged him through the throng, Agamemnon wounded him beneath his bossed shield with his bronze-tipped spear, and loosed his limbs. Then he stood beside him and cut his head off over Iphidamas. There, at the hand of Atreus' son the king, Antenor's sons fulfilled their doom and passed into the house of Death.

Agamemnon wandered then among the lines of other men with shield and sword and great stones, while the warm blood still gushed from his wound; but when the wound dried and the bleeding ceased, sharp pain seized the mighty son of Atreus. As when the keen shaft falls on a woman in labor, the piercing shaft sent by the Eileithyiae who excite the pangs of birth, Hera's daughters, who bring bitter pains, so sharp pains seized the mighty son of Atreus. He leaped to his chariot and bade the charioteer drive to the hollow ships, for he was racked at heart. He gave a piercing cry, shouting to the Danaans: "Friends, leaders and counselors of the Argives, do you now keep from the seafaring ships the violent strife, since Zeus the counselor has not allowed me to battle with the Trojans all day long."

So he spoke, and the driver lashed the fair-maned horses to the hollow ships, and they flew not unwillingly. Their chests were flecked with foam, and they were spattered with dust beneath, as they bore the tortured king far from the battle.

When Hector saw Agamemnon depart, he called with a loud shout to Trojans and Lycians: "Trojans and Lycians and close-fighting Dardanians, be men, my friends, and remember furious valor. The best warrior has departed, and Zeus, Cronus' son, has given me great glory. Drive the single-hoofed horses straight at the mighty Danaans, that you may gain a higher glory."

So speaking, he aroused the might and heart of each. As when a hunter sets his white-toothed hounds upon a wild boar or a lion, so Hector, Priam's son, like Ares, bane of mortals, set the great-hearted Trojans on the Achaeans. He himself strode with high hopes among the first and plunged into the fray like a loud-roaring storm that rushes down and churns the violet sea.

Whom first, whom last, did Hector, Priam's son, then slay when Zeus gave him glory? Asaeus first, and Autonous and Opites and the Dolopian, Clytius' son, and Opheltius and Agelaus, Aesymnus and Orus and steadfast Hipponous. These leaders of the Danaans he slew, and then the throng; as when the West Wind scatters clouds from the brightening South Wind, striking them with a heavy gale—many a huge wave rolls, and much foam is scattered aloft from the wind's roaring blast that drives ships far off their course—so the crowded heads of the men fell before Hector.

Then destruction would have raged and irreparable deeds been done and the Achaeans would have fallen into their ships in rout, had not Odysseus called to Tydeus' son, Diomedes: "Son of Tydeus, what has befallen us that we forget our furious valor? Come here, dear friend, and take your stand by me, for we shall be disgraced if Hector of the glancing helmet takes the ships."

Mighty Diomedes answered him and said: "I will indeed stay and endure, but we shall do little good, since cloud-gathering Zeus intends to give strength to the Trojans rather than to us."

He spoke, and thrust Thymbraeus from his chariot to the

ground, striking him in the left breast with his spear, while Odysseus slew Molion, the prince's godlike squire. They left them then, since they had ceased from war and the two of them spread havoc, ranging through the press. As when two boars with high hearts fall upon hunting dogs, so, turning back, they slew the Trojans, while the Achaeans gladly caught their breath, escaping godlike Hector.

Then they caught a chariot and two of the host's best warriors, the two sons of Merops of Percote, who was skilled beyond all men in divination and would not permit his sons to march to man-destroying war, but they would not obey him, for the fate of dark death led them on. Tydeus' son, Diomedes, famed with the spear, deprived them of breath and spirit and took away their glorious arms. And Odysseus slew Hippodamus and Hypeirochus.

Then the son of Cronus, looking down from Ida, stretched taut their battle lines on either side, and they slew one another. Tydeus' son wounded Agastrophus, heroic son of Paeon, in the hip joint with his spear, for his team was not close by for him to flee, and he had been much misled in mind, for his squire held the horses far away, while he rushed among the foremost ranks on foot until he lost his life. But Hector quickly saw Diomedes and Odysseus in the ranks and rushed upon them with a shout, and with him followed the battalions of the Trojans. When Diomedes of the mighty war cry saw him, he shuddered and said at once to Odysseus, close at hand: "That cursed mighty Hector rolls upon us. Let us stand and defend ourselves upon the spot."

So speaking, he drew back his long-shadowed spear and cast it, nor did he miss, aiming for the helmet's top upon his head, but bronze was turned by bronze, nor pierced to the fair skin, warded off by the threefold crested helmet which Phoebus Apollo gave him. Hector quickly sprang a vast distance back and mixed with the throng; he fell upon his knees and with his stout hand leaned upon the earth. And black night veiled his eyes. But while Tydeus' son followed the spear's course far through the foremost ranks to the spot where it had come to earth, Hector regained his breath and, leaping back into a chariot, drove back into the throng and evaded his black doom. Rushing toward him with his spear, mighty Diomedes said to him: "This time, dog, you have again escaped from death, though doom was close upon you. Now Phoebus Apollo saved you, to whom you doubtless pray when you go toward the din of spears. Yet will I slay you, though it be later that I meet you, if some god be my helper too. Now I shall go after the others, whomever I may find."

So speaking he slew Paeon's son, famed with the spear. But Alexander, fair-haired Helen's husband, leaning against a pillar on the man-built tomb of Ilus, Dardanus' son, an elder of the people in days of old, drew his bow against the son of Tydeus, shepherd of the people. Diomedes was stripping mighty Agastrophus' gleaming breastplate from his chest and his shield from his shoulders, and his heavy helmet. And Alexander bent the bow's center piece and shot him in the flat of his right foot, nor did the shaft fly from his hand in vain. The arrow drove straight through and fixed itself in the ground. Then laughing very sweetly, he sprang from his ambush and boasting cried: "You are hit; the shaft sped not in vain. Would I had hit you in the lower belly and taken your life. Then would the Trojans have had rest from evil, who shudder at you like bleating goats before a lion."

But fearlessly the mighty Diomedes said to him: "Archer, gossip, curlylocks, flirt, if you would face trial man to man with arms, your bow and thick-flying arrows would not avail you. Now, having scratched the surface of my foot, you make your idle boast. I care no more than as if a woman or a witless child should hit me. Dull is the shaft of a man without worth or valor, whereas a weapon from my hand, though it touch but little, is sharp and lays a man dead at once; both his wife's cheeks are torn in grief, and his children are fatherless; staining the earth with blood, he rots, and around him are more birds than women."

So he spoke, and Odysseus, famed with the spear, came close and stood in front of him, and he, sitting down behind Odysseus, drew the sharp arrow from his foot, and a grievous pain passed through his flesh. He climbed into his chariot and bade his charioteer drive toward the hollow ships, for he was racked at heart.

Odysseus, famed with the spear, was left alone, nor did any of the Argives stay at his side, since fear had seized them all. Troubled, he said to his great-hearted soul: "Ah, what will become of me? It will be a great disgrace if I flee in fear of the multitude; yet it will be worse if I am caught alone; the son of Cronus has put the other Danaans to flight. But why does my soul say this to me? For I know that cowards depart from war, but he who excels in battle must stand firm, whether he be hit or hit another."

While he was debating this in heart and mind, the lines of

Trojan shieldmen were advancing, and they hemmed him in their midst, holding their bane [1] among them. As when hounds and stout huntsmen surge about a boar as it comes from a deep thicket, whetting its white tusks against its curved jaws, and the hunters rush around it to a sound of gnashing tusks, and they at once await the beast, dreadful though it be, so then the Trojans surged about Odysseus, dear to Zeus. First, lunging with his sharp spear, he wounded blameless Deiopites above the shoulder, then he slew Thoön and Ennomus, then he thrust Chersidamas with his spear beneath the navel, as he rushed up in his chariot, and he fell in the dust and grasped the earth in his outstretched hand. He let them lie, and wounded with his spear Hippasus' son Charops, own brother of wealthy Socus. Socus, the godlike mortal, came to his aid and stood close by and said: "Odysseus, greatly praised for craft or toil, this day either you shall exult over Hippasus' two sons, having slain such men and stripped them of their arms, or, struck by my spear, you shall lose your own life."

So speaking, he thrust at his balanced shield, and the heavy spear passed through the shining shield and stuck fast in the richly wrought breastplate, cutting all the skin from his ribs, but Pallas Athena would not suffer it to reach the man's vitals. Odysseus knew that it had not reached a fatal spot, and drawing back he said to Socus: "Wretch, utter destruction is upon you. You have indeed stopped me from battling with the Trojans, but I say that death and black fate shall befall you here this day, and that slain by my spear you shall give glory to me and your soul to Hades of the famous steeds."

He spoke, and the other turned and started back in flight. But as he turned, Odysseus plunged his spear into his back between the shoulders, and it pressed through his chest. He clanged as he fell, and godlike Odysseus exulted over him: "Socus, son of Hippasus the prudent tamer of horses, the lot of death overtook you first, nor could you escape it, nor shall your father and queenly mother close your eyes even in death, but carrion birds shall peck them out as wings beat swift about you. But me, if I die, the godlike Achaeans shall inter."

So speaking, he drew out of his flesh and his bossed shield the heavy spear of prudent Socus. As it was withdrawn, the blood sprang forth, and his spirit was distressed. And when the great-hearted Trojans saw Odysseus' blood, a shout arose throughout the host, and all advanced upon him. Then he

[1] I.e., Odysseus, who had been their bane.

drew back and called to his companions. Thrice then he called, as great a shout as mortal head can hold, and thrice did Menelaus, dear to Ares, hear his shouting. At once he called to Ajax, who was close at hand: "Ajax, Zeus-born son of Telamon, leader of men, there comes to me the cry of stout-hearted Odysseus, as if the Trojans had cut him off in the mighty conflict and were overpowering him, he being alone. Let us go through the press, for it is better to protect him. I fear lest he suffer ill, left alone amid the Trojans, brave as he is, and a great loss befall the Danaans."

So speaking he led the way, and the godlike mortal followed. Then they found Odysseus, dear to Zeus, and the Trojans were rushing about him like tawny jackals on the mountains about a wounded antlered stag, which some man has wounded with an arrow from a bowstring. The stag has escaped him, fleeing on its feet so long as its blood is warm and its knees will lift, but when the swift arrow overcomes it, the ravening jackals devour it in some shady grove among the mountains. But then some god brings a ravenous lion there, and the jackals scatter while the lion devours the stag. So then about prudent, versatile Odysseus many brave Trojans gathered, while the hero, lunging with his spear, kept off the cruel day. Then Ajax drew near, bearing a shield like a city wall, and stood close by. And the Trojans scattered to every side. Then warlike Menelaus took Odysseus' hand and led him from the press until his squire drove his chariot close.

But Ajax leaped upon the Trojans and slew Doryclus, Priam's bastard son, and then wounded Pandocus, and he wounded Lysander and Pyrasus and Pylartes. As when a flooded stream pours plainward, swollen by snow among the mountains, forced on by rain from Zeus, and it carries down many dry oaks and many pines, and empties much silt into the sea, so glorious Ajax then drove all before him on the plain, slaying men and horses. Nor had Hector yet learned it, since he was fighting on the left of the whole battle, by the banks of the river Scamander, where men's heads were falling thickest and an unending shout arose about great Nestor and warlike Idomeneus. Hector joined with them, doing wonders of spearcraft and horsemanship and routing the companies of the young men. But not even yet would the godlike Achaeans have withdrawn from their onward way had not Alexander, husband of fair-haired Helen, stopped Machaon, shepherd of the people, in the midst of his valorous deeds, hitting him in the right shoulder with a three-barbed arrow. The Achaeans, breathing might, feared for him, lest when the battle line surged back the foe might capture him. At once Idomeneus said to godlike Nestor: "Nestor, Neleus' son, great glory of the Achaeans, quick, mount your chariot and let Machaon mount beside you, and drive your single-hoofed horses with all speed toward the ships. For a physician is worth many other men to cut out arrows and sprinkle healing drugs upon a wound."

So he spoke, nor did the Gerenian horseman Nestor disobey him. At once he mounted his chariot, and beside him stepped Machaon, son of Asclepius, the blameless physician. He lashed the horses, and not unwillingly they flew to the hollow ships, for so it pleased their hearts.

But Cebriones, as he strode at Hector's side, noticed the Trojans in rout and said to him: "Hector, we strive here with the Danaans on the tumultuous battle's edge, but the other Trojans are routed in confusion, both chariots and men. Ajax, Telamon's son, drives them before him; I know well it is he, for he bears a broad shield on his shoulders. Come, let us too drive our chariot and horses thither, where most of all the charioteers and foot soldiers, stirring bitter strife, are slaying one another, and where ceaseless shouts arise."

So speaking, he cut the fair-maned horses with a whistling lash, and feeling the blow they quickly bore the swift chariot between the Trojans and Achaeans, trampling on shields and bodies. The whole axle was spattered underneath with blood, as was the rim about the chariot, which was sprayed with drops of blood from the horses' hoofs and from the tires. Hector was eager to enter the press of men and leap into it and break it up, and he caused an evil din among the Danaans and rested little from the spear play. But he ranged then among the ranks of other men with spear and sword and great stones, and avoided battle with Ajax, Telamon's son.

Now high-throned Father Zeus aroused fear in Ajax. He stood in a daze and put his shield of seven ox hides behind him and drew back, peering among the press like a wild beast, turning often about, setting one knee past the other in short steps. As dogs and farmhands drive a tawny lion from a cattle yard, and watching all night keep him from seizing the fat cattle, and he, craving for meat, attacks, but accomplishes nothing, for in his face from their stout hands fly javelins and burning faggots, which he fears for all his eagerness, and with the dawn he goes away with troubled heart, so Ajax then with troubled heart withdrew before the Trojans, much against his will, for he feared for the ships of the Achaeans. As when an ass, passing a field, proves too much for boys—a lazy beast, on whose sides many a club has been broken: he goes and grazes on the deep grass while the boys beat him with cudgels, but their strength is feeble, and they can hardly drive him out even when he has had his fill of fodder—so then the high-hearted Trojans and their many allies ever followed great Ajax, Telamon's son, pricking at the center of his shield with their spears. Ajax sometimes remembered furious valor, and turning about held back the companies of horse-taming Trojans, and sometimes he turned to flee. But he kept them all from going to the swift ships, and he himself raged as he stood again and again between Trojans and Achaeans. Of the spears from their mighty hands some in their onward course stuck fast in his great shield, many plunged to the ground midway before touching his white flesh, despite their eagerness to sate themselves with it.

When Eurypylus, Euaemon's glorious son, saw him hardpressed by many shafts, he went and stood beside him and thrust with his shining spear and hit Phausius' son Apisaon, shepherd of the people, in the liver below the midriff, and at once his knees were loosed. Eurypylus rushed forward and stripped his armor from his shoulders. But when godlike Alexander saw him stripping off Apisaon's armor, he at once drew his bow against Eurypylus and hit him in the right thigh with an arrow. The shaft broke and weighed down his thigh. He shrank back into the throng of his companions, avoiding his fate, and he called out piercingly, shouting to the Danaans: "Friends, leaders and counselors of the Argives, turn and stand and ward off the pitiless day from Ajax, who is overwhelmed by missiles, nor do I think he will escape from tumultuous war. Come, stand and face them around great Ajax, Telamon's son."

So spoke the wounded Eurypylus, and they stood close about him, resting their shields on their shoulders and lifting their spears. Ajax came toward them, and turned and stopped when he reached the throng of his companions.

So they fought, like shining fire. But the Neleian horses, sweating, bore Nestor from the battle and Machaon, too, shepherd of the people. Swift-footed, godlike Achilles saw and noted him, for he stood on the stern of his wide-bellied ship, watching the hard toil and tearful onset. At once he spoke to his comrade Patroclus, calling from the ship, and Patroclus, hearing him from the tent, came out, like to Ares; and this was the beginning of misfortune for him. The brave son of Menoetius first said to Achilles: "Why do you call me, Achilles? What need have you of me?"

Swift-footed Achilles answered him and said: "Godlike son of Menoetius, dear to my heart, now I think the Achaeans will fall at my knees in supplication, for a need no longer endurable has come upon them. Go now, Patroclus, dear to Zeus, ask Nestor whom he brings there wounded from the battle. From the rear it seems in all ways like Machaon, Asclepius' son, but I could not see the man's eyes, for the horses rushed by me, speeding onward."

So he spoke, and Patroclus obeyed his dear companion and went running past the tents and ships of the Achaeans.

When the others reached the tent of Neleus' son, they stepped out upon the all-nourishing earth, and Eurymedon, the squire, loosed the old man's horses from the chariot. The men dried the sweat from their shirts, standing in the wind by the shore of the sea. Then they went into the tent and sat down in chairs. Hecamede of the lovely tresses mixed a posset for them, the daughter of great-hearted Arsinous, she whom the old man had taken from Tenedos when Achilles sacked it. The Achaeans set her aside for him because he surpassed all in council. She first set before them a fair table, highly polished, with dark blue feet, and on it placed a basket of bronze with an onion in it as relish with the wine. She set out yellow honey, too, and sacred barley meal, and a fair cup which the old man brought from home, set with studs of gold. It had four handles, and two golden doves were feeding on the sides of each, and there were two bases underneath. Another could hardly lift it from the table full, but old Nestor raised it without trouble. In it the godlike woman mixed Pramnian wine and water, and grated goat's cheese upon it with a grater of bronze, and sprinkled white barley upon it, and bade them drink, when she had prepared the posset. After the two had drunk and quenched their parching thirst, they were taking delight in speech with one another when Patroclus stood in the doorway, a godlike man. When the old man saw him, he arose from his shining chair and took him by the hand and brought him in and pressed him to sit down. But Patroclus, for his part, refused and said: "This is no time for sitting, Zeus-nurtured father, nor shall you so persuade me. Revered and dreadful is the one who sent me to learn who is that man you bring back wounded. But I recognize him myself; I see Machaon, shepherd of the people. And now I am returning as messenger to Achilles to bear him word. Well you know, Zeus-nurtured father, how dread the man is, for he would be quick to blame even the blameless."

Then the Gerenian horseman, Nestor, answered him: "Why then does Achilles pity thus the sons of the Achaeans who are struck by missiles? Does he know nothing of our grief, how great it is, that has arisen in the camp? For our best men lie on the ships, hit and wounded. Tydeus' son, the mighty Diomedes, has been hit, and Odysseus, famed with the spear, is wounded, and Agamemnon. Eurypylus has been shot in the thigh with an arrow, and this other one I brought but now from battle, shot by an arrow from the string. Yet Achilles, for all his valor, cares not and has no pity for the Danaans. Is he then waiting until the swift ships, close by the sea, shall burn with blazing fire despite the Argives, and we ourselves be slain, one on another? For my strength is not what it once was in my pliant limbs.

"Would I had still the youth and strength as when dispute arose between the men of Elis and ourselves about some cattle lifting, when I slew Itymoneus, Hypeirochus' valiant son, who dwelt in Elis, as I drove away our booty. Defending his cattle, he was struck by a javelin from my hand as he stood in the front ranks, and down he fell and the peasants fled in all directions. We gathered our plunder from the plain, and very much of it there was—fifty herds of cattle and as many flocks of sheep, as many droves of swine and as many wide herds of goats, and one hundred and fifty sorrel horses, all mares, many with foals beneath them. We drove them to Neleian Pylos, reaching the town by night. Neleus rejoiced at heart that much had fallen to me on going while but a youth to war.

"When dawn appeared, the heralds loudly called that all should come who had debts owing them in glorious Elis. The leading men among the Pylians assembled and made the division, for the Epeians owed damages to many, since we in Pylos, being few, had been ill used. For mighty Heracles had come and used us ill in former years and had slain all our nobles, for we were twelve sons of blameless Neleus, and of them I alone was left, and all the rest had perished.

"The bronze-clad Epeians in their arrogance scorned us and worked evil. The old man took out a herd of cattle and a great flock of sheep, choosing three hundred and their herdsmen. For a great debt was owed to him in glorious Elis— four prize-winning horses with their chariot, which went to seek the prize, for they were to run for a tripod; but Augeias, king of men, retained them there and sent away the driver, grieving for his horses. The old man, angered at these words and deeds, took for himself boundless booty; the rest he gave to the people to divide, lest any of his men go wanting his due share. We discussed it all, and offered sacrifices to the gods about the city, and on the third day, the Epeians all came, in great numbers themselves, with single-hoofed horses, in all haste, and among them came the sons of Molione in their armor, still boys, not yet well versed in furious valor.

"There is a city called Thryoessa, on a steep hill, far away upon the Alpheus, a border town of sandy Pylos. This they were besieging, eager to overthrow it. But when they had traversed the entire plain, Athena came speeding from Olympus in the night, a messenger to us to arm, and roused the people throughout Pylos, who were not unwilling, but very eager for war. But Neleus would not let me arm, and he hid my horses, for he said I did not yet know aught of the works of war. Yet even so I shone among our horsemen, though I was on foot, since so Athena led the strife. There is a river called Minyeius which flows into the sea close by Arene— there we horsemen of the Pylians awaited the bright dawn, and the companies of foot came streaming in. Arming in all haste, we marched from there by noontime to Alpheus' sacred river. There we sacrificed fair victims to almighty Zeus, and a bull to Alpheus and a bull to Poseidon, but to bright-eyed Athena a cow from the herd. Then we ate by companies throughout the camp and lay down, each in his armor, along the river's course. The high-hearted Epeians surrounded the city, eager to overthrow it, but before them stood the heavy work of Ares, for when the radiant sun stood above the earth, we met in battle, praying to Zeus and to Athena.

"When the strife of Pylians and Epeians raged, I was the first to slay a man, the spearman Moulius, and I carried off his single-hoofed horses; he was Augeias' son-in-law, having wed his eldest daughter, Agamede, who knew all the herbs the broad earth bears. As he came on, I smote him with my spear of bronze and he fell in the dust. I leaped into his chariot and took my place then in the foremost ranks. The high-hearted Epeians fled in all directions when they saw fall the man who led their charioteers and was their best in battle. I rushed upon them like a black tempest and I took fifty chariots, and beside each two mortals bit the dust, slain by my spear. Now would I have slain the youthful sons of Actor and Molione, had not their father, the wide-ruling Earth-shaker,[1] saved them from battle, hiding them in a thick mist. Then Zeus gave great power to the Pylians, for we pursued them over the broad plain, slaying them and gathering their fair armor until we brought our horses to Bouprasius, rich in wheat, and the Olenian rock and the place called Alesium's hill. There Athena turned back the host. There I slew my last man and left him; but the Achaeans drove their swift horses back from Bouprasius toward Pylos, and all gave glory to Zeus among gods and among men to Nestor.

"So I was that day, if ever, among heroes. But Achilles will profit of his valor all alone. He will, I think, weep much hereafter when the host has perished. Dear friend, surely Menoetius gave you these commands that day when he sent you from Phthia to Agamemnon. I and the godlike Odysseus were within and heard well what commands he gave you in the hall. We had come to Peleus' well-built house, gathering the men throughout fertile Achaea. There we found the hero Menoetius at home, and you yourself, and with you Achilles. The aged horseman Peleus was burning a bull's rich thighs in the courtyard to Zeus, who rejoices in the thunder. He held a golden goblet, pouring gleaming wine upon the burning sacrifice. You and Achilles were making ready the bull's meat when we stood in the doorway. Surprised, Achilles started up and took us by the hand and led us in and bade us sit down, and he duly set before us offerings of hospitality, which are the right of guests. When we had taken pleasure of food and drink, I spoke the first, bidding you follow us. You two were very willing, but they two gave you many an order. Old Peleus bade his son Achilles ever to excel and be pre-eminent above the rest. And these are the orders Menoetius, Actor's son, gave you: 'My child, Achilles is superior in birth, but you are older; yet he is far the stronger. Give him wise words, counsel him and guide him well, and he will heed you in the good at last.' So ordered the old man, but you forget. Yet even now you could say this to wise-hearted Achilles in the hope that he will heed. Who knows but what with God's help you might stir his heart by your persuasion? A friend's persuasion does some good. If in his heart he shuns some prophecy and his queenly mother told him one from Zeus, still let him send you forth and let the rest of the host of Myrmidons go with

[1] There is a discrepancy in the lads' paternity.

you, in the hope that you might be a light to the Danaans.
And let him give you his fair arms to wear to war, on the
chance that taking you for him the Trojans may refrain from
battle and the warlike sons of the Achaeans catch their
breath, pressed as they are. For even a brief space is a breathing spell in war. And easily could you who are unwearied
drive men wearied by battle back toward the city from the
ships and tents."

So he spoke and stirred the heart within Patroclus' breast,
and he started to run past the ships to Aeacus' son Achilles.
But when Patroclus, as he ran, came by the ships of godlike
Odysseus, where stated assemblies met and where stood their
altars to the gods, there Eurypylus, Euaemon's Zeus-born son,
met him, wounded in the thigh by an arrow, limping from
battle. The heavy sweat ran down his head and shoulders, and
dark blood trickled from his grievous wound, but his mind
was clear. When Menoetius' valiant son beheld him, he pitied
him, and in his pity spoke to him winged words: "Unhappy
leaders and counselors of the Danaans, so were you fated, far
from your friends and native land, in Troy, to sate the swift
dogs with your gleaming fat. Come, tell me this, Zeus-nurtured
hero Eurypylus, will the Achaeans still hold huge Hector or
will they soon perish at his hand, slain by his spear?"

The wounded Eurypylus answered him: "No longer, Zeus-
born Patroclus, will there be any defense for the Achaeans,
but they will fall among the black ships. For all who were
once the bravest lie on the ships, hit and wounded at the
Trojans' hands. The Trojans' strength forever rises. Now do
you save me, take me to my black ship, cut out the arrow
from my thigh, wash the dark blood from it with warm water,
and sprinkle healing herbs upon it—good herbs they say you
learned from Achilles, whom Chiron taught, the most righteous of the Centaurs. Of our physicians Podaleirius and
Machaon, one, I believe, lies wounded in the tents, himself
in need of a blameless physician, and the other faces sharp
Ares on the Trojan plain."

Then Menoetius' valiant son addressed him: "How could
these things be? What shall we do, brave Eurypylus? I go to
tell wise-hearted Achilles a command Gerenian Nestor, bulwark of the Achaeans, gave me. Yet not even so will I
abandon you in your distress."

So speaking, he clasped the shepherd of the people beneath
the chest and took him to his tent. When his squire saw it, he
spread ox hides beneath him. There Patroclus stretched him

out and with a knife cut the keen, sharp arrow from his thigh
and washed away the dark blood with warm water. He rubbed
in his hands a bitter root and laid it on the wound to ease
the pain, and it stopped all his pangs. Then the wound dried
and the bleeding ceased.

BOOK XII

So AMONG THE TENTS the valiant son of Menoetius was tending the wounded Eurypylus, but the Argives and the Trojans fought on in throngs. Nor was the ditch of the Danaans and the wide wall above it to hold for long, the wall they had built as a defense for the ships, and the ditch they had driven around it, yet gave no glorious offerings to the gods that the wall might guard the swift ships and rich booty it encompassed. Against the will of the immortal gods was it built; and it did not long stand firm. As long as Hector lived and Achilles still cherished his wrath and the city of King Priam was still unsacked, so long did the great wall of the Achaeans stand firm. But when all the best of the Trojans had died, and of the Argives many had been slain and many still were left, and the city of Priam was sacked in the tenth year and the Argives had gone back in their ships to their dear native land, then indeed Poseidon and Apollo took counsel to sweep away the wall, bringing against it the might of all the rivers that flow from Ida's mountains to the sea—Rhesus and Heptaporus and Caresus, and Rhodius and Granicus; and Aesepus and bright Scamander, and Simoïs by whose banks many ox-hide shields and crested helmets fell in the dust, and a race of heroes halfdivine. Phoebus Apollo turned the mouths of all these streams together, and for nine days he drove their flood against the wall, and Zeus rained continuously, that he might the sooner thrust the wall out to sea. The Earth-shaker himself, trident in hand, was leader, and swept out upon the waves all the foundations of logs and stones which the Achaeans had laid with toil, and he made a smooth plain beside the strong-flowing Hellespont, and he covered the wide beach with sand again, after he had swept away the wall. And the rivers he turned back to flow in the channels where formerly they poured their fair-flowing water.

So were Poseidon and Apollo to do in time to come. But then war and the din of battle blazed about the well-built wall, and the beams of the towers rattled as they were hit; and the Argives, overwhelmed by Zeus' scourge, were driven back and penned by the hollow ships in fear of Hector, the mighty deviser of rout, but he fought as before, like a whirlwind. As when among the hounds and huntsmen a boar or lion turns, exulting in his strength, and they, forming ranks like a wall, stand facing him, and thick and fast the spears thrust from their hands, yet his noble heart fears not, nor trembles, and his own valor slays him; often he turns, trying the ranks of men, and wherever he charges, there the ranks of men will yield; so Hector, going throughout the press, turned, bidding his comrades cross the ditch. The swift-footed horses dared not, but whinnied loudly, standing on its very edge, for the broad ditch scared them off, not being easy to leap or cross from close at hand, for it had steep, overhanging banks on either side along all its length, and had sharp stakes above it which the sons of the Achaeans planted, tall and closely spaced, a defense against their foes. A horse dragging a fair-wheeled chariot could not easily enter it, and the foot soldiers wondered if they could accomplish it. Then Polydamas, standing by bold Hector, said: "Hector and you other chiefs of Trojans and allies, we are fools to drive swift horses through the ditch. It is very hard to cross; sharp stakes stand over it, and by them is the wall of the Achaeans. There is no chance here to enter the ditch or fight with chariots. It is narrow, and I think we will come to grief in it. If, in his grudge against them, high-thundering Zeus puts them to rout and wishes to aid the Trojans, then I would wish that this might come to pass at once —that the Achaeans perish nameless here away from Argos— but if they turn again and there is a drive back from the ships and we rush into the deep ditch, then I think not even any messenger would go back to the city from the hands of the Achaeans once they rally. Come, let us all do as I say. Let the squires hold the horses at the ditch and let us all on foot and under arms follow Hector in a body. Then the Achaeans will not face us if the bonds of doom are on them."

So spoke Polydamas, and his timely speech pleased Hector. Promptly he jumped with his weapons from his chariot to the ground. Nor did the other Trojans gather in their chariots, but all leaped out when they saw godlike Hector. Then each one bade his squire keep his horses in good order there beside the ditch, and they themselves separating and forming their ranks followed their leaders in five companies.

The most of them, the bravest, the most eager to break the wall and fight by the hollow ships, advanced with Hector and blameless Polydamas. Cebriones followed them as third com-

mander, and Hector left beside the chariots another, inferior
to Cebriones. Paris, Alcathous, and Agenor led the second
wave, and two sons of Priam, Helenus and godlike Deiphobus,
led the third. Third in command was heroic Asius—Asius, son
of Hyrtacus, whom his great shining horses bore from Arisbe
on the river Selleis. The fourth wave was led by Anchises'
brave son Aeneas, and with him were the two sons of Antenor,
Archelochus and Acamas, well skilled in every form of battle.
Sarpedon took command of the glorious allies and chose to
aid him Glaucus and warlike Asteropaeus, who seemed to him
decidedly the best of the others, after himself, for he stood out
among them all. When they had formed close ranks with their
well-made ox-hide shields, they quickly moved straight on the
Danaans, and thought they would not halt but would fall upon
the black ships.

Then the other Trojans and far-famed allies obeyed the
counsel of blameless Polydamas, but not Asius, son of Hyrtacus, chief of men, who, unwilling to leave his horses there and
his squire who drove them, advanced on the swift ships with
them, fool that he was, nor was he fated to escape his evil
doom and return from the ships to wind-swept Ilium, glorying
in his chariot and horses. Before that, ill-omened fate enwrapped him beneath the spear of Idomeneus, Deucalion's
glorious son, for he drove to the left of the ships when the
Achaeans were withdrawing from the plain with chariots and
horses. Through that point they were driving their chariots and
horses, and he found the doors of the gates unclosed and the
long bolt unshot; rather, men held them open in hope that
they might help safely to the ships some comrade fleeing from
war. Straight at these he drove his horses, and his men came
after with loud cries, for they thought that the Achaeans would
hold no longer but would fall back on the black ships—fools
that they were, for they found in the gates two of the bravest
men, the high-spirited sons of Lapith spearmen, Peirithous'
son, mighty Polypoetes, and Leonteus, like to Ares, bane of
mortals. These two stood before the lofty gates like high-
crowned oaks upon the mountains, that abide the wind and
showers all their days, supported by long, deep roots. So these
two, trusting in their mighty hands, awaited the onslaught of
great Asius, nor did they flee before him. His followers raised
their dried ox-hide shields aloft and rushed on the well-built
wall with a great battle cry about lord Asius and Iamenus and
Orestes and Adamas, Asius' son, and Thoön and Oenomaus.
Now as long as the two Lapiths were within the gates they

urged the well-greaved Achaeans to make a stand before the ships, but when the Danaans saw the Trojans rushing on the wall, a cry of fear arose from them, but those two rushed out before the gates and fought like wild boars, who on the mountain meet the onset of a noisy throng of men and dogs, and, rushing sideways, shatter the trees about them, hewing them off at the roots, and a clash of tusks arises until someone hits and kills them. So the shining bronze upon their breasts resounded, as they were hit in front, for they fought right sturdily, trusting in their men above them and in their own strength. And the men hurled stones from the well-built towers, defending themselves, their tents and the swift-faring ships. The stones fell to the ground like snowflakes that a tempestuous wind, driving the shadowy clouds, pours thick upon the fertile earth. So poured the missiles from the hands of Achaeans and of Trojans too, and the helmets and bossed shields rang hollow beneath the blows of millstones. Then Asius, son of Hyrtacus, groaned and smote his thighs and cried indignantly: "Father Zeus, now would it seem that you prove wholly false, for I thought the brave Achaeans were not to hold back our might and invincible hands. But like pliant wasps or bees that make their hive upon some rugged road and will not leave their hollow home but face the huntsmen and protect their young, so these men, though but two, refuse to quit the gates until they either slay or are slain."

So he spoke, nor did he by thus speaking move the heart of Zeus, for it was to Hector that his heart wished to give glory.

But others gave battle at the other gates, and it is hard for me to tell all these things as though I were a god, for everywhere about the wall of stone portentous fire arose. The Argives, though disheartened, fought for their ships perforce, and all the gods were sad at heart who were the Danaans' helpers in the strife. And the Lapiths joined in war and battle.

Then Peirithous' son, mighty Polypoetes, thrust Damasus with his spear through the helmet with its sidepieces of bronze. The bronze helmet did not stop the bronze point, which crushed the bone. The brains were scattered about within and he slew him despite his bold attack. Then Polypoetes slew Pylon and Ormenus. Leonteus, scion of Ares, smote Antimachus' son Hippomachus, striking him in the belt with his spear. Then, dragging his sharp sword from its scabbard, he rushed through the press and in close combat smote Antiphates first, and he lay stretched on his back upon the ground. Then in quick succession he brought down Menon and Iamenus and Orestes all to the fertile earth.

While they were stripping them of their gleaming armor, the young men who followed with Polydamas and Hector, they who were the most numerous and brave and the most eager to break the wall and burn the ships with fire, these still stood hesitant beside the ditch. For as they pressed forward to cross, a bird flew over them, a high-soaring eagle, cutting the host off on the left, holding in his talons a huge, blood-red serpent, alive and still writhing, not yet forgetful of battle, for twisting back it struck the bird that held it in the breast, close by the neck, and the eagle, in the anguish of the pain, cast the serpent from him earthwards, and it fell in the midst of the press, while the eagle, with a shriek, flew off with the blast of the wind. The Trojans shuddered when they saw the gleaming serpent lying in their midst, a portent of aegis-bearing Zeus. Then Polydamas stood close to bold Hector and said: "Hector, you always rebuke me in some way when I speak before assemblies, even though I give good counsel, since you say it is by no means right for a man of the people to demur either in council or in war, but ever to increase your power; yet now I will speak out what seems to me the best. Let us not go to fight the Danaans around the ships, for thus I think it shall come to pass, if in truth it was to the Trojans that this bird came as they pressed on to cross the ditch, this high-soaring eagle, cutting the host off on the left, holding in his talons a huge, blood-red serpent, alive—and he cast it away at once, before he reached his eyrie, nor did he accomplish his purpose to give it to his young—so we, if with great strength we break down the gates and wall of the Achaeans, and the Achaeans give way, shall return from the ships along the same road in disorder, for we shall leave behind us many of the Trojans, whom the Achaeans will slay with their bronze, defending their ships. So would the seer reply who was wise of heart concerning omens and whom the people obeyed."

Then Hector of the glancing helmet looked at him scornfully and said: "Polydamas, these words you speak no longer please me. You know how to conceive some better speech than this. If you really utter this in earnest, then the gods themselves have deprived you of your senses, that you bid us forget the counsels of loud-thundering Zeus, the promises he gave me and confirmed himself. You bid us heed long-winged birds, which I regard not nor consider, whether they fly to the right toward the dawn and the sun, or to the left toward the misty darkness. Let us obey the counsel of great Zeus, who rules all mortals and immortals. There is one best omen, to fight for our native land. Why do you fear war and conflict? For even though all the rest of us are slain by the Argive ships, you have no fear of perishing, for your heart cannot abide the foe, nor is it warlike. But if you hold back from combat or, persuading any other by your words, turn him from battle, you shall die at once, smitten by my spear."

So speaking, he led the way and they followed him with a tremendous shout; and Zeus, who rejoices in the thunder, sent from the Idaean mountains a blast of wind which bore the dust straight toward the ships; and he bewildered the mind of the Achaeans and gave glory to the Trojans and to Hector. Trusting in his omens and their might, they tried to break the great wall of the Achaeans. They strove to pull down the walls of the towers and tear down the battlements, and they pried up the jutting pillars which the Achaeans had first set in the earth to be buttresses of the towers. These they drew out, and hoped to break the wall of the Achaeans. Yet not even now would the Danaans fall back from their path, but, fencing the battlements with ox hides, they hurled missiles from them at the foe who came up to the wall.

Both the Ajaxes went everywhere upon the walls giving encouragement, arousing the might of the Achaeans, speaking with soft words to one, with hard words chiding another, whomever they saw wholly letting up from battle: "Friends, good, bad, and indifferent among the Argives, since all men are not alike in war, now there is work for all, and surely you know this yourselves. Let no man when he hears the battle cry turn back toward the ships but press on forward, and urge on one another, in hope that Olympian Zeus, the lord of lightning, will grant we may push back the assault and send the foe in flight toward the city."

So shouting, they roused the battle of the Achaeans. As flakes of snow fall thick upon a winter's day when Zeus the counselor has begun to snow, revealing to men these weapons of his, and putting the winds to sleep, he snows unceasingly until he covers the lofty mountain peaks and the high forelands and the lotus-bearing plains and the rich works of men— the snow falls on the shores and havens of the hoary sea, but the breaking wave holds it back; over all else it casts its cloak, when the snow of Zeus falls heavily—so thick flew stones from either side, some on the Trojans, some from Trojans on Achaeans, as they threw at one another, and along the whole wall rose the din.

Not even then would the Trojans and glorious Hector have broken the gates of the wall and the long bar, had not Zeus the counselor aroused his son Sarpedon against the Argives like a lion against crooked-horned cattle. At once he raised before him his balanced shield, fairly beaten out of bronze, which the smith had beaten out and had riveted within it many ox hides with golden pins continuous around the edge. Holding this before him, brandishing two javelins, he started forward like a lion, born among the mountains, that has long lacked meat, and its lordly spirit bids it go even to some compact farmstead to make a raid upon the flocks, and even if it finds the herdsmen there keeping watch over the flocks with dogs and spears, yet it is unwilling to be frightened from the fold without a trial, and either it springs upon the flock and bears away its prey, or is itself hit by a dart from some swift arm among the foremost ranks, so then the spirit of godlike Sarpedon sent him forth to charge upon the wall and burst the battlements. At once, he said to Glaucus, Hippolochus' son: "Glaucus, why are we held in special honor in place and meat and cups more numerous, in Lycia? Why do all look on us as gods and why do we possess a great domain upon the banks of Xanthus, fair with fruit and plowland bearing wheat? It is for this that we now must stand among the foremost Lycians and face the raging battle, so that some one of the armored Lycians may say: 'Not without glory do our sovereigns reign in Lycia, eat the rich flocks and drink wine choice and honeysweet; but so too have they noble might when they fight among the foremost Lycians.' Dear friend, if fleeing from this war we could become both ageless and immortal, neither would I myself fight among the foremost nor would I send you into man-ennobling war, but now, since surely ten thousand dooms of death stand over us, which mortals may not flee nor shun, let us go, whether we shall give someone glory or someone give fame to us."

So he spoke, and Glaucus did not turn back nor did he fail to heed him. Straight on they went, leading the great host of Lycians, and Peteos' son Menestheus shuddered when he saw them, for they advanced upon his tower, bringing evil; and he looked along the wall of the Achaeans, hoping to see one of the leaders who would ward off the attack from his companions. Close by he spied the two Ajaxes, insatiate of war, standing still, and Teucer just coming from his tent, but all his shouting could not reach them, so great was the din, and the clamor rose to heaven as shields and helmets with their horse-hair crests were struck and the gates as well, for these had all been shut, and the foe stood before them and strove to break them down and force an entrance. At once he sent the herald Thoötes to the Ajaxes: "Go, godlike Thoötes, run and call Ajax, or rather both of them, for that would be by far the best of all, since soon there will be utter ruin here, for here the leaders of the Lycians have charged, who even formerly were very bold in mighty conflict. But if there also toil and strife have come upon them, then let valiant Telamonian Ajax come alone, and let the skilled bowman Teucer follow with him."

So he spoke, and the herald failed not to obey him when he heard. He ran along the wall of the bronze-clad Achaeans and went and stood before the Ajaxes and quickly spoke to them: "Ajaxes, leaders of the bronze-clad Achaeans, the dear Zeus-nurtured son of Peteos bids you go there to share his toil at least a little time—preferably both of you, which would be by far the best of all, since soon there will be utter ruin there, for the leaders of the Lycians have charged, who even formerly were very bold in mighty conflict. And if here also toil and strife have arisen, then let valiant Telamonian Ajax come alone, and let the skilled bowman Teucer follow with him."

So he spoke, and great Telamonian Ajax did not fail to heed. At once he spoke winged words to Oileus' son: "Ajax, you and mighty Lycomedes stand here and stir the Danaans up to fight with power. I will go there and share the conflict, and I will come straight back when I have given them good aid."

So speaking, Telamonian Ajax set off, and Teucer, his brother, his own father's son, went with him; with them Pandion carried Teucer's curving bow. Just as they reached great-hearted Menestheus' tower, passing inside the wall—and they came to men hard-pressed—the mighty leaders and counse-lors of the Lycians were storming the battlements like a black tempest; so they threw themselves into the fight, and the battle cry arose.

Telamonian Ajax was the first to kill a man, Sarpedon's comrade great-hearted Epicles, hitting him with a jagged stone which lay within the wall beside the battlements, a great one, and the topmost of the pile. Not easily could a man as mortals are today hold it in his two hands, even in the prime of life, but Ajax lifted it aloft and hurled it and shattered Epicles' four-ridged helmet and crushed his whole skull. He fell like a diver from the high tower, and his spirit left his bones. And as Glaucus, Hippolochus' mighty son, rushed forward, Teucer from the lofty tower shot him with an arrow where he saw his shoulder bared. He made him cease from battle. Glaucus leaped from the wall stealthily, lest some of the Achaeans see him shot and boast over him. And Sarpedon grieved when Glaucus went away, as soon as he perceived it. Yet he did not forget the battle, but hit and wounded Thestor's son Alcmaon with his spear and drew out the blade, and Alcmaon, following the spear, fell-prone, and his armor, cunningly wrought of bronze, rattled upon him. Then Sarpedon grasped the parapet with his mighty hands and pulled, and it all came away; the wall above was bared, and made a way for many.

But Ajax and Teucer hit Sarpedon at the same moment, Teucer with an arrow in the shining strap that held his all-enveloping shield and ran about his chest; but Zeus warded the fates from off his child, lest he be slain beside the sterns of the ships; Ajax lunged and struck his shield, but the spear did not go through, but staggered him in his assault. He drew back a little from the parapet, yet did not entirely retreat, since his spirit hoped to gain renown. He turned and called to the godlike Lycians: "Lycians, why do you thus slacken in your furious valor? For all my strength, it is hard for me alone to break through and make a pathway by the ships. Come, follow close behind me; the more the doers, the better the deed."

So he spoke, and they, respecting their lord's command, pressed closer round their counsel-bearing king. The Argives, on the other side, strengthened their companies within the wall, and the task appeared a heavy one to both. For neither could the mighty Lycians break through the Danaans' wall and make a pathway by the ships, nor could the Danaan spearmen push back the Lycians from the wall when once they had attained it. As two men dispute their boundaries, with measuring rod in hand in a plowland they have held in common, and in a small space they wrangle for a fair division, so the battlements divided the two sides, and over them they smote the curved, ox-hide shields and fluttering targets on one another's breasts. Many were wounded in the flesh by the pitiless bronze —any among the fighters who turned and bared his back— and many through the shield itself. Towers and parapets were sprinkled everywhere with the blood of Trojans and Achaeans both. Yet not even so could they cause a rout of the Achaeans, but they stood balanced as an honest spinner holds her scales, who takes a weight and wool and lifts the scales, balancing them fairly, to win a poor wage for her children's sake. So evenly was drawn the strength of war and battle for them both until Zeus granted highest glory to Hector, Priam's son, who first broke through the wall of the Achaeans. He gave a piercing shout, crying to the Trojans: "Rise, horse-taming Trojans, break the Argives' wall and hurl upon their ships portentous fire."

So he spoke, rallying them. All of them gave ear and rushed as one man upon the wall, and they climbed the towers, pointed spears in hand. Hector picked up and bore a stone which lay before the gates, broad at the bottom, sharp above. The two best men among the people, as mortals are today, could not easily lift it to a wagon from the ground, but he swung it easily alone; the son of crooked-counseled Cronus made it light for him. As when a shepherd easily carries a ram's fleece in one hand and the weight troubles him little, so Hector lifted the stone and bore it toward the close-set portals that shut fast the gates—double and lofty. Two bars that shot from opposite sides held them within, and one key made them fast. Hector went and stood close by, set himself firm on widespread feet, that the missile might be no weaker, and hurled it at the center of the gates, and he broke both the hinges. The stone of its own weight fell within, and the gates rang aloud, nor did the bars hold, but the portals split to this side and that beneath the stone's impact, and glorious Hector sprang within, his face like swift night. He shone in the fearful bronze which clad his flesh, and he held two javelins in his hand. None save the gods could have met and checked him when he leaped within the gates; his eyes burned bright with fire. Turning, he bade the Trojans in their throngs to cross the wall, and they obeyed his urging; speedily some crossed the wall and others pressed through the well-built gates themselves, and the Danaans fled among the hollow ships, and a ceaseless din arose.

BOOK XIII

WHEN ZEUS had brought the Trojans and Hector close to the ships, he left them beside the ships to bear the toil and woe unceasingly, and he himself turned his shining eyes away, gazing afar at the land of the horse-rearing Thracians and the Mysians, who fight in close array, and the noble Hippemolgi, who live on milk, and the Abii, most righteous of men. No longer did he turn his shining eyes toward Troy, for he did not believe in his heart that any one of the immortals would go to aid either Trojans or Danaans.

Yet the mighty Earth-shaker kept no careless watch, for gazing in wonder at the war and battle he sat high on the loftiest peak of wooded Samothrace. Thence all Ida lay plain before him, and plain before him lay Priam's city and the ships of the Achaeans. He had risen from the sea and gone and sat there; he pitied the Achaeans as they were worsted by the Trojans, and he was greatly angered at Zeus.

At once he went down from the rugged mountain with quick strides, and the long ridges and the woods trembled beneath the immortal feet of Poseidon as he passed. Three strides he made, and with the fourth he reached his goal, Aegae, where in the depths of the sea his glorious house is built, golden and glittering, indestructible forever. There he came, and put to his chariot his bronze-hoofed horses, swift-flying, with manes of gold. He clad himself in gold and grasped a well-wrought golden whip, and mounted his chariot and set out across the waves. The creatures of the sea arose on all sides from the depths and gamboled near him, nor did they fail to know their lord. With joy the sea parted before him, and the horses flew right swiftly; the bronze axle was not even wet beneath, and with easy stride they bore him toward the ships of the Achaeans.

There is a broad cavern in the depths of the deep sea, midway between Tenedos and rugged Imbros. There earth-shaking Poseidon stopped the horses and loosed them from the chariot and cast before them ambrosial food to eat. He case golden hobbles about their feet, unbreakable, unloosable, that they might continually there await their master's return, and he himself departed for the camp of the Achaeans.

The Trojans, like a flame or tempest, followed in a body with unceasing eagerness after Hector, Priam's son, their shouts an indistinguishable tumult. They hoped to take the ships of the Achaeans and slay beside them all the bravest. But Poseidon, who surrounds and shakes the earth, came from the deep sea and roused the Argives, likening himself in body and unwearying voice to Calchas. First he addressed the two Ajaxes, who were eager of themselves: "Ajaxes, do you two now save the host of the Achaeans; remember valor and not chilling rout. Elsewhere I have no fear of the invincible hands of the Trojans, who have crossed the great wall in a throng, for the well-greaved Achaeans will hold them all. But I am most dreadfully afraid that something may befall us here where Hector leads the way, raging like a flame of fire, boasting himself the son of mighty Zeus. May some one of the gods put it into your mind to stand here firmly and urge on the rest. Then you could thrust him back from the swift-faring ships for all his drive, even though the Olympian himself arouse him."

So spoke he who surrounds and shakes the earth, and striking them both with his staff, he filled them with mighty strength and made their limbs light, their feet and their hands above. As a swift hawk soars aloft, mounting from some high, sheer cliff, and swoops to chase some other bird across the plain, so Poseidon the earth-shaker rushed from them. Swift Ajax, Oileus' son, was first to recognize him, and at once he said to Ajax, Telamon's son: "Ajax, since some one of the gods who dwell upon Olympus likens himself to the seer and bids us fight beside the ships—for it is not Calchas, the seer who understands the flight of birds; I easily recognized the shape of his feet and shins as he departed; the gods are easily known—my own spirit, too, within my breast yearns more for war and battle, and my feet beneath are eager and my hands above."

Telamonian Ajax answered him and said: "So too now are my invincible hands eager as they grasp the spear; my strength has risen and my feet beneath are quick with eagerness. I even seek to fight alone with Hector, Priam's son, who drives on relentlessly."

So they spoke to one another, joyous in the delight of battle which the god had put into their heart. Meanwhile, he who surrounds the earth was rousing from the rear the

Achaeans who were refreshing their spirit by the swift ships. Their limbs were weak with bitter weariness, and grief had seized their hearts as they beheld the Trojans who had crossed the great wall in force. As they watched them, the tears poured from their eyes, for they thought they should not escape disaster. But the Earth-shaker went among them and easily roused their mighty companies. He went first with his commands to Teucer and Leitus and heroic Peneleos and Thoas and Deipyrus and Meriones and Antilochus, raisers of the battle cry. Arousing them, he spoke winged words: "Shame on you, Argives, young striplings. I trusted you to save the ships by your fighting; but if you draw back from wretched war, the day of our defeat by the Trojans has now dawned. Fools, this is a great wonder that my eyes behold, such as I never thought should come to pass, that the Trojans should attack our ships, they who formerly were like timid does that wander through the wood defenseless, food for jackals and leopards and wolves, and have no joy in combat. So formerly the Trojans had no wish to face the mighty hands of the Achaeans, not for a moment. But now they are fighting far from the city by the hollow ships, through our leader's baseness and the slackness of our men, who, angry with him, are unwilling to defend the swift-faring ships but are slain among them. But even if the heroic son of Atreus, wide-ruling Agamemnon, is in truth wholly at fault, because he grossly insulted the swift-footed son of Peleus, it is by no means possible for us to give up war. Let us quickly set things right. The hearts of the good are tractable. It is no longer right for you, all the bravest of the host, to relax your furious valor. I would not myself quarrel with a man who, being a weakling, withdraws from war, but I am angry at heart with you. My friends, you will soon bring on some greater evil by this slackness. But now let each man take shame to his heart, and indignation, for great is the strife that has arisen. Hector of the mighty war cry fights powerfully beside the ships; he has burst the gates and their great bar."

So rousing them, he who surrounds the earth stirred the Achaeans, and mighty companies fell in about the two Ajaxes, such as neither Ares could scorn, if he came upon them, nor Athena, who rouses the nations. For those picked for bravery stood to face the Trojans and glorious Hector, spear joined to spear and shield overlapping shield. Shield pressed on shield, helmet on helmet, man on man. The plumes of horsehair touched the bright crests as they shook their heads, so close they stood by one another. The spears bent as they brandished them in their mighty hands and their minds looked forward in their eagerness for battle.

The Trojans pressed forward in a body, and Hector led them eagerly straight on, like a stone rolling from a cliff, which a stream in winter flood thrusts from the edge, breaking in ceaseless rain the supports of the ruthless stone. Leaping high, it flies along, and its thunder fills the wood; it runs on steadily without stopping until it strikes the plain, and then it rolls no more for all its speed. So Hector for a time threatened to go easily through the tents and ships of the Achaeans to the sea, slaying as he went. But when he came to the close-drawn companies, he stopped when just before them. The sons of the Achaeans facing him thrust with their swords and their spears, sharp at both ends, and drove him from them, and he gave ground, reeling. He called out loudly, shouting to the Trojans: "Trojans and Lycians and close-fighting Dardanians, stand by; the Achaeans shall not hold me long, however close they pack themselves together. I think they will fall back before my spear, if it was really the greatest of the gods, Hera's loud-thundering husband, who aroused me."

So speaking, he aroused the might and spirit of each man. Deiphobus, Priam's son, strode among them with high heart and held before him his balanced shield, stepping lightly and advancing under its shelter. Meriones aimed his shining spear at him, nor did he miss, but hit him on the balanced ox-hide shield. The long spear did not pierce through; well before that its shaft was broken at the socket, for Deiphobus held the ox-hide shield before him, fearing in his heart the spear of wise-hearted Meriones. Then the hero Meriones drew back into the throng of his companions, dreadfully angry for his lost victory and his broken spear, and he set out beside the tents and ships of the Achaeans to bring a long spear that had been left within his tent.

The others went on fighting, and a ceaseless cry arose. Teucer, Telamon's son, was first to slay a man, the spearman Imbrius, son of Mentor of the many steeds; he dwelt in Pedaeum, before the coming of the sons of the Achaeans, and wedded Priam's bastard daughter Medesicaste. But when the curved ships of the Danaans came, he went again to Ilium and was pre-eminent among the Trojans and dwelt near Priam, who honored him as much as his own sons. Telamon's son wounded him beneath the ear with his long spear and drew the spear out. He fell like an ash tree which on some far-seen mountain top is cut down by the bronze and bows its shining leaves to earth; so fell he, and his armor, wrought cunningly of bronze, rattled upon him. Teucer rushed forward, eager to strip his armor from him, and Hector cast his shining spear against him as he rushed. But he looked up and dodged the bronze spear by but a little. Hector with his spear struck Amphimachus, Actorian Cteatus' son, in the chest as he went into combat; he fell with a crash and his armor clanged upon him. Then Hector rushed to snatch from great-hearted Amphimachus' head the helmet that fitted closely to his temples, and Ajax thrust with his shining spear at Hector, but his flesh was nowhere bared, being all hid by dreadful bronze. He hit the boss of the shield and pushed him by his mighty strength, and Hector drew back from both the bodies, and the Achaeans dragged them off. Stichius and godlike Menestheus, leaders of the Athenians, brought Amphimachus into the host of the Achaeans, and the two Ajaxes, eager in their furious valor, brought Imbrius. As two lions snatch a goat from sharp-toothed dogs and carry it into the thick undergrowth, holding it in their jaws high off the ground, so the two helmed Ajaxes held him up and stripped him of his armor. The son of Oileus cut his head from his soft neck, in his rage because of Amphimachus, and turned and sent it rolling through the throng; it fell before the feet of Hector in the dust.

Then was Poseidon angered at heart for his grandson, fallen in the dreadful strife, and he set out beside the tents and ships of the Achaeans to urge on the Danaans, and he prepared woe for the Trojans. Toward him came Idomeneus, famed with the spear, coming from his comrade, who had just returned to him from battle, wounded in the hollow of the knee by the sharp bronze. Him his comrades carried, and Idomeneus, having given orders to the physicians, was on the way to his own tent, for he still desired to face the battle. The mighty Earth-shaker addressed him, likening his voice to that of Andraemon's son Thoas, who ruled over the Aetolians in all Pleuron and steep Calydon and was reverenced by the people as a god: "Idomeneus, counselor of the Cretans, what has become of the threats the sons of the Achaeans uttered against the Trojans?"

Idomeneus, leader of the Cretans, answered him: "Thoas, no man now is at fault, so far as I know, for we all know how to fight. None is seized by cowardly fear, nor does anyone, yielding to reluctance, shun evil war. Surely it must be the pleasure of the almighty son of Cronus that the Achaeans perish nameless here, away from Argos. But, Thoas, as you were brave before and are wont to urge on any other you see slacking, do not now cease from battle; give orders to every man."

Then Poseidon the earth-shaker replied to him: "Idomeneus, may that man never return home from Troy but be here the sport of dogs who this day willingly gives over fighting. Come, take your weapons and go. In this we must hasten if we are to be of help, though only two. Even cowards' courage joined is of avail, and we know how to battle with the best."

So speaking, the god departed through the toil of heroes, and Idomeneus, when he reached his well-built tent, donned his fair armor and grasped his spears and set forth like the lightning which the son of Cronus grasps in his hand and hurls from radiant Olympus, showing a sign to mortals, and its beams are very bright. So the bronze gleamed upon his breast as he ran forth. His brave squire Meriones met him, still close to the tent, for he was going to get his brazen spear. Mighty Idomeneus said to him: "Meriones, Molus' son, swift of foot, dearest of comrades, why have you come here, leaving war and strife? Have you been wounded? Does the point of some missile hurt you? Or have you come as someone's messenger to me? I myself do not desire to sit within the tent but to do battle."

Prudent Meriones replied to him: "Idomeneus, counselor of the bronze-clad Cretans, I came to get a spear, if any has been left within your tent. For the one I had before broke as I hurled it against the shield of insolent Deiphobus."

Idomeneus, leader of the Cretans, said to him: "If it be spears you wish, you will find one to twenty standing within my tent against the shining side-walls of the entrance—Trojan spears which I take from those I slay. For I do not believe in fighting men while standing at a distance; therefore have I spears and bossed shields and helmets and bright-gleaming breastplates."

Prudent Meriones answered him: "Beside my tent and my black ship I too have many Trojan spoils, but they are not near to fetch. No more have I, I swear, forgotten valor, but stand among the first in man-ennobling battle when the strife of war arises. Any other of the bronze-clad Achaeans might

more likely fail to see me fighting, but you yourself, I think,
know of it well."

Idomeneus, leader of the Cretans, answered him: "I know
how brave you are. What need for you to talk of that? For
if all the bravest of us beside the ships were mustered for an
ambush—where men's valor is best seen, where the coward
and the brave are both revealed, for the coward's hue is ever
changing and the spirit in his breast will not be checked
to let him sit unmoving but he keeps shifting, standing now
on one foot, now on the other, and his heart beats loudly in
his breast as he thinks about his fate, and his teeth begin
to chatter, but the brave man's color does not change nor
is he very frightened when first he takes his place amid the
heroes' ambush, and he prays that he soon may mix in hot and
bitter strife—your mighty hands could not be blamed. And
if in combat you were hit or wounded, the shaft would fall
not on your neck behind or on your back, but would find
your breast or belly as you pressed ahead amid the combat
of the foremost lines. But come, let us speak no more of this,
standing like children, lest someone be greatly angered. Go to
my tent and take a mighty spear."

So he spoke, and Meriones, like swift Ares, quickly took
the bronze spear from the tent and followed after Idomeneus, greatly concerned about the battle. As Ares, bane of
mortals, goes to war, and his dear son Rout follows him,
mighty and fearless, who turns the stoutest-hearted warrior
to flight—from Thrace the armored pair follow the Ephyri
or the great-hearted Phlegyes, yet give not ear to both sides,
but grant glory to the one—so Meriones and Idomeneus,
chiefs of men, went forth to war, armed in gleaming bronze.
Meriones first said to his companion: "Son of Deucalion,
where do you wish to enter combat? On the right of the
whole army, in the center, or on the left? For I believe the
long-haired Achaeans do not fall so short in battle anywhere
as on the left."

Then Idomeneus, leader of the Cretans, answered him:
"There are others to ward off the foe in the center of the
line of ships—the two Ajaxes and Teucer, who is best of
the Achaeans in archery and brave in close combat as well.
They can drive Hector, Priam's son, back far enough, for
all his love of battle and his mighty strength. It will be hard
for him, eager though he is for battle, to overcome their
mighty and invincible hands and set the ships afire, unless
Cronus' son himself hurl a flaming brand on the swift ships.

No man could make the great Telamonian Ajax yield, no mortal man who ate Demeter's grain, who could be hurt by bronze or by great stones. Ajax would not yield even to Achilles, breaker of men—that is, not in close combat, for in speed of foot no man can vie with Achilles. Let us head this way toward the army's left, that we may know at once whether we shall give glory to some other or he to us."

So he spoke, and Meriones, like swift Ares, led the way, until they came to that part of the army whither Idomeneus had urged him go.

But when the Trojans saw Idomeneus, flamelike in his valor, him and his squire with their well-wrought arms, a shout arose through the ranks and all rushed toward him; and among them all a common strife arose about the sterns of the ships. As when gusts of shrill winds blow hard, on the day when there is most dust upon the roads, and the winds together raise a great cloud of dust, so their battle met, and they were eager at heart to slay one another in the press with the sharp bronze. The man-destroying battle bristled with the long, flesh-biting spears they held. Eyes were blinded by the gleam of bronze from shining helmets, freshly polished breastplates, and bright shields as men advanced together. Right stout of heart would be the man who rejoiced then to behold that toil and felt no qualms.

Thus the two mighty sons of Cronus brought grievous woes upon the heroes through their divided purpose. Zeus wished victory for Hector and the Trojans, to bring honor to swift-footed Achilles, yet he did not wish the Achaean host to perish utterly in front of Ilium, but was honoring Thetis and her stout-hearted son. But Poseidon went among the Argives and encouraged them, rising unnoticed from the hoary sea. For he was grieved to see them worsted by the Trojans and he was mightily angered at Zeus. They were of one blood and of one father, but Zeus was the first-born and knew the more. Therefore Poseidon avoided giving open aid but in human form ever roused men throughout the host unnoticed. Above both sides they drew the cord of mighty strife and common war, unbreakable, unyielding, that loosed the knees of many men.

Then Idomeneus, gray-headed though he was, urged on the Danaans, and leaping on the Trojans, roused their fear. For he slew a man who lived among them, Othryoneus from Cabesus, who had lately come, on tidings of the war, and had asked for the fairest of Priam's daughters, Cassandra,

without bridal gifts, but promised a great deed—to drive
the Achaeans forth from Troy against their will. Old Priam
promised and consented to bestow her, and Othryoneus was
fighting, trusting in that promise. Idomeneus aimed his shining spear at him and hit him as he came high-striding on.
The bronze breastplate he wore did not protect him, and
the spear pierced the center of his belly, and he fell with
a crash. Idomeneus cried boastingly above him: "Othryoneus, I praise you above all mortals if you fulfill all the
promises you made to Dardanus' son Priam, and he promised you his daughter. We too would make such a promise
to you, and keep it, to give you the fairest of the daughters
of the son of Atreus, bringing her from Argos for your
wedding, if with us you will sack the fair-lying citadel of
Ilium. Come with me, that on board the seafaring ships we
may get together on the marriage, since we are not stingy
with our dowries."

So speaking, the hero Idomeneus dragged him by the feet
through the mighty conflict. Asius came to protect him,
on foot, before his horses; his squire held them so they were
forever breathing on his shoulder. He was eager at heart to
hit Idomeneus, but the latter was too quick for him and
struck him with his spear in the throat beneath the chin
and drove the bronze straight through. He fell as when an
oak falls or a poplar or a tall pine, which among the mountains carpenters cut down with freshly whetted axes to be
timber for a ship; so he lay stretched before his horses and
his chariot, grasping the bloody dust. His squire lost what
wits he had before and dared not turn back the horses to
avoid the hands of his foes. Steadfast Antilochus thrust him
through the middle with a spear. The bronze breastplate he
wore did not protect him; the spear struck the center of his
belly. Gasping, he fell from the well-wrought chariot, and
Antilochus, son of great-hearted Nestor, drove the horses
from among the Trojans into the ranks of the well-greaved
Achaeans.

Deiphobus, distressed for Asius, came very close to Idomeneus and hurled his shining spear at him. But Idomeneus
looked up and dodged the bronze spear, for he was covered
by the balanced shield he carried, inlaid with hides of cattle
and with flashing bronze and set with two handles. He
squeezed himself entirely behind it, and the bronze spear
flew over him. The shield resounded dully as the spear grazed
it. Yet Deiphobus did not hurl it to no purpose from his

heavy hand, but hit Hippasus' son Hypsenor, shepherd of the people, below the midriff in the liver, and his knees were loosed at once. Deiphobus exulted mightily, giving a great shout: "Asius lies not unavenged, but I think that even as he goes to Death, the mighty keeper of the gate, he will rejoice in spirit, since I have given him an escort."

So he spoke, and the Argives grieved to hear his boast; above all, he roused the ire of prudent Antilochus. Yet not even in his anger did he forget his comrade, but ran and stood astride him and held his shield before him. Then two faithful comrades, Mecisteus, Echius' son, and godlike Alastor, stooped down and bore Hypsenor, groaning heavily, to the hollow ships.

But Idomeneus did not slacken in his great might, and desired ever to wrap some Trojan in black night or fall crashing himself in warding off destruction from the Achaeans. Now the heroic Alcathous was the dear son of Zeus-nurtured Aesyetes and son-in-law of Anchises, for he married the eldest of his daughters, Hippodameia, whom her father and queenly mother loved most in their heart of those in their home, for she surpassed all of her age in beauty and works and wisdom; therefore the best man in broad Troy wedded her. Him Poseidon now brought low at Idomeneus' hands, blinding his bright eyes and binding his glorious limbs. For he could neither run away nor dodge, but stood unmoving as a pillar or high-foliaged tree, while heroic Idomeneus thrust his spear square at his breast and broke the coat of bronze upon him, which formerly had kept destruction from his flesh. Now, pierced by the spear, he gave a hollow cry. He fell with a crash and the spear stuck in his heart, which made the very spear butt quiver with its beating. And there, then, mighty Ares stopped the weapon's forward course. Idomeneus exulted mightily, with a great shout: "Deiphobus, shall we call it even, when three are slain for one? Since it is you who boast thus, blind in your folly, stand yourself and face me, that you may know what sort of son of Zeus I am who come here—Zeus, who begot Minos first, ruler in Crete, and Minos begot a son, blameless Deucalion, and Deucalion begot me, lord over many warriors in broad Crete. Now our ships have brought hither woe to you, your father, and the other Trojans."

So he spoke, and Deiphobus was of two minds, whether he should draw back and take some one of the high-hearted Trojans as his comrade or should try his luck alone. On thinking, it seemed better to him to go and get Aeneas. He found him standing at the battle's very rear. For he was ever angry with godlike Priam because he paid him no honor for all his valor among the warriors. Deiphobus stood close to him and spoke winged words: "Aeneas, counselor of the Trojans, now you must help your brother-in-law if you are touched at all by grief. Follow me, let us protect the body of Alcathous, who once as your brother-in-law cherished you in his home when you were small. Idomeneus, famed with the spear, has slain him."

So he spoke, and he roused the spirit in Aeneas' breast, and he went with great zeal for war to seek Idomeneus. But Idomeneus was not seized by fear like some small child; he waited as a wild boar on the mountain, confident in its valor, waits in some lonely spot for a great noisy throng of men approaching, and the bristles on its back arise, its eyes gleam fire, and it whets its teeth, eager to fight off dogs and men as well. So waited Idomeneus, famed with the spear, and gave no ground, as Aeneas, hastening to help, approached. But he called to his comrades, looking toward Ascalaphus and Aphareus and Deipyrus and Meriones and Antilochus, raisers of the war cry. Urging them on, he spoke to them winged words: "Come here, my friends, and help me, who am alone. I am dreadfully afraid of swift-footed Aeneas, who is approaching to attack me. He is very strong at slaying men in battle. Then, too, he is in the flower of youth, when strength is greatest. Would that I had the age to match my spirit. For then at once either he or I should gain great glory."

So he spoke, and they all stood close together with one spirit in their breasts, leaning their shields against their shoulders. And Aeneas, on the other side, called to his companions, looking toward Deiphobus and Paris and godlike Agenor, who with him were leaders of the Trojans; and after them followed the soldiers as sheep follow a ram from pasture to watering place and the shepherd rejoices in his heart; so did the heart of Aeneas rejoice in his breast when he saw the companies of infantry that followed with him.

Then about Alcathous they met in close combat with their long spears, and the bronze upon their breasts rang dreadfully as men thrust at one another in the press. Two warriors above all the rest longed to cut one another's flesh with the pitiless bronze—Aeneas and Idomeneus, both like Ares. Aeneas first made a cast against Idomeneus, but he looked up and dodged the bronze spear, and Aeneas' spear point fell quivering in the ground, now that it had sped from his stout hand in vain. But Idomeneus struck Oenomaus in the center of the belly and broke the convex surface of his breastplate, and the bronze pierced his entrails. He fell in the dust and grasped the earth with his outstretched hand. Idomeneus withdrew from the body his long-shadowed spear, but he was unable to strip the rest of the fair armor from his shoulders, for he was pressed by the missiles. For the joints of his feet were no longer firm as he attacked, either to rush forward after his own weapon or to avoid another's. Therefore he stood steadfast and warded off the pitiless day, and his feet would no longer swiftly bear him in flight from war. As he step by step withdrew, Deiphobus cast his shining spear at him, for his anger at him still endured. But then again he missed him, and struck Ascalaphus, Enyalius' son, with the spear, and the mighty spear drove through the shoulder. He fell and grasped the earth in his outstretched hand. Not yet had loud-shouting, mighty Ares learned that his son had fallen in the mighty strife. He sat on Olympus' summit under golden clouds, restricted by the will of Zeus, where the other immortal gods as well were barred from war.

Then about Ascalaphus they met in close combat. Deiphobus seized the shining helmet from the body, but Meriones, like swift Ares, leaped upon him and struck his arm with his spear, and the plumed and crested helmet fell booming to the ground from his hand. Meriones leaped forward again like a vulture and dragged his stout spear from Deiphobus' upper arm and fell back into the throng of his companions. But Deiphobus' own brother, Polites, threw his arms about Deiphobus' waist and led him forth from the tumultuous battle until he came to his swift horses, which stood with his squire and skillfully wrought chariot to the rear of the war and battle. These bore him to the city as he groaned heavily in great distress, and the blood ran down his freshly wounded arm.

The rest fought on, and an unceasing shout arose. Then Aeneas rushed on Aphareus, Caletor's son, and with his sharp spear cut his throat where it was turned to him. His head sank to one side, and shield and helmet followed, and life-destroying death poured over him. Antilochus, watching sharply, rushed up and thrust at Thoön as he turned away; he cut right through the artery which runs straight up the back into the neck. Straight through it he cut, and Thoas fell backward in the dust, stretching out both hands to his

dear comrades. Antilochus rushed upon him and stripped
the armor from his shoulders, glancing anxiously about. The
Trojans standing around him rained blows from all sides on
his broad, gleaming shield, yet were unable to scratch Antilochus' tender flesh within with pitiless bronze. For Poseidon the earth-shaker protected Nestor's son, even amid
many missiles. Never was he free of fear, but he kept turning toward them; nor was his spear at rest, but turned and
thrust in every quarter. In his heart he aimed either to throw
it at someone or to fight at close quarters.

But as he thrust through the press he was not unnoticed
by Adamas, Asius' son, who struck his shield in the center
with the sharp bronze, attacking from close at hand, but
dark-haired Poseidon made vain the spear point, begrudg-
ing him Antilochus' life. The spear point remained there in
Antilochus' shield like a fire-hardened stake, and half of it
dragged on the ground. Adamas shrank back into the throng
of his companions, avoiding his fate; but as he withdrew,
Meriones followed him and smote him with his spear between the genitals and naval, where Ares is most grievous
to wretched mortals. There he drove his spear, and falling
upon it, Adamas gasped like an unwilling bull that cowherds
lead away, binding it by force with twisted cords upon the
mountains. So did he gasp when struck—a little, not for very
long, until heroic Meriones came close and drew the spear out
of his body and darkness veiled his eyes.

Helenus smote Deipyrus at close quarters on the temple
with a great Thracian sword and struck off his crested helmet. It fell bounding on the ground, and some one of the
battling Achaeans picked it up as it rolled at his feet. Then
dark night enwrapped Deipyrus' eyes.

The son of Atreus, Menelaus of the mighty war cry, was
grieved and advanced threateningly on Helenus, the heroic
leader, brandishing his sharp spear, and Helenus grasped
the center of his bow. Both of them let fly together, one
with his sharp spear and the other with an arrow from his
bowstring. Then Priam's son hit Menelaus with his arrow in
the chest on the convex portion of this breastplate, and the
bitter arrow flew aside. As when beans or black chick-peas
leap from a broad winnowing fan on a great threshing floor
before a shrill breeze and the winnower's stroke, so far flew
the bitter arrow, turned from the breastplate of glorious
Menelaus. But Atreus' son, Menelaus of the mighty war cry,
struck Helenus in the hand with which he held his polished

bow. The bronze spear drove straight through the hand into the bow. He shrank back into the throng of his companions, avoiding his fate and letting his hand hang down as the ashen spear dragged after him. Great-hearted Agenor drew it from his hand and bound the hand with a tight-twisted strand of wool, in a sling, which a squire held for the shepherd of the people.

Then Peisander made straight for glorious Menelaus. An evil fate led him to the end of death, to be slain at your hands, Menelaus, in dread strife. When they came close to one another in their onset, the son of Atreus missed and his spear was turned aside, and Peisander thrust at the shield of glorious Menelaus but could not drive the bronze straight through, for the broad shield checked the spear and its shaft broke off; yet he rejoiced in his heart and hoped for victory. But the son of Atreus drew his silver-studded sword and leaped upon Peisander, and the latter drew from behind his shield his battle-ax, fairly made of bronze on a long, well-polished helve of olive wood. They drew near one another, and Peisander drove at the ridge of his helmet with its thick horsehair plume, just below the crest itself, but Menelaus smote him as he came on, in the forehead, just above the bridge of the nose. The bones cracked and his eyes, all bloody, fell in the dust on the ground at his feet, and he fell backward. Menelaus set his heel upon his chest and stripped him of his arms, and boasting said: "This is the way you shall leave the ships of the Danaans with their swift steeds, you overweening Trojans, insatiate of dreadful battle; nor are you lacking the other infamy and shame of the deeds you have done me, evil dogs, who had no fear at heart of the stern wrath of Zeus, loud-thundering god of hospitality, who shall some day destroy your lofty town—you who went rashly off with my own wedded wife and many treasures, when she herself had entertained you. And now you wish to hurl baneful fire on the seafaring ships and slay the brave Achaeans, but you shall yet cease, for all your love of Ares. Father Zeus, they say thou art above all in wisdom, whether men or gods, and all these things arise from thee. What strange favor this is that thou showest to insolent men, these Trojans, whose might is ever wanton, nor can they ever have enough of the strife of equal war. There is satiety in all things—sleep and love, sweet song and blameless dancing, of which a man would rather have his fill than of war, but the Trojans are insatiable of battle."

So speaking, blameless Menelaus stripped the bloody armor from the body and gave it to his comrades, and he himself set forth again and mingled with the foremost fighters.

There Harpalion, son of King Pylaemenes, leaped upon him. He had followed his dear father to war at Troy, nor did he come back to his native land. He now with his spear struck the shield of Atreus' son in the center from close at hand, but could not drive the bronze straight through, and he drew back among the throng of his companions, avoiding his doom, glancing in all directions, lest someone strike his flesh with bronze. Meriones shot a bronze-tipped arrow at him as he withdrew and hit him in the right buttock. The arrow pierced straight through the bladder beneath the bone. He lay back there in the arms of his dear comrades, breathing out his life and stretched out on the earth like a worm, and his dark blood ran out and soaked the earth. The great-hearted Paphlagonians tended him, and placing him in a chariot brought him in sorrow to holy Ilium; with them went his father, weeping; but there was no quit-money for his son's death.

Paris was greatly angered in spirit at his death, for Harpalion had been his friend among the many Paphlagonians. Angered for him, he shot a bronze-tipped arrow. There was a certain Euchenor, son of the seer Polyidos, rich and brave, dwelling in Corinth. He well knew his baneful fate when he went aboard the ship, for the good old man Polyidos had often told him that he would either die of a grievous illness in his halls or be slain by the Trojans among the ships of the Achaeans. Therefore he avoided both the heavy fine[1] of the Achaeans and the grievous illness, so that he might not suffer sorrows in his heart. Paris shot him below the jaw and ear, and his spirit quickly departed from his limbs, and hateful darkness seized him.

So they fought like blazing fire; but Hector, dear to Zeus, had not heard nor did he know at all that his men were being cut to pieces to the left of the ships by the Argives. And glory might soon have come to the Achaeans, so well did he who holds and shakes the earth urge on the Argives, and add his own strength to the defense. Hector, indeed, remained where first he had leaped through the gates and wall, breaking the close ranks of the Danaan shieldmen, where the ships of Ajax and Protesilaus were drawn up on

---

[1] I.e., for failure to go to Troy.

the shore of the gray sea. There where the wall had been built lowest, there men and horses were boldest in the fray.

There the Boeotians and long-robed Ionians, the Locrians and Phthians and illustrious Epeians held Hector as he drove eagerly upon the ships, yet they could not drive back glorious, flamelike Hector, though some were the chosen men of the Athenians. Their leader was Peteos' son Menestheus, and with them went Pheidas and Stichius and brave Bias. The Epeians were led by Phyleus' son Meges and by Amphion and Dracius. At the head of the Phthians were Medon and steadfast Podarces. Medon was the bastard son of godlike Oileus and was Ajax' brother. He dwelt in Phylace, apart from his native land, for he had slain a man, the brother of his stepmother Eriopis, Oileus' wife. Podarces was the son of Iphiclus the son of Phylacus. These, in their armor, at the head of the great-hearted Phthians, fought in defense of the ships, along with the Boeotians. Ajax, Oileus' swift son, had not yet moved an inch from the side of Ajax, Telamon's son. As two red oxen with like spirit draw a well-made plow in fallow land, and much sweat pours out at the base of their horns—the polished yoke alone holds them apart as they drive along the furrow, and the plow marks off the limit of the field—so those two stood side by side. Many good men followed Telamon's son as comrades, receiving his shield from him when sweaty weariness came upon his knees. But the Locrians did not follow the great-hearted son of Oileus, for their heart could not abide close combat. For they had no helmets of bronze with horsehair plumes, nor rounded shields, nor spears with ashen shafts. They had followed him to Ilium, trusting in their bows and the well-twisted sheep's wool with which they then slung many shots and broke the Trojans' ranks. So now the men of Telamon's son, in the front lines, with arms of cunning craftsmanship fought off the Trojans and brazen-armored Hector, and the Locrians shot their missiles from the rear, unseen. Nor did the Trojans remember the joy of battle at all, for the arrows wrought confusion among them.

Then would the Trojans have fallen back shamefully from ships and tents toward wind-swept Ilium, had not Polydamas stood by bold Hector's side and said: "Hector, you do not easily heed advice. Because God gave you skill in war above all others, therefore you wish to be wiser than the rest in council too. Yet you cannot claim all things for yourself. To one God gives the work of war, to one the dance, to another

lyre and song, and in another's breast far-thundering Zeu
implants a noble mind, whereof many men may profit; h
saves many men, and he himself knows best. So I will sa
what seems to me the best, for a circle of war is every
where ablaze about you, and the great-hearted Trojan.
having crossed the wall, are some of them standing alod
with their weapons, while others are fighting few agains
many, scattered among the ships. Draw back and summo
all your best men here. Then we could consider our whol
plan, whether we should fall upon the many-oared ships, i
God grant us strength, or whether we should fall back fror
the ships still unharmed. For I fear lest the Achaeans mak
good their loss of yesterday, since there remains beside th
ships a man insatiate of battle, who, I think, will no longe
wholly refrain from war."

So spoke Polydamas, and his seemly speech pleased Hec
tor. Promptly he jumped with his weapons from his chario
to the ground, and addressing him spoke winged words
"Polydamas, do you hold all the best men here. I will g
there and face the battle and then return at once, whe
I have given them proper orders."

So he spoke, and set forth looking like a snow-cappe
mountain, shouting and flying through the Trojans and thei
allies. They all rushed toward Panthous' son, manly Poly
damas, when they heard Hector's voice. But Hector wan
dered among the foremost fighters, seeking to find Deipho
bus and mighty lord Helenus, Asius' son Adamas, and Asius
Hyrtacus' son. He found them, but no longer untouched by
harm or death; some lay by the sterns of the Achaeans
ships, having lost their lives at the Argives' hands; others
had been struck and wounded within the wall. The god
like Alexander, fair-haired Helen's husband, he soon found
on the left flank of the lamentable battle encouraging his
comrades and urging them on to fight. Standing close.
he addressed him in insulting terms: "Vile Paris, fairest of
face, woman-mad, seducer, where are Deiphobus and mighty
lord Helenus, Asius' son Adamas, and Asius, Hyrtacus' son?
Where is Othryoneus? Now is all steep Ilium doomed, from
summit to foundation. Now is your utter destruction certain."

The godlike Alexander answered him: "Hector, since you
are disposed to blame the blameless, some other day I shall
be more inclined to rest from war, as my mother did not
bear me wholly without valor. From the moment when you
roused your comrades' battle by the ships, we here have

never ceased to fight the Danaans. The comrades whom you seek are slain. Only Deiphobus and mighty lord Helenus have departed, both wounded in the hand by the long spears, but Cronus' son kept death from them. Now lead wherever heart and spirit bid you; we shall follow readily, and I think we will not lack for valor, so far as we have strength. No man, however eager, can fight beyond his strength."

So speaking, the hero won over his brother's mind. They set out then to the place where the fray and strife were thickest, around Cebriones and blameless Polydamas and Phalces and Orthaeus and godlike Polyphetes and Palmys and Ascanius and Morys, Hippotion's two sons, who had come as substitutes from fertile Ascania with the previous dawn. Then Zeus roused the battle. They advanced like a blast of violent wind, which rushes earthward before Father Zeus' lightning and meets the ocean with a wondrous din, as breaker after foaming breaker rolls in shining order on the resounding sea. So the Trojans in serried rank on rank, gleaming with bronze, followed their chiefs. Priam's son Hector, like Ares, bane of mortals, led the way. Before him he held his balanced shield, well set with hides, with a thick coat of beaten bronze. Upon his temples shook a shining helmet. Leaping forward, he tried the hostile ranks in all directions, to see if they would yield before him as he advanced behind his shield. But he could not shake the spirit in the breasts of the Achaeans. First Ajax challenged him, advancing with long strides: "Come hither, fool. Why do you vainly try to frighten the Argives? We Achaeans are not inexperienced in battle, but have been worsted by the bitter scourge of Zeus. I suppose you hope at heart to sack the ships. But our hands too are ready to protect them. Much sooner will your fair-lying town be captured and laid waste beneath our hands. I tell you that the day is close when in your flight you shall pray Father Zeus and the rest of the immortals that your fair-maned horses may be swifter than hawks as they bear you toward the city, raising the dust upon the plain."

As he said this, a bird flew on his right, a high-soaring eagle, and the host of the Achaeans cheered, heartened by the omen. Glorious Hector answered: "Ajax, random speaker, braggart, how you talk. Would I were all my days the son of aegis-bearing Zeus, would queenly Hera had borne me, and would I were reverenced as Athena and Apollo are, as surely as this day brings woe to all the Argives, and you shall be among them, if you dare abide my long spear, which shall rend your delicate flesh. You shall feed full the Trojans' dogs and birds with fat and flesh when you fall beside the ships of the Achaeans."

So speaking, he led the way, and they followed with a wondrous din, and the men cheered from the rear. The Argives cheered on their side, nor did they forget their valor, but abode the onslaught of the Trojans' best. And the shout of both mounted to the ether and to the radiance of Zeus.

BOOK XIV

Now NESTOR did not fail to hear the shouting, though he was drinking. He spoke winged words to Asclepius' son: "What do you think is the meaning of this, godlike Machaon? There is a greater shout of mighty men beside the ships. You sit here now and drink the gleaming wine until fair-haired Hecamede shall heat a hot bath and wash away the gore, while I go quickly to some observation point and learn."

So speaking he took the cleverly fashioned shield of his son, horse-taming Thrasymedes, which lay in the tent, shining with bronze. Thrasymedes had his father's shield. He took a mighty spear, tipped with sharp bronze, and stood outside the tent and quickly saw a shameful sight, the one side in confusion, the other, the high-hearted Trojans, rushing wildly after them; and the wall of the Achaeans was torn down. As when a great surge swells up uncertainly upon a silent sea, foreboding the swift paths of shrill winds, and it rolls to neither side until a decisive gale sweeps down from Zeus, so the old man pondered, divided in his mind whether to go toward the throng of Danaans, with their swift steeds, or toward Atreus' son Agamemnon, shepherd of the people. In his thought, this seemed to him to be better, to go toward Atreus' son. But the rest slew one another in combat; and the stubborn bronze struck on their flesh as they pierced one another with swords and with spears pointed at both ends.

The Zeus-nurtured kings met Nestor as they came from their ships, as many as had been smitten by the bronze—Tydeus' son and Odysseus and Atreus' son Agamemnon. For their ships were drawn up far from the battle, on the shore of the gray sea. They had pulled them as the first upon the plain, but had built the wall beyond the hindmost.[1] For, wide as it was, the shore could not hold all the ships, and the men were crowded. Therefore they had dragged the vessels row beyond row and filled the wide mouth of the

---

[1] The ships seem to have been pulled up stern first, the leaders' ships on the edge of the sea, the rest inland beyond them.

whole strand, as much as the low headlands bounded. So, the kings came together, leaning on their spears, to look upon the battle and the shouting, and their spirits grieved within their breasts. Old Nestor met them and terrified the spirit in the breasts of the Achaeans. Mighty Agamemnon spoke to him and said: "Nestor, Neleus' son, great glory of the Achaeans, why have you left man-destroying war and come hither? I fear lest mighty Hector carry out his threat, which once he made when speaking among the Trojans, that he will not return from the ships to Troy until he burn the ships with fire and slay ourselves. So he spoke, and now all this will come to pass. Yes, and now other well-greaved Achaeans nurse anger at me in their hearts, even as Achilles, and will not fight by the ships' sterns."

Then the Gerenian horseman Nestor answered him: "This has all happened already, and not even high-thundering Zeus himself could alter it, for the wall of the Achaeans has fallen, which we were confident would be an unbreakable bulwark for the ships and for ourselves. They make stubborn and unceasing war by the swift ships, nor could you any longer tell, however hard you looked, from which direction the Achaeans are put to flight, in such confusion are they slain, and the clamor mounts to heaven. Let us consider what is to be done, whether thought will be of any help. But I do not bid us enter battle, for one cannot fight if wounded."

Agamemnon, king of men, replied to him: "Nestor, since they are fighting by the ships' sterns, and the wall we built avails us not, not even the ditch, at which the Danaans suffered much, and hoped at heart that it would be an unbreakable bulwark for the ships and for themselves, such must be the pleasure of almighty Zeus, that the Achaeans perish nameless here, away from Argos. For I knew when he willingly defended the Danaans and I know now when he exalts the others like the blessed gods and has bound our mighty hands. Come, let us all do as I say. Let us drag down all the first row of ships that are drawn up close by the sea and let us launch them all on the shining ocean, and let us moor them in deep water with their anchors until the divine night descend, in the hope that then the Trojans will hold back from war. Then we could launch all the ships. It is no disgrace to flee from evil, not even by night. 'Tis better for him who flees and escapes evil than for him who is caught."

But looking scornfully at him, many-wiled Odysseus said:

"Son of Atreus, what word has escaped the barrier of your teeth? Accursed one, would that you commanded some other, inglorious army, and did not rule us, to whom Zeus has given from youth to age to wind up grievous wars until we perish, each of us. Are you so eager to leave the wide-wayed city of the Trojans, for the sake of which we suffer many ills? Be silent, lest some other of the Achaeans hear this proposal, which no man would allow to pass his lips at all who knew in his heart how to speak suitably and who was a scepter bearer and was obeyed by as many men as you command among the Argives. Now I wholly scorn your thoughts, such things you say, bidding us, when war and battle have begun, to drag our well-benched ships to sea, that all the more the Trojans' wishes may be granted, that they win the victory in spite of everything and that bitter destruction fall on us. For the Achaeans will not hold out in the battle if the vessels are dragged seaward, but they will look away and cease from battle. Then will your plan be ruined, you leader of men."

Then Agamemnon, king of men, answered him: "Odysseus, you have struck me right to the heart with your harsh reproach. Yet the sons of the Achaeans were not unwilling to heed my command to drag the well-benched vessels seaward. Would there now might be someone, young or old, to suggest a better plan than this; I would welcome him."

Then Diomedes of the mighty war cry said to them: "The man is close at hand—we shall not have long to seek him—if you are willing to heed him and are not each one provoked and angry because I am youngest in birth among you, for I can boast myself son of a valiant father—Tydeus, whom the heaped earth hides in Thebes. For to Portheus three blameless sons were born—they dwelt in Pleuron and steep Calydon—Agrius and Melas, and the third was Oeneus the horseman, my father's father. He was pre-eminent among them for his valor. He remained there, but my father settled in Argos, after wandering; for such, I suppose, was the will of Zeus and the other gods. He took a wife from among the daughters of Adrastus and dwelt in a house rich in substance, having great plenty of wheat-bearing plowlands and many orchards round about and many flocks. He surpassed all the Achaeans in skill with the spear—you must know whether that be really true. Therefore you could not call me base of birth and cowardly, nor scorn my propasal if I speak it well. Let us, though wounded, join the fight perforce, but let us then ourselves hold back from conflict, out of range of missiles, lest any receive wound on wound. Let us rouse the rest and send them on, those who have been humoring their hearts by standing back and shirking battle."

So he spoke, and they readily listened and obeyed him. And they set out with Agamemnon, king of men, commanding.

Now the glorious Earth-shaker kept no fruitless watch, but followed them, in likeness of an aged man. He seized the right hand of Agamemnon, Atreus' son, and uttering winged words addressed him: "Son of Atreus, now, I suppose, Achilles' cruel heart rejoices in his breast as he beholds the slaughter and panic of the Achaeans, since he has no feelings, not the least. So may he perish, and may God ruin him. But with you the blessed gods are no longer wholly angry; even yet the leaders and counselors of the Trojans shall raise the dust of the wide plain, and you yourself shall see them flying toward the city from the ships and tents."

So he spoke, and raised a mighty shout, rushing across the plain. As great a shout as nine or ten thousand men could raise in war, joining the strife of Ares, so great a shout the mighty Earth-shaker sent from his chest; and in the heart of each Achaean he roused unfailing might for war and strife.

Hera of the golden throne beheld this with her own eyes from Olympus' peak where she was standing. At once she recognized her brother and brother-in-law as he hastened about amid the man-ennobling battle, and her heart rejoiced. She saw Zeus seated on the highest peak of many-fountained Ida, and he was hateful to her soul. Ox-eyed, queenly Hera pondered how she might beguile the mind of aegis-bearing Zeus, and this seemed the best plan to her heart—to make herself fair and go to Ida, in the hope that he might desire to lie with her in love and she might pour on his eyes and prudent heart a warm and gentle sleep. She started for her chamber, which her dear son Hephaestus had built for her, fitting the tight doors to the posts and locking them with a secret bolt no other god could open. There she went and shut the shining doors. First, with ambrosia she washed all stains from off her lovely flesh and anointed herself with sweet, ambrosial oil she had, all fragrant; were it only shaken in the house of Zeus, with its bronze threshold, the odor would reach even to earth and heaven. With it she anointed her fair flesh, and combing her hair with her hands, she plaited fair, shining, ambrosial tresses on her immortal head. She clothed herself in an ambrosial gown Athena had made and pressed for her, adorning it with many intricate designs. She pinned it with golden brooches at the breast and girt herself with a belt that bore a hundred tassels, and she put in her well-pierced ear lobes earrings with three drops, as dark as mulberries, and radiant grace shone from them. Goddess of goddesses, she veiled herself in a new and lovely veil, white as the sun, and on her shining feet she bound fair sandals. When she had decked herself in all her ornaments, she issued from the chamber, and calling Aphrodite apart from the other gods, she said to her: "Would you listen to me, dear child, in what I have to say, or would you refuse, angered at heart because I aid the Danaans, you the Trojans?"

Then Zeus' daughter Aphrodite answered her: "Hera, reverend goddess, daughter of great Cronus, say what you have in mind. My spirit bids me do it if I can, and if it may be done."

Then queenly Hera with crafty purpose said to her: "Give me the loveliness and charm whereby you conquer all immortals and mortal men as well. For I am going to visit the ends of the bounteous earth, Ocean, the parent of the gods, and Mother Tethys, who reared me well and cherished me in their home, receiving me from Rhea, when far-thundering Zeus banished Cronus beneath the earth and the barren sea. Them I am going to visit, and I shall compose their endless quarrels, for it is a long time now that they have slept apart, since anger seized their hearts. If I could win their hearts by words and bring them to lie together, I should ever be dear and honored in their eyes."

Laughter-loving Aphrodite said to her: "It is neither possible nor seemly to deny your plea, for you sleep in the arms of almighty Zeus."

So speaking, she loosed from her waist the embroidered girdle, subtly fashioned, wherein all her charms are wrought. Therein are love and longing and persuasive converse, which steals the senses even of the closest thinkers. She put it in Hera's hands and said to her: "There, put this subtly fashioned girdle in your bosom. In it all things are wrought, I think your way will not be fruitless in whatever is your heart's desire."

So she spoke, and ox-eyed, queenly Hera smiled, and smiling put the girdle in her bosom.

Then Zeus' daughter Aphrodite went to her home, but

Hera left the crest of Olympus in great haste, traversing Pieria and lovely Emathia, and rushed to the snowy mountains of horse-raising Thrace, to their highest peaks, nor did her feet once touch the earth. From Athos she crossed the surging deep and came to Lemnos, the city of godlike Thoas. There she met Sleep, Death's brother, and took his hand and spoke and said to him: "Sleep, ruler of all gods and of all men, you have heard my plea before, so heed me now again, and I shall be grateful to you all my days. Put Zeus' shining eyes to sleep beneath his brows for me, as soon as I have lain by his side in love. I will give you gifts—a fair golden throne, indestructible forever. Hephaestus, my lame son, will make it carefully and will set a footstool underneath it whereon you may rest your shining feet at banquets."

. Sweet Sleep answered her and said: "Hera, reverend goddess, daughter of great Cronus, any other of the eternal gods I could easily put to sleep, even the streams of the river of Ocean, who is the parent of all. But Zeus, the son of Cronus, I could not approach, nor could I put him to sleep, unless he himself should bid me. For a command of yours at another time has made me wise, the day when that high-hearted son of Zeus[1] sailed from Ilium, after destroying the city of the Trojans. Then I put to sleep the mind of aegis-bearing Zeus, pouring my sweetness over it, and devised evil in your heart against his son, arousing blasts of violent winds upon the sea, and bore him then to fair-lying Cos, far from all his friends. When Zeus awoke, he raged with anger, hurling all the gods about his house, and sought for me above all, and would have hurled me to oblivion from heaven to sea had I not been saved by Night, subduer of gods and men. I went to her in flight, and he gave up, though angry still. For he feared to do anything that would displease swift Night. And now you bid me do this other impossible deed."

Then ox-eyed, queenly Hera said to him: "Sleep, why do such thoughts run through your mind? Do you think far-thundering Zeus will aid the Trojans even as he grew angry for his own son Heracles? Come; I will give you one of the younger Graces to wed and to be called your wife."

So she spoke, and Sleep rejoiced and answered her: "Come now, swear to me by the inviolable water of Styx, and with one hand touch the bountiful earth, and with the other the

[1] I.e., Heracles.

shining sea, that we may have to witness all the gods below
who dwell with Cronus, that you will give me Pasithea, one
of the younger Graces, whom I have longed for all my days."

So he spoke, and the white-armed goddess Hera did
not fail to heed. She swore as he had bidden, naming all
the gods below in Tartarus, who are called Titans. When
she had sworn and ended her oath, the two departed, leaving the towns of Lemnos and Imbros. They cloaked themselves in mist and easily made their jouney. They came to
many-fountained Ida, mother of beasts, to Lectus, where
first they left the sea. Then they passed over the dry land,
and the treetops of the forest swayed beneath their feet.
Then Sleep paused, before the eyes of Zeus could see him,
and mounted a very lofty pine tree, which was the tallest
at that time on Ida and towered into the ether through the
air. There he sat, covered with pine branches, like a clear-
voiced mountain bird the gods call chalcis but men call the
nighthawk.

But Hera quickly mounted Gargarus, a peak of lofty Ida,
and cloud-gathering Zeus caught sight of her. When he saw
her, love filled his prudent heart as when they first were
joined in love and bedded unbeknownst to their dear parents. He stood before her and spoke and addressed her:
"Hera, where were you hastening as you came here from
Olympus? Your horses and chariot are not here for you to
ride."

With crafty purpose queenly Hera said to him: "I am
going to visit the ends of the bounteous earth, Ocean, the
parent of the gods, and mother Tethys, who reared me well
and cherished me in their home. Them I am going to visit,
and I shall compose their endless quarrels, for it is a long
time now that they have slept apart, since anger seized their
hearts. My horses stand ready at the foot of many-fountained
Ida to bear me over dry and wet. Now for your sake I have
come hither from Olympus, lest you be angry with me hereafter if, without a word, I go to deep-flowing Ocean's home."

Cloud-gathering Zeus answered her and said: "Hera, you
can go there later. But for us two, come, let us take our
pleasure, lying together in love, for never yet has love for
goddess or for woman so flooded and overwhelmed my heart
within my breast, neither when I fell in love with Ixion's
wife, who bore Peirithous, like to the gods in wisdom; nor
when I loved Acrisius' daughter, Danae of the fair ankles,
who bore Perseus, pre-eminent above all heroes; nor when

I loved the daughter of far-famed Phoenix, who bore me Minos and godlike Rhadamanthus; nor when I loved Semele or Alcmene in Thebes—the latter bore a son, stout-hearted Heracles, and Semele bore Dionysus, joy of mortals; nor when I loved the lady Demeter of the lovely tresses, nor glorious Leto, nor you yourself, as now I love you and sweet longing seizes me."

With crafty purposes queenly Hera said to him: "Most dreadful son of Cronus, what sort of word is this that you have uttered? If now you wish to lie in love upon the peaks of Ida, all will be plainly seen. How would it be if one of the eternal gods should see us sleeping and go and tell all the gods? I could not rise from the bed and go to your house; it would be shameful. But if you really wish and your heart is set upon it, you have a chamber which your dear son Hephaestus built for you and fitted the doors tightly to the posts. There let us go and lay us down, since bed is now your pleasure."

Then cloud-gathering Zeus answered her and said: "Hera, fear not lest any god or man shall see it, such a golden cloud I shall throw about us; not even Helios could see us, whose light is sharpest for discerning."

So spoke the son of Cronus, and took his wife in his arms. Beneath them the divine earth caused fresh grass to grow and dewy lotus and crocus and hyacinth flowers, thick and soft, which held them high, far off the ground. Therein they lay, and drew about them a fair golden cloud that dropped a sparkling dew.

So the Father slept quietly on Gargarus' peak, overwhelmed by sleep and love, and held his wife in his arms. But sweet Sleep went running toward the ships of the Achaeans to tell the news to him who holds and shakes the earth, and he stood close by and addressed to him winged words: "You may readily aid the Danaans now, Poseidon, and give them glory for a little time, while Zeus still slumbers. For I have wrapped soft sleep about him, and Hera beguiled him to lie down in love."

So speaking, he passed on to the glorious tribes of men, and all the more he set Poseidon on to aid the Danaans. At once Poseidon made a mighty leap into the foremost ranks and gave command! "Argives, shall we again resign the victory to Hector, Priam's son, that he may take our ships and gain him glory? So he says and boasts, because Achilles remains with angry heart beside the hollow ships. He will not be so greatly missed if the rest of us urge one another to defense. Come, let us all do as I say. Take up the best and largest shields within the camp, cover your heads with burnished helmets, and take in hand the longest spears, and let us go. I will lead the way, and I think that Hector, Priam's son, will not stand up to us for all his eagerness. If there be any man steadfast in battle who has a small shield on his shoulder, let him give it to some worse soldier and put on a larger shield."

So he spoke, and they readily listened and obeyed him. The kings themselves, though wounded, marshaled them—Tydeus' son and Odysseus and Agamemnon, Atreus' son. They went to all and exchanged their warlike arms—the brave put on brave weapons, and they gave to the worse the worse. Then when they had clad their flesh in flashing bronze, they started out. Earth-shaking Poseidon led them, holding in his stout hand a keen and dreadful sword, like lightning. No man may meet him in the fearful heat of combat; fear restrains all heroes.

Glorious Hector on the other side was driving up the Trojans. Then dark-haired Poseidon and glorious Hector tightened war's most dreadful strife, one helping the Trojans and the other the Argives. The sea surged up to the tents and ships of the Argives, and the lines met with a great cheer. The wave of the sea roars not so loud upon the shore, when it rolls from the deep before the harsh blast of Boreas; a shining fire's roar is not so loud in mountain glens when it rises to burn the woods; a wind among the lofty oaks roars not so loud—which roars the loudest in its wrath—as was the voice of Trojans and Achaeans in their dreadful shout when they rushed against each other.

Glorious Hector first hurled his javelin at Ajax, since he was turned straight toward him. Nor did he miss, striking him where two straps crossed upon his chest, one of his shield and the other of his silver-studded sword; the straps protected his soft flesh. Hector was angered that his sharp weapon had fled from his hand in vain, and he shrank back into the throng of his companions, avoiding his fate. As he departed, great Ajax, Telamon's son, picked up one of the many stones that rolled at their feet as they fought, props for the swift ships. With it he struck Hector in the chest, above the shield rim, near the neck. It spun him like a top when it hit him, and he spun round and round. As when an oak falls roots and all beneath the bolt of Father Zeus, and

a dreadful smell of sulphur rises from it, and whoever sees
it from close by loses all courage, and terrible is great Zeus'
thunderbolt, so mighty Hector quickly fell in the dust upon
the earth and dropped his spear from his hand, and his
shield and helmet fell upon him, and his cleverly wrought
armor of bronze rattled about him. The sons of the Achaeans
ran up to him with a great shout, hoping to drag him off,
and they hurled many a javelin at him. But none could
hit or wound the shepherd of the people, for before that
the bravest had stood beside him—Polydamas, Aeneas, godlike Agenor, Sarpedon, leader of the Lycians, and blameless
Glaucus. Nor did any of the rest neglect him, but they held
their well-rounded shields before him. His comrades lifted him
in their hands and bore him from the strife, until he came
to his swift horses, which stood with his squire and cleverly
wrought chariot to the rear of the war and the battle. These
bore him, groaning heavily, toward the city.

But when they came to the fair-flowing river, eddying
Xanthus, which immortal Zeus begot, there they lifted him
from the chariot to the ground, and poured water on him.
He came to his senses and opened his eyes again, and rising
on his knees spat out dark blood. Then he lay back again
upon the ground and black night veiled his eyes, for the
missile still quelled his spirit.

When the Argives saw Hector depart, they leaped the
more upon the Trojans and remembered the joy of battle.
Then, by far the first of them, swift Ajax, Oileus' son, leaped
upon Satnius and wounded him with his sharp spear. He
was Enops' son, whom a blameless Naiad bore to Enops when
he tended cattle on the banks of the Satnioeis. Oileus' son,
famed with the spear, approached him and wounded him
in the flank. He fell back, and about him Trojans and Danaans joined in a mighty battle. Spear-brandishing Polydamas,
Panthous' son, came forward as his defender and struck Prothoenor, son of Areilycus, in the right shoulder. The mighty
spear thrust through the shoulder, and he fell and grasped
the earth in his outstretched hand. Polydamas, with a loud
shout, boasted exceedingly: "I think the shaft leaped not in
vain from the stout hand of Panthous' high-hearted son.
Some one of the Argives received it in his flesh, and I think
that leaning on it he will go down to the house of Death."

So he spoke, and grief fell upon the Argives as he boasted.
Especially did he arouse the spirit of prudent Ajax, Telamon's
son, for Prothoenor had fallen closest to him. Quickly he cast

his shining spear at Polydamas as he went away. Polydamas himself avoided black fate by darting sideways, but Archelochus, Antenor's son, got it, for the gods had planned his death. The spear struck him where his head and neck were joined, at the highest vertebra, and cut both muscles. His head and mouth and nose reached the ground much sooner than his shins and knees as he fell. Then Ajax called to blameless Polydamas: "Think, Polydamas, and tell me truly, is not this man worthy to die in revenge for Prothoenor? He seems to me no coward and no coward's get, but brother of horse-taming Antenor, or his son, for the family likeness is very close."

So he spoke, knowing him well, and grief seized the Trojans' spirit. Then Acamas, standing above his brother, wounded Boeotian Promachus with his spear, as the latter was dragging the corpse by the feet. Acamas, with a loud shout, boasted over him exceedingly: "Noisy Argives, insatiate of threats. Not we alone shall have labor and woe, but you too at times shall thus be slain. See how your Promachus sleeps, worsted by my spear, so that the blood-price for my brother goes not long unpaid. Even for this does a man pray that a kinsman be left in his halls to be an avenger of ruin."

So he spoke, and grief fell on the Argives as he boasted. Particularly did he arouse the spirit of prudent Peneleos, who rushed on Acamas. The latter did not abide lord Peneleos' onslaught, but Peneleos wounded Ilioneus, son of Phorbas, rich in flocks, whom Hermes loved most of the Trojans and to whom he gave wealth. Ilioneus was the only son his mother bore to Phorbas. Peneleos wounded him beneath the brow in the roots of the eye and put out the pupil. The spear passed through the eye and the bone at the back of the head, and he spread out both his arms and sat down. Then Peneleos drew his sharp sword and drove it through his neck and cut off his head and helmet onto the ground, and still the stout spear stayed in his eye. Peneleos held the head up like a poppy bloom and showed it to the Trojans, and boasting called: "Trojans, tell good Ilioneus' dear father and mother for me to mourn within their halls. No, nor shall the wife of Promachus, Alegenor's son, rejoice in her dear husband's homecoming when we sons of the Achaeans return with our ships from Troy."

So he spoke, and a trembling seized the limbs of all, and each glanced here and there to see how he might flee from sharp destruction.

Tell me now, ye Muses who have your home upon Olympus, who first of the Achaeans took bloodstained spoils when the famed Earth-shaker turned the battle. First, Ajax, Telamon's son, wounded Hyrtius, Gyrtius' son, leader of the stout-hearted Mysians. Antilochus slew Phalces and Mermerus Meriones killed Morys and Hippotion, and Teucer slew Prothoön and Periphetes. Then Atreus' son wounded Hyperenor, shepherd of the people, in the flank, and the bronze entered his bowels, rending them, and his soul rushed hastening through the open wound, and darkness veiled his eyes. But Ajax slew the most, Oileus' swift son, for none was like him to follow running after trembling men when Zeus roused fear among them.

BOOK XV

BUT WHEN in their rout they had passed the palisade and the ditch and many had been slain at the hands of the Danaans, the rest drew up beside the chariots, and were halted, pale with fear and wholly routed. Then Zeus awoke at the side of Hera of the golden throne, upon the peaks of Ida, and arose with haste and saw the Trojans and Achaeans, the former scattered and the Argives rushing after, with lord Poseidon in their midst. He saw Hector lying on the plain and his comrades seated around him while he was seized by grievous panting and lay senseless, vomiting blood, since it was by no means the weakest of the Achaeans who had hit him. When the father of gods and men saw this, he pitied him, and with a dreadful frown he said to Hera: "Your evil-working wiles, impossible Hera, have made the godlike Hector cease from battle and have routed his men. I do not know but what you may be first again to reap the fruit of your grievous wrongdoing and I shall beat you. Do you not remember when I hung you from on high, and fastened two anvils to your feet, and cast about your arms an unbreakable bond of gold? You hung in the ether and the clouds, and the gods on high Olympus were indignant but could not approach you and release you. Whomever I caught I seized and flung from my threshold until he fell faint to earth. Yet not even thus was my soul lightened of its endless grief for godlike Heracles. With Boreas' help you won the storm winds' aid and sent him out upon the restless sea with evil purpose, and brought him then to fair-lying Cos. I saved him thence and brought him again to horse-rearing Argos, though he had suffered much. I shall again remind you of these things, that you may cease from your deceits and may know whether love's bed will avail you, wherein you joined me, coming from the gods, and tricked me."

So he spoke, and ox-eyed, queenly Hera shuddered and spoke to him winged words: "By earth and wide heaven above and the flowing water of Styx, which is the greatest and most dreadful oath among the blessed gods, and by your sacred head and our own bridal bed, by which I never would swear rashly, it is not by my will that earth-shaking Poseidon troubles Hector and the Trojans and helps the others. Surely his own heart rouses him and drives him on. When he saw the Achaeans hard pressed by the ships, he pitied them. But I would advise him too to go the way you lead, dark-clouded one."

So she spoke, and the father of gods and men smiled and spoke winged words in answer: "If in truth, ox-eyed, queenly Hera, you were hereafter to sit among the immortals in harmony of thought with me, then Poseidon, even though he wished far otherwise, would turn his mind at once after your heart and mine. So if you are speaking truthfully and frankly, go now to the ranks of the gods and bid Iris come hither, and Apollo, famed for his bow, that she may go among the host of the bronze-clad Achaeans and tell lord Poseidon to cease from war and go to his own home, and that Phoebus Apollo may urge Hector into battle, breathe strength into him again and make him forget the pains that distress his heart, and that he may again turn back the Achaeans, starting cowardly rout among them, that they may flee and fall among the many-oared ships of Peleus' son Achilles. The latter will rouse his comrade Patroclus, and glorious Hector will slay Patroclus with his spear before Ilium, when Patroclus has slain the other warriors in great numbers, and among them my son, godlike Sarpedon. In anger for Patroclus, godlike Achilles will slay Hector. From then on I shall cause a continual, unceasing rout back from the ships, until the Achaeans take steep Ilium through Athena's counsels. But until then I will not abate my wrath nor suffer any other of the immortals here to aid the Danaans—until the wish of Peleus' son be accomplished, as first I promised him and nodded confirmation with my head, on that day when the goddess Thetis touched my knees, beseeching me to honor Achilles, the sacker of cities."

So he spoke, and the white-armed goddess Hera did not disobey. She passed from Ida's mountains to long Olympus. And as a man's swift fancy speaks, when after traversing much of the earth, he thinks in his sagacious heart, "Would I were there, or there," and he longs for many things, so swiftly in her eagerness flew queenly Hera. She came to steep Olympus and found the immortal gods assembled in the house of Zeus. On seeing her, they all arose, and pledged her with their cups. The others she let be, but accepted a cup from fair-cheeked Themis, for she came running first to meet her and addressed to her winged words: "Hera, why have you come? You seem distraught. Surely Cronus' son, your own husband, has badly frightened you."

Then the white-armed goddess Hera answered her: "Do not ask me all about this, Themis. You yourself know how overweening and how harsh his spirit is. Do you begin the equal feast for the gods within the halls. Of these things you shall hear along with the other immortals—what evil deeds Zeus threatens. Not all hearts will be equally delighted, I dare say, whether of men or gods, if even now any can still feast in pleasure."

So speaking, queenly Hera took her seat, and the gods in Zeus' house were troubled. She smiled with her lips, but her forehead above her dark brows was joyless and she spoke to all with indignation: "We are fools, who in our folly are angry with Zeus. We still desire to approach him and check him by words or force, but he sits apart and cares not for us nor heeds us. For he says that among the immortal gods he is beyond dispute supreme in strength and might. Therefore accept whatever ill he sends to each of you. For even now I think that sorrow is destined for Ares, for his son has perished in battle, Ascalaphus, dearest of men to him, he whom mighty Ares calls his own."

So she spoke. Then Ares struck his stalwart thighs with downturned hands and said in grief: "Begrudge me not, you dwellers on Olympus, the right to go to the ships of the Achaeans and avenge the murder of my son, even though it be my fate to be struck by Zeus' thunderbolt and lie amid the dead in blood and dust."

So he spoke, and bade Terror and Rout to yoke his horses, and he himself put on his gleaming armor. Now would even greater wrath and anger have been roused in Zeus against the immortals had not Athena, fearing for all the gods, rushed through the doorway and left the throne on which she sat. She took the helmet from Ares' head and the shield from his shoulders and she took the bronze spear from his mighty hand and set it down. Then with her words she rebuked impetuous Ares: "Madman, crazed in mind, you are lost! Surely your ears hear to no purpose and your mind and sense of right are dead. Do you not understand what the white-armed goddess Hera said, who is just now come from Olympian Zeus? Or do you wish yourself to suffer many woes and return to Olympus perforce, for all your grief, while you beget great mischief for the rest? For he will at once leave the high-hearted Trojans and Achaeans and come to Olympus to vent his rage on us.

He will lay hold on guilty and guiltless each in turn. Therefore
I bid you give up your anger for your son. For many a better
man than he in might of hands has been slain and will be slain
hereafter. It is hard to save the lineage and offspring of all
mankind."

So speaking, she forced impetuous Ares to sit down on his
throne. But Hera called Apollo forth from the house, and Iris,
who is messenger for the gods, and addressing them spoke
winged words: "Zeus bids you go to Ida in all haste. When you
come there and look on Zeus' face, do whatever he commands
and bids you."

So speaking, queenly Hera went back and sat down on her
throne, but the other two flew in haste. They came to many-
fountained Ida, mother of beasts, and found there the far-
thundering son of Cronus seated on the peak of Gargarus.
Around him was wreathed a fragrant cloud. The two came
and stood before cloud-gathering Zeus, nor was he angry at
heart when he saw them, since they had quickly obeyed the
commands of his dear wife. To Iris first he addressed winged
words: "Go, swift Iris, and bear all this message to lord Poseidon, and be no false messenger. Bid him cease from war and
battle and join the ranks of the gods or enter the shining sea.
If he does not obey my commands but disregards them, let
him consider then in heart and mind that not even with his
strength will he dare abide my onslaught, since I boast myself
far his superior in strength and his senior in birth, though his
heart heedlessly claims equal rights with me, at whom the
others shudder."

So he spoke, and swift, wind-footed Iris did not disobey, but
went down from Ida's mountains to holy Ilium. As snow or
chill hail flies from the clouds before the rush of sky-born
Boreas, so quickly in her eagerness swift Iris flew, and standing close, addressed the famous Earth-shaker: "Dark-haired
holder of earth, I have come here bringing you a message from
aegis-bearing Zeus. He bade you cease from war and battle
and join the ranks of the gods or enter the shining sea. If you
do not obey his commands, but disregard them, he threatens
to come here himself and fight hand to hand with you, and he
bade you avoid his hands, since he boasts himself far your
superior in strength and your senior in birth, though your heart
heedlessly claims equal rights with him, at whom the others
shudder."

Greatly angered, the famous Earth-shaker addressed her:
"Indeed, mighty as he may be, he has spoken with arrogance,

if by force and against my will he plans to restrain me who am his equal in honor. We are three brothers, sprung from Cronus, born of Rhea, Zeus and I and the third one, Hades, who rules over those beneath the earth. All things were divided in three ways and each one had his share of honor. When the lots were cast, mine was the gray sea, to dwell therein forever, and Hades drew the misty realms of shadows. Zeus drew broad heaven, amid the air and clouds. But earth and high Olympus are still held by all in common. Therefore I will not live after the mind of Zeus. Let him, though mightier, abide in peace in his appointed third. Let him not try to scare me by might of hand as though I were a weakling, for it were better to upbraid with dreadful words his sons and daughters whom he himself begot, who will perforce give ear when he commands."

Then swift, wind-footed Iris answered him: "Dark-haired holder of earth, shall I bear this harsh and violent word from you to Zeus, or will you change it? For the hearts of good men may be changed. You know how the Furies ever side with the elder."

Then Poseidon the earth-shaker addressed her: "Divine Iris, this word of yours is meetly spoken. For it is well when a messenger knows what is right. But this dreadful sorrow strikes to my heart and spirit whenever he is pleased to chide with wrathful words one of equal place and rights. But now I shall yield despite my anger, but I shall tell you this also, and I threaten it with all my heart—if, disregarding me and Athena, the driver of spoil, and Hera and Hermes and lord Hephaestus, he spares steep Ilium and will not sack it or give great might to the Argives, let him know this, that our anger will be unappeasable."

So speaking, the Earth-shaker left the Achaean host and went and entered the sea, and the Achaean heroes missed him. Then cloud-gathering Zeus addressed Apollo: "Go now, dear Phoebus, to brazen-armored Hector. For already he who holds and shakes the earth has departed into the bright sea, avoiding our harsh wrath, else others too would have learned of our battle, even they who are gods below with Cronus. But this was far better both for me and for himself, that he sooner yielded before my hands despite his anger, since it would not have been settled without sweat. But take the tasseled aegis in your hands, and brandishing it hard, rout the Achaean heroes. And let glorious Hector be your care, unerring one. Arouse great might in him until the Achaeans in rout gain the ships and the Hellespont. Then I will contrive deeds and words so that the Achaeans too in turn may catch their breath from toil."

So he spoke, and Apollo rebelled not against his father, but went down from Ida's mountains like a swift hawk, a slayer of doves, which is swiftest of winged creatures. He found the son of prudent Priam, godlike Hector, sitting up, no longer lying prostrate. He had just regained his senses and recognized his comrades round about him. His gasping and his sweat had ceased, for the will of aegis-bearing Zeus had roused him. Apollo the Warder stood close by and said: "Hector, Priam's son, why do you sit swooning far from the others? Has some sorrow come upon you?"

Weakly, Hector of the glancing helmet said to him: "Who art thou, most excellent of gods, who questionest me face to face? Dost thou not know that by the sterns of the ships of the Achaeans Ajax of the mighty war cry smote me on the chest with a stone as I slew his comrades, and made an end to my furious valor? Indeed, I thought to pass among the dead within Death's house this very day as I breathed out my life."

Then lord Apollo the unerring said to him: "Take courage now; such a comrade has the son of Cronus sent you from Ida to stand beside you and protect you, Phoebus Apollo of the golden sword, even me, who have guarded you before, both you and your steep city. Come now, urge many horsemen to drive their swift horses against the hollow ships. I will go ahead and smooth the whole way for the horses and will rout the heroic Achaeans."

So speaking, he breathed great might into the shepherd of the people. As when a horse from his stall, well fed at the manger, breaks his tether and runs galloping over the plain, accustomed to bathe in a fair-flowing river—proud he is; he holds his head high, and the mane flows about his shoulders, and his knees quickly bear him, trusting in his beauty, to the haunts and pasture of the mares; so Hector plied swift feet and knees, urging on the horsemen, when he heard the voice of the god. But as for the Danaans—just as dogs and country-men drive some antlered stag or a wild goat, but some steep rock and densely shaded wood protect it, and their fate is not to find him, but at their clamor a well-maned lion appears in the road and routs them all at once despite their eagerness— so the Danaans for a time followed in unending troops, thrust-ing with their swords and their spears, sharp at both ends. But when they saw Hector advancing on the warriors' lines, they were afraid and the spirit of all fell at their feet.

Then Thoas spoke to them, Andraemon's son, far best of the Aetolians, skilled with the javelin, valiant in close combat; few of the Achaeans could better him in council when the young men vied among themselves with words. With wise and kindly thought for them he spoke and said: "Ah, it is a great wonder that my eyes behold. Hector has escaped his fate and risen once more. The heart of each of us had hoped him dead beneath the hand of Telamonian Ajax. But once more some one of the gods defended and saved Hector, who has loosed the knees of many Danaans, as now I think he will again. For not without the aid of loud-thundering Zeus does he stand thus eagerly in the first line. Come, let us all do as I say. Let us bid the multitude return toward the ships and let us ourselves, all who boast ourselves the bravest in the army, make a stand, in the hope that at first we may meet and hold him back, raising our spears. I think that despite his eagerness he will fear at heart to enter the throng of Danaans."

So he spoke, and they readily listened and obeyed him. The men about Ajax and lord Idomeneus and Teucer and Meriones and Meges, peer of Ares, closed their ranks, calling on their bravest, and faced Hector and the Trojans. But the multitude retired toward the ships of the Achaeans.

The Trojans forced their way forward in a body, and Hector led them with long strides. Before him went Phoebus Apollo, a cloud about his shoulders. He bore the raging aegis with its shaggy border, dreadful and glorious, which Hephaestus the smith gave to Zeus to wear into the rout of men. With this in his hands, Apollo led the host.

The Argives in a body awaited them, and a sharp cry arose from either side, and the arrows leaped from the string. Many spears sped from brave hands, some to fix themselves in the flesh of youths swift in battle, and many to fall and stand in the earth between the ranks before they touched white flesh, for all their eagerness to sate themselves with it. As long as Phoebus Apollo held the aegis idle in his hands, the missiles of both sides flew thick and fast and the men fell. But when he looked in the face of the Danaans, with their swift horses, and shook the aegis and gave a piercing cry himself, he melted the spirit in their breasts and they forgot furious valor. As two beasts put to flight a herd of cattle or a great flock of sheep in the darkness of the black night, coming on them suddenly,

when no herdsman is at hand, so the frightened Achaeans
were routed. For Apollo sent panic upon them and gave glory
to the Trojans and to Hector.

Then man slew man as the conflict scattered. Hector slew
Stichius and Arcesilaus, the one the leader of the bronze-clad
Boeotians, the other the faithful comrade of great-hearted
Menestheus. Aeneas killed Medon and Iasus. Medon was the
bastard son of godlike Oileus and was Ajax's brother. He
dwelt in Phylace, apart from his native land, for he had slain
a man, the brother of his stepmother Eriopis, Oileus' wife.
Iasus was the leader of the Athenians and was called son of
Sphelus, Boucolus' son. Polydamas slew Mecisteus, Polites,
and Echius in the first fray, and godlike Agenor slew Clonius.
Paris hit Deiochus from behind in the lower part of the
shoulder as he fled among the foremost fighters, and he drove
the bronze straight through.

While they were despoiling them of their arms, the Achaeans, rushing into the sunken ditch and the palisade, fled this
way and that and were forced within the wall. But Hector
with a loud shout commanded the Trojans: "Rush for the
ships; let be the bloody spoils. Whomsoever I see far from the
ships on the other side I will slay on the spot, nor shall his
kinsmen and kinswomen give him in death the meed of fire,
but the dogs shall worry him before our city."

So speaking, he swung the lash upon his horses from his
shoulder, calling to the Trojans in the ranks. With a cry, they
all drove on with him the steeds that drew their chariots, in a
dreadful din. Before them, Phoebus Apollo easily tore down
with his feet the banks of the steep ditch and threw them into
its center and made a bridge and pathway long and wide, as
far as a spear flies when a man hurls it in a test of strength.
There they poured forward in their companies, and before
them went Apollo with the precious aegis. Very easily he tore
down the wall of the Achaeans; as a child, when it builds its
foolish playthings by the sea, easily with feet and hands destroys again its castles in the sand, so thou, bright Phoebus,
didst destroy much toil and labor of the Argives and didst stir
up rout among them.

So they halted beside the ships and stood their ground,
shouting to one another; and holding up their hands to all
the gods, each offered fervent prayer. Nestor, the bulwark of
the Achaeans, prayed most of all, lifting his hands toward the
starry heavens: "Father Zeus, if ever any of us, even in Argos
rich in wheat, burning fat thighs of bull or ram, prayed to come

home, and thou didst promise and nod assent, remember this, and keep from us the cruel day, Olympian, and suffer not the Achaeans to be so worsted by the Trojans."

So he spoke in prayer, and Zeus the counselor thundered loudly, hearing the prayer of the aged son of Neleus.

But when the Trojans heard the thunderclap of aegis-bearing Zeus, they leaped the more upon the Argives and remembered the joy of combat. As a great billow of the wide-wayed sea breaks down over a ship's bulwarks driven on by the might of the wind, which most increases waves, so the Trojans poured over the wall with a great shout, and driving their horses on, fought hand to hand beside the sterns with spears sharp at both ends, they from their chariots and the Achaeans with long pikes from the high, black ships where they had climbed—jointed pikes which lay on the ships for naval combat, shod at the tip with bronze.

So long as Achaeans and Trojans fought around the wall away from the swift ships, Patroclus sat in the tent of manly Eurypylus and delighted him with conversation and spread on his grievous wound drugs to heal the dark pains. But when he saw the Trojans rush the wall, and when the shout and flight of the Danaans began, he groaned and struck his thighs with downturned hands and sorrowing said: "Eurypylus, I can stay here with you no longer, however much you wish it, for a great struggle has begun. Let your squire care for you; I shall hasten to Achilles to urge him to do battle. Who knows but that with God's help I may persuade and stir his heart? A comrade's advice is good."

When he had thus spoken, his feet bore him away, but the Achaeans stood firm against the oncoming Trojans, yet could not push them back from the ships though they were fewer. Nor could the Trojans break through the ranks of the Danaans and reach the tents and ships. But as a chalk line keeps straight a ship's timber in the hands of a skillful workman, who is well versed in all wisdom through Athena's counsels, so straight was drawn their battle line. So they fought in groups about the different ships, but Hector made for glorious Ajax. The two struggled for one ship, and the one could not drive the other away and set fire to the ship, nor could the other push him back, since a god was urging him on. Then as Caletor, Clytius' son, was bearing fire toward the ship, glorious Ajax hit him in the breast with his spear. He fell with a crash, and the firebrand fell from his hand. When Hector saw his nephew fallen in the dust before the black ship, he called with a loud cry to Trojans and Lycians: "Trojans and Lycians and close-fighting Dardanians, do not yet withdraw from battle at this pass, but save Clytius' son, lest the Achaeans strip him of his armor where he fell in the space between the ships."

So speaking, he thrust at Ajax with his shining spear, and missed him, but with the sharp bronze struck Lycophron in the head above the ear as he stood close by Ajax. He was Mastor's son and Ajax' squire, a Cytherian, who dwelt with Ajax, since he had slain a man in holy Cythera. He fell backward from the ship's stern to the dusty earth, and his limbs were loosed. Ajax shuddered and called to his brother: "Dear Teucer, our faithful comrade Mastor's son is slain, whom we revered as much as our own parents when he came from Cythera and dwelt within our halls. Great-hearted Hector slew him. Where are your swift-slaying arrows and your bow that Phoebus Apollo gave you?"

So he spoke, and Teucer understood and ran and stood close beside him, holding in his hand his curved bow and his quiver full of arrows; very swift were the missiles that he sent against the Trojans. He hit Cleitus, Peisenor's glorious son, comrade of Polydamas the goodly son of Panthous, as he held the reins in his hands. He was busy with his horses; for as a favor to Hector and the Trojans he held the horses at the spot where the squadrons milled about in greatest numbers. Evil soon befell him, and none of them, for all their wish, could keep it from him. For the arrow, rich in groans, struck him in the neck from behind. He slipped from the chariot, and the horses, rattling the empty chariot, started back. Lord Polydamas quickly noticed it and was the first to meet the horses. He gave them to Astynous, Protiaon's son, and gave him many orders to hold the steeds close by and watch them well, but he himself went back and joined the foremost ranks.

Teucer took another arrow against brazen-armored Hector, and would have stopped him from battle beside the ships of the Achaeans if striking him as he did his deeds of valor he had taken his life away. But he could not evade the sharp mind of Zeus, who guarded Hector and robbed Telamonian Teucer of his glory. He broke the well-twisted string on the good bow as he drew it against Hector, and the arrow, heavy with bronze, flew wild, and the bow fell from his hand. Teucer shuddered and said to his brother: "Ah, a god completely foils our plan of battle and has struck the bow from my hand and broken the freshly twisted string, which I tied on early this morning that it might often bear the leaping arrows."

Then great Telamonian Ajax answered him: "Dear brother, let the bow and the many arrows go, since a god who bears a grudge against the Danaans spoiled them. Take a long spear in your hands and a shield upon your shoulder and fight off the Trojans and arouse the other men. Let it not be without a struggle that they take the well-benched ships, although they beat us; and let us recall the joy of battle."

So he spoke, and Teucer put the bow inside his tent. Upon his shoulders he set a fourfold shield, and on his mighty head he put a well-wrought helmet with a horsehair crest; the plume nodded dreadfully above it. He took his mighty spear, tipped with sharp bronze, and set forth, and running very quickly went and stood at Ajax' side.

When Hector saw Teucer's missiles thwarted, he cried to Trojans and Lycians with a mighty shout: "Trojans and Lycians and close-fighting Dardanians, be men, my friends, and remember furious valor amid the hollow ships, for I have seen a very brave man's missiles thwarted by Zeus. Easily recognizable is the power of Zeus to men, both to those to whom he grants a more excellent glory and to those whom he lessens and will not defend, as now he lessens the Argives' might and helps us. Come, fight all together by the ships. Whoever of you is shot or struck and meets his death and doom, let him die; no shameful thing it is to die in defense of one's country, but his wife and his children are safe thereafter, and his home and his estate are undisturbed, if only the Achaeans depart with their ships to their dear native land."

So speaking, he aroused the might and spirit of each man. Ajax, on the other side, called to his comrades: "For shame, Argives, now is the crisis, whether we perish or save ourselves and thrust back danger from the ships. Do you hope that if Hector of the glancing helmet takes the ships each man will reach his native land on foot? Do you not hear Hector urging on all his men in his eagerness to set fire to the ships? He invites them not to come to a dance but to fight. We have no better course or plan than this—to join at close quarters with hands and might. It is better to die or live, once and for all, than to be long wearied thus in dreadful combat to no purpose by the ships at the hands of men inferior."

So speaking, he aroused the might and spirit of each man. Then Hector slew Schedius, Perimedes' son, leader of the

Phocians, and Ajax slew Laodamas, chief of the foot soldiers, Antenor's glorious son. Polydamas despoiled Otus of Cyllene, comrade of Phyleides and ruler of the great-hearted Epeians. When Meges saw this, he rushed upon him, but Polydamas swerved to the side and Meges missed him, for Apollo would not suffer that Panthous' son be slain amid the foremost fighters. But Meges wounded Croesmus with a spear in the center of his chest, and he fell with a crash. Meges stripped the armor from his shoulders. Then Dolops leaped upon him, well skilled with the spear, Lampus' son, whom Lampus best of men begot, Lampus, Laomedon's son. Well versed in furious valor, Dolops struck from close at hand the shield of Phyleus' son full on the center with his spear, but the close-set breastplate protected him, which he wore all set with convex plates. This Phyleus once brought from Ephyre, from the Selleis River. For his friend Euphetes, king of men, had given it to him to wear to war, a defense against the foe. So now it kept destruction from the body of his son. Then Meges struck with his sharp spear the topmost crest of Dolops' bronze helmet with its horsehair plume and broke off the horsehair crest. Freshly dyed with purple, it all fell in the dust upon the earth. While Dolops remained there and fought with him and still hoped for victory, warlike Menelaus came to Meges' defense. He stood on one side with his spear, unseen, and struck Dolops in the shoulder from behind. The point thrust eagerly through his chest, pushing forward, and he fell on his face. The two went to strip his bronze armor from his shoulders, but Hector gave command to all his brothers, and specially rebuked mighty Melanippus, Hicetaon's son. At one time he had pastured cattle with shambling gait in Percote, while the foe were far away; but when the curved ships of the Danaans came, he came again to Ilium and was pre-eminent among the Trojans, and he dwelt with Priam, who honored him as much as his own sons. Hector rebuked him and spoke and said to him: "Shall we thus give way, Melanippus? Is your heart not moved at your cousin's slaying? Do you not see how they are coming after Dolops' arms? Follow me; we cannot fight the Argives from afar; sooner either we slay them or they seize steep Ilium from top to bottom and enslave her citizens."

So speaking, he led the way, and the other followed him, a godlike man. But great Ajax, Telamon's son, urged on the Argives: "My friends, be men, set honor in your hearts and think of your repute with one another in the mighty strife. For of men who value honor, more are saved than slain, whereas for them that flee there is neither glory nor escape."

So he spoke, and they themselves were eager to ward off the foe. They took his words to heart and ringed the ships with a wall of bronze, and Zeus aroused the Trojans against them. Menelaus of the mighty war cry urged on Antilochus: "Antilochus, none of the Achaeans is younger than yourself, nor swifter of foot, nor as brave as you in battle. You might leap out and strike down some hero of the Trojans."

So speaking, he rushed away, but he had aroused the other, who leaped out from the foremost lines and hurled his shining spear, glancing around him. The Trojans gave way before the hero as he cast, nor did he hurl his shaft in vain, but struck Hicetaon's son, high-hearted Melanippus, in the breast beside the nipple, as he went to battle. He fell with a crash, and darkness veiled his eyes. Antilochus rushed upon him like a dog which rushes on a wounded fawn that a hunter has shot and has loosed its limbs as it leaps from its hiding place. So, Melanippus, did Antilochus, stanch in battle, leap upon you to strip you of your arms. But he did not escape the eye of god-like Hector, who came running through the strife to meet him. Antilochus, swift warrior though he was, did not await him but fled like some beast that has done harm, one that has slain a dog or cowherd by the cattle, and flees before the throng of men can gather. So fled Nestor's son, and the Trojans and Hector with a fearful shout poured after him their grief-laden missiles. But he turned and stopped when he reached the throng of his companions.

The Trojans, like ravening lions, rushed toward the ships and carried out the commands of Zeus, who roused their great might continually and cast a spell on the minds of the Argives and took away their glory, while he urged the others on. For his heart was set on giving glory to Hector, Priam's son, that he might cast upon the curved ships portentous, unwearying fire, and might fulfill Thetis' presumptuous prayer in its entirety; this was what Zeus the counselor awaited, to see the glare of a blazing ship. For from that moment on he planned to cause a repulse of the Trojans from the ships and to give glory to the Danaans. With such intent, he aroused Hector, Priam's son, amid the hollow ships, although he was already most eager of himself. He raged like spear-brandishing Ares, or like a destructive fire upon the mountains, in the thickets of a deep wood. He foamed at the mouth, and his eyes gleamed beneath his dreadful brows, and the helmet shook dreadfully upon his temples as he fought; for Zeus himself from heaven was his protector, who gave him honor and glory alone among many men. For he was fated to be short-lived, since already Pallas Athena was bringing upon him the day of his doom beneath the might of Peleus' son. He wished to test and break the ranks of men where he saw the throng the thickest and the weapons best. Yet even so he lacked the power to break them, for all he was so eager, for they stood firm as a tower, like a high, steep rock, close by the gray sea, which abides the swift ways of the shrill winds and the swelling waves that break in foam against it; so the Danaans firmly abode the Trojans and would not flee. Then Hector, all gleaming with fire, leaped into the press and fell on them as a wave falls on a swift ship, roused quickly by the winds beneath the clouds. The ship is all hidden by foam, and a dreadful blast of wind roars in the sail, and the sailors tremble at heart with fear, for by only a little are they carried forth from death; so was the spirit torn in the breasts of the Achaeans. Like a savage lion coming upon cattle which are feeding in vast numbers in a great marshy meadow, and among them is a herdsman who is not yet well skilled in fighting a wild beast over the slaughter of crooked-horned cattle—he keeps pace always with the foremost cattle or the hindermost, while the lion leaps on those in the center and devours a cow, and all of them are frightened—so then the Achaeans were utterly terrified by Hector and Father Zeus, all of them, and Hector slew one alone, Mycenaean Periphetes, Copreus' dear son, who had often gone as messenger from King Eurystheus to mighty Heracles. He was a son better in all excellence than his much inferior father, both in swiftness of foot and in battle, and in mind he was among the first men of Mycenae. He then gave higher glory to Hector, for as he turned back he stumbled on the rim of his own shield which reached to his feet and was a bulwark against missiles. Tripped by this, he fell backward, and the helmet rang dreadfully on his temples as he fell. Hector quickly saw it, and ran and stood close by him and plunged his spear into his breast and slew him, close by his dear companions. Grieved though they were for their companion, they could not help him, for they themselves were terribly afraid of godlike Hector.

The Achaeans arrived within the line of ships, and the outermost vessels encircled them, those that had been drawn up first, but the Trojans poured after them. The Argives withdrew perforce from the first ships, but halted in a body beside the tents, nor did they scatter through the camp, for shame and fear restrained them, as they called out unceasingly to one another. Gerenian Nestor, furthermore, the bulwark of the Achaeans, besought each man in the name of his parents: "Friends, be men, and cherish in your hearts a sense of shame before the rest of mankind. Remember each of you his wife, his birthright, and his parents, both he whose parents live and he whose are dead. Here on their behalf, though they are not with us, I beg you to stand firm and not to turn in rout."

So speaking, he aroused the might and heart of each, and from their eyes Athena drove the strange cloud of mist, and light streamed bright upon them from either side—from the ships and from leveling war. And they saw Hector of the mighty war cry and they saw their companions, both those who had fallen back and fought not, and those who did battle by the swift ships.

Nor was the great-hearted Ajax longer content in spirit to stand on the spot where the other sons of the Achaeans fell back. He stepped with long strides over the decks of the ships and brandished in his hands a great polished pike, jointed with ferrules and twenty-two cubits long. As when a man well skilled in riding, who has harnessed together four horses out of many, rushes from the plain and drives toward a great city along a public highway, and many men and women marvel at him, and he continually leaps safely from one steed to another, and the horses fly, so Ajax passed with long strides across many decks of the swift ships, and his voice reached the heavens, and ever shouting dreadfully, he bade the Achaeans defend their ships and tents. Nor did Hector remain amid the din of the Trojans with their close-set breastplates. But as a shining eagle swoops upon a flock of birds as they feed beside a river, geese or cranes or long-necked swans, so Hector rushed straight on against a dark-prowed ship and urged his men along with him.

Again a sharp battle was joined beside the ships. You would think them unwearying and untiring as they met in battle, so eagerly did they fight. This was their thought as they struggled: the Achaeans thought they would not escape from disaster but perish, whereas each Trojan's heart within his breast hoped to burn the ships and slay the Achaean heroes. Such were their thoughts as they stood against each other. Then Hector grasped the stern of a seafaring ship, fair and swift-sailing, which had brought Protesilaus to Troy but took him not back to his dear native land. About his ship Achaeans and

Trojans slew one another in close combat. Nor did they from afar abide the shower from the bows or the darts, but they stood close and with one spirit fought with sharp axes and hatchets and with great swords and spears sharp at both ends. And many fair, dark-hilted swords fell to the ground, some from the hands and some from the shoulders of the struggling men, and the black earth ran with blood. But when Hector had seized the ship by the stern, he would not let go, grasping the curved tip of the sternpost in his hands and crying to the Trojans: "Bring fire, and all together raise the battle cry. Now Zeus has given us a day worth all the rest, to seize the ships which came here against the will of the gods and wrought us many woes, through the cowardice of the elders, who, when I wished to fight at the ships' sterns, held me back and restrained the men. But if far-thundering Zeus then marred our senses, now he himself commands us and drives us on."

So he spoke, and they rushed the more fiercely upon the Argives. And Ajax stood firm no longer, for he was hard-pressed by the missiles, but drew back a little, thinking of death, to the seven-foot helmsman's bench, and left the deck of the fair-lined ship. There he stood, keeping sharp watch and ever with his spear fending off from the ships whichever Trojans brought unwearying fire. Ever with dreadful roar he commanded the Danaans: "Friends, Danaan heroes, squires of Ares, be men, my friends; remember furious valor. Do we think there are many comrades behind us or any compact wall to ward off destruction from our men? There is no walled city close at hand where we might defend ourselves, with the people to turn the tables. Rather, we stand on the plain of the Trojans with their close-set breastplates, our backs to the sea, far from our native land. Therefore deliverance lies in our own hands, not in faintness in the battle."

So he spoke, and eagerly attacked with his sharp spear. Whoever of the Trojans approached the hollow ships with blazing fire to please Hector who urged them on, him would Ajax wound, waiting for him with his long spear, and he wounded twelve men at close quarters before the ships.

BOOK XVI

So THEY FOUGHT about the well-benched ship. But Patroclus stood beside Achilles, shepherd of the people, shedding warm tears, like a dark-watered spring which pours its dusky waters over some sheer cliff. Seeing him, swift-footed, godlike Achilles pitied him and spoke to him winged words: "Why do you weep, Patroclus, like some little girl, who runs beside her mother and bids her take her up, clinging to her robe and hindering her as she would hurry on, and looking tearfully up at her until she takes her up? Like her, Patroclus, do you shed soft tears. Are you trying to tell something to the Myrmidons, or to me myself, or have you alone had news from Phthia? They say Menoetius, Actor's son, is still alive and that Aeacus' son Peleus still lives among the Myrmidons. We should indeed mourn the death of both of them. Or do you pity the Argives, as they perish upon the hollow ships for their own transgression? Speak out, hide nothing in your mind, so that we both may know."

Then, horseman Patroclus, you sighed heavily and said to him: "Achilles, Peleus' son, by far the best of the Achaeans, be not angry, so great a woe has overwhelmed the Achaeans. All those who were once the bravest lie hit and wounded on the ships. Hurt is Tydeus' son, the mighty Diomedes, and Odysseus, famed with the spear, is wounded, and Agamemnon too, and hurt is Eurypylus by an arrow in the thigh. The physicians, with their many drugs, are tending them, dressing their wounds. But you are inflexible, Achilles. May no such anger seize on me as you with your dread bravery cherish. What profit shall any other have of you, though he be born hereafter, if you do not ward off disgraceful disaster from the Argives? Cruel one, the horseman Peleus was not your father, nor Thetis your mother. The gray sea and the steep rocks gave you birth, for your mind is harsh. But if you dread some prophecy in your heart, or if your queenly mother told you one from Zeus, yet send me at least quickly forth and arouse the rest of the host of the Myrmidons, in the hope that I may be a light to the Danaans. Give me your armor to wear upon my shoulders, in the hope that the Trojans, mistaking me for you, may hold back from battle, and the warlike sons of the Achaeans may catch their breath, worn as they are. For even a brief space is a breathing spell in war. Unwearied as we are, we might easily with a shout push back the wearied soldiers toward the city from the ships and tents."

So he spoke in supplication, the great fool, for it was to be his own evil death and doom for which he prayed. Greatly distressed, swift-footed Achilles said to him: "Ah, Zeus-born Patroclus, what sort of talk is this? I care for no oracle that I know of, nor has my queenly mother told me one from Zeus. But this dreadful anger strikes to my heart and soul, when a man desires to rob one who is his equal and to take away his prize, because he surpasses him in power. It is a dreadful source of wrath to me, since I have suffered grief at heart. The maid whom the sons of the Achaeans set aside as a prize for me, whom I won with my spear as I sacked her well-walled city, this woman the mighty Agamemnon, Atreus' son, tore from my arms as though I were some unregarded wanderer. But let us pass by what has happened. It is not really possible to rage unceasingly within my heart. I had not thought to cease my anger before the war cry and the battle reached my ships. But put my glorious armor on your shoulders and lead the war-loving Myrmidons to battle, if indeed a dark cloud of Trojans has victoriously engulfed the ships and the Argives have their backs to the sea beach, with but a little share of space remaining. The whole city of the Trojans has marched forth with courage, for they do not see the front of my shining helmet close at hand. They would quickly flee and fill the ditches with their dead if mighty Agamemnon should be reconciled with me. Now they are fighting around the camp. For no spear rages in the hands of Diomedes, Tydeus' son, to ward off destruction from the Danaans, nor have I yet heard the voice of Atreus' son speaking from his hateful head. But man-slaying Hector's voice rings out, calling orders to the Trojans, and they fill the whole plain with their war cry as they conquer the Achaeans in battle. So, Patroclus, fall on them mightily, and ward off destruction from the ships, lest they burn the ships with gleaming fire and take away our dear return. Now obey the purpose of the words I impress upon your mind, so that you may win me great honor and glory among all the Danaans and they may send back the lovely maiden and proffer generous gifts as well. When you have driven them from the ships, come back. And if Hera's loud-thundering husband grant that you win glory, seek not to fight far from me with the war-loving Trojans. You will dishonòr me the more. Nor do you, exulting in war and strife as you slay the Trojans, lead on toward Ilium, lest some one of the eternal gods from Olympus enter the combat, for Apollo the Warder loves them much. But turn back, when you have set the light of victory among the ships, and let them struggle on the plain. Father Zeus, and Athena, and Apollo, would that not one of all the Trojans might escape death, nor any of the Argives, but that we two might cheat destruction, so that we alone might break the sacred crown of Troy."

So they spoke to one another. Now Ajax stood firm no longer, for he was driven back by the missiles; the will of Zeus and the shots of the noble Trojans overwhelmed him. As his shining helmet was struck about his temples, it gave a dreadful ringing. He was continually struck upon the helmet's well-made cheek pieces, and his left shoulder was weary from holding continuously his gleaming shield. Yet they could not shake the shield before him, for all the force they lent their weapons. A ceaseless, painful panting racked him, and sweat poured down all his limbs in streams, nor could he ever get his breath. Woe was piled on woe in every shape.

Tell me now, ye Muses who have your home upon Olympus, how fire first fell upon the ships of the Achaeans.

Hector stood close by and smote with his great sword the ashen spear of Ajax on the shaft below the point, and broke it off. Then Telamonian Ajax brandished the docked spear vainly in his hands, while the bronze tip fell crashing to the earth far from him. In his blameless heart Ajax knew this for the work of the gods, and shuddered—knew that high-thundering Zeus was baffling utterly his skill in combat and that Zeus desired victory for the Trojans. So he drew back from the missiles. The Trojans threw unwearying fire on the swift ship and the unextinguishable flame poured over her as the fire enwrapped her stern.

So fire enfolded the ship's stern, and then Achilles smote his thighs and said to Patroclus: "Up, Zeus-born Patroclus, driver of horses, for I see the roar of devouring fire beside the ships. Up, lest they take the ships and there be no escape. Arm yourself quickly, and I will muster the men."

So he spoke, and Patroclus donned the flashing bronze. First he put on his shins fair greaves, fitted with silver ankle clasps. Next he strapped on his chest the intricately fashioned, starry breastplate of Aeacus' swift-footed son. About his shoulders he threw his silver-studded sword of bronze, and then his great, stout shield. On his mighty head he set his well-wrought helmet, with its horsehair crest, and the plume nodded dreadfully above it. He took two stout javelins, well fitted to his hand. Only the heavy, huge, strong spear of the blameless son of Aeacus he did not take. No other of the Achaeans could wield it, for it was Peleus' ashen spear, which Cheiron gave Achilles' dear father on Pelion's peak, to be the death of heroes. Then Patroclus bade Automedon to yoke the horses quickly, Automedon, whom he honored most after Achilles, breaker of men, for he was the most trustworthy to await his call in battle. For him Automedon yoked the swift horses, Xanthus and Balius, who flew like the winds. The whirlwind Podarge bore them to Zephyr as she pastured in a meadow by the stream of Ocean. In the side-traces he put blameless Pedasus, whom Achilles captured when he took Eëtion's city and who, though mortal, ran with the immortal horses.

Achilles went among the Myrmidons and helped them all to arm with their weapons in their tents. Like wolves that feed upon raw flesh, in whose breasts is valor unquenchable, who slay and devour a great antlered stag upon the mountains, and all their chops are red with blood, and they go in a pack to lap the black surface of some dark-watered spring with slender tongues, belching up blood and gore—the spirit in their breasts is fearless, and their bellies are sucked in—such were the leaders and counselors of the Myrmidons as they marched about the brave squire of Aeacus' swift-footed son, and among them stood warlike Achilles, urging on the horses and the shieldmen.

Fifty were the swift ships that Achilles, dear to Zeus, led to Troy, and in each were fifty heroic comrades at the oars. He had named five leaders whom he trusted to give commands, and he himself, with his great power, was king. One company was led by Menesthius of the gleaming breastplate, son of Spercheius, the river fed by Zeus. Peleus' daughter, fair Polydora, bore Menesthius to unwearying Spercheius, a woman wed to a god, but by report to Borus, Perieres' son, who wedded her openly, giving boundless marriage gifts. Another company was led by warlike Eudorus, son of an unwed mother. To him Phylas' daughter Polymele, fair in the dance, gave birth. The mighty slayer of Argus loved her when he beheld her among the maids who did a choral dance to sounding Artemis of the golden arrow. And gracious Hermes went at once with her into an upper chamber and lay with her in secret and she gave him a glorious son, Eudorus, who excelled in race or battle. But when Eileithyia, who brings the birth pangs, brought him to the light and he beheld the sun's rays, mighty Echecles, Actor's son, took her to his home, giving countless bridal gifts, and old Phylas reared the child well and cherished him, loving him as if he had been his own son. The third company warlike Peisander led, Maemalus' son, who, after the comrade of Peleus' son, was pre-eminent in sword-play among the Myrmidons. The old horseman Phoenix led the fourth company, the fifth Alcimedon, Laerces' blameless son. When Achilles had drawn them all up in order with their leaders, he gave them forceful orders: "Myrmidons, let none of you forget the threats you uttered by the swift ships against the Trojans, during all my wrath, when each of you asked me: 'Unhappy son of Peleus, did your mother feed you on gall, cruel one, that you hold your unwilling comrades by the ships? Let us sail home again with our seafaring ships, since this evil wrath has fallen upon your heart.' Thus you spoke to me often, gathering round. Now the great work of combat is at hand, which once you so desired. Now let each man with valiant heart do battle with the Trojans."

So speaking, he aroused the might and spirit of each. The lines drew closer when they heard the king. As when a man erects with close-set stones the wall of some high mansion, shunning the wind's might, so helmets and bossed shields fitted together. Shield pressed on shield, helmet on helmet, man on man. The plumes of horsehair touched the bright crests as they shook their heads, so close they stood by one another. Before them all two men put on their armor, Patroclus and Automedon, both with one spirit, to fight before the Myrmidons. But Achilles stepped into his tent and opened the cover of a fair and cunningly fashioned chest, which silver-footed Thetis put on his ship to take with him, filling it full of shirts and wind-proof cloaks and woolen rugs. There was his well-wrought cup. From it no other man drank the bright wine, nor did he pour libation from it to any of the gods save Father Zeus. Taking it from the chest, he cleansed it first with sulphur and then washed it in fair streams of water, and himself washed his hands and poured the shining wine. Then he stood in the center of the court and prayed, and looking up to heaven poured the wine, nor was he unseen by Zeus, who rejoices in the thunder: "Lord Zeus, Pelasgian, Dodonian, who dwellest afar and dost rule storm-swept Dodona; around thee dwell the Selli, thy spokesmen, who wash not their feet and make their bed upon the ground; thou hast heard my prayer before and hast honored me and greatly chastised the host of the Achaeans; fulfill now this wish of mine as well. For I myself shall remain in the space about the ships, but my comrade I am sending with many Myrmidons to battle. Grant him glory, far-thundering Zeus; make brave the heart within his breast, so that Hector too may know whether our comrade knows how to fight alone as well, or whether his arms rage only then invincible when I go into Ares' mill. But when he has repelled the battle and the shouting from the ships, may he come back to the swift ships unscathed, with all his armor and his close-fighting comrades."

So he spoke in prayer, and Zeus the counselor heard him. But the father granted him one thing and refused the other. He granted that Patroclus should drive the war and battle from the ships, but refused that he come back safe from battle. Achilles, when he had poured a libation and made prayer to Father Zeus, went back into his tent and put the cup back in the chest, and went and took his stand before the tent, still wishing in his heart to see the dreadful combat of the Trojans and Achaeans.

Under arms, they marched with great-hearted Patroclus as they charged with high hopes upon the Trojans. They poured out suddenly, like wasps along the road, which boys have angered in their heedless way, the little fools, forever teasing them and causing general grief to many. If some traveler stir the wasps unwittingly, as he passes by, the whole swarm pours out and fights bold-heartedly to defend its young. With their heart and spirit, the Myrmidons poured from the ships, and an unceasing shout arose. Patroclus, with a loud cry, commanded his companions: "Myrmidons, comrades of Achilles, Peleus' son, be men, my friends, and remember furious valor, that we may do honor to the son of Peleus, who is by far the bravest of the Argives beside the ships—and so are we, his close-fighting followers—and that Atreus' son, wide-ruling Agamemnon, may know his fatal folly, that he paid no honor to the best of the Achaeans."

So speaking, he aroused the might and spirit of each, and they fell in a mass upon the Trojans. The ships re-echoed dreadfully the shouts of the Achaeans. But when the Trojans saw Menoetius' valiant son, himself and his squire as well, resplendent in their armor, the hearts of all were troubled and their ranks were shaken, for they thought that beside the ships the swift-footed son of Peleus had put away his wrath and chosen friendship. Each one glanced around him to see how he might escape sharp destruction.

Patroclus first thrust with his shining spear straight through their center, at the place where most of them were rushing wildly, beside the stern of the ship of great-hearted Protesilaus. He struck Pyraechmes, who had led the Paeonian charioteers from Amydon on the wide-flowing Axius. Him he hit in the right shoulder, and he fell groaning on his back in the dust, and his Paeonian comrades were put to flight about him, for Patroclus filled them all with fear by slaying their leader, who was the best in battle. He drove them from the ships and quenched the blazing fire. The ship was left there half-burned, and the Trojans fled with a fearful outcry, and among the hollow ships the Danaans poured out against them, and an unceasing din arose. As when from the high peak of some great mountain Zeus the thunderer drives away a heavy cloud, and all the lookouts and high headlands and the dells stand out, and the boundless ether opens to the depths of heaven, so the Danaans, having driven back the blazing fire from the ships, paused a short time to catch their breath, but there was no pause in war, for not yet had the Trojans been driven in headlong flight from the black ships by the Achaeans, dear to Ares, but still resisted, though withdrawing from the ships perforce.

Then man slew man among the leaders, as the conflict scattered. First, Menoetius' mighty son with his sharp spear struck Areilycus in the thigh as he turned, and the bronze drove straight through. The spear broke the bone, and he fell prone to earth. Then warlike Menelaus wounded Thoas in the breast, where his shield had left it bare, and he loosed his limbs. Phyleides bided his time as Amphiclus rushed on him, and thrusting before the other could, he struck his thigh where the muscle is thickest. The sinews split about the spear blade, and darkness veiled his eyes. Of Nestor's sons, Antilochus wounded Atymnius with his sharp spear, and the bronze spear drove through his flank, and he fell forward. Maris, angered for his brother, rushed close in upon Antilochus with his spear and stood before the body. But godlike Thrasymedes at once thrust at his shoulder, before he could wound Antilochus, nor did he miss. The spear point tore away the upper arm from the muscles and shattered the bone completely. He fell with a crash, and darkness veiled his eyes. So the two, slain by two brothers, went to Death's house—Sarpedon's noble comrades, the spearmen sons of Amisodarus, who reared the raging Chimaera that

was a woe to many men. Ajax, Oileus' son, attacked Cleobulus
and took him alive, baffled in the tumult, but he loosed his
might at once, striking his neck with the hilted sword. The
whole sword was warm with blood, and on his eyes fell dark
death and mighty doom. Peneleos and Lycon ran together,
for they had missed each other with their spears, and both had
cast their javelins in vain. Therefore they next ran together
with swords. Then Lycon struck the ridge of Peneleos' horsehair crest, and the sword broke at the hilt. Peneleos smote him
in the neck below the ear; the whole sword was buried, and
his head hung down held only by the skin, and his limbs were
loosed. Meriones, with his swift feet, overtook Acamas and
wounded him in the right shoulder as he entered his chariot.
He fell from the chariot, and a mist overspread his eyes. Idomeneus struck Erymas in the mouth with the pitiless bronze,
and the brazen spear pierced straight through below the brain,
and his white bones were shattered. His teeth were dashed
out and both his eyes were filled with blood, and he poured
forth a stream of gore from his nostrils and his gaping mouth,
and a dark cloud of death enwrapped him.

These leaders of the Danaans slew each his man. As ravenous wolves fall upon lambs or kids, choosing them from the
flocks which have been cut off in the mountains through the
shepherd's folly, and the wolves, seeing it, seized them at once
since they have a timid heart, so the Danaans fell upon the
Trojans, and the Trojans remembered shrieking rout and forgot their furious valor.

Great Ajax ever strove to cast his javelin at brazen-armored
Hector, but the latter, with his skill in war, his broad shoulders
covered by his ox-hide shield, watched the arrows' whistling
and the din of spears. He recognized the shifting fortune of
the battle, but even so stood fast and strove to save his faithful
comrades.

As when a cloud goes through the heavens from Olympus,
from the clear ether, when Zeus sends a squall, so from the
ships went shouts and terror. Nor did the Trojans fall back in
good order. Swift-footed horses bore Hector and his arms
away, and he left the Trojan soldiers, whom the ditch held
back against their will. And in the ditch many swift chariot
horses broke their masters' chariots at the pole's end and left
them. But Patroclus followed after, urging on the Danaans
impatiently and devising evil for the Trojans. They, in clamor-
ing rout, filled all the roads when they scattered. Above them
spurts of dust spread underneath the clouds, and the single-

hoofed horses ran at full stretch back toward the city from the ships and tents. Patroclus gave a shout and drove toward the place where he saw the army most confused. Men fell headlong from their chariots beneath the axles, and the chariots turned over rattling. The swift, immortal horses that the gods gave as a glorious gift to Peleus leaped straight across the ditch, rushing forward, and Patroclus' spirit urged him after Hector, for he wished to smite him, but Hector's swift horses bore him off. As when the whole black earth is drenched by a downpour on a day in late summer, when Zeus pours rain most violently in his wrath and anger at men who do violence to the laws and twist them in the market place and drive justice out, heeding not the eye of the gods—all the rivers run in roaring spate to the dark sea, down from the mountains headlong, wasting the works of men—so great a tumult made the Trojan horses as they ran.

Now when Patroclus had mown down the first companies, he hurled the Trojans back toward the ships nor would he let them reach the city as they wished. He chased and slew them between the ships and the river and the lofty wall, and took revenge for many men. Then he smote Pronous first with his shining spear where his breast was left bare by his shield, and he loosed his limbs. And Pronous fell with a crash. Then next Patroclus attacked Thestor, Enops' son, who sat cowering in his polished chariot, for he had lost his wits, and the reins had slipped from his hands. Patroclus stood close by and smote him with his spear on the right of his jaw and pierced his teeth. He hooked him on the spear and dragged him across the chariot's rim as when a man sits on a jutting rock and drags a mighty fish from the sea by a line and gleaming bronze. So he dragged him from the chariot gasping on the shining spear, and threw him on his face, and his spirit left him as he fell. Then, as Erylaus rushed upon him, Patroclus smote him full in the head with a stone and his skull was split and crushed to pieces within his heavy helmet. Prone to the earth he fell, and life-destroying death poured over him. Then Patroclus brought Erymas and Amphoterus and Epaltes and Tlepolemus, Damastor's son, and Echius and Pyris and Ipheus and Euippus and Polymelus all of them in quick succession to the fertile earth.

When Sarpedon saw his unbelted comrades slain at the hands of Menoetius' son Patroclus, he called out in reproach to the godlike Lycians: "Shame on you, Lycians; whither are you fleeing? Be quick now. For I shall meet this man that I may learn who it is that prevails and has done much evil to the Trojans, since he has loosed the knees of many noble men."

So he spoke, and with his weapons leaped from his chariot to the ground. Patroclus, on the other side, when he saw him, leaped from his chariot. Like vultures with crooked claws and curving beaks which on some lofty rock fight screaming harshly, so shouting they rushed on one another. When the son of crooked-counseled Cronus saw them, he was filled with pity and said to Hera, his sister and his wife: "Alas, that it is fated for Sarpedon, dearest of men to me, to die beneath the hands of Menoetius' son Patroclus. My heart is torn at the choice as I debate in mind whether to snatch him living from tearful battle and set him down in the rich land of Lycia or now to let him fall beneath the hands of Menoetius' son."

Then ox-eyed, queenly Hera answered him: "Most dreadful son of Cronus, what is this that you propose? Do you wish to release from Death, the bringer of woe, a mortal man, long given over to fate? Do so, but by no means shall all we other gods approve. Another thing I will tell you, and do you turn it over in your heart. If you send Sarpedon to his home alive, beware lest some other of the gods also desire to send his dear son from the mighty conflict. For many sons of the immortals are fighting around Priam's great city; in them you will arouse a dreadful anger. But if he is dear to you and your heart pities him, let him be slain in the mighty conflict at the hands of Menoetius' son Patroclus. But when his soul and life depart from him, send Death and sweet Sleep to bear him until they reach the land of broad Lycia. There his brethren and friends will give him solemn burial with tomb and monument, for such is the portion of the dead."

So she spoke, and the father of gods and men failed not to heed her. But he sent a bloody rain upon the earth in honor of his dear son whom Patroclus was to slay in fertile Troy, far from his native land.

When they came close to one another in their onset, Patroclus smote far-famed Thrasymelus, brave squire of lord Sarpedon, in the lower belly and loosed his limbs. And Sarpedon, the second to attack, missed Patroclus with his shining spear but wounded the horse Pedasus in the right shoulder with his spear. The horse shrieked as he breathed out his life and fell screaming in the dust, and his spirit flew away. The two others reared apart and the yoke groaned and the reins became tangled, since the trace horse lay in the dust. For this Automedon, famed with the spear, found a remedy. He drew his keen sword from his sturdy thigh and rushed up and cut free the trace horse, nor did he linger. The two steeds were set aright and pulled in harness. Then the two heroes met again in soul-devouring strife.

Sarpedon missed again with his shining spear, and the blade of the spear flew over the left shoulder of Patroclus and struck him not. Next Patroclus rushed in with the bronze. Not in vain did the weapon fly from his hand but struck where the midriff closes round the throbbing heart. Sarpedon fell as an oak falls, or a poplar, or a tall pine, which carpenters cut down on the mountains with freshly whetted axes to be timber for a ship. So he lay stretched before the horses and the chariot, clutching the bloody dust. As a lion comes upon a herd and slays a bull, tawny and great of heart, among the cattle of shambling gait, and he dies bawling beneath the lion's jaws, so the leader of the Lycian shieldmen raged at his own slaying by Patroclus; and he called to his dear comrade: "Dear Glaucus, most war-like of warriors, now you must indeed be both spearman and dauntless warrior. Now let evil war be your desire, if only you be quick. First go everywhere and arouse the leading heroes of the Lycians to fight about Sarpedon. Then do you yourself strive for me with the bronze. For I shall be forever all your days a shame and a disgrace to you if the Achaeans strip off my armor where I fell before the ships. Hold stoutly and rouse all our men."

As he spoke, the end of death enwrapped his eyes and nostrils, and Patroclus put his heel upon his chest and drew the spear out of his flesh, and his midriff followed with it; he drew out his soul and the spear blade together. And the Myrmidons held Sarpedon's panting horses there, though they wished to flee, once they had left their master's chariot.

A dreadful grief fell upon Glaucus when he heard Sarpedon's voice, and his heart was moved that he could not help him. He seized his own arm in his hand and pressed it, for he was pained by the wound given him by Teucer's arrow as he rushed toward the high wall, when Teucer saved his comrades from destruction. Then he spoke in prayer to the unerring Apollo: "Hear me, Lord, who art surely either in Lycia's rich land or in Troy. Wherever thou art, thou canst give ear to a man in such trouble as that which has come to me. For I have this grave wound, and my arm is pierced with sharp pangs, nor can my blood be stanched, and my shoulder is made heavy. I cannot hold my spear firmly, nor go and fight my foes. The best of men has perished, Sarpedon, son of Zeus, and Zeus de-

fends not even his own son. Heal then, Lord, this grave wound
of mine and still my pain and give me strength, that I may call
to my Lycian comrades and bid them fight, and that I myself
may fight over the body of the fallen."

So he spoke in prayer, and Phoebus Apollo heard him. At
once he stopped his pain and dried the dark blood in the
grievous wound and filled his heart with might. Glaucus knew
in his heart and rejoiced that the great god had quickly heard
him when he prayed. First he went among the leading men of
the Lycians on all sides, urging them to fight over Sarpedon.
Then he went with long strides after the Trojans, after Polydamas, Panthous' son, and godlike Agenor, and he went after
Aeneas and Hector of the brazen harness. Standing close to
them, he spoke winged words: "Hector, now you have wholly
forgotten your allies, who for your sake are losing their lives
far from friends and native land. You are not willing to defend
them. Sarpedon, leader of the Lycian shieldmen, lies dead,
he who protected Lycia by his judgments and his strength.
Brazen Ares has slain him with a spear, at the hands of Patroclus. Come, my friends, stand by, and in your hearts resolve
that the Myrmidons shall not take away his armor and mutilate his body in their anger for all the Danaans who perished,
those we slew with our spears by the swift ships."

So he spoke, and grief unbearable utterly overcame the Trojans, unendurable, since Sarpedon was the city's bulwark, even
though a stranger. For many men had followed him, and
among them he was best in battle. The Trojans moved in haste
upon the Danaans, and Hector led them in anger for Sarpedon's sake. But Patroclus of the shaggy heart roused the
Achaeans. First he addressed the two Ajaxes, though they
were eager of themselves: "Ajaxes, now may you find pleasure
in defense, being even such as you were before among the
heroes, or even braver. That man lies dead who first leaped
over the wall of the Achaeans—Sarpedon. If we could but
capture and mutilate his body and strip the armor from his
shoulders and slay with pitiless bronze one of the comrades
who defend him!"

So he spoke, and they were eager to make a defense. When
both sides had strengthened their lines—Trojans and Lycians
and Myrmidons and Achaeans—they met in combat over the
body of the fallen, shouting dreadfully. Loud rang the armor
of men. Zeus spread baneful night above the mighty conflict,
that there might be baneful toil of battle over his dear son.

First the Trojans drove back the bright-eyed Achaeans, for

he who was by no means the worst man among the Myrmidons was hit—the son of great-hearted Agacles, godlike Epeigeus. He was formerly lord in fair-lying Boudeium, but when he had slain his noble nephew, he fled as a suppliant to Peleus and silver-footed Thetis, and they sent him to follow Achilles, breaker of men, to Ilium of the fair steeds, that he might battle with the Trojans. Now as he touched the body, glorious Hector struck him in the head with a stone, and his skull was split and crushed within his heavy helmet. He fell forward on the body, and life-destroying death poured over him. Grief seized Patroclus for his slain companion, and he went straight through the front ranks like a swift hawk that frightens daws and starlings. So, straight for the Trojans and Lycians did you rush, horse-driving Patroclus, and you were angry at heart for your companion. Patroclus hit Sthenelus, Ithaemenes' dear son, in the neck with a stone and crushed the muscles. Then the front ranks and glorious Hector gave way. As far as the cast of a long hunting spear that a man throws to test himself in sport or in war in the face of murderous foes, so far the Trojans gave way, and the Achaeans pushed them. Glaucus, leader of the Lycian spearmen, was the first to rally, and he slew great-hearted Bathycles, Chalcon's dear son, who, when he dwelt in Hellas, was conspicuous among the Myrmidons for wealth and fortune. Glaucus thrust him in the center of the chest with his spear, turning suddenly when Bathycles overtook him in pursuit. Bathycles fell with a crash, and heavy grief came upon the Achaeans that a great man had fallen. The Trojans rejoiced greatly and came and stood in throngs about him, nor did the Achaeans forget valor, but brought their might to bear upon them. Then Meriones took a helmed hero of the Trojans, Laogonus, the brave son of Onetor, who was priest of Idaean Zeus and was reverenced by the people as a god. He hit him beneath the jaw and ear. Quickly his spirit departed from his limbs and hateful darkness seized him. Aeneas cast a bronze spear at Meriones, for he hoped to hit him below the shoulder as he advanced. But he looked up and dodged the brazen spear, for he ducked forward, and the long spear buried itself in the ground behind him and its butt quivered, and mighty Ares took away its might. So Aeneas' spear point went quivering into the earth, since it had sped from his mighty hand in vain, and Aeneas was angry at heart and called: "Meriones, though you be a dancer, my spear would soon have stopped you utterly if I had hit you."

Meriones, famed with the spear, answered him: "Aeneas, however mighty one may be, it is hard to quench the power of all men who face you in self-defense, for you too are mortal. If I should hit you squarely with the sharp bronze, quickly then, though you be strong and trust your hands, you would give glory to me and your soul to Hades of the famous steeds."

So he spoke, and the mighty son of Menoetius rebuked him: "Meriones, why do you speak thus, brave man that you are? Dear friend, the Trojans will not draw back from the corpse before reproachful words. Before that, the earth shall hide someone. For the issue of war resides in hands, the issue of words in council. Therefore it is best for us not to enlarge on words but to fight."

So speaking, he led the way, and the godlike mortal followed him. As the din of woodcutters arises in a mountain's glens and can be heard afar, so their din arose from the wide-wayed earth, the din of their bronze and leather and well-made ox-hide shields, as they thrust with their swords and spears sharp at both ends. Not even an observant man could still have recognized godlike Sarpedon, since he was covered with darts and blood and dust from his head clear to his toes. Still they fought about the body, as flies buzz in a barnyard about the full milk pails in the springtime, when the milk drenches the pails. So they fought about the body, nor did Zeus once turn his gleaming eyes away from the mighty conflict, but watched them continually and pondered in his heart, considering many things about the slaying of Patroclus, whether glorious Hector should at once slay him too with the bronze there in the mighty conflict over godlike Sarpedon and should strip the armor from his shoulders, or whether he should increase the bitter toil for yet more men. As he considered, this seemed to him the better—that the brave squire of Achilles, Peleus' son, should once more drive the Trojans and brazen-armored Hector to the city and should take the lives of many. First of all, he inspired in Hector an unvalorous spirit; he mounted his chariot and turned in flight and bade the other Trojans flee, for he recognized the sacred scales of Zeus. Then not even the brave Lycians remained, but all fled when they saw their king struck to the heart and lying among the host of dead, for many had fallen over him when the son of Cronus drew taut the mighty conflict. The Achaeans stripped the gleaming armor of bronze from the shoulders of Sarpedon, and Menoetius' valiant son gave it to his comrades to carry to the hollow ships. Then cloud-gathering Zeus said to Apollo: "Come now, dear Phoebus, get Sarpedon out of range and cleanse him of black blood, and then carry him far away and wash him in the river's stream and anoint him with ambrosia and clothe him in ambrosial raiment. And send him with an escort swift to bear him, the twin brothers Sleep and Death, who will soon set him in the rich land of broad Lycia, where his brethren and friends will give him solemn burial with tomb and monument, for such is the portion of the dead."

So he spoke, nor did Apollo fail to heed his father. He went down from the Idaean mountains to the dreadful strife and straightway lifted godlike Sarpedon out of range of the missiles and carried him far away and washed him in the river's stream and anointed him with ambrosia and clothed him in ambrosial raiment. Then he sent him with an escort swift to bear him, the twin brothers Sleep and Death, who quickly set him down in the rich land of broad Lycia.

Patroclus, with an order to his horses and Automedon, went after the Trojans and Lycians, and greatly did he err, poor fool. If he had kept the command of Peleus' son he would have escaped black death's evil fate. But ever stronger than the mind of men is that of Zeus; sometimes he puts even a brave man to flight and easily takes away victory, yet sometimes of himself he urges a man to battle. He it was who then aroused the spirit in Patroclus' breast.

Whom then did you slay first, whom last, Patroclus, when the gods called you deathwards? First Adrastus and Autonous and Echeclus and Perimus, Megas' son, and Epistor and Melanippus; then Elasus and Moulius and Pylartes—these he slew; each of the rest remembered flight.

Then the sons of the Achaeans would have taken high-gated Troy by the hands of Patroclus, for he raged forward and about him with his spear, had not Phoebus Apollo stood upon the well-built tower with evil purpose toward him, aiding the Trojans. Thrice Patroclus reached the corner of the lofty wall and thrice Apollo forced him back, striking his gleaming shield with immortal hands. But when a fourth time Patroclus reached forward, like a god, Apollo gave a dreadful shout and spoke to him winged words: "Draw back, Zeus-born Patroclus. It is not fated that the brave Trojans' city should now be overthrown by your spear, nor even by Achilles, who is better far than you."

So he spoke, and Patroclus fell far back, avoiding the wrath of the unerring Apollo.

But Hector checked his single-hoofed horses in the Scaean

gates; for he debated whether he should drive them back and
fight again in the tumult or should call to the people to gather
within the wall. As he pondered this, Phoebus Apollo stood
beside him, in the likeness of a strong and mighty man, Asius,
who was a maternal uncle of horse-taming Hector, own
brother of Hecuba, and son of Dymas, who dwelt in Phrygia
by Sangarius' streams. In this man's likeness Apollo, son of
Zeus, addressed him: "Hector, why do you cease from battle?
You ought not. Would I were as much your better as I am
your inferior. Surely then you would withdraw from battle at
your cost. Come, drive your strong-hoofed horses after Patroclus, in the hope that you may take him, and Apollo may give
you glory."

So speaking, the god went back among the strife of heroes,
and glorious Hector ordered prudent Cebriones to whip the
horses into battle. But Apollo went and entered the fray and
sent a disastrous tumult on the Argives and gave glory to the
Trojans and to Hector. Hector let the other Danaans be and
did not slay them, but drove his strong-hoofed horses after
Patroclus. And Patroclus, on the other side, leaped from his
chariot to the ground, holding his spear in his left hand; in
the other he grasped a shining, jagged stone, which his hand
covered. He braced himself and threw it; neither did he withdraw much from his foe, nor did he hurl the missile in vain,
but hit Hector's charioteer Cebriones, the bastard son of far-
famed Priam, as he held the reins of the horses. He hit him in
the forehead with the sharp stone. The stone crushed both his
brows, nor did the bone hold firm. His eyes fell to the ground
in the dust before his feet. Like a diver he plunged from the
well-made chariot and his spirit left his bones. In scorn you
said to him, horseman Patroclus: "Well, well, the man is fast,
he dives so easily. If he were on the fishy deep this fellow
could feed many men, diving from his ship for oysters, even
though it were stormy, so easily he now dives from his chariot
on the plain. Even among the Trojans they have divers."

So speaking, he strode toward the hero Cebriones, with the
spring of a lion which, ravaging the stall, is wounded in the
chest, and his own valor destroys him. So you, Patroclus,
leaped eagerly upon Cebriones, and Hector on the other side
leaped from his chariot to the ground. The two contended over
Cebriones like two lions who battle on some mountain peak
for a slain doe, both of them hungry and both high of heart.
So the two raisers of the war cry, Menoetius' son Patroclus,
and glorious Hector, rushed about Cebriones eager to cut one

another's flesh with the pitiless bronze. Hector, when he had seized the corpse's head, would not let go, and Patroclus opposite him held to a foot. And then the rest of the Trojans and Danaans joined in mighty battle.

As Eurus and Notus strive with one another to shake a deep wood in a mountain's glens—a wood of oaks and ash and slender cornel trees, which toss their tapering branches at each other with a fearful din and the noise of those that break—so the Trojans and Achaeans rushed on and slew each other, and neither thought of baneful flight. Many sharp spears were planted about Cebriones, many winged arrows leaping from the string, and many great stones smote the shields of those that fought about him. And in the whirls of dust the vast man vastly lay, his horsemanship forgotten.

As long as the sun was astride the heavens, the weapons struck both sides and soldiers fell, but when the sun passed on to ox-loosing time, then the Achaeans were superior beyond their fate. They dragged the hero Cebriones out of range of the missiles away from the tumult of the Trojans and stripped the armor from his shoulders, and Patroclus rushed forward toward the Trojans with an evil purpose. Thrice then he darted forward, like swift Ares, with a dreadful shout, and thrice he slew nine men. But when a fourth time he rushed forward like a god, then, Patroclus, the end of life appeared to you. For dreadful Phoebus met you in the mighty conflict. But Patroclus did not see him as he passed through the tumult, for he was shrouded in thick mist as he came toward him. The god stood behind Patroclus and smote his back and broad shoulders with his palm, and Patroclus' eyes whirled round and round. Then Phoebus Apollo threw the helmet off Patroclus' head, and the plumed and crested helmet rattled as it rolled beneath the horses' feet, and its horsehair crest was fouled with blood and dust. Before that time no god had suffered the helmet with its horsehair crest to be fouled with dust, but it had guarded the head and handsome brow of the godlike warrior Achilles. Now Zeus gave it to Hector to wear upon his head, but his death was close upon him. In Patroclus' hands the long-shadowed spear was shattered—all of it, heavy, huge, strong, well-tipped. From his shoulders the fringed shield with its strap fell to the ground, and his breastplate was undone by lord Apollo, son of Zeus. Doom seized his mind, and his glorious limbs grew feeble and he stood astounded. From close behind a Dardanian struck him with a sharp spear in the back between the shoulders, Panthous' son Euphorbus, who surpassed all of his age with the spear and in horsemanship and swiftness of foot. Even on that day he had brought down twenty men from their chariots, though coming with a chariot for the first time himself, learning the art of war. He it was who first cast a missile against you, horseman Patroclus, but did not slay you; rather, he ran back and mingled with the throng, dragging his ashen spear from your flesh, nor did he abide Patroclus even when unarmed in conflict. And Patroclus, overwhelmed by the god's blow and the spear, shrank back into the throng of his companions, avoiding his fate.

When Hector saw great-hearted Patroclus drawing back, wounded by the sharp bronze, he drew close to him through the lines and wounded him with his spear in the lower flank and drove the bronze through. He fell with a crash, and brought great sorrow to the host of the Achaeans. As when a lion has worsted a tireless boar in conflict, when, with high hearts, they battle for some scant spring upon a mountain's peaks and both would drink, and the lion with his might overcomes the quickly panting boar, so Hector, Priam's son, deprived Menoetius' brave son of his life with the spear, from close at hand, after he had slain many. Boasting, Hector spoke to him winged words: "Patroclus, surely you thought to reach our city and take away the day of freedom from the Trojan women and lead them in your ships to your own dear native land, fool that you are. Before them, Hector's swift horses stretch their feet to battle. And I myself am outstanding with the spear among the Trojans, I that ward off from them the day of doom. The vultures shall eat you here, poor wretch, nor shall Achilles, for all his valor, help you, he who, though he remained behind, doubtless gave you many an order as you went: 'Horse-driving Patroclus, come not back to my hollow ships until you split upon the breast of Hector his tunic red with blood.' So he doubtless spoke to you and moved your foolish heart."

Then in your weakness you addressed him, horseman Patroclus: "Great are your boasts now, Hector. For Zeus, Cronus' son, and Apollo have given you victory, they who slew me easily. For they themselves have stripped the armor from my shoulders, but if twenty like you had met they would all have perished here, slain by my spear. But a baneful fate and the son of Leto slew me, and, among men, Euphorbus. You are third in my slaying. Another thing I will tell you, and do you turn it over in your heart. You shall not yourself live long; already Death stands close beside you, and mighty fate, to be slain by the hands of Achilles, Aeacus' blameless son."

As he said this, the end of death enwrapped him, and his soul fled from his limbs and passed into the house of Death, bewailing its fate, forsaking manliness and youth. And glorious Hector spoke to him, even when dead: "Patroclus, why do you foretell sudden death for me? Who knows whether Achilles, son of fair-haired Thetis, will not be the first to lose his life, slain by my spear?"

So speaking, he set his heel upon him and drew the spear from the wound and pushed him from the spear upon his back. Immediately he set out with the spear after Automedon, the godlike squire of the swift-footed son of Aeacus, for he wished to smite him, but he was borne away by the swift, immortal horses that the gods gave as glorious gifts to Peleus.

BOOK XVII

Nor did Atreus' son Menelaus, dear to Ares, fail to see Patroclus slain in the conflict. He went through the front ranks armed in gleaming bronze and stood over Patroclus as a cow on her first bearing stands above her calf and lows, having known no birth before. So fair-haired Menelaus stood over Patroclus and held his spear and his balanced shield before him, eager to slay whoever should come to face him. Nor did Panthous' son Euphorbus with the good ashen spear fail to notice the fall of blameless Patroclus. He stood close by him and said to Menelaus, dear to Ares: "Zeus-nurtured son of Atreus, Menelaus, leader of the host, fall back, abandon the body, leave the bloodstained spoils. For none of the Trojans and their famous allies was before me in striking Patroclus with a spear in the mighty conflict. Therefore let me gain noble glory among the Trojans, lest I strike you and take away your honey-sweet life."

Greatly angered, fair-haired Menelaus said to him: "Father Zeus, it is not right to boast unduly. Neither the leopard's might nor the lion's nor that of the baleful-hearted boar, whose spirit in his breast beats highest in its strength, can equal the pride of the sons of Panthous with their good ashen spears. Mighty Hyperenor, the tamer of horses, did not profit by his youth when he scorned me to my face and said I was the worst warrior among the Danaans. Not on his own feet, I think, did he go to rejoice his wedded wife and goodly parents. So then shall I loose your might too, if you stand face to face with me. I bid you withdraw and fall back into the throng and stand not against me, before you suffer ill. But a thing done, even a fool can know."

So he spoke, but he could not persuade him, and Euphorbus said to him in answer: "Now, Zeus-nurtured Menelaus, you will surely atone for my brother whom you slew—and boasting you proclaim it—and you made his wife a widow in the chamber of their new home and brought his parents grief and lamentation indescribable. I should be a consolation to the poor souls in their mourning if I brought your head

270

and armor and put them in the hands of Panthous and godlike Phrontis. But the struggle shall no longer be untried nor
uncontested, whether in valor or in flight."

So speaking, he thrust at Menelaus' balanced shield. But
the bronze did not break through, and the point was bent
in the stout shield. Atreus' son Menelaus next lunged with
the bronze, praying to Father Zeus, and he struck him in
the lower throat as he drew back, and he pressed the blow
home, trusting in his heavy hand. The point passed straight
through his soft neck, and he fell with a crash and his armor clanged upon him. Blood wet his hair, fair as the Graces,
and his curling locks bound in gold and silver. As a man
rears a flourishing olive shoot in some lonely spot where
abundant water wets it, and it grows luxuriantly and the
blasts of all the winds shake it, and it swells with white
bloom, but a wind comes suddenly in a strong squall and
wrests it from its place and stretches it upon the earth, such
was Panthous' son Euphorbus of the good ashen spear when
Atreus' son Menelaus had slain him and stripped him of his
armor.

As when some mountain-nurtured lion, trusting in his valor,
seizes the best cow of a pasturing herd and takes her neck
first in his mighty teeth and breaks it, and then rends her
and gulps down her blood and all her entrails—around him
dogs and herdsmen shout wildly from a distance yet will
not draw close, for pale fear grips them hard—so the spirit
in the breasts of none of them dared face glorious Menelaus. Then Atreus' son would easily have borne off the glorious armor of Panthous' son had not Phoebus Apollo begrudged
him it and aroused against him Hector, like to swift Ares.
Apollo likened himself to a man, Mentes, leader of the Ci-
cones, and addressing Hector, spoke to him winged words:
"Hector, now you are running thus in hopeless pursuit of
the horses of the prudent son of Aeacus. They are hard for
mortal men to master and to drive, for any other than Achilles,
whom an immortal mother bore. Meanwhile, Menelaus,
Atreus' warlike son, bestriding Patroclus has slain the bravest
of the Trojans, Panthous' son Euphorbus, and has ended his
furious valor."

So speaking, the god went back through the strife of men,
and dreadful grief encompassed the black heart of Hector.
He glanced along the lines and at once recognized Menelaus
stripping off the glorious armor, and Euphorbus lying on the
ground, blood flowing from the wound that had been dealt

him. Then Hector went through the front lines, armed in gleaming bronze and shouting loudly, like Hephaestus' flame, that is unquenchable. Nor did his loud cry go unheard by Atreus' son. Angered, he said to his great-hearted soul: "Alas, if I leave the fair armor and Patroclus, who lies here for my honor's sake, I fear lest whoever of the Danaans see it blame me. But if, for very shame, I fight alone with Hector and the Trojans, I fear lest many surround me, who am but one. Hector of the glancing helmet is leading all the Trojans hither. But why does my soul say this to me? When a man wishes to fight against heaven's will with a mortal whom a god honors, soon a great woe is rolled upon him. Therefore none of the Danaans will censure me if he sees me yielding before Hector, since he fights with a god behind him. But if I could find Ajax, good at the war cry, the two of us would go back and remember valor, even against a god, in the hope that we might drag away the body for Achilles, Peleus' son. That would be the least of evils."

While he debated this in heart and mind, the Trojans' lines advanced and Hector led them. Menelaus fell back and left the body, turning frequently about like a well-maned lion, which dogs and men drive from a farmyard with spears and shouts; his valiant heart is chilled within his breast, but he leaves the yard unwillingly. So fair-haired Menelaus fell back from Patroclus, but turned and stopped when he reached the throng of his companions, looking for great Ajax, Telamon's son. At once he caught clear sight of him on the left of the whole battle, encouraging his comrades and urging them on to fight, for Phoebus Apollo had inspired a dreadful fear in them. Menelaus started running, and when he reached him said immediately: "Ajax, let us hasten this way, dear friend, to the dead Patroclus, in the hope that we may bear at least his naked body to Achilles; for Hector of the glancing helmet has his armor."

So he spoke, and aroused the spirit of prudent Ajax. He went through the front ranks, and fair-haired Menelaus went beside him. When Hector had taken the glorious armor from Patroclus, he dragged him off, that he might cut the head from his shoulders with the sharp bronze and might carry the body away and give it to the Trojan dogs. But Ajax drew near, bearing his shield that was like a city wall, and Hector went and drew back into the throng of his companions and mounted his chariot and gave the fair armor to the Trojans to bear to the city, to be his own great glory. Ajax held his broad shield over Menoetius' son and stood like a lion over his cubs when huntsmen meet him as he leaves the young ones in a wood, and he exults in his strength and draws down his whole brow, hiding his eyes. So Ajax bestrode heroic Patroclus, and Atreus' son, Menelaus, dear to Ares, stood on the other side, nursing great sorrow in his breast.

Glaucus, Hippolochus' leader of the Lycians, looked scornfully at Hector and rebuked him with harsh words: "Hector, best in looks, you are sadly lacking in battle. Your noble reputation is false, for you are a coward. Consider now how you may save the city and its stronghold alone with the soldiers born in Ilium. For none of the Lycians at least will go to fight the Danaans for the city's sake, since there has been no thanks for fighting always pitilessly against the foe. How could you save a worse mortal in the throng, coward, when you left your friend and comrade Sarpedon to be a prey and booty to the Argives—a man who was a great help both to the city and to yourself while he was living? But now you have not even courage to protect him from dogs. Therefore, if any of the Lycian warriors will obey me, we shall go home, and utter destruction shall appear for Troy. If only there were now in the Trojans might and courage immovable, such as enters into men who for their native land face toil and battle with the foe, we should at once drag Patroclus into Ilium. And if he should come in death to the great city of King Priam and we should drag him from the battle, the Argives would at once release the fair armor of Sarpedon and we could take his body into Ilium. For dead is the squire of that man who is far the bravest among Argives by the ships and among their close-fighting squires. But you did not dare stand face to face with greathearted Ajax, meeting his eye in the clamor of the foe, nor to fight squarely against him, since he is better than you."

Hector of the glancing helmet looked at him scornfully and said: "Glaucus, why, being what you are, do you speak with insolence? My friend, I thought you the superior in wisdom to all others who dwell in fertile Lycia; but now I scorn your sense completely, so you talk, saying that I do not abide huge Ajax. I fear not, I assure you, battle or din of horses. But the mind of aegis-bearing Zeus is ever stronger, who sometimes puts even a brave man to flight and easily takes victory away, yet sometimes of himself urges a man to battle. Come here, friend, stand by me and watch the work, whether I shall be a coward all day long, as you say, or whether I shall hold back some one of the Danaans, though he be eager in valor to fight for the dead Patroclus."

So speaking, he called to the Trojans with a mighty shout: "Trojans and Lycians and close-fighting Dardanians, be men, my friends, and remember furious valor until I put on the fair armor of blameless Achilles, which I took by force from Patroclus when I slew him."

So speaking, Hector of the glancing helmet went forth from fierce war. He ran, and following his comrades on swift feet found them very quickly, not yet far away, as they were bearing to the city the glorious arms of Peleus' son. He stood apart from lamentable battle and exchanged the armor. His own he gave to the war-loving Trojans to bear to holy Ilium, and he donned the immortal armor of Achilles, Peleus' son, which the heavenly gods had given his dear father, and Peleus, aging, gave it to his son; but the son did not grow old in his father's armor.

As Zeus the cloud-gatherer saw him from afar, clad in the armor of the godlike son of Peleus, he shook his head and said to his own spirit: "Wretched man, no thought of death have you, though it draws near you. But you don the immortal armor of a noble hero, before whom others tremble. His comrade you slew, gentle and strong, and stripped the armor from his head and shoulders in no seemly fashion. However, for the present I will grant you great power as a recompense for the fact that Andromache shall not receive from you, as you come home from battle, the glorious armor of the son of Peleus."

So spoke the son of Cronus, and nodded his black brow, and changed the armor to fit Hector's body. Ares, the dread god of battle, entered into him, and his limbs were filled within by valor and might. After his famous allies he sped, shouting loudly, and appeared to them all-gleaming in the armor of Peleus' great-hearted son. He went and stirred each with words, Mesthles and Glaucus and Medon and Thersilochus and Asteropaeus and Deisenor and Hippothous and Phorcys and Chromius and Ennomus, the augur. Stirring them up, he spoke winged words: "Hear me, ye myriads of tribes of allies who dwell round about us. Not because I wanted numbers or needed them did I gather each of you here from your cities, but so that you might eagerly defend the Trojans' wives and their tender children from the war-loving Achaeans. With this purpose I exhaust my people for gifts and food and enlarge the heart of each of you. Therefore, turning now straight forward, let each man find death or safety, for so ends war's dalliance. Whoever drags Patroclus, dead though he be, into the midst of the horse-taming Trojans, and Ajax yields to him, shall receive from me half the spoils, and half I myself shall have, and his glory shall be as great as mine."

So he spoke, and they at once charged heavily on the Achaeans, lifting their spears. Their hearts greatly hoped to drag the body away from beneath Ajax, Telamon's son, fools that they were. Many were those whose lives he took away over Patroclus. Then Ajax said to Menelaus of the mighty war cry: "Dear friend, Zeus-nurtured Menelaus, I have no longer any hope that we two by ourselves shall get home again from war. Nor do I fear so much for Patroclus' body, which shall soon sate the Trojans' dogs and birds, as I fear for my own head, lest aught befall it, and for yours, since Hector, cloud of war, envelops everything, and before us utter destruction looms. Come, call the bravest of the Danaans, if any will give ear."

So he spoke, nor did Menelaus of the mighty war cry fail to heed him. He called out clearly, shouting to the Danaans: "Dear leaders and counselors of the Argives, you that with Atreus' sons, Agamemnon and Menelaus, drink at the common cost and each command your soldiers—and honor and glory from Zeus attend you—it is difficult for me to search out each of the leaders, so great a strife of war is kindled. But let each come of himself and have shame at heart that Patroclus should become a sport of Trojan dogs."

So he spoke, and swift Ajax, Oileus' son, gave sharp attention and was first to come running toward him through the strife, and after him Idomeneus and Idomeneus' squire Meriones, like man-slaying Enyalius. Who could carry in his mind the names of the rest who after these roused the battle of the Achaeans?

The Trojans pressed forward in a mass, and Hector led them. As when at the mouth of some swift river fed by Zeus a great wave roars against the stream, and the high rocks shout around as the brine spurts upward, with such a shout the Trojans marched. But the Achaeans stood around Menoetius' son with one spirit, fenced by their shields of bronze. Cronus' son poured a thick mist over their bright crests, since he had been no foe of Menoetius' son before, while he was living and was the squire of the son of Aeacus. Zeus hated to see him become the prey of Trojan dogs at his foes' hands. Therefore he roused his comrades to defend him.

First the Trojans drove back the bright-eyed Achaeans, who left the body and fell trembling back. Yet the high-hearted Trojans slew none of them with their spears, eager though they were, but tried to drag away the body. But the Achaeans were to be absent but for a short time, for very quickly Ajax rallied them, he who after Peleus' blameless son surpassed the other Danaans in looks and deeds. He went through the front lines in valor like a wild boar, which easily scatters dogs and bold youths upon the mountains as it turns upon them in the glens. So the son of noble Telamon, glorious Ajax, easily strode among the Trojans' ranks and scattered them who had moved about Patroclus and had highest hopes of dragging him to their city and of winning fame.

The glorious son of Pelasgic Lethus, Hippothous, dragged the body by one foot through the mighty conflict, binding a strap around the ankle sinews, doing pleasure to Hector and the Trojans. Evil at once befell him, which no one could ward off, eager though he were. Telamon's son rushed upon him through the throng and struck him. at close quarters through his helmet with its cheek pieces of bronze. The helmet, with its thick horsehair crest, broke beneath the spear point, struck by a good spear and a sturdy hand. The bloody brains gushed up to the spear's socket through the wound, and his might was loosed and he let the foot of great-hearted Patroclus fall from his hands to the ground, and fell himself close to him, face forward on the body, far from fertile Larissa; nor did he repay to his dear parents the cost of his nurture, and his life was short as he fell by the spear of great-hearted Ajax.

Hector in turn thrust at Ajax with his shining spear, but Ajax looked up and dodged the spear by but a little; but Hector hit Schedius, great-hearted Iphitus' son, by far the best of the Phocians, who had his home in famed Panopeus, ruling over many men—he struck him below the center of the collarbone, and the sharp bronze point drove straight through beside the lower part of his shoulder. He fell with a crash, and his armor clanged upon him.

Ajax in turn hit Phorcys, Phaenops' prudent son, in the center of the belly as he stood above Hippothous. He broke the convex portion of his breastplate and the bronze pierced his entrails. He fell in the dust and clutched the earth with outstretched hand. At that the front lines and glorious Hector fell back, and the Argives gave a mighty cheer and dragged away the dead men, Phorcys and Hippothous, and stripped the armor from their shoulders.

Then the Trojans, overcome by cowardice before the Achaeans, dear to Ares, would have entered Ilium, and the Argives would have won glory even beyond the fate of Zeus by their own strength and might. But Apollo himself aroused Aeneas, likening himself to Periphas the herald, Epytus' son, who at his old father's side was growing old as herald, wise at heart with kindly wisdom. Likening himself to him, Apollo, son of Zeus, said to Aeneas: "Aeneas, how could you ever protect steep Ilium against the will of a god like other heroes I have seen trusting in their strength and might and in their manhood and in their numbers, though their people were but few? Zeus wishes victory to us far more than to the Danaans, yet you tremble constantly and will not fight."

So he spoke, and Aeneas looked at him and knew unerring Apollo and cried out to Hector with a mighty shout: "Hector, and you other leaders of the Trojans and allies, shameful this is now, to enter Ilium overcome by cowardice before the Achaeans, dear to Ares. Even now some one of the gods stands by me and says that highest Zeus, deviser of battle, has come to our aid. So let us march straight on the Danaans, nor let them bear the dead Patroclus to the ships in peace."

So he spoke, and leaped forward far beyond the foremost ranks and took his stand. They rallied and stood to face the Achaeans. Then Aeneas wounded with his spear Laeocritus, Arisbas' son, the noble comrade of Lycomedes. And as he fell, Lycomedes, dear to Ares, pitied him and went and stood close by him and cast his shining spear and hit Hippasus' son Apisaon, shepherd of the people, in the liver, below the midriff, and his knees were loosed at once. He had come from fertile Paeonia and was the best in battle after Asteropaeus.

As he fell, warlike Asteropaeus pitied him and rushed with eagerness to battle with the Danaans, but he could succeed no longer, for they had closed in with their shields on every side, standing about Patroclus, and held their shields before them. For Ajax had gone to all of them with many orders. He ordered that none draw back from the corpse, and none stand to fight beyond the rest of the Achaeans, but that they should stand firm about him and give battle hand to hand. So huge Ajax ordered, and the ground grew wet with crimson blood, and the corpses of Trojans and high-spirited allies and Danaans alike fell close together, nor did the latter fight a bloodless battle, yet far fewer perished, for they remembered ever to ward off from one another grim destruction in the throng.

So they fought, like blazing fire, nor could you call the sun safe, nor the moon, for they were veiled in battle's cloud, where the bravest stood about the dead son of Menoetius. The other Trojans and well-greaved Achaeans fought unmolested under the clear sky, and the sharp rays of the sun spread over them, and no cloud rose from all the earth or mountains. They fought, then rested, and stood far from each other, shunning each other's grief-laden missiles. But those in the center suffered woe from darkness and from war, and were tormented by the pitiless bronze—all who were the bravest. But two men had not yet heard of blameless Patroclus' death, two valiant men, Thrasymedes and Antilochus, who still thought he was fighting with the Trojans, alive amid the din of the front ranks. These two, guarding against the death and rout of their companions, were fighting far away, since Nestor had so commanded when he sent them from the black ships to war.

As for the rest, the great contest of their bitter strife arose throughout the day. Each man's knees and shins and feet below, and his hands and eyes, were smeared with sweat and weariness as they strove ever mercilessly over the brave squire of Aeacus' swift-footed son. As when a man gives the hide of a great bull to the people to stretch, all soaked with fat, and they take it and stand about in a circle stretching it, and the moisture disappears at once, and the fat soaks in, as many pull, and it is all stretched thoroughly, so both sides dragged the corpse this way and that, in a small space. They hoped eagerly at heart, the Trojans to drag it to Ilium, the Acheans to drag it to the hollow ships, and a wild turmoil rose round about it; nor could Ares who rouses the nations, nor Athena, find fault with the fight on seeing it, not even if very angry.

So bitter a conflict of men and horses did Zeus stretch that day over Patroclus. Nor even yet did godlike Achilles know Patroclus to be dead, for they were fighting far from the swift ships, beneath the Trojans' wall. Hence he never imagined in his heart that Patroclus was dead but that having pressed forward to the gates he would come back alive, since he did not in the least expect that they would sack the city without him, or even with him, for he had often heard this from his mother, listening apart, when she reported to him the plan of mighty Zeus. But indeed his mother had not told him then how much evil was ordained, that his very dearest friend was doomed.

But the others continually crowded forward with their pointed spears about the body and slew each other. And thus would one of the bronze-clad Achaeans say: "My friends, no glory to us would it be to go back to the hollow ships; sooner may the black earth open for us here. That would be far better for us, if we give up this man to the horse-taming Trojans to drag to their city and win glory."

And thus in turn would some one of the great-hearted Trojans exclaim: "My friends, even if it be fated that we all alike must die beside this man, let no one yet fall back from battle."

So someone would say, and rouse the might of each. So they fought, and the iron din rose to a heaven of bronze through the barren air. The horses of the son of Aeacus, far from the battle, wept when first they learned their driver had fallen in the dust before man-slaying Hector. Automedon, Diores' valiant son, struck them often with the quick whip and addressed them many times with gentle words and many times with threats, but they would neither go back to the ships by the Hellespont, nor would they follow the Achaeans into battle, but as a pillar holds firm that stands upon the tomb of some dead man or woman, so firmly they remained with the fair chariot, dropping their heads to the ground, and warm tears fell from their eyelids to the earth as they mourned in their sorrow for their driver, and their thick manes were wet where they flowed beside the pads beneath the yoke on either side.

The son of Cronus pitied them when he saw them mourning, and shook his head, saying to his heart: "Unhappy ones, why did we give you to King Peleus, a mortal, whereas you are age-less and immortal? Was it that you might suffer sorrow among unhappy men? For nothing is more wretched than man, of all the things that breathe and walk upon the earth. Hector, Priam's son, shall not drive you and your skillfully wrought chariot; no, for I will not allow it. Is it not enough that he has the armor and boasts vainly? I will put might into your knees and hearts, that you many bear Automedon in safety from the battle to the hollow ships, for I will give the Trojans glory still to slay and slay until they reach the well-benched ships and the sun sets and holy twilight falls."

So speaking, he breathed strong might into the horses. Shaking the dust from their manes onto the ground, they lightly bore the swift chariot toward the Trojans and Achaeans. And Automedon fought against the Trojans, though grieved for his companion, dashing with the horses like a vulture after geese. For lightly would he flee from the Trojans' battle din; then lightly rush upon them pressing through the numerous throng. But he could not slay men when he rushed in their pursuit, for being alone in the sacred chariot he could not attack with his spear and hold in the swift horses. At last a comrade saw him, Alcimedon, son of Laerces, Haemon's son. He stood behind the chariot and called to Automedon: "Automedon, what god put vain counsel in your heart and took away your good sense, so that you fight thus alone in the first line of combat with the Trojans? Your comrade has been slain, and Hector himself rejoices, wearing on his shoulders the armor of the son of Aeacus."

Automedon, Diores' son, addressed him: "Alcimedon, what other of the Achaeans is your peer to tame and guide the immortal horses' might?—except Patroclus, equal of a god in wisdom while he lived. But now death and fate have found him out. Take you the whip and gleaming reins, and I will dismount from the chariot to fight."

So he spoke, and Alcimedon mounted the swift chariot and quickly grasped the whip and reins, and Automedon leaped down. Glorious Hector noticed it and quickly said to Aeneas, who was close at hand: "Aeneas, counselor of the bronze-clad Trojans, I noticed there the horses of Aeacus' swift-footed son appearing in battle with bad drivers. I might hope to capture them if you are willing in your heart, since if the two of us attacked they would not dare to stand and face us and give battle."

So he spoke, nor did the brave son of Anchises disobey him, and the two went forward, their shoulders covered with tough, dry ox hide with much bronze wrought upon it. Chromius and godlike Aretus both went with them, and their hearts hoped greatly to slay the men and drive away the proud-necked horses—fools, for not unbloodied were they to turn back from Automedon. The latter offered a prayer to Father Zeus, and his black breast was filled with strength and valor. At once he addressed Alcimedon, his

faithful comrade: "Alcimedon, do not hold the horses far
from me, but breathing on my very back. For I do not think
that Hector, Priam's son, will check his might before he
slay us and mount Achilles' fair-maned horses and rout the
ranks of Argive heroes or himself be slain among the foremost."

So speaking, he called the Ajaxes and Menelaus: "Ajaxes,
leaders of the Argives, and Menelaus, entrust the body to
the bravest to stand over it and ward off the ranks of heroes;
and from us, the living, too, ward off the cruel day. For
hither through tearful war charge Hector and Aeneas, who
are the bravest of the Trojans. But these things lie upon the
knees of the gods; I shall make my cast; the rest shall be
the care of Zeus."

So speaking, he drew back his long-shadowed spear and
cast it and struck the balanced shield of Aretus. The shield
did not ward off the spear, and the bronze pierced through
and drove into his lower belly through his belt. As when a
strong man with a sharp ax strikes a pastured ox behind the
horns and cuts through all the sinew and the ox falls, leaping
forward, so he leaped forward and fell on his back, and the
spear, quivering with all its sharpness in his bowels, loosed
his limbs. Then Hector hurled his shining spear against Automedon, but the latter looked up and dodged the brazen
spear, for he bent forward, and the long shaft plunged into
the ground behind him, and the spear butt quivered. Then
and there mighty Ares stilled its might. Then they would
have rushed at one another hand to hand with swords, had
not the two Ajaxes parted them for all their eagerness.
Through the throng they came, upon their comrade's summons, and Hector and Aeneas and godlike Chromius drew
back in fear of them and left Aretus lying there, wounded
at heart. Automedon, like swift Ares, stripped off his armor
and spoke a boasting word: "I have eased my heart a little
of its grief for the slain son of Menoetius, though I have
slain a man inferior."

So speaking, he took the bloody spoils and put them in the
chariot and mounted it himself, his feet all bloodied and his
hands above, like a lion which has devoured a bull.

Once more above Patroclus the mighty strife was joined,
grievous and tearful, and Athena roused the conflict, coming
down from heaven, for far-thundering Zeus had sent her to
arouse the Danaans, for now his will had turned. As Zeus
stretches a bright rainbow in heaven for mortals, to be an

omen of war or a chill storm that stops men from their work on earth and harms the flocks, so wrapping herself in a dark cloud she entered the army of the Achaeans and aroused each man. First she spoke to stir up Atreus' son, mighty Menelaus—for he was near her—likening herself in body and unwearying voice to Phoenix: "It will be a shame and a reproach to you, Menelaus, if the swift dogs drag the faithful comrade of noble Achilles beneath the Trojans' wall. Hold stoutly, and urge on all the host."

And Menelaus of the mighty war cry said to her: "Phoenix, ancient, aged father, would that Athena would give me the strength and would ward off the rain of missiles; then I should be willing to stand by and guard Patroclus, for his death greatly grieved my heart. But Hector has the dreadful might of fire and never leaves off slaying with bronze, for Zeus gives him the glory."

So he spoke, and the bright-eyed goddess Athena rejoiced, that to her first of all the gods he prayed. She put might in his shoulders and his knees, and in his breast the daring of the fly, which though brushed off desires still to bite a man's flesh, and human blood is its delight. Such a creature's courage filled his black heart, and he bestrode Patroclus and cast his shining spear. There was among the Trojans one called Podes, son of Eëtion, a rich and valiant man. Hector honored him most of all the people, since he was his dear companion at the feast. Him fair-haired Menelaus struck in the belt, as he rushed on in flight, and the bronze drove straight through. He fell with a crash; but Menelaus, Atreus' son, dragged the body from among the Trojans into the midst of his companions.

Then Apollo urged Hector on, standing close by in the shape of Phaenops, Asius' son, who of all his friends abroad was dearest to him, dwelling in Abydus. Likening himself to him, Apollo the Warder said: "Hector, who else among the Achaeans could fear you any longer when you have fled thus from Menelaus, who was before now a soft spearman? Now he has alone snatched a corpse and gone with it from the Trojans' midst and slain your faithful comrade, a brave man among the foremost ranks, Podes, Eëtion's son."

So he spoke, and a black cloud of grief enveloped Hector, and he went through the front ranks armed in gleaming bronze. Then the son of Cronus took the flashing, tassled aegis and hid Ida behind clouds and gave a mighty flash and thunderclap and shook the aegis and gave victory to the Trojans, but the Achaeans he drove in rout.

First to begin the rout was Peneleos the Boeotian. For he was wounded by a grazing blow on the top of his shoulder as he turned ever forward, and the spear of Polydamas cut him to the bone, for Polydamas had hurled it from close at hand. And Leitus, too, did Hector wound in the wrist from close at hand—great-hearted Alectryon's son—and stopped him from combat. He looked about with a shudder, since he no longer hoped in heart to fight the Trojans, spear in hand. But as Hector rushed after Leitus, Idomeneus struck him in the breastplate on the chest, beside the nipple. The long spear broke in the shaft, and the Trojans shouted. Then Hector cast his spear at Idomeneus, Deucalion's son, as he stood in his chariot, but missed him by a little. However he hit Coeranus, Meriones' squire and charioteer, who had come with him from goodly Lyctus—for Meriones came at first on foot when he left the curved ships, and would have given great glory to the Trojans, had not Coeranus quickly driven up the swift horses. He came as the light to him and warded off the cruel day, but himself lost his life before man-slaying Hector, who hit him beneath the jaw and ear, and the spear point knocked his teeth out and cut his tongue in two. He fell from the chariot and dropped the reins to the ground. Meriones bent down and picked them up from the plain in his own hand and said to Idomeneus: "Ply the lash, now, until you come to the swift ships. You yourself know that the strength of the Achaeans is no more."

So he spoke, and Idomeneus lashed the fair-maned horses to the hollow ships, for indeed fear fell upon his soul.

Zeus did not escape the notice of great-hearted Ajax and Menelaus when he gave decisive victory to the Trojans. Great Telamonian Ajax was the first to speak: "Now even a very fool could know that Father Zeus himself supports the Trojans. All their missiles hit the mark, whoever hurls them, be he bad or good; Zeus guides them all alike; whereas all ours fall to the ground in vain. Even so, let us consider the best plan, how we shall both drag off the body and ourselves get home to be a joy to our dear comrades, who surely are distressed as they look hither and think that man-slaying Hector's might and invincible hands will not halt again, but will fall upon the swift ships. Would there were some comrade to report this with all speed to Peleus' son, since I believe he has not even

learned the bitter news that his dear friend is dead. But
I cannot see such a man among the Achaeans, for men and
horses both are veiled in mist. Father Zeus, save the sons of
the Achaeans from the cloud, and clear the skies, and
grant our eyes to see. Slay us in light, since to slay us is
now thy pleasure."

So he spoke, and the Father pitied him as he shed tears.
At once he scattered the mist and pushed away the cloud.
The sun shone forth, and all the battle was revealed. Then
Ajax said to Menelaus of the mighty war cry: "Look now,
Zeus-nurtured Menelaus, if possibly you may see Antilochus
still living, great-hearted Nestor's son. Urge him to go swiftly
to wise-hearted Achilles to say that his dearest friend is dead."

So he spoke, and Menelaus of the mighty war cry did not
disobey. He set out like a lion from a farmyard, a lion
weary of worrying the dogs and men who watch all night
and will not let him choose the fattest cattle. Eager for
meat, he advances, but in vain, for a hail of javelins from
stout arms meets him, and blazing faggots, which he fears
for all his haste; and at dawn he departs with murderous
heart. So Menelaus of the mighty war cry left Patroclus,
much against his will. For he feared greatly lest the Achaeans
in their grievous rout might leave Patroclus as booty to the
foe. He gave many an order to Meriones and the Ajaxes:
"Ajaxes, leaders of the Argives, and Meriones, let each man
now remember poor Patroclus' gentleness. For he knew how
to be kind to all while living, but now death and fate have
found him out."

So speaking, fair-haired Menelaus departed, glancing in
all directions, like an eagle, which they say sees most keenly
of all winged creatures under heaven. A swift-footed hare,
cowering under a leafy bush, cannot escape its eye, even
when it is far above, and it swoops down upon him and
quickly seizes him and takes his life. So then your eyes,
Zeus-nurtured Menelaus, turned gleaming everywhere among
the throng of your many companions, hoping to see the
son of Nestor still alive. Quickly they saw him on the left
of all the battle, encouraging his comrades and urging them
on to fight. Standing close beside him, fair-haired Menelaus
said: "Antilochus, come here, Zeus-nurtured, that you may
hear grim tidings, that I wish had not befallen. For I think that
you yourself have already seen and known that the god is
sending a flood of war upon the Danaans and that victory
is the Trojans'. The best of the Achaeans is slain—Patroclus

—and great grief has fallen upon the Danaans. Do you run quickly to the ships of the Achaeans and tell Achilles, in the hope that he may with all speed bring the naked body in safety to the ship. But as for the armor, Hector of the glancing helmet has it."

So he spoke, and Antilochus was struck with horror as he heard the news. Long was he speechless, and his eyes were filled with tears, and his mighty voice was choked. Yet not even so did he neglect the command of Menelaus. He went running off and gave his armor to his blameless comrade Laodocus, who turned the single-hoofed horses for him close at hand.

His feet bore him weeping from the battle, to take the evil tidings to Peleus' son Achilles. Nor was your spirit willing, Zeus-nurtured Menelaus, to defend the hard-pressed companions from whom Antilochus departed, and the Pylians missed him much. But Menelaus sent godlike Thrasymedes to them, and himself went back to the heroic Patroclus. He ran and stood beside the Ajaxes and said to them at once: "I have sent him to the swift ships, to go to swift-footed Achilles. Yet I do not think Achilles will come now, for all his wrath at godlike Hector. For he could not fight naked with the Trojans. Let us devise the wisest plan, so that we may drag away the body and ourselves escape from death and fate amid the Trojans' tumult."

Then great Telamonian Ajax answered him: "All you have said is fitting, most glorious Menelaus. Do you and Meriones stoop down right quickly and raise the body and bear it from the strife. Meanwhile we two behind you will fight the Trojans and godlike Hector, like-named, like-hearted, even as formerly we stood together and abode sharp Ares."

So he spoke, and they raised the body in their arms, high, high above the earth. The Trojan host behind them shouted to see the Achaeans lift the body, and they rushed on them like dogs who rush before hunters on a wounded boar. For a time they run, eager to rend him, but when, sure of his strength, he turns upon them, they draw back and flee in fear in all directions. So the Trojans for a time followed in an endless throng, thrusting with swords and spears sharp at both ends, but when the Ajaxes turned and stood to face them, their color changed and none dared rush forward to do battle for the corpse.

So hastily they bore the body from battle to the hollow ships. And war raged against them fierce as a fire that rises and rushes on a city of men in sudden conflagration, and the houses shrivel in the mighty flame, and the wind's force sets it roaring. So the unceasing din of horses and of spearmen followed them as they came on. As mules, putting forth great strength, draw from a mountain down a rocky path a beam or a great ship's timber, and their heart is racked with weariness and sweat as they hasten on, so hastily they bore the corpse. In the rear, the Ajaxes held back the foe, as a wooded headland, stretching through a plain, holds back the water, and even holds the troublous streams of mighty rivers and deflects at once the currents of all to wander over the plain, nor can they break it, though they flow with all their might. So the Ajaxes ever kept back the Trojans' battle, but the latter followed close upon them, two most of all: Aeneas, Anchises' son, and glorious Hector. As a cloud of starlings or of jackdaws flies screaming incessantly when they see a hawk approaching, which brings death to small birds, so the warriors of the Achaeans went screaming incessantly before Aeneas and Hector and forgot the conflict. Many fair weapons fell round about the ditch, as the Danaans fled, but there was no pause in the battle.

BOOK XVIII

SO THEY FOUGHT, like blazing fire, but swift-footed Antilochus went with his message to Achilles. He found him before the straight-horned ships, imagining in his heart those things which had indeed befallen. In his grief, Achilles said to his great-hearted soul: "Alas, why are the long-haired Achaeans rushing again in wild confusion toward the ships across the plain? May the gods not bring to pass the bitter sorrow to my heart that my mother once foretold me, when she said that the bravest of the Myrmidons would leave the sun's light at the Trojans' hands while I was yet alive. Menoetius' valiant son is surely dead, unhappy man, yet I bade him come back to the ships when he had driven off the blazing fire, and not to strive in might with Hector."

While he pondered thus in heart and mind, the son of noble Nestor drew close to him, shedding warm tears, and told his bitter news: "Alas, son of prudent Peleus, sad is the message you shall hear, which I would had never happened. Patroclus lies dead, and they are fighting above his naked body. But as for the armor, Hector of the glancing helmet has it."

So he spoke, and a dark cloud of grief enwrapped the other. In both his hands he took black dust and poured it on his head and fouled his handsome face. Dark ashes settled on his fragrant shirt. Vast in the dust he vastly lay and tore his tumbled hair with his own hands. The servant women whom Achilles and Patroclus had borne off as booty grieved at heart and set up a loud keening and ran out the door and gathered about prudent Achilles and all beat their hands upon their breasts, and the limbs of each were loosed beneath her. On the other side, Antilochus shed tears of grief, holding Achilles' hands, for he feared lest he cut his throat with the iron, so groaned his noble heart. Dreadfully he cried aloud in grief, and his queenly mother heard him, as she sat in the depths of the sea beside her aged father. Then she wailed, and the goddesses gathered round her, all Nereus' daughters who were in the deep. There were Glauce and Thaleia and Cymodoce, Nesaea and Speio, and Thoe and ox-eyed Halia, and Cymothoe and Actaea and Limnoreia and Melite and Iaera and Amphithoe and Agave, Doto and Proto and Pherousa and Dynamene, Dexamene and Amphinome and Callianeira, Doris and Panope and far-famed Galateia, Nemertes and Apseudes and Callianassa. There were Clymene and Ianeira and Ianassa, Moira and Oreithyia and fair-tressed Amatheia, and the rest of Nereus' daughters who were in the ocean's depths. The silver-shining cave was full of them. All beat their breasts, and Thetis led their lamentations: "Listen, sister Nereids, that you may all hear and know well what woes are in my heart. Unhappy that I am, who to my bane have borne a hero. For I bore a blameless and a mighty son, above all heroes. He shot up like a sapling. Him whom I had reared, like a tree on the orchard's slope, I sent in the curved ships to Ilium to battle with the Trojans. I shall not welcome him returning home to Peleus' house. Yet while he lives and looks on the sun's light, he suffers, nor can I help him though I go to him. But I will go to see my dear child and hear what grief has come upon him as he stayed away from war."

So she spoke, and left the cave, and they went with her, weeping, and about them broke a billow of the sea. When they came to fertile Troy, they climbed together up the shore where the ships of the Myrmidons were drawn up in close ranks about swift Achilles. His queenly mother stood beside him, as he groaned heavily, and with a sharp cry she took her son's head in her hands and mourning spoke to him winged words: "Child, why do you weep? What grief has come upon your heart? Speak out; do not conceal it. Zeus has granted what you prayed for with uplifted hands, that all the sons of the Achaeans might be hemmed in at the ships' sterns, for need of you, and that they might suffer things unwished for."

And groaning heavily, swift-footed Achilles said to her: "Mother, those prayers the Olympian has fulfilled for me. But what pleasure is there for me in these things when my dear comrade is dead?—Patroclus, whom I honored beyond all my comrades, as much as my own head. Him I have lost; and his gigantic armor, a wonder to behold, and fair, Hector stripped from him when he slew him. The gods gave it as a glorious gift to Peleus on that day when first they placed you in a mortal warrior's bed. Would you had dwelt there amid the sea's immortals and Peleus had wed a mortal wife. Now they have otherwise ordained, that the grief within your breast may be past measure for your son when he shall die, he whom you shall not welcome coming home again, since my spirit will not let me live nor mix with men unless Hector be first smitten by my spear and lose his life and pay for his slaying and despoiling of Menoetius' son Patroclus."

Thetis answered him in tears: "You will be swift of doom, my child, from what you say. For your fate is appointed straightway after Hector."

In great distress, swift-footed Achilles said to her: "May I die at once, since I was not to protect my comrade at his slaying. Very far from his native land he perished, and lacked for me to be the warder-off of doom. Now, since I shall not go to my dear native land, nor was I the light of deliverance to Patroclus nor to my other comrades who were slain in multitudes by glorious Hector, but sit beside the ships a useless burden of the earth—I who am in battle such as no other of the bronze-clad Achaeans, though there are others better in council—may strife perish from the midst of gods and men, and anger, which brings to rage even the wisest, and sweeter far than flowing honey grows like smoke within men's breasts. So Agamemnon, king of men, just now aroused my anger—but let us skip the past, however grieved, quelling perforce the spirits in our breasts. Now I go to find Hector, the slayer of that dear head. My fate I will accept whenever Zeus and the other immortal gods desire to accomplish it. Not even the mighty Heracles escaped his fate, though he was most dear to lord Zeus, Cronus' son. But fate and the bitter wrath of Hera overcame him. So I as well, if a like fate be set for me, shall lie when I shall fall. But now may I gain a noble glory and bring loud weeping to some one of the deep-bosomed daughters of Tros or Dardanus as she wipes the tears from her soft cheeks with both her hands, and may they know that I have long refrained from war. Keep me not from battle, though you love me, nor shall you so persuade me."

Then the silver-footed goddess Thetis answered him: "It is in truth no evil thing, my child, to ward off utter destruction from one's hard-pressed comrades. But your fair, gleaming armor of bronze is in the hands of Trojans; Hector of the glancing helmet himself rejoices to wear it on his shoulders. Yet I do not think he will long glory in it, since death is close upon him. But go not yet into the mill of Ares, until you see me coming hither. For with the dawn and rising sun I shall come bearing you fair arms from lord Hephaestus."

So speaking, she left her son, and turning to her sisters of the sea she said: "Do you plunge into the sea's broad bosom, to visit the old man of the sea and the house of our father, and tell him everything. I am going to high Olympus, to Hephaestus the famous craftsman, in the hope he may be willing to give my son glorious, radiant armor."

So she spoke, and they at once plunged beneath the billow of the sea, but the silver-footed goddess Thetis went to Olympus, to bring to her dear son the glorious armor.

Her feet bore her to Olympus, while the Achaeans, fleeing before Hector with a dreadful shout, came to the ships and the Hellespont. Nor were the well-greaved Achaeans likely to have dragged the body of Patroclus, squire of Ares, out of the range of missiles, for he was found again by soldiers and chariots and by Hector, Priam's son, in valor like a flame. Thrice glorious Hector grasped him by the feet from behind, eager to drag him off, and loud the Trojans cheered. Thrice the two Ajaxes, clothed in furious valor, drove them back from the body. But Hector, sure in his courage, would now rush upon them through the din, and now would stand and give a mighty shout, but he fell not back at all. As shepherds of the farm cannot drive back from a dead body a tawny lion, greatly hungered, so the two crested Ajaxes could not frighten Hector, Priam's son, from the corpse. Now he would have dragged it off and won glory unquenchable had not swift, wing-footed Iris come running to Peleus' son with a message to prepare himself for battle. She came without Zeus' knowledge or that of the other gods, for Hera sent her. Close by she stood and spoke winged words: "Up, son of Peleus, most dreadful of all warriors. Protect Patroclus, for whose sake a dreadful strife is joined before the ships. They are slaying one another, some defending his dead body, whereas the others, the Trojans, rush up to carry it away toward wind-swept Ilium. Glorious Hector is most eager to drag it off; his spirit bids him cut the head from the soft neck and impale it upon stakes. Up, lie here no longer. Let shame fall on your soul that Patroclus should become a sport for Trojan dogs. Yours the disgrace if his corpse return defiled."

Swift-footed, godlike Achilles answered her: "Goddess Iris, who of the gods sent thee as a messenger to me?"

Wing-footed, swift Iris said to him in turn: "Hera sent me, the glorious wife of Zeus. Neither high-throned Zeus nor any other knows of it, of the immortals who dwell upon snow-capped Olympus."

Swift-footed Achilles answered her and said: "How can I go into the fray? They have my arms. And my dear mother forbade me to prepare myself for battle until I should see her coming, for she promised to bring fair armor from Hephaestus. I know of no other's glorious armor that I might put on, unless it be the shield of Ajax, son of Telamon. But he too, I hope, himself is mingled with the foremost fighters, slaying with his spear about the dead Patroclus."

Wind-footed, swift Iris said to him in turn: "We too know well that they have your glorious armor. Yet even so, go to the ditch and show yourself to the Trojans, in the hope that in fear of you the Trojans may refrain from battle, and the warlike sons of the Achaeans catch their breath, pressed as they are. For even a brief space is a breathing spell in war."

So speaking, swift-footed Iris departed, and Achilles, dear to Zeus, arose. About his mighty shoulders Athena cast the tasseled aegis, and the goddess of goddesses wreathed a golden cloud about his head, and from it caused a gleaming flame to burn. As when smoke rising from some city mounts to heaven, from some far island around which fight the foe, and all the day the warriors come from their city to prove themselves in war, and with the setting sun the signal fires flare out in countless numbers, and the gleam mounts swiftly up for dwellers round about to see, in the hope that they may come with their ships to save them from destruction, so the radiance mounted to heaven from Achilles' head. He went forth from the wall and stood beside the ditch, nor did he mix with the Achaeans, for he honored his mother's wise command. There he stood and shouted, and at a distance Pallas Athena raised her voice. It roused ungovernable panic in the Trojan ranks. As clear as is the trumpet's voice when sounded by murderous foes who have beset a city, so clear was then the voice of Aeacus' son. When they heard the brazen voice of Aeacus' son, the hearts of all were dismayed; the fair-maned horses turned back their chariots, for they foreboded sorrow in their hearts. And the charioteers were stricken when they saw unwearying fire burning dreadfully above the head of the great-hearted son of Peleus, for the bright-eyed goddess Athena set it burning. Thrice godlike Achilles gave a mighty shout across the trench, and thrice the Trojans and their glorious allies were confounded. Then and there twelve of the bravest mortals perished beside their spears and chariots. Meanwhile the Achaeans gladly drew Patroclus back from the range of missiles and placed him on a bier, and his dear companions stood above him weeping. With them went swift-footed Achilles, shedding warm tears when he saw his faithful comrade lying upon the litter, wounded by sharp bronze. He had sent him with horses and chariots to battle, but did not receive him coming home again.

Then queenly Hera sent the unwearying sun to Ocean's stream before he was ready to depart. So the sun set, and the godlike Achaeans ceased from mighty conflict and from war that levels all.

The Trojans on the other side withdrew from mighty battle and loosed their swift horses from the chariots. They gathered in council before making their meal. Standing they held their council, nor did any dare sit down. For a trembling held them all, that Achilles had appeared after he had long ceased from painful battle. Prudent Polydamas, Panthous' son began to speak to them, for he alone saw into past and future. He was Hector's companion—they had been born on the same night—but the one was far superior in words, the others with the spear. He, with wise and kindly thought for them, spoke and said: "Think carefully on either course, my friends. For I bid you now go to the city and not await the glorious dawn upon the plain beside the ships. We are far from the wall. So long as that man was angry with godlike Agamemnon, the Achaeans were easier to fight. I too rejoiced to sleep by the swift vessels, hoping to capture the curved ships. But now I am dreadfully afraid of the swift-footed son of Peleus. Such is the violence of his spirit, that he will not be willing to stay upon the plain, where both Trojans and Achaeans share the fury of Ares in their midst, but he will fight for the city and its women. Come, let us go to the city; listen to me, for thus shall it be. Now ambrosial night has made the swift-footed son of Peleus pause. If he find us here tomorrow when he rushes on us with his arms, each shall know him well. Gladly shall he who escapes win his way to holy Ilium, but many of the Trojans shall the dogs and vultures eat. May the tale of such things be far from my ear. If we heed my words, though grieved, we shall hold our force through the night in the assembly and the city will be guarded by her towers and high gates and the tall, well-fashioned portals joined and bolted fast. Early, with the dawn, girt with our armor, we shall stand upon the towers. The worse for him, if he desires to leave the ships and fight with us about the wall. He shall go back to the ships when he has given his proud-necked horses all their fill of every kind of running, as he wanders back and forth before the town. But his spirit will not let him force his way within, nor shall he ever storm the city; before that day the swift dogs shall eat him."

Then Hector of the glancing helmet looked at him scornfully and said: "Polydamas, these words you speak please me no longer, you who bid us fall back and gather in the city. Have you not had your fill of close confinement within towers? In former times all mortal men called Priam's city rich in gold and rich in bronze. But now the fair treasures are gone from our homes, and many goods have been sold away to Phrygia and lovely Maeonia, since great Zeus grew angry. And now, when the son of crooked-counseled Cronus has given me to win glory by the ships and to press the Achaeans back against the sea, do not you, fool, set forth such thoughts among the people. None of the Trojans will comply, for I will not permit it. Come, as I say, let all of us obey. Now eat your supper in the field by companies. Remember your guard, and let each man be vigilant. Whoever of the Trojans is exceeding weary of his wealth, let him gather it and give it to the people to consume in common. It is better that any one of them profit by it than that the Achaeans should. Early, with the dawn, girt with our armor, let us raise sharp Ares by the hollow ships. If it be true that godlike Achilles has arisen beside the ships, it shall be the worse for him if he so wish. I shall not flee before him from tumultuous war, but shall stand and face him squarely, whether he shall carry off a mighty victory or I may. Enyalius is impartial and often slays the slayer."

So Hector spoke, and the Trojans cheered in answer, poor fools, for Pallas Athena took away their senses. For they cheered Hector, who gave them evil counsel, but no one cheered Polydamas, who gave them good advice. Then they took supper throughout the army, but the Achaeans mourned Patroclus all the night with lamentations. The son of Peleus led them in their loud lament, laying upon his comrade's breast his own man-slaying hands, and mourning loud and long, like a strong-bearded lion whose whelps a deer hunter has stolen from a dense thicket. The lion returns too late, and grieves, and tracks the man through many valleys in the hope of finding him, for very bitter is the anger that has seized it. So, groaning heavily, Achilles cried out to the Myrmidons: "Alas, vain was the word I uttered on that day to hearten heroic Menoetius in our halls. I said that I would bring his glorious son back to him in Opoeis, when he had plundered Ilium and won his share of booty. But Zeus does not fulfill all purposes for men. For it is fated that we both shall stain the same earth scarlet here before Troy, since neither aged Peleus, the horseman, nor my mother Thetis shall receive me in their halls come safely home, but the earth shall hold me here. And now, Patroclus, since I shall be later than you to pass beneath the earth, I shall not bury you until I bring hither armor and head of Hector, your great-hearted slayer. Twelve glorious sons of Trojans shall I kill before your pyre, in anger at your slaying. And as long as you shall lie unburied by the curved ships, deep-bosomed daughters of Tros and Dardanus shall mourn you night and day with streaming tears, women whom we ourselves have won by force and the long spear when we sacked rich towns of mortal men."

So speaking, godlike Achilles bade his companions set a great tripod on the fire, that they might quickly cleanse Patroclus of his bloody gore. They set the tripod for bath water on the blazing fire and poured in water and took wood and kindled it below. The fire played round the tripod's belly and the water warmed. When the water was boiling in the shining bronze, then they washed the body and anointed it with olive oil and filled the wounds with ointment nine years old. They placed it on a bed and wrapped it in a linen robe from head to foot and spread a white cloak over it. Then around swift-footed Achilles the Myrmidons mourned Patroclus all the night with lamentations. And Zeus said to Hera, his sister and wife: "You have succeeded, ox-eyed, queenly Hera, in arousing swift-footed Achilles. It would seem that the long-haired Achaeans spring from you."

Then ox-eyed, queenly Hera answered him: "Most dread son of Cronus, what sort of word is this that you have uttered? Surely even a man might do as much for any warrior, even one who is a mortal and does not have much wisdom. Why, then, should not I, who boast myself best of the goddesses on two counts, both by my birth and because I am called your wife and you rule over all the immortals— why should not I in anger at the Trojans work them harm?"

So they spoke with one another. But silver-footed Thetis

came to Hephaestus' home—indestructible, star-set, outstanding among the immortals, made of bronze and built by the
club-footed god himself. She found him sweating as he
hastened round the bellows. For he had made twenty tripods,
all to stand about the walls of his well-founded hall. He had
set golden wheels upon the base of each, that they might of
themselves go to the divine council and come back to his
home, a wonder to behold. They were so far complete, but
had not yet their handles. These he was preparing and was
beating out the rivets. While he was working on these with
his cunning mind, the silver-footed goddess Thetis drew near
him. Charis of the shining headband, whom the renowned
lame god had wed, came from the house and saw her. She put
her hand upon her and spoke and said to her: "Why, dear,
honored Thetis of the trailing robe, have you come to our
house? You have not often come before. But come in, that
I may offer you our hospitality."

So speaking, the goddess of goddesses led the way. Then
she seated Thetis upon a silver-studded chair, fair and subtly fashioned, and there was a footstool for her feet beneath.
She called Hephaestus, the famed workman, and spoke a
word with him: "Hephaestus, come in here. Thetis has
need of you." Then the famed god of the mighty arms replied to her: "Awful and reverend is the goddess in our
house, she who saved me when pain seized me after my
long fall at my dog-faced mother's wish, who desired to hide
me because I was lame. Then had I suffered grief at heart,
had not Eurynome and Thetis taken me in their arms—Eurynome, daughter of encircling Ocean. With them for nine
years I forged much cunning handiwork—brooches and spiral
armbands and cups and necklaces, within a hollow cave.
Around me ran the stream of Ocean murmuring with foam,
an endless flow. No other among gods or mortal men knew
this, but Thetis and Eurynome who saved me knew it. And
Thetis now has come to our house. I am therefore bound to
repay to fair-tressed Thetis all I owe her for having saved
my life. Do you now offer her fair hospitality, while I put
away my bellows and all my gear."

The dread god spoke, and rose up puffing from his anvil
block, limping, and his thin legs moved beneath him. He
set the bellows back from the fire and gathered all the tools
he worked with in a silver box. With a sponge he wiped off
his face and both his hands, his mighty neck, and hairy
chest, and put on a shirt and took up his stout staff and

started limping from the room. Two golden handmaids went beside their lord, like living maidens. There is a mind in their breasts, and voice and strength, and they have skill in handiwork from the immortal gods. They hurried along, giving their lord support, and he hobbled close to Thetis and sat down in a shining chair. He put his hand upon her and spoke and said to her: "Why, dear honored Thetis of the trailing robe, have you come to our house? You have not often come before. Speak out your purpose; my spirit bids me fulfill it if I can and it is so ordained."

Then Thetis answered him, in tears: "Hephaestus, has any of all the goddesses who dwell upon Olympus suffered in her heart sad woes to match the pain Zeus, Cronus' son, has given me among all the rest? For out of all the other daughters of the Sea he made me subject to a man, Aeacus' son Peleus, and I endured a mortal's bed, though much against my will. He lies burdened with wretched age within his halls, and I now have other sorrows, since he gave me a son to bear and rear, above all heroes. He shot up like a sapling. Him whom I had reared like a tree on the orchard's slope I sent in the curved ships to Ilium to battle with the Trojans. I shall not welcome him returning home again to Peleus' house. Yet while he lives and looks on the sun's light, he suffers, nor can I help him though I go to him. The maiden whom the sons of the Achaeans chose to be his prize mighty Agamemnon took from his arms. In grief for her was he eating out his heart, but the Trojans hemmed the Achaeans in beside the ships' sterns and would not let them forth, and the elders of the Argives besought him and named many glorious gifts. Then he refused to ward off ruin himself, but put his armor on Patroclus and sent him into battle and gave him many men. All day they fought around the Scaean gates, and now they would this very day have sacked the city had not Apollo slain Menoetius' valiant son in the front lines, after he had done much harm. So he gave Hector glory. Therefore I come now to your knees, in hope you may be willing to give my early-fated son a shield and helmet and fair greaves with ankle pieces and a breastplate. For what he had, his faithful comrade lost when he was slain by the Trojans, and my son lies on the ground, grieving at heart."

Then the renowned lame god answered her: "Take courage. Let not these things disturb your mind. Would that I could as surely hide him away from Death the bringer of woe when dread fate comes upon him, as he shall have fair arms of such a sort that any one of numerous mankind will marvel when he sees them."

So speaking, he left her there and went back to his bellows. He turned them on the fire and bade them fall to work. Twenty bellows all blow on the melting pits, sending out a strong blast for every need—now to help him when in haste and now to end the task according to his will and profit. He threw into the fire hard copper and tin and precious gold and silver. Then he placed a great anvil on the block and seized a mighty hammer in one hand and grasped the tongs in the other.

First he made a great, stout shield, adorning it on every side, and put a threefold glittering, shining rim about it, and fastened to it a silver strap. There were five layers in the shield itself, and on it he set many devices with his cunning skill.

On it he fashioned earth and sea, the unwearying sun and the full moon, and all the wondrous signs that wreathe the heavens—the Pleiades and Hyades, mighty Orion, and the Bear, that they also call the Wain, which turns in the same place watching Orion, and has alone no share in Ocean's baths.

On it he fashioned two towns of mortal men, most fair. In one there was a wedding feast, and they were escorting the brides from their chambers through the city by the light of shining torches, and the wedding hymn rose loudly. Dancing boys whirled round and round, and in their midst the flutes and lyres made music. The women, each in her doorway, watched with wonder. The people were gathered in the market place, where a dispute had arisen, and two men were quarreling about the blood-price of some murdered man. One said that he had given all, explaining it to the people; the other denied receiving it; and each was eager to win his case before the judge. The people applauded both, as both sides had supporters. Heralds held back the people, and the old men sat upon polished stones in a sacred circle and held the staves of loud-voiced heralds in their hands. Leaning on these, they rose and gave their verdict, each in turn. In the center lay two talents of gold, to give to him who spoke the straightest verdict.

About the other city sat two armies, gleaming in their armor. Their purpose lay between two choices, to destroy the town or each to take the half of all the wealth the

lovely city held within it. But the citizens would not yet
yield and were arming for an ambush. Their dear wives and
tender children stood upon the wall to guard it, and with
them those men upon whom age had come. The warriors
were starting out, led by Ares and Pallas Athena, both
wrought in gold and clad in golden garments, and both fair
and tall, and splendid in their arms, as gods should be. The
soldiers were of lesser stature. When they came to the place
where it suited them to set their ambush, by the river, at the
watering place of all the flocks, there they sat down, wrapped
in gleaming bronze. Two lookouts lay apart from the soldiers,
waiting to see the sheep and crooked-horned cattle. These
soon appeared, and with them came two herdsmen, playing on
Panpipes, with no thought of treachery. When the men caught
sight of them, they rushed upon them and quickly then cut
off the herds of cattle and the fair flocks of shining sheep and
slew the herdsmen by them. But when the besiegers, sitting
before the assembly place, heard the great din about the cattle,
they straightway leaped up behind high-stepping horses
and drove toward it, arriving in a moment. Then they formed
their lines and fought a battle by the river's bank and hurled
their bronze-tipped spears at one another. Strife and Uproar
moved among them, and baneful Fate as well, keeping one
man alive though wounded, another free from wounds, while
she dragged by the feet amid the din another who had
perished, and she wore upon her shoulders a robe all red-
dened with men's blood. Like living men they joined and
fought, and dragged dead bodies from each other.

On it he placed a soft fallow earth, a rich plowland, wide
and thrice plowed. Many plowmen plowed thereon this
way and that, turning their teams about. And when they
had turned and reached the field's edge once again, a man
stepped up and put into their hands a cup of honey-sweet
wine; and they turned again along the furrows, eager to
reach once more the edge of the deep fallow land. The
earth was black behind them, and like earth freshly plowed,
though wrought in gold. It was a very wondrous work.

On it he placed a royal field. Here reapers moved with
sharp sickles in their hands. Some handfuls fell to earth
along the swath, and others the sheave binders tied with
bands of straw. Three binders followed, and behind came
children gleaming, who never ceased to give them armfuls.
The king stood in their midst in silence by the swaths, holding
his staff and glad at heart. Heralds were preparing dinner

underneath a distant oak, and were dressing a great bull which they had sacrificed; and the women were strewing much white barley on the meat as a dinner for the reapers.

On it he placed a fair golden vineyard, heavy-laden with fruit. There were dark clusters on it, and it was all held on silver vine props. Around it he made a ditch of blue enamel and a fence of tin. There was only one pathway through it, along which the vintagers would go when they harvested the vineyard. Light-hearted youths and maidens bore the honey-sweet fruit in woven baskets. In their midst a lad played on his lyre a tune to set one dreaming, and in a delicate voice sang a fair Linus song. Stamping in unison, they followed with shouts and dancing, beating the measure.

On it he placed a herd of straight-horned cattle. These were wrought in gold and tin, and pressed lowing from the barnyard to their pasture on a singing river by a bed of waving reeds. Four herdsmen in gold went with the cattle, followed by nine swift-footed dogs. Two grim lions had caught a bellowing bull among the foremost cattle, and he was bawling loudly as they dragged him off, and dogs and youths went after him. The lions, having broken the hide of the great bull, were gulping down the entrails and dark blood, and the herdsmen vainly set on the swift hounds with their urgings. The dogs shrank from biting the lions, but stood close by and barked and then fell back.

On it the renowned lame god placed a great pasture of sheep in a fair glen—folds and roofed huts and pens.

On it the renowned lame god placed a dancing floor like that which once in broad Cnossus Daedalus made for Ariadne of the lovely tresses. There youths and dearly courted maidens danced, holding each other's wrists. The maids wore robes of fine linen and the lads well-woven shirts, just touched with olive oil. The maidens wore fair garlands and the lads bore golden daggers, hanging from silver belts. Sometimes they ran most easily on skillful feet, as when a potter sits and fits his hand about his wheel and tries it, if it run; sometimes they ran in lines toward one another. A great throng stood in delight about the charming dance, and among them a divine bard played on his lyre, and two tumblers, beginning their sport, spun through their midst.

On it he placed the great might of Ocean around the outer rim of the well-wrought shield.

When he had made the great and mighty shield, he made

for him a breastplate brighter than the gleam of fire, and he
made for him a heavy helmet fitted to the temples, fair and
subtly fashioned, and he set a golden crest upon it, and
made him greaves of pliant tin.

When the renowned lame god had fashioned all the armor, he took it and laid it before Achilles' mother, and
she swept like a hawk down from snow-clad Olympus, bearing the glittering armor from Hephaestus.

BOOK XIX

DAWN IN SAFFRON MANTLE rose from Ocean's streams to bring light to immortals and to men. And Thetis came to the ships bringing the gifts from the god. She found her dear son weeping loudly as he lay, holding Patroclus, and many comrades mourned around him. The goddess of goddesses stood in their midst and put her hand upon him and spoke and said to him: "My child, let us leave him lying there, for all our grief, since after all he was slain by the gods' will. Receive this glorious armor from Hephaestus—most fair, such as no man yet has borne upon his shoulders."

So speaking, the goddess put down the armor before Achilles, and all the cunning handiwork rattled loudly. Fear fell on all the Myrmidons, nor did any dare to look straight at the armor, but they trembled. But as Achilles gazed at the arms he grew the angrier, and his eyes shone dreadfully beneath his brows, like flame; yet he rejoiced as he held in his hands the glorious gifts of the god. But when he had pleased his heart with gazing at the cunning work, he at once spoke winged words to his mother: "Mother, the god has sent gifts fitting to be the work of the immortals, such as no mortal man could make. Now, therefore, I will arm myself, but I am dreadfully afraid lest meanwhile flies enter the wounds made by the bronze upon Menoetius' valiant son, and there breed worms and corrupt his body—since his life has been destroyed—and the flesh all rot away."

Then the silver-footed goddess Thetis answered him: "My child, let not these things concern your heart, for I will try to ward off the wild swarms from him, the flies that devour mortals slain in battle. For even though he lie for a full year, his flesh shall still be firm or even firmer. Do you call the Achaean warriors to an assembly, renounce your anger against Agamemnon, shepherd of the people, and arm at once for war, clothing yourself in valor."

So speaking, she inspired in him might with abundant courage, and through Patroclus' nostrils she dropped ambrosia and ruddy nectar, that his flesh might remain firm.

Then godlike Achilles went along the seashore shouting
dreadfully and roused the Achaean warriors. Even those who
before had stayed among the ships, pilots who held the rud-
ders of the ships or those who were stewards upon the ships
and distributed the food, even these came this time to the
assembly, because Achilles had appeared after having long
held back from painful battle. Two squires of Ares came limping, leaning on spears—Tydeus' son, steadfast in battle, and
godlike Odysseus, for they still had painful wounds. They came
and sat down in the first row of the assembly. Then last of all
came Agamemnon, king of men, wounded as well, for even
him had Coön, Antenor's son, wounded with his bronze-tipped
spear in mighty conflict. When all the Achaeans were gathered, swift-footed Achilles arose and spoke to them:

"Son of Atreus, was it better for us both, you and myself,
when with angry hearts we raged in soul-devouring wrath
about a maiden? Would that Artemis had slain her with an
arrow on the day when I chose her after laying waste Lyrnessus. Then so many of the Achaeans would not have seized
the vast earth in their teeth at the hands of our foes, because
of my wrath. For Hector and the Trojans this was the better,
but I think the Achaeans will long remember my wrath and
yours. But what has been let us pass by, grieved though we
be, mastering perforce the spirit in our breasts. Now I will
cease from my anger, nor should I rage unrelentingly forever.
Come, urge the long-haired Achaeans quickly into battle, that
I may once more face and try the Trojans, if they wish to
sleep close by the ships. I think any among them will gladly
bend his knees in weariness if he escapes from hostile battle
from before our spears."

So he spoke, and the well-greaved Achaeans rejoiced that the
great-hearted son of Peleus had renounced his wrath. Then
Agamemnon, king of men, spoke to them from where he sat,
without arising in their midst: "Friends, Danaan heroes,
squires of Ares, it is well to listen to a man when he has risen,
nor should one interrupt him, for that is hard even for the
skilled. How could one hear or speak in a great din of warriors? Even a clear-voiced orator is hindered. To Peleus' son I
will declare myself, but do you other Argives give me heed
and each of you mark well my words. Often the Achaeans
made this proposal to me and reproached me; but I am not at
fault, but Zeus and Fate and the Fury that walks in darkness,
who inspired a savage, fatal folly in my heart in the assembly
on that day when I took away Achilles' prize myself. But

what could I do? A goddess brings all things to pass, the reverend daughter of Zeus, blind Folly, who misleads all, the baneful one. Her feet are soft, for she walks not on the earth but strides upon the heads of men, harming mankind and she snares one or another. And she once blinded Zeus, though they say he is best of men and gods. Yet even him Hera once tricked with a woman's wiles on that day when Alcmena was to bear the mighty Heracles in fair-crowned Thebes. Boasting he said to all the gods: 'Hear me, all ye gods and goddesses, that I may speak that which the spirit in my heart compels me. From that race of men who are of my own blood, Eileithyia, who brings the labor pains, this day shall reveal unto the light a man who shall rule over all that dwell about him.'

"With crafty purpose, queenly Hera said to him: 'You deceive yourself, nor shall you bring to pass your boast. Come now, Olympian, swear to me a mighty oath: that from men who are by race of your own blood, he who this day falls between a woman's feet shall rule over all that dwell about him.'

"So she spoke, and Zeus did not perceive her crafty purpose, but swore a great oath and then was greatly duped. Hera left Olympus' peak in haste and quickly reached Achaean Argos, where she knew the strong wife of Perseus' son Sthenelus to be. She was pregnant with a dear son, and her seventh month had come. Him Hera brought to the light, even before his time, but checked Alcmena's labor and held back Eileithyia. And bearing the news herself, she said to Zeus the son of Cronus: 'Father Zeus, lord of the gleaming lightning, I will drop a word in your heart. Already a goodly man is born, who shall reign over the Argives—Eurystheus, son of Perseus' son Sthenelus, your descendant; it is not unfitting for him to rule the Argives.'

"So she spoke, and a sharp pain smote his deep heart. Straightway he seized blind Folly by her head with its shining locks, being angered at heart, and he swore a mighty oath that blind Folly who deludes all should never come again to Olympus or the starry heaven. So speaking, he whirled her about in his hand and cast her from starry heaven, and quickly she came to the works of men. He ever groaned at the thought of her when he saw his dear son doing some shameful task in the labors set him by Eurystheus. So I, when great Hector of the glancing helmet was slaying the Argives at the sterns of the ships, could not forget blind Folly, by whom I was deluded in the first place. But since I was deluded and Zeus took away my senses, I wish to make amends and to give boundless recompense. Arise and go to battle, and arouse the other soldiers. As for gifts, I am here to offer you all those that godlike Odysseus promised yesterday in your tent when he went there. If you wish, wait, though eager for battle, and my squires shall take the gifts from my ships and bear them to you, that you may see that I will give you satisfaction."

Swift-footed Achilles answered him and said: "Most glorious son of Atreus, Agamemnon, king of men, to send the gifts as is seemly, if you so desire, or to keep them, rests with you, but now let us at once remember the joy of combat. For we must not spin out time with trifles here, nor waste it, for a great work is still undone. Just as each shall see Achilles slaying the ranks of Trojans with brazen spear in the front lines, so let each of you bear this in mind and fight his man."

Many-wiled Odysseus answered him and said: "Brave though you are, godlike Achilles, do not thus urge the sons of the Achaeans fasting toward Ilium to fight the Trojans, since the strife will be for no short time when once the companies of men are joined and a god breathes might into both sides. Bid the Achaeans taste of food and wine by the swift ships, for therein is strength and valor. For a man cannot fight hand to hand all day until the setting sun, hungry for food. Even though he be eager at heart to fight, yet his limbs grow heavy unawares, and thirst and hunger come upon him and his knees grow weary as he goes. But the man who has had his fill of wine and food will fight all the day long with his enemies; his heart is brave within his breast and his limbs do not weary before all have ceased from war. Come, dismiss the soldiers and bid them make their meal. Let Agamemnon, king of men, bring out the gifts into the midst of the assembly, that all the Argives may see them with their own eyes and you may rejoice in heart. And let him stand among the Argives and swear an oath to you that he has never mounted her bed nor lain with her, as is the way, my lord, of men and women. And may your spirit in your heart be gentle to him. And let him then appease you with a rich banquet in the tents, that you may lack nothing of your due. Son of Atreus, thereafter you will be juster even in another's eyes. For it is not unseemly for a king to conciliate a man when he himself was first in anger."

Then Agamemnon, king of men, addressed him: "I rejoice to hear your words, son of Laertes. For you discoursed and spoke of everything in order. That oath I am willing to swear, and my spirit bids me do so, nor shall I forswear myself before the god. Let Achilles remain here for the moment, eager though he be for war, and you others all remain together, that the gifts may come from the tent and we may take our oaths. On you yourself I lay this order and command—choose the best youths of all the Achaeans and bring from my ship all the gifts we promised yesterday to give Achilles, and lead forth the women. Let Talthybius quickly prepare me in the broad army of the Achaeans a boar to sacrifice to Zeus and Helios."

Swift-footed Achilles answered him and said: "Most glorious son of Atreus, Agamemnon, king of men, you would do better to make these preparations at another time, when there is some respite from the war and such might dwells not in my breast. But now some lie slain, overcome by Hector, Priam's son, when Zeus gave him glory; yet you are urging men to food. I would now urge the sons of the Achaeans to battle, fasting and hungry, but would urge them to prepare a great banquet with the setting sun, when we have wiped out our disgrace. Sooner than that no drink or food could pass my throat, since my comrade is dead, who lies in my tent, smitten by sharp bronze, his feet turned toward the door, and round about him his companions mourn. All these preparations concern me not at heart—only slaughter, blood and the labored groans of men."

Many-wiled Odysseus answered him and said: "Achilles, son of Peleus, by far the greatest of the Achaeans, you are mightier than I and not a little better with the spear, but I could excel you much in wisdom, since I was earlier born and know the more. Therefore let your heart endure to listen to my words. Men soon have their fill of strife, from which the bronze lays low much straw upon the earth and very little grain, when Zeus tips his scales, he who is the steward of mankind in war. The Achaeans cannot mourn the dead with their bellies, for too many are they who fall with every day; when could one catch his breath from toil? We must bury him who dies, keeping our hearts untouched by pity, and weeping only for that day alone. But as many as are left from hateful war should remember drink and food, that we may ever unceasingly fight all the more against our foes, clothing ourselves in stubborn bronze. Let no one of the soldiers hold back awaiting another summons, for the summons is this: Ill will it be for anyone left by the Argives' ships. Rather let us move in a body against the horse-taming Trojans and arouse sharp Ares."

So he spoke, and took with him the sons of glorious Nestor, and Phyleus' son Meges, and Thoas and Meriones and Creon's son Lycomedes, and Melanippus. They set out for the tent of

Agamemnon, Atreus' son. So then the word was no sooner spoken than the work was done. They bore from the tent the seven tripods which Agamemnon had promised him, and twenty gleaming caldrons and twelve horses. And at once they led forth seven women skilled in faultless work, and the eighth was fair-cheeked Briseis. Odysseus weighed out ten talents of gold altogether, and then led the way, and the rest of the leaders of the Achaeans brought gifts and put them down in the midst of the assembly, and Agamemnon rose. Talthybius, godlike in voice, stood beside the shepherd of the people, holding a boar. Atreus' son drew in his hand the sacrificial knife that ever hung beside the great scabbard of his sword, and making a first offering of bristles from the boar, raised his hands to Zeus and prayed. All the Argives sat in proper silence in their place, listening to the king, and he, looking up to the broad heaven, spoke in prayer: "Be thou my first witness, Zeus, loftiest and mightiest of gods, and Earth and Sun and Furies, who punish beneath the earth such men as are forsworn, that I have not laid hand upon the maid Briseis, using either the pretext of bed or any other, but that she is undefiled within my tent. If any of these things be false, may the gods send me many evils—such as they send on any who take their name in vain."

So he spoke, and cut the boar's throat with the cruel bronze. Talthybius whirled the beast about and cast him into the great gulf of the sea, food for the fish. Then Achilles arose and said to the war-loving Argives: "Father Zeus, great folly hast thou given men. Never would the son of Atreus have aroused so thoroughly the spirit within my breast, never have led the maid implacably away against my will; but surely Zeus willed that death should fall on many of the Achaeans. Now come to the dinner, that we may engage in battle."

So he spoke, and dismissed the quickly scattering assembly. They dispersed, each to his ship, and the great-hearted Myrmidons busied themselves with the gifts and went bearing them to the ship of godlike Achilles. Some they placed in the tents, and there they left the women, but the horses the noble squires drove to the herd.

Then Briseis, peer of golden Aphrodite, when she saw Patroclus, slain by the sharp bronze, cast herself upon him wailing shrilly, and tore her breast and soft neck and fair face with her own hands. Then this woman, like to the goddesses, said, weeping: "Patroclus, dearest to this sad heart, I left you alive when I departed from this tent, but on my return I find you dead, O best of soldiers. So woe comes ever close on woe for me. The husband to whom my father and queenly mother gave me I saw slain by the sharp bronze before our city, and the three dear brothers, whom my own mother bore, all met their day of death. But you would not even let me weep when swift Achilles slew my husband and sacked godlike Mynes' city, but said you would make me the wedded wife of godlike Achilles and take me in his ships to Phthia and hold my wedding feast among the Myrmidons. Therefore I mourn you without ceasing, dead, but forever dear."

So she spoke, weeping, and the women wailed in answer, with Patroclus as their pretext, but each for her own woes. Around Achilles gathered the elders of the Achaeans, beseeching him to eat, but he refused with groans: "I beg you, whoever of my dear comrades will heed me, do not bid me satisfy my heart with food or drink, since this dreadful woe has come upon me. I shall stay and endure until sunset none the less."

So speaking, he sent away the other kings, but the two sons of Atreus remained, and godlike Odysseus and Nestor and Idomeneus and the old horseman Phoenix, trying to cheer him in his bitter grief. But he could not be cheered at all in spirit until he entered the jaws of bloody war. Remembering, he drew a deep and sobbing sigh, and said: "There was a time when you, ill-starred one, dearest of comrades, yourself would set a dainty meal beside me in my tent with speed and neatness, when the Achaeans were hastening to bring lamentable war upon the horse-taming Trojans. Now you lie slain, while my heart in longing for you goes hungry for food and drink which lie within. Nothing worse can I suffer, not even should I hear of my father's death, who surely now sheds soft tears in Phthia for lack of such a son as I, who fight in a foreign land with the Trojans for the sake of dreadful Helen, or should I hear of the death of my dear son, who is being reared in Scyrus, if indeed the godlike Neoptolemus is still alive. For formerly my heart within my breast had hope that only I should perish here in Troy, far from horse-taming Argos, and that you would go back to Phthia that you might bring my son from Scyrus in a swift, black ship and show him everything— my property and slaves and the great, high-roofed house. For I believe that Peleus is really dead already, or, with but little life, is burdened by hateful age, ever waiting for the bitter news from me when he shall know me dead."

So he spoke, weeping, and the old men wailed in answer, remembering what each had left in his own halls. When the son of Cronus saw them mourning, he was filled with pity, and straightway to Athena spoke winged words: "My child, you have entirely forsaken your warrior. Is Achilles no longer of the least concern to your heart? For before the straight-horned ships he sits, weeping for his dear comrade. The others have gone to dinner, but he is hungry and unfed. Go, distill nectar and lovely ambrosia into his breast, that hunger may not come upon him."

So speaking, he urged on the already eager Athena. She, like a wide-winged, clear-voiced sea bird, darted down from heaven through the ether. Then while the Achaeans were arming at once throughout the camp, she distilled nectar and lovely ambrosia into Achilles' breast, that joyless hunger might not come upon his knees. She herself then departed to her mighty father's well-built house, and the Achaeans poured forth from the swift ships. As when from Zeus snowflakes fall thick and fast, bitterly cold beneath the blast of ether-born Boreas, so thickly then the brightly gleaming helmets and bossed shields and strong breastplates and ashen spears poured from the ships. The brightness rose to heaven, and all the earth laughed round about beneath the gleam of bronze. A din arose from the warriors' feet, and in their midst godlike Achilles armed himself. He gnashed his teeth and his eyes shone like flames of fire, but his heart was full of grief unbearable. In wrath against the Trojans he put upon him the god's gifts, which Hephaestus had toiled to make for him. First he put about his shins the fair greaves, fitted with silver ankle pieces, and secondly he fastened the breastplate on his chest and threw the silver-studded sword of bronze about his shoulders. Then he took the great, stout shield, from which there flashed a radiance like the moon's. As when to sailors out at sea there shines the light of a blazing fire which burns high on the mountains in some sheepfold, and the winds bear them against their will over the fishy deep away from those they love, so from Achilles' fair and subtly fashioned shield the radiance rose to heaven. He lifted the mighty helmet and set it on his head. The horsehair plume gleamed like a star, and the golden strands shook round about it where Hephaestus had set them thick around the crest. Godlike Achilles tested the arms upon himself to see if they fitted him and if his glorious limbs had play in them. They were like wings to him, and lifted the shepherd of the people. He took from the spear case his father's spear, heavy and huge and strong, which no other of the Achaeans could wield, for Achilles alone knew how to brandish it, the Pelian spear of ash which Cheiron had given his dear father on the peak of Pelion, to be the death of heroes. Automedon and Alcimus prepared and yoked the horses. They placed fair collars on them and put bits in their jaws and drew the reins back to the well-joined chariot. Automedon took in his hand the shining whip, which fitted it, and leaped to the chariot. Behind him went Achilles in his armor, shining like beaming Hyperion. He shouted dreadfully to his father's horses: "Xanthus and Balius, Podarge's far-famed sons, plan to bring your driver in other fashion safely back into the throng of Danaans when we have had our fill of war, and leave him not there like Patroclus, dead."

Then the swift-footed horse Xanthus spoke to him beneath the yoke and quickly hung his head, and all his mane escaped from the neck pad and fell beside the yoke and reached the ground. The white-armed goddess Hera gave him speech: "This time we shall still surely save you, mighty Achilles, but your day of doom is close. We are not at fault, but a great god and mighty Fate. It was not through our sloth or slowness that the Trojans stripped the armor from Patroclus' shoulders. The mightiest of the gods, whom fair-haired Leto bore, stood among the foremost fighters and gave Hector glory. We two could run swiftly as Zephyr's blast, which men say is the swiftest, but for you it is fated to be slain with violence by a god and by a man."

When he had spoken thus, the Furies stopped his speech, and swift-footed Achilles answered with a mighty sigh: "Xanthus, why do you foretell my death? You need not. Well now do I know it is my fate to perish here, far from my dear father and my mother. Yet even so I will not stop until I have driven the Trojans to have their fill of war."

So he spoke, and with a shout drove his single-hoofed horses among the foremost.

BOOK XX

So THE ACHAEANS ARMED themselves beside the curved ships about you, son of Peleus, insatiate of battle; and the Trojans likewise on the other side, at the rise of the plain. But Zeus bade Themis call the gods to an assembly from the crest of many-valed Olympus, and she went everywhere and bade them come to the house of Zeus. None of the rivers was absent save Ocean, none of the nymphs who dwell in the fair groves and in the springs of the rivers and in the grassy meadows. They entered the house of Zeus, the cloud-gatherer, and sat in the polished porches which for Father Zeus Hephaestus had made with his cunning skill.

So they had gathered in the house of Zeus. Nor did the Earth-shaker disobey the goddess, but came to them from the sea and sat down in their midst and asked the will of Zeus: "Lord of the gleaming lightning, why have you called the gods to an assembly? Are you considering something about the Trojans and Achaeans? For now is their battle and war flame closest."

Zeus, the cloud-gatherer, answered him and said: "Earth-shaker, you know the purpose in my breast, for which I summoned you. I have care for them, even though they perish. But I shall remain here seated in a valley of Olympus, whence I can gaze to my own heart's content. The rest of you go away to join the Trojans and Achaeans and give your aid to either as the mind of each inclines. For if Achilles alone shall fight against the Trojans, not even for a little while shall they hold back Peleus' swift-footed son. Even before, they trembled when they saw him. And now that he is dreadfully angered for his comrade's sake, I fear lest he storm even the wall before the time appointed."

So spoke the son of Cronus, and aroused unceasing strife. The gods went their way to the war divided in counsel. Hera and Pallas Athena and Poseidon, the holder of the earth, and Hermes the helper, who excels with his clever wits, set out for the assembly of the ships, and Hephaestus went with them, exulting in his strength, limping, but with his slender shins in rapid motion. Ares of the glancing helmet went to the Trojans, and with him Phoebus of the unshorn locks and Artemis, the huntress, and Leto and Xanthus and laughter-loving Aphrodite.

While the gods were apart from mortal heroes, the Achaeans won great glory because Achilles had appeared after he had long refrained from painful battle. A dreadful trembling seized the limbs of every Trojan in their fear when they beheld Peleus' swift-footed son shining in his armor, like Ares bane of mortals. But when the Olympians entered the press of heroes, mighty Strife arose, who rouses the nations, and Athena shouted—now she would stand by the deep ditch outside the wall, and now on the loud-thundering headlands she would give a mighty shout. Ares shouted from the other side, like a dark-storm wind, giving sharp orders from the city's summit to the Trojans, and again running over Callicolone by the Simoïs.

So the blessed gods brought both sides together with their urgings, and in their midst themselves broke into heavy strife. The father of gods and men thundered fearfully from on high, and Poseidon shook the vast earth below and the steep summits of the mountains. All the feet and peaks of many-fountained Ida trembled, and the Trojans' city, and the ships of the Achaeans. Aidoneus, king of the underworld, trembled below, and started from his throne in fear and cried aloud, lest Poseidon the earth-shaker break open the earth above him and the dark and dreadful mansions which even the gods hate be revealed to mortals and immortals. Such was the din that arose when the gods met in their strife. Facing lord Poseidon stood Phoebus Apollo with his winged arrows, and facing Enyalius was the bright-eyed goddess Athena. Hera was faced by Artemis, huntress of the golden arrows and the sounding chase, sister of the Unerring One. Facing Leto stood Hermes the savior and helper, and facing Hephaestus was the great, deep-eddying river whom the gods call Xanthus but men call Scamander.

So gods moved face to face with gods, but Achilles desired most to plunge into the throng and meet with Hector, Priam's son. For his heart bade him above all to sate with Hector's blood the warrior Ares of the bull's-hide shield. Apollo, who rouses the nations, at once aroused Aeneas to face Peleus' son, and inspired in him great might. He likened his own voice to that of Priam's son Lycaon, and in his semblance Apollo, son of Zeus, addressed Aeneas: "Aeneas, counsel-bearer of the Trojans, where are your threats which you made among the wine cups to the leaders of the Trojans, that you would fight with Peleus' son Achilles hand to hand?"

Aeneas answered him and said: "Son of Priam, why do you bid me to do that against my will—to fight hand to hand with the high-hearted son of Peleus? This will not be the first time that I shall stand face to face with swift-footed Achilles; even before, he drove me with his spear from Ida when he attacked our cattle and sacked Lyrnessus and Pedasus. But Zeus saved me, giving me strength and nimble knees. Else I would have died at the hands of Achilles and Athena, who went before and gave him glory and bade him slay the Leleges and Trojans with his spear of bronze. Therefore a man cannot fight Achilles hand to hand, for one of the gods is ever beside him to ward off destruction. Besides, his shaft flies straight and falters not before it reaches human flesh. If a god made equal the odds of war, he would not win so very easily, not even though he boasts himself to be all bronze."

Then lord Apollo, son of Zeus, said to him: "Warrior, you too may boast of the immortal gods; they say you are a son of Zeus' daughter Aphrodite, whereas Achilles sprang from a lower goddess, for Aphrodite is of Zeus and Thetis of the old man of the sea. Carry the stubborn bronze straight against him and let him not turn you aside at all by shameful words and threats."

So speaking, he inspired great might in the shepherd of the people and he went through the front ranks armed in gleaming bronze. Nor did Anchises' son escape the eye of white-armed Hera as he went to face the son of Peleus amid the throng of warriors. She called the gods together and said to them: "Consider in your hearts, Poseidon and Athena, how these things shall be. There goes Aeneas, armed in gleaming bronze, to face the son of Peleus, and Phoebus Apollo sent him. Come, let us turn him back at this point, or else then let one of us stand also at Achilles' side and give to him great strength, and let him lack naught in spirit, that he may know that the mightiest of the immortals love him and that the rest are useless as the wind, who have long been keeping war and combat from the Trojans. We have all descended from Olympus to take our part in this battle, that he may suffer nothing at the Trojans' hands this day. Later he shall suffer those things that Fate spun for him with her thread at his birth, the day his mother bore him. If Achilles hear not these things from the gods' voice, he will be afraid when some god meets him face to face in battle. The gods are dangerous to see in their own proper shape."

Then Poseidon the earth-shaker answered her: "Hera, be not angry beyond reason; you must not. I would not wish to bring us other gods together in strife, since we are far stronger. Let us go from the pathway to some vantage point and there sit down, and war shall be the care of men. But if Ares or Phoebus Apollo begin to fight or if they hold back Achilles and will not let him fight, then shall angry strife arise between us and them; and I think they will very quickly withdraw and go back to Olympus to the assembly of the other gods, overcome perforce beneath our hands."

So speaking, the dark-haired god led the way to the high-encircling wall of godlike Heracles which the Trojans and Pallas Athena made for him so that he could take refuge in flight from the sea monster whenever it drove him from the shore toward the plain. There Poseidon and the other gods sat down and drew an impenetrable cloud around their shoulders. The others sat down on the other side of Calli-colone, around thee, gleaming Phoebus, and Ares the sacker of cities.

So they sat on either side, devising their plans, but they hesitated to begin painful war with one another, and Zeus, seated on high, was in command.

The whole plain was filled with men and horses, and it flashed with bronze and the earth quaked beneath their feet as they rushed together. Two men, by far the best, came together between the lines, eager for battle—Aeneas, Anchises' son, and godlike Achilles. Aeneas had been the first to advance in threatening fashion, nodding his heavy helmet. He held his stout shield before his chest and brandished his spear of bronze. Peleus' son rushed to meet him from the opposite side, like a ravenous lion which a whole township of men hunt down in eagerness to slay. At first he goes unheeding, but when one of the valiant young men hits him with a spear he crouches, jaws agape, and foam forms on his teeth and his stout heart groans within his breast and he lashes his flanks on both sides with his tail and works himself up to battle and glaring gives a mighty leap straight forward in the hope that he may slay one of the men or die himself in the first onslaught. So Achilles' might and commanding spirit urged him to come face to face with great-hearted Aeneas. When they came close to one another in their onset, swift-footed godlike Achilles first addressed the other: "Aeneas, why have you come forward and taken your stand so far before the throng? Does your spirit bid you battle with me in the hope to rule with Priam's sway over the horse-taming Trojans? But even if you slay me, Priam will not put his power in your hands, for he has sons and he is firm and is not light of wits. Or have the Trojans set apart for you above all the rest a pleasant patch of vineyard and of plowland, for you to cultivate if you slay me? I think you will be hard put to do it. Once already I have routed you, I claim, before my spear. Or do you not remember when I found you alone and drove you from your cattle quickly on swift feet down Ida's mountains? Then you fled without a backward glance; you fled thence to Lyrnessus, but I sacked that too, attacking with Athena's aid and that of Father Zeus, and I took away the day of freedom from the women whom I seized, and led them captive. But you, Zeus and the other gods protected. But I do not think that he will save you now, as you think in your heart. I bid you withdraw and fall back among the throng and stand not face to face with me, before you suffer ill. Even a fool knows a thing when it is done."

Aeneas answered him and said: "Son of Peleus, think not by words to frighten me like some small child, since I myself am also skilled in speaking taunts and evil words. We know each other's birth, we know each other's parents, as we hear the ancient tales of mortal men. You will never see mine, nor I yours. They say you are blameless Peleus' offspring and that your mother was fair-tressed Thetis, daughter of the sea. I boast that I am the son of great-hearted Anchises and my mother is Aphrodite. One of these couples shall weep for their son this day, for I think we shall not be parted thus by foolish words and so withdraw from battle. But if you wish to learn these things, that you may know our race—and many are the men who know it—in the first place cloud-gathering Zeus begot Dardanus and founded Dardania, since holy Ilium was not yet built upon the plain, a city of mortal men, but they still dwelt upon the foot of many-fountained Ida. Dardanus begot a son, King Erichthonius, who was the wealthiest of mortal men. Three thousand mares of his pastured in the meadow, rejoicing in their frisking colts. Boreas loved them as they pastured, and likening himself to a black-maned stallion mated with them, and they conceived and bore twelve colts. When these bounded over the wheat-giving earth, they ran upon the tips of the ears of grain, yet did not tread them down, and when they bounded over the broad back of the sea they ran upon the breaking surface of the hoary brine. Erichthonius begot Tros, the Trojans' king, and from Tros sprang three blameless sons, Ilus, Assaracus, and godlike Ganymede, who was the fairest ever born of mortal men. Him the gods snatched away to pour the wine for Zeus, for his beauty's sake, that he might dwell with the immortals. Ilus begot a son, blameless Laomedon, and Laomedon begot Tithonus and Priam, Lampus and Clytius and Hicetaon, scion of Ares. Assaracus begot Capys and he begot a son Anchises, and Anchises me, whereas Priam begot godlike Hector. That is the race and blood of which I boast myself to be. But Zeus makes valor wax and wane in warriors as he will, for he is mightiest of all. Come now, let us talk thus no longer like small children, standing in the central combat of the battle. For either side has many a reproach to cast, nor could a ship with a hundred benches bear their burden. Supple is the tongue of mortals and in it are many words of every sort, and wide the field of speech on every side. Such words you speak, such answer may you hear. But why must we vex each other face to face with wrath and carpings, like women who in soul-destroying wrath meet in mid-street to strive with one another, with many truthful words and many not, and anger speaks them all? You will not by words turn me from my eagerness for valor before we meet in single combat with the bronze. Come, let us the sooner taste one another with our bronze-tipped spears."

He spoke, and hurled his mighty spear into Achilles' dreadful shield, and the shield rang loudly about the spear's point. The son of Peleus held his shield away from him with his stout arm in fear, for he thought the long-shadowed spear of the great-hearted Aeneas would easily drive through, fool that he was, nor did he realize in heart and soul that the god's glorious gifts are not easily harmed, nor do they yield. Nor did the mighty spear of the prudent Aeneas then break the shield, for the gold checked it, the gift of the god. But it drove through two layers and there were still three left, since the club-footed god had laid on five, two bronze, and two within of tin and one of gold, wherein the ashen spear was held.

Next Achilles hurled his long-shadowed spear and struck Aeneas on his rounded shield, below the outer rim, where the bronze ran thinnest and a very thin bull's hide was stretched upon it. And the Pelean spear of ash ran through and the shield cracked before it. Aeneas crouched and held the shield away from him in fear. The lance passed swiftly across his shoulder and fixed itself in the earth after driving through both

circles of the man-protecting shield. Aeneas, having dodged the
long spear, stood upright, and immeasurable pain flowed down
upon his eyes in his fear because the missile had fixed itself
close by him. Then Achilles drew his sharp sword and eagerly
rushed upon him with a fearful shout and Aeneas picked a
stone up in his hand, a weighty mass which two men, as men
now are, could never carry, but even alone he handled it with
ease. Then, as Achilles rushed ahead, Aeneas would have
struck him with the stone on the helmet or the shield, which
kept off sad death from him, and Peleus' son would have soon
taken away his life with the sword, had not Poseidon, shaker
of the earth, taken sharp notice. At once he spoke to the immortal gods: "I am troubled for great-hearted Aeneas, who
shall soon be slain by Peleus' son and pass into the house of
Death because, poor fool, he obeyed the words of Apollo the
unerring, nor shall the god ward off at all his sad destruction.
But why now, when he is blameless, does he suffer woe without reason because of others' sorrows, even though he ever
gives offerings pleasing to the gods who dwell in the wide
heaven? Come, let us lead him away from death, lest Cronus'
son be angry if Achilles should slay him. It is fated that he
escape, lest seedless in oblivion perish the race of Dardanus,
whom Cronus' son loved beyond all the children that were
born to him of mortal women; for in this time the son of
Cronus has come to hate the race of Priam, and now mighty
Aeneas and his children's children shall rule the Trojans who
shall be born hereafter."

Then ox-eyed, queenly Hera answered him: "Earth-shaker,
consider for yourself in your heart whether you shall save
Aeneas or let him perish for all his valor at the hands of Peleus'
son Achilles. But Pallas Athena and I swore many oaths among
all the immortal that we would not ward off the evil day from
the Trojans, not even when all Troy should burn with devouring fire and the warlike sons of the Achaeans kindle it."

When Poseidon the earth-shaker heard this, he set out amid
the battle and the clash of spears and came where Aeneas and
the famed Achilles were. At once he shed a mist over the eyes
of Peleus' son Achilles, and he drew the ashen spear, well
tipped with bronze, out of the shield of great-hearted Aeneas
and placed it before Achilles' feet, and whisked Aeneas from
the earth, raising him aloft. Lifted by the god's hand, Aeneas
leaped over many lines of heroes and of horses and came to
the very edge of the furious combat, where the Caucones were
arming themselves for battle. Poseidon the earth-shaker drew

close to him and addressing him spoke winged words: "Aeneas, who of the gods bids you so rashly fight hand to hand with Peleus' overweening son, who is stronger than you and dearer to the immortals? Come, fall back whenever you shall meet him, lest you pass into Death's house before your time. When Achilles has met his death and doom, then take courage to fight among the foremost, for no other of the Achaeans shall destroy you."

So speaking, he left him there, when he had told him all. And at once he drove from Achilles' eyes the wondrous mist, and he stared wide-eyed. Then in sorrow he said to his great-hearted soul: "Great is this wonder that my eyes behold, for the spear lies there upon the ground, nor do I see anyone at whom I cast it, eager to slay him. Truly Aeneas must be dear to the immortal gods, though I thought his boasting vain and empty. Let him go. He will no longer have the spirit to test me out, since he was but now happy to escape from death. Come, I will give my orders to the war-loving Danaans and try the other Trojans as I meet them face to face."

He spoke, and leaped to the ranks and gave his orders to each man: "Stand now no longer far from the Trojans, godlike Achaeans, but let man meet man and battle with them all. Not even Ares, though he is an immortal god, nor Athena could enter such a maw of battle and support the toil. So far as I have power in hands and feet and strength, I will not slacken, not in the least, but I will press right through the line, and I think none of the Trojans shall rejoice, whoever comes close to my spear."

So he spoke, to rouse them. And glorious Hector called to the Trojans with a shout, and bade them go to face Achilles: "High-hearted Trojans, fear not Peleus' son. I too could fight with words even against the immortals, but with the spear it is hard, since they are much the mightier. Nor shall Achilles set the seal to all his words; some he shall accomplish, but some he shall leave half done. Him I shall go to face, though his hands were like to fire, and his might to flashing iron."

So he spoke, to rouse them, and the Trojans raised their spears against the foe. The warriors' might was mingled and their cry arose. Then Phoebus Apollo stood at Hector's side and said: "Hector, do not yet fight alone against Achilles, but await him in the throng amid the din, lest he hit you or strike you with his sword from close at hand."

So he spoke, and Hector once more joined the throng of men, frightened to hear the god's voice speaking. Achilles, his

heart clad in valor, leaped upon the Trojans with a dreadful
shout, and first he slew Iphition, Otrynteus' noble son, leader
of many soldiers, whom a Naiad bore to city-sacking Otrynteus
under snow-capped Tmolus, in the rich land of Hyde. As he
rushed forward, godlike Achilles hit him with his spear square
in the head, and it was split quite in two. He fell with a
crash and godlike Achilles boasted over him: "There you lie,
Otrynteus' son, most terrible of all men. Here is your death,
but your birthplace is by the Gygaean lake, where is your ancestral estate, by Hyllus with its fish and by the eddying
Hermus."

So he spoke, boasting, and darkness veiled Iphition's eyes.
Him the chariots of the Achaeans cut with their tires in the
foremost combat, but Achilles next struck Demoleon, Antenor's son, a good defender from battle, in the temple,
through the helmet with its bronze cheek-guard, nor did the
bronze helmet check the blow, but the point pierced it and
crushed the bone, and his brains were scattered about within,
and Achilles slew him despite his bold attack.

Then he wounded Hippodamas in the back with his spear
as he fled before him after leaping from his chariot. He
gasped, and vomited forth his life as a bull vomits when
dragged before the altar of the lord of Helice, as young men
drag it on and the Earth-shaker rejoices in them. So he
vomited as his guiding spirit left his bones. Then Achilles with
his spear set out after godlike Polydorus, Priam's son. Him
his father would not allow to fight because he was the youngest among the sons of his begetting and was the dearest to
him, surpassing all in speed of foot. Even then in his folly he
ran among the foremost warriors, showing off his speed of
foot until he lost his own dear life. Swift-footed, godlike
Achilles hit him with a javelin as he sped by, square in the
back, where the gold clasps of his belt were joined and his
double breastplate met. The spear's point pierced through by
his navel, and he fell on his knees with a cry, and a dark
cloud enwrapped him, as sinking down he clasped his bowels
to him in his hands.

When Hector saw his brother Polydorus holding his bowels
in his hands and sinking to the earth—saw that a mist had
overspread his eyes—he could no longer bear to wander long
far off, but brandished his sharp spear and came like a flame
to meet Achilles. And when Achilles saw him, he leaped up
and said in prayer: "The man who most pierced my heart is

close at hand, he who slew my honored comrade. May we no longer shrink from one another on the dykes of war."

He spoke, and, with a scornful look, addressed the godlike Hector: "Come closer, that you may the sooner reach destruction's bounds."

But Hector of the glancing helmet felt no fear and said to him: "Son of Peleus, think not to frighten me like a child with words, since I myself know well the way to utter jeers and insults; I know that you are brave and I much your inferior. But these things lie on the knees of the gods, whether, though your inferior, I shall take away your life with my spear's cast, since my spear too has a sharp point."

He spoke, and drawing back his spear he cast it, but Athena breathed very softly and with her breath turned it back from glorious Achilles, and it came back to godlike Hector and fell before his feet. Then Achilles rushed impetuously forward with a dreadful shout, eager to slay him. But Apollo snatched Hector away, right easily, as a god would, and hid him in thick mist. Thrice then swift-footed godlike Achilles rushed upon him with his spear of bronze, and thrice he smote deep mist. But when the fourth time he rushed forward like a god, he gave a dreadful shout and spoke winged words: "This time again you have escaped death, dog, though doom came close to you. Now Phoebus Apollo saved you, to whom you doubtless pray when you go toward the din of spears. Yet will I slay you, though it be later that I meet you, if some god be my helper too. Now I shall pursue the rest, whomever I may find."

So speaking, he wounded Dryops with a javelin square in the neck, and he fell before his feet. Him he let lie, and checked Demouchus, Philetor's brave and mighty son, hitting him in the knee with a spear, and afterwards he pierced him with his great sword and took away his life. Then he attacked Laogonus and Dardanus, Bias' sons, and thrust them both from the chariot to the ground, hitting one with the spear and striking the other with his sword from close at hand. And Tros, Alastor's son—he came to clasp his knees in the hope that he would spare him and take him captive and then let him go alive and would not slay him, out of pity for one of like age, poor fool, nor did he know that he was not to persuade him; the hero was not sweet of spirit nor gentle of heart but very impetuous—Tros clasped his knees in his arms, hoping to plead with him, but he thrust the sword into his liver. His liver slipped from the wound and dark blood from it flooded his whole lap and darkness veiled his eyes as he gasped for breath. Achilles stood by Moulius and thrust him in the ear, and the bronze point drove straight through the other ear. He struck Agenor's son Echeclus square in the head with his hilted sword and the whole sword was warmed with blood, and on his eyes fell dark death and mighty doom. Next Achilles pierced Deucalion through the arm with the bronze spear point, where the elbow's tendons meet, and Deucalion awaited him, his arm weighed down, seeing death before him, and Achilles struck his neck with the sword and cast the helmed head afar. The marrow spurted out from the vertebrae and he lay stretched upon the ground. Then Achilles set out after the blameless son of Peires, Rhigmus, who had come from fertile Thrace. He hit him in the middle with a javelin, and the bronze stuck in his belly, and he fell from his chariot. As his squire Areithous was turning away the horses, Achilles struck him in the back with a sharp spear and pushed him from the chariot and the horses were panic-stricken.

As a portentous fire rages through the deep glens of a parched mountain and the deep wood is kindled, and a buffeting wind wheels the flame in all directions, so he charged in all directions with his spear, like a god, rushing across the slain, and the black earth ran with blood. As when one yokes broad-browed bulls to tread out white barley on a well-built threshing floor, and the grain is easily husked beneath the feet of the loud-lowing bulls, so great-hearted Achilles' single-hoofed horses trod on bodies and shields alike. His axle was all spattered beneath with blood, and so too his chariot rim, where drops from the steeds' hoofs and the tires struck it. But Peleus' son pressed on to win glory, and his invincible hands were stained with gore.

BOOK XXI

But when they came to the ford of the fair-flowing river, eddying Scamander, whom immortal Zeus begot, then Achilles split them and drove some on to the plain toward the city, by the road on which the Achaeans had fled in their panic on the previous day, when glorious Hector raged. Along that road some poured in rout, and Hera spread a deep mist before to check them. The other half were forced into the deep-flowing river with its silver eddies, and fell in with a mighty splashing. The steep bed of the river roared, and the banks around rang loudly, and they, with cries, swam round and round, whirled in the eddies. As when locusts rise before a rushing fire to flee to some river, and the unwearying fire burns and flares up suddenly, and they take refuge in the water, so before Achilles, the singing stream of deep-eddying Xanthus was filled with men and horses in confusion.

There on the bank the Zeus-born hero left his spear leaning against some tamarisks, and himself leaped in like a god, holding only his sword, and plotting evil in his heart; and he struck around him on all sides. A ghastly groan arose from those struck by his sword, and the water grew red with blood. As other fish, fleeing before a great-mawed dolphin, fill the recesses of some safe harbor in their fear, for he devours any he may catch, so the Trojans in the streams of the dread river cowered beneath the banks. And when Achilles' hands were tired with slaying, he chose twelve living youths out of the river as a blood price for the dead Patroclus, Menoetius' son, and he led them forth, startled as fawns, and bound their hands behind them with well-cut thongs which they themselves had worn upon their tight-twisted coats of mail. He gave them to his comrades to lead back to the hollow ships, and then he rushed on again, eager to slay.

Next he met a son of Dardanian Priam fleeing from the river, Lycaon, whom he had once led captive, all unwilling, from his father's orchard, when he made a raid by night;

Lycaon was cutting new shoots from a fig tree with sharp bronze, to serve as chariot rims, and godlike Achilles had come upon him, an evil unforeseen. That time Achilles had sent him by ship to goodly Lemnos and had sold him there, and Jason's son had given the purchase money. A foreign friend had freed him thence and had given much to do it—Eëtion of Imbros—and he had sent him to bright Arisbe, and thence he had escaped and reached his father's house. Eleven days he had rejoiced his heart among his friends, coming from Lemnos, and on the twelfth the god cast him again into Achilles' hands, who was to send him to the house of Death, reluctant as he was to go. When, therefore, swift-footed, godlike Achilles saw him quite unarmed, without a helmet or a shield, nor had he even a spear, but had thrown all these upon the ground, for sweat distressed him as he fled from the river and weariness overcame his knees, then in surprise, Achilles said to his great-hearted soul: "A great wonder is this my eyes behold. The great-hearted Trojans I slew shall rise again from the misty darkness, even as this man has come fleeing the pitiless day, after being sold to sacred Lemnos. The gray sea's width could not contain him, though it holds many back against their will. Now shall he taste our spear point, that I may know within my heart and learn whether he shall return from there as well, or whether the life-giving earth shall hold him, she that holds even the mighty."

So he pondered, waiting, and Lycaon drew near him in confusion, eager to clasp his knees and wishing much in spirit to escape from evil death and his dark fate. Godlike Achilles lifted his long spear, eager to wound him, but he ran under it and bent and clasped his knees. The spear flew over his shoulder and fixed itself in the ground, eager to have its fill of human flesh. With one hand Lycaon clasped Achilles' knees in supplication, and with the other held the pointed spear, nor would he let it go. Speaking, he addressed to him winged words: "I clasp your knees, Achilles; consider me and have pity; you see in me, Zeus-nurtured one, a suppliant deserving of consideration, for you were the first with whom I ate Demeter's meal on that day when you took me in the goodly orchard and sent me far from father and friends and sold me into sacred Lemnos, and I brought you a hundred oxen's price. Now I have been released on paying thrice that ransom and this is the twelfth day since I returned to Ilium after many woes.

Now cruel fate has put me in your hands again. I must certainly be hated by Father Zeus, who has given me to you again. My mother bore me to be short in days. Laothoe, daughter of old Altes—Altes, who is king of the war-loving Leleges in steep Pedasus on Satnioeis. His daughter Priam wed, and many others did he wed as well. Two of us were born of her, and you will cut the throats of both. For the other, godlike Polydorus, you slew among the first foot soldiers when you hit him with your sharp spear. And now my evil fate will come. For I think not to escape your hands, since the god has sent you on me. Another thing I will tell you, and do you turn it over in your heart. Slay me not, since I am not from the same womb as Hector, who slew your gentle, stalwart comrade."

So the glorious son of Priam spoke to him in suppliant words, but he heard a harsh reply: "Fool, offer me no ransom; no, nor mention it. For before Patroclus met his day of doom it was then more pleasing to my heart to spare the Trojans, and many I took alive and sold; but now there is none who shall escape from death, whomever the god throws into my hands before Ilium—none of all the Trojans, and especially of Priam's sons. No, die—you too, my friend. Why do you grieve this way? Even Patroclus died, who was a man far nobler than you. Do you not see how fair I am myself, and tall? I come of a brave father, and a goddess mother bore me. Yet over me too hang death and mighty doom. There shall be a dawn or afternoon or midday when someone shall take away my life in battle, hitting me with a spear or an arrow from the string."

So he spoke, and then Lycaon's knees and very heart were loosed. He let go of the spear and sank down, spreading out both his arms. Achilles drew his sharp sword and struck him above the collarbone, beside the neck, and the two-edged sword sank in him to the hilt. He lay stretched prone upon the ground and the dark blood ran from him and wet the earth. Then Achilles took him by the foot and threw him for the river to bear away, and boasting over him spoke winged words: "Lie there now with the fish, who will lick the blood from off your wound and mourn you not. Nor shall your mother lay you in your bed and weep for you, but eddying Scamander shall bear you to the sea's broad bosom. Many a fish, leaping in the wave, shall dart through the black ripple and eat the white fat of Lycaon. Die, Trojans, until we take the citadel of holy Ilium, you fleeing and I behind you slaying. Nor shall the broad-flowing river with its silver eddies save you, to which you offer many bulls and cast into its eddies living, single-hoofed horses; even so you shall die an evil death until you all atone for Patroclus' death and the slaughter of the Achaeans whom you slew by the swift ships, apart from me."

So he spoke, and the river grew angrier at heart and debated in his mind how he might make godlike Achilles cease from battle and might ward off destruction from the Trojans. Meanwhile Peleus' son, carrying his long-shadowed spear, was leaping on Asteropaeus, Pelegon's son, eager to slay him. Pelegon was begotten by broad-flowing Axius and Periboea, eldest of Acessamenus' daughters, for the deep-eddying river lay with her. On him Achilles charged, and Asteropaeus stood facing him in the river's bed, holding two spears. Xanthus put strength in his heart, since he was angered at the warrior dead whom Achilles slew so pitilessly along his course. When they came close to one another in their onset, swift-footed, godlike Achilles first addressed him: "Who on earth are you of the heroes that you dare come face to face with me? Unhappy those whose sons meet with my might."

Pelegon's glorious son replied to him: "Great-hearted son of Peleus, why do you ask my birth? I am from fertile Paeonia, far away, leader of the long-speared Paeonians. This is now the eleventh dawn since I came to Ilium. My race is from the wide-flowing Axius, the fairest water that flows on earth, Axius, who begot Pelegon, famed with the spear, and he, they say, begot me. Now then, let us fight, glorious Achilles."

So he spoke, threatening, and godlike Achilles raised his Pelian, ashen spear, while heroic Asteropaeus cast two spears at once, since he was ambidextrous. With one spear he struck the shield, but did not pierce it, for the gold, the god's gift, checked the spear. With the other he grazed the lower part of Achilles' right arm, and the dark blood rushed out, but the spear passed by his body and fixed itself in the earth, eager to sate itself with flesh. Then Achilles next hurled his straight-flying, ashen spear at Asteropaeus, being eager to kill him. But he missed him, and struck the high bank and drove the ashen spear for half its length firmly into the bank. Then the son of Peleus drew his sharp sword from his thigh and leaped upon him eagerly, and Asteropaeus could not draw Achilles' ashen spear from the

jutting bank with his stout hand. Thrice he shook it in his
eagerness to withdraw it, and thrice his strength ran out.
The fourth time he wished in his heart to bend and break
the ashen spear of the son of Aeacus, but before that Achilles deprived him of his life with his sword from close at
hand, for he hit him in the navel, and all his bowels
gushed out on the ground, and darkness veiled his eyes
as he gasped. Achilles leaped on his chest and stripped
off his armor and, boasting, cried: "So lie. It is hard to fight
the children of Cronus' mighty son, even for one begotten
of a river. You said you were the son of a broad-flowing
river, but I boast that I am of the race of mighty Zeus. The
man who begot me rules over many Myrmidons, Peleus, son
of Aeacus, and Aeacus was the son of Zeus. Therefore, as
Zeus is mightier than the seaward-flowing rivers, so is Zeus'
race mightier than a river's. You have a great river right beside
you, if he can help you, but it is impossible to fight Zeus
the son of Cronus, with whom neither mighty Achelous vies,
nor the great strength of deep-flowing Ocean, from whom
flow all rivers, every sea, and all the springs and the deep
wells. Yet even he fears the lightning of great Zeus and the
dread thunder, when it roars from heaven."

He spoke, and drew the bronze spear from the jutting
bank and left him lying there upon the sand, now that he
had taken away his life; and the black water wet him.
Upon him the eels and fish fell to their work, tearing and
chewing away the fat above his kidneys, but Achilles went
after the Paeonian charioteers, who were still fleeing beside
the eddying river as they saw their best man mightily slain
in mighty combat beneath the hands and sword of Peleus'
son. Then he slew Thersilochus and Mydon and Astypylus,
Mnesus and Thrasius and Aenius and Ophelestes. And now
swift Achilles would have slain yet more of the Paeonians,
had not the deep-eddying river spoken to him in anger,
likening himself to a man, and called from his deep eddy:
"Achilles, you pass all men in power, and you pass them in
base deeds, for the gods themselves ever defend you. If
Cronus' son has granted you to slay all Trojans, drive them
away from me and do your dread deeds on the plain. For
my lovely streams are full of bodies, nor can I pour my
current into the shining sea, being blocked by bodies, but
you slay unheeding. Come now, let be; I am astonished, best
of soldiers."

Swift-footed Achilles answered him and said: "It shall be

as you bid, Zeus-born Scamander. But I will not cease to slay the haughty Trojans until I shut them in the city and try my might in close combat with Hector, whether he shall slay me or I him."

So speaking, he rushed on the Trojans like a god, and then the deep-eddying river addressed Apollo: "Ah, god of the silver bow, offspring of Zeus, you have not observed the will of Cronus' son, who gave you many an order to stand by and guard the Trojans until late evening falls and spreads its shadow on the fertile plowland."

He spoke, and Achilles, famed with the spear, leaped from the jutting bank into his middle. In a swelling surge the river rushed upon him, and roaring roused up all his streams and rolled along the many bodies which lay in him in full plenty and which Achilles slew. With a bull-like roar he tossed them out on the dry land, but the living he tried to save in his fair streams, hiding them in the wide, deep eddies. A wave rose about Achilles with a dreadful roar, and the stream struck his shield and pushed him, nor could he find firm footing. He seized in his arms a tall, fair-growing elm, but the tree fell roots and all, and tore the whole bank away and covered the fair current with its tangled roots, and blocked the stream itself, falling in entirely. Achilles rose from the eddy in haste and rushed to fly on swift feet over the plain in fear, but the great god did not relent, and with black surface rushed in his pursuit, that he might make godlike Achilles cease from combat and might ward off destruction from the Trojans. The son of Peleus rushed a spear's cast away, with the speed of a black eagle, the hunter, which is mightiest and swiftest of all things that fly. Like him he rushed, and the bronze rang dreadfully upon his breast. He ran from the flood on a slanting course, and the river, flowing after, followed with a mighty roar. As when a ditch digger, mattock in hand, clears a way for the water from some dark-watered spring through crops and gardens and throws the rubbish from the channel, and the rushing water sweeps along the pebbles, and it murmurs as it swiftly flows downhill and runs ahead of him who leads it, so the stream's wave forever overtook Achilles, swift though he was—for gods are mightier than men. As often as swift-footed, godlike Achilles made to stop and face his foe and learn if all the immortals dwelling in broad heaven were after him, a great wave of the Zeus-fed river would splash down on his shoulders, and he would leap high, pained at heart. The river wearied his knees, running swiftly across his course and washing away the ground beneath his feet. The son of Peleus cried out and looked to the broad heaven: "Father Zeus, how is it that no one of the gods would undertake to save me, in my pitiful plight, from the river? From now on let anything happen to me. No other of the heavenly ones is so guilty in my eyes as my dear mother, who beguiled me with lies. She said that beneath the armored Trojans' walls I should die by the swift shafts of Apollo. How I wish Hector had slain me, he who was reared the best man of all. Then a brave man had slain me and a brave had he despoiled. Now it has proved my fate to be caught in a shameful death, overwhelmed by a mighty river, like a lad tending swine, whom a torrent sweeps down as he crosses it in winter."

So he spoke, and very quickly Poseidon and Athena came and stood close behind him and made themselves in body like to men, and taking each a hand of his in theirs they gave him courage with their words. Poseidon the earth-shaker was the first to speak: "Son of Peleus, tremble not so much, nor fear, for such as we are come your helpers from among the gods, even Pallas Athena and I, with Zeus' approval, for it is not your fate to fall before a river. This stream shall soon retire, and you yourself shall know it. We have some shrewd advice for you, if you will heed it. Hold not your hands from leveling war until you pen the Trojan soldiery, whoever flees, within the famous walls of Ilium. When you have taken Hector's life away, go back to the ships. We give you glory for the winning."

When the two had spoken thus, they departed to join the immortals. But Achilles went on into the plain, for the gods' command had greatly stirred him. The plain was all filled with the flood waters, and much fair armor of slain warriors and many bodies floated there. He lifted his knees high as he rushed straight up against the current, nor could the wide-flowing river check him, for Athena inspired in him great strength. Nor did Scamander abate his might, but grew the angrier at Peleus' son and reared his billows' crest on high and called with a shout to Simoïs: "Dear brother, let us together check this hero's might, since soon he will sack lord Priam's mighty city, and the Trojans will not abide amid the turmoil. Help me at once, and fill your channels with water from the springs; cause all the river beds to swell, and raise a mighty billow; make a great din of logs and stones, that we may stop this wild man, who now has power, and whose purpose apes the gods'. I declare that neither his might nor beauty shall avail him, nor his fair armor, which shall lie hidden in mud at the bottom of the mere. And the man himself I shall wrap in sand, pouring great plenty of gravel around him, nor shall the Achaeans know how to gather up his bones, in such a heap of slime shall I enshroud them. Here shall his tomb be raised, nor shall there be any need to cover him with a mound when the Achaeans hold his funeral."

So he spoke, and rushed upon Achilles in a raging flood, surging aloft, roaring with foam and blood and corpses. The dark billow of the Zeus-fed river rose towering up and was about to wash away the son of Peleus, but Hera gave a mighty cry in her fear for Achilles, lest the great, deep-eddying river wash him down, and at once she called out to Hephaestus, her dear son: "Up, club-footed one, my child, for it was against you that we thought eddying Xanthus was matched in battle. Go quickly to the rescue and give your fire wide play. Meanwhile, I shall go to stir up from the sea a harsh tempest of the West Wind and swift South which will burn the heads and armor off the Trojans as it bears the evil flames. For your part, burn the trees along the banks of Xanthus and hurl the fire against him too, nor let him by gentle words or threats turn you aside. Nor do you slacken in your might until I call aloud to you; then check the unwearying fire."

So she spoke, and Hephaestus made ready the portentous fire. At first the fire burned on the plain and consumed many dead who lay thick upon it, slain by Achilles, and all the plain was dried and the shining water checked. As when the North Wind in autumn quickly dries a newly drenched orchard, and glad is he who tills it—so all the plain was dried and the corpses burned. Then Hephaestus turned his shining flames toward the river. Burned were the elms, the willows and the tamarisks, and burned the lotus and the rushes and the marsh grass, which grew in plenty by the river's lovely channels. The eels and fish in the eddies were afflicted and leaped this way and that in the fair channels, tormented by the heat of many-skilled Hephaestus. The mighty river was burned and spoke and cried: "Hephaestus, none of the gods can vie with you, nor would I fight with you when you burn thus with fire. Cease from your wrath; let godlike Achilles drive the Trojans even now forth from their city. What have I to do with wrath or rescue?"

He spoke, burned by the fire, and his fair streams seethed. As a pot filled with melting fat of a well-fed hog boils within when hurried by much fire, bubbling up everywhere, with dry wood laid beneath it, so his fair streams burned with fire and the water boiled, nor would he flow, but was checked to suffer in the mighty heat of many-skilled Hephaestus. Then he uttered winged words with many a prayer to Hera: "Hera, why did your son fall on my stream to harm it of all others? I am not so much at fault as all the rest who help the Trojans. But really I will cease, if you command me, and let him cease as well. And furthermore, I will swear never to ward off the evil day from the Trojans, not even when all Troy shall burn, blazing with devouring fire, and the warlike sons of the Achaeans kindle it."

When the white-armed goddess Hera heard this, she at once addressed Hephaestus, her dear son: "Hephaestus, glorious son, hold back. It is not seemly so to mishandle an immortal god for mortals' sake."

So she spoke, and Hephaestus quenched the portentous fire, and the wave rolled once more down its lovely streams.

When Xanthus' might was conquered, then they both ceased, for Hera checked them, angry though she was. But heavy, grievous anger fell on other gods, and the spirit in their hearts was divided against one another. They fell upon each other with a mighty roar, and the broad earth groaned and the high heaven rang about them: Zeus heard it as he sat upon Olympus, and his heart laughed with joy when he saw the gods meet in anger. Not long then did they stand apart, for shield-piercing Ares took the lead and was first to rush upon Athena, holding his brazen spear. He spoke, reviling: "Why, dog-fly, do you drive the gods in strife against each other with your stormy courage? Why does your great heart spur you? Do you not remember when you set Diomedes, Tydeus' son, to wounding, and yourself openly seized your spear and thrust at me and tore my fair flesh? Therefore I think you now shall pay for what you did to me."

So speaking, he thrust at the dreadful, tasseled aegis, which even Zeus' thunderbolt cannot destroy. Bloodstained Ares thrust at it with his long spear, but Athena drew back and seized a stone in her strong hand, a black stone lying on the plain, both rough and huge, which men of old had placed to mark a plowland's boundary. With this she struck impetuous Ares on the neck and loosed his limbs. Seven plethra he covered, fallen, and his hair was fouled with dust, and his armor clanged upon him.

Pallas Athena laughed, and boasting over him spoke winged words: "Poor fool, not even yet have you realized how much better I boast myself to be—that you match your strength with mine. So you might fully satisfy your mother's grudge, for in her anger she devises evil for you, because you abandoned the Achaeans and defend the insolent Trojans."

So speaking, she turned away her gleaming eyes. Zeus' daughter Aphrodite took his hand and led him off, as he gave many a groan, and scarcely could he catch his breath. As the white-armed goddess Hera saw her, she spoke at once winged words to Athena: "Ah, child, of aegis-bearing Zeus, Atrytone, there is that dog-fly leading man-destroying Ares out of dread battle through the din. Go, follow them."

So she spoke, and Athena hastened after them with joyful heart, and coming up to them she struck with her stout hand Aphrodite's breast, and her knees and heart were loosed upon the spot. So both of them lay upon the fertile earth, and Athena, boasting over them, spoke winged words: "Now would that all who aid the Trojans were as you when they battled the armored Argives, as bold and as enduring as Aphrodite when she came as Ares' aid to face my might. Then had we long had rest from war, having sacked the well-built city of Ilium."

So she spoke, and the white-armed goddess Hera smiled. Then the mighty Earth-shaker said to Apollo: "Phoebus, why do we stand aside? It is not fitting when others have begun. This will be the greater shame: that we return without fighting to Olympus to the house of Zeus with its bronze threshold. Lead on, for you are younger; it is not fitting for me, since I was earlier born and know the more. Fool, what a thoughtless heart you had. Do you not even now remember the woes we alone among the gods endured about Ilium when we came from Zeus to brave Laomedon and served him for a year for stated hire, and he gave us his commands? I built a broad and very handsome wall about the Trojans' city, that the city might be impregnable. And, Phoebus, you herded crooked-horned cattle with their shambling gait in the dells of wooded, many-valed Ida. But when the glad

seasons brought round our hire's payment, then dread Laomedon defrauded us of all our pay and sent us off with
threats. He threatened to bind our feet and hands above
and send us to distant isles, and promised to shear off our
ears with bronze. So we went off with angry hearts, in
rage about our hire, which he had promised and not paid.
For this you now thank his people, nor do you work with
us that the insolent Trojans be overwhelmed in utter ruin,
with their children and their wedded wives."

Then lord Apollo the Warder said to him: "Earth-shaker,
you could not call me sound of sense if I should fight with
you for the sake of wretched mortals, who, like the leaves,
now flourish with the flame of life, eating the fruit of the
field, now lifeless waste away. Let us cease at once from
battle; and let them strive by themselves."

So speaking, he turned back, for he shrank from coming
to grips with his father's brother. But his sister, the mistress of wild beasts, Artemis the huntress, chided him bitterly, uttering words of reproach: "You are fleeing, Warder,
and leaving all victory to Poseidon, and have given him an
unearned glory. Fool, why do you vainly keep your useless
bow? Let me not hear you now still boasting in our father's
halls, as formerly among the immortal gods, that you can
fight Poseidon face to face."

So she spoke, and Apollo the warder answered her not.
But the revered wife of Zeus was angered and chided the
archeress with reproachful words: "How can you now wish,
you shameless vixen, to stand before me? I am a hard one
for you to match in might, though you do bear the bow,
since Zeus made you a lion to women and granted you to
slay whomever you wish. Yes, it is better to slay the beasts
and the wild does upon the mountains than to battle with
might against those stronger than yourself. But if you wish
to learn about war, that you may well know how much
the better I am since you match your strength with mine—"

She spoke, and seized both Artemis' wrists in her left
hand and with her right hand dragged the bow and quiver
from her shoulders, smiling, and struck her with them about
the ears as she dodged this way and that, and the swift
shafts fell out of the quiver. Weeping, the goddess ran off
to the side, like a dove that flees into a crevice in a hollow
rock before a hawk, nor is she fated to be taken. So Artemis
fled weeping, and left her bow and arrows there. Then the
guide, the slayer of Argus, said to Leto: "Leto, I will not

fight with you, for it is hard to contend with the wives of
cloud-gathering Zeus. You may cheerfully boast among the
immortal gods to have beaten me with mighty force."

So he spoke, and Leto gathered up the curved bow and
the arrows, which had fallen in all directions in a whirl of
dust. She took them and went after her daughter, and the
latter came to Olympus to the house of Zeus with its bronze
threshold and sat in tears upon her father's knees, like a
small maid, and her ambrosial garments shook upon her
body. Her father, Cronus' son, clasped her to him and, gently
laughing, said to her: "Who now of those in heaven has
done this thing to you, dear child, as though you had openly
done wrong?"

The fair-crowned goddess of the echoing chase answered
him: "Your wife, the white-armed Hera, struck me, Father,
she from whom strife and contention come to the immortals."

So they spoke to one another. Meanwhile, Phoebus Apollo
entered holy Ilium, for he was concerned for the wall of
the well-built city, lest the Danaans pierce it on that day
before their time. But the other gods, who live forever,
went to Olympus, some angry and some greatly proud, and
they sat down beside their father, who is shrouded in dark
clouds. Meanwhile, Achilles was slaying both the Trojans
themselves and their single-hoofed horses. As when smoke
rises from a burning city and reaches the broad heavens—
the anger of the gods has made it mount—and brings labor
to all and to many woe, so Achilles brought labor and woe
to the Trojans.

And the aged Priam stood upon the god-built tower and
gazed on huge Achilles, while before him Trojans ran in
scurrying rout, and valor there was none. He gave a groan
and descended from the tower to the ground, arousing the
far-famed gate keepers along the wall: "Hold the gates open
with your hands until the soldiers reach the city in their
flight, for Achilles is close at hand there as he routs them.
Now will there be deadly deeds, I think. But when they
are safe within the walls and catch their breath, then shut
again the closely fitting gates, for I am fearful lest that dreadful man leap within the wall."

So he spoke, and they opened the gates and pushed away
the bolts, and the opened portals brought deliverance. Meanwhile, Apollo leaped forth to face Achilles, that he might
ward off destruction from the Trojans. These fled straight

for the city and the lofty wall, rough in the throat with
thirst, and dusty from the plain, but Achilles followed eagerly
with his spear, and a mighty madness still possessed his
heart, and he wished to win him glory.

Then would the sons of the Achaeans have captured Troy
of the lofty gates, had not Phoebus Apollo stirred up godlike Agenor, a man who was Antenor's blameless, mighty
son. The god cast courage into his heart and himself leaning
against an oak tree and hidden in thick mist stood beside
him to keep from him the heavy fates of death. As Agenor
saw Achilles, sacker of cities, he stopped, and as he waited
seethed with many fears, and in his trouble he said to his
great-hearted soul: "If I flee before mighty Achilles as the
others fled in panic, he will take me even then and behead
me in my cowardice. And if I let them flee before Peleus'
son Achilles and myself run in flight in the other direction
from the wall to the Ilian plain, until I come to Ida's valleys
and plunge into the thickets, there in the evening I might
wash me in a river and cleanse the sweat from me and come
again to Ilium—but why does my soul say this to me? May he
not see me leaving the city for the plain and, starting after,
overtake me with his swift feet; no longer then will it be
possible to avoid my death and doom, for he is exceedingly
mighty beyond all men. But what if I go to meet him before
the city? Indeed he too has flesh the bronze can wound; there
is but one soul within him, and men say that he is mortal,
though Zeus, Cronus' son, gives him glory."

So speaking, he gathered himself and waited for Achilles,
and his valiant heart within him surged for war and battle.
As a panther moves from a deep thicket to face a hunter
and trembles not nor fears at heart when it hears the bay-
ing of hounds; and if the hunter wound or hit it first, though
pressed by the spear, it still fails not in valor until it
attack the hunter or be slain—so the son of noble Antenor,
godlike Agenor, refused to flee until he had made trial of
Achilles. He held his balanced shield before him and aimed
his spear at Achilles and gave a mighty shout: "I am sure
you had high hopes in heart, glorious Achilles, that on this
day you would sack the city of the lordly Trojans, fool
that you are. There are yet many woes to suffer for her
sake. For we within are many men and brave, who will fight
for Ilium before our dear parents and our wives and sons. And
here you shall meet your fate, although you are so dreadful
and so brave a warrior."

He spoke, and hurled the sharp spear from his heavy hand and struck him in the shin below the knee, nor did he miss. Achilles' greave of new-wrought tin rang dreadfully, but the bronze leaped back from the impact and did not pierce through, for the god's gift repelled it. Then the son of Peleus rushed on godlike Agenor; but Apollo would not yet allow him to gain glory, but snatched away Agenor and hid him in thick mist and sent him to go quietly away from war. Meanwhile, he kept the son of Peleus from the soldiers by a trick. For the Warder, likened in all respects to Agenor, stood in his way, and Achilles started to run after him. While he pursued him over the wheat-bearing plain, turning him along the deep-eddying river Scamander as he ran but a little ahead —Apollo deceived him by his trick, so that he might continually hope to overtake him with his running—so long the other Trojans in their panic came thronging gladly to the city, and the town was filled with those it sheltered. They could not even bear to wait for one another outside the city and the wall or to learn who had escaped and who had died in battle, but they poured in haste into the city, whomsoever feet and knees could save.

BOOK XXII

So, THROUGHOUT THE CITY, having fled like fawns, they were wiping away the sweat and drinking and slaking their thirst, as they leaned on the fair battlements. Meanwhile the Achaeans drew near to the wall, resting their shields upon their shoulders. But Hector's dire fate bound him to remain there before Ilium and the Scaean gates. Then Phoebus Apollo said to Peleus' son: "Why, son of Peleus, do you pursue me with swift feet, being yourself a mortal, and I an immortal god? Not even yet have you known me, that I am a god, and you are violently enraged. You have now no care for your toil about the Trojans whom you put to rout, and who are gathered in the city while you retire hither. You will not slay me, since I am not fated to be slain."

Greatly angered, swift-footed Achilles said to him: "You have beguiled me, Warder, most dangerous of all gods, turning me hither, away from the wall. Otherwise had many more bitten the earth with their teeth before reaching Ilium. Now you have deprived me of great glory and saved them with ease, since you feared no punishment hereafter. Indeed, I would avenge myself upon you if the power were mine."

So speaking, he strode off toward the city in his pride, rushing like a prize-winning horse with its chariot, as it runs easily, stretching out across the plain. So Achilles plied swift feet and knees.

Old Priam was the first to see him, all shining as he rushed across the plain, like the star that rises with the autumn, and its rays shine bright to many men in the darkness of the night. Orion's Dog they call it, and it is the brightest, but an evil omen, and it brings much fever to unhappy mortals. So his bronze gleamed upon his breast as he ran on. The old man groaned and raised his hands aloft and beat his head and cried out with a mighty groan in supplication to his beloved son, who stood before the gates, insatiably eager to do battle with Achilles. The old man stretched his hands out to him and spoke piteous words:

"Hector, dear child, please do not await this man alone, far from the others, lest you quickly meet your fate, overcome by Peleus' son, since he is much the stronger, the cruel man. Would the gods loved him as I do; then would the dogs and vultures soon devour him as he lay dead and a great grief would pass from my heart. For he has bereft me of many noble sons, slaying them or selling them to distant islands. Even now there are two sons, Lycaon and Polydorus, whom I cannot see among the Trojans gathered in the city. Laothoe bore them to me, that queen of women. If they are in his camp alive, we shall ransom them with bronze and gold; it lies within, for the famous old man Altes gave much to his daughter. But if they are already dead and in the house of Hades, it is a great grief to my heart and to their mother, to us who begot them. But the grief will be less lasting to the rest of the people unless you too perish, slain at Achilles' hands. Come, enter within the wall, my child, that you may save the Trojan men and women and not give great glory to the son of Peleus, and be yourself deprived of your dear life. Still more, have pity on me, wretched and ill-starred, yet still living. For Cronus' son, our father, will destroy me with a bitter doom upon the threshold of old age, when I have looked on many woes, my sons destroyed, my daughters dragged away, my chambers ravaged, the tender children dashed to the ground in dreadful conflict and my sons' wives dragged off by the harsh hands of the Achaeans. Me, last of all, the ravening dogs will drag away before the door, when someone by thrust or cast of the sharp bronze has taken the spirit from my limbs. The dogs I reared in my halls, fed from my table, and set to guard my door shall drink my blood, mad at heart, and lie in my courtyard. All things become a young man as he lies slain in war, cleft by the sharp bronze; dead though he be, all things are fair, whatever shows. But when dogs insult the gray head and private parts of an old man as he lies slain, that is indeed the most piteous sight for wretched mortals."

So spoke the old man, and he grasped his gray hairs with his hands and tore them from his head; yet he could not move the heart of Hector. The mother on the other side lamented and shed tears, loosening the fold of her robe, and with her other hand she held up her breast and weeping spoke winged words to him: "Hector, my child, revere this and have pity on me, if ever I gave you this breast that brought

forgetfulness of care. Remember these things, dear child, and
ward off our enemy from within the walls, nor stand as
champion against him, stubborn one, for if he slays you I
shall not weep for you as you lie upon your bed, dear child,
even I who bore you, nor shall your richly dowered wife.
Far away from us, beside the Argives' ships, the swift dogs
will devour you."

So the two weeping spoke to their dear son with many a
supplication, but they could not move the heart of Hector.
He stood and awaited the approach of huge Achilles. As
a mountain serpent by its hole awaits a man, when it has
fed on noisome herbs and a dreadful rage has entered it
and it gives a baleful glance as it coils about its hole, so
Hector with unconquerable might would not withdraw, but
propped his shield against the jutting tower and in his anguish said to his great-hearted soul: "If I enter the gates
and walls, Polydamas will be the first to heap reproach upon
me, he who bade me lead the Trojans to the city during
the fatal night now past, when godlike Achilles arose. But
I would not heed him, and far better would it be. Now,
since I have destroyed the people by my blind folly, I am
ashamed before the Trojans and the Trojan women with
their trailing robes, lest some other, inferior to me, say:
'Hector brought ruin on the people by his trust in his own
strength.' So they will say, and then it were far better for
me to face Achilles and slay him and so return, or myself
to perish gloriously before the city. Or what if I put down
my bossed shield and heavy helmet and lean my spear
against the wall and go myself and meet blameless Achilles
and promise him to give Helen to the sons of Atreus to
take away, and with her all the possessions Alexander
brought in his hollow ships to Troy, which was the beginning of the quarrel, and furthermore to divide among the
Achaeans all else this city hides and thereafter require from
the Trojans an oath on the part of the elders to hide nothing but to divide in two parts all the wealth the lovely
city holds—but why does my soul say this to me? Let me
beware lest I go and reach him but he show me neither mercy
nor honor, and slay me unarmed, helpless as a woman, when
I have put off my armor. There is no way now to chat with
him from oak or rock, like lass and lad, as lass and lad chat
on together. Better to meet in anger with all speed. Let us
see to which the Olympian will give the glory."

So he debated, lingering, and Achilles drew close to him

like Enyalius, the god of war with waving plume, brandishing over his right shoulder his dreadful Pelian spear of ash. The bronze upon his body shone like the gleam of blazing fire or of the rising sun. Hector, when he saw him, fell to trembling, nor could he endure to stay there any longer, but left the gates behind and ran in flight. As a hawk upon the mountains, swiftest of birds, easily swoops upon a trembling dove, and the dove flies out from under, and the hawk, with a shrill cry, keeps darting at her, and his spirit bids him seize her, so Achilles sped eagerly straight for him, and Hector fled along the wall and plied swift knees. Past the lookout and the wind-swept fig tree, out from below the wall they swept, along the wagon road, and came to two fair-flowing springs where the two sources of eddying Scamander rise. One flows with warm water, and a smoke rises from it as from a gleaming fire. The other in the summertime flows forth like hail or chill snow or ice upon the water. There beside them are the broad washing troughs, fairly made of stone, where the wives and the fair daughters of the Trojans had been wont to wash their gleaming garments in the former days of peace, before the coming of the sons of the Achaeans. Past these they ran, one fleeing and the other in pursuit behind. A good man fled before, but a far better pursued him swiftly, for they strove not for an animal for sacrifice nor an ox hide, which are the prizes for a foot race among men, but they ran for the life of Hector, tamer of horses. As when single-hoofed horses run very swiftly around the goalpost and a great prize is offered, a tripod or a woman, when some man has died, so the two ran thrice round Priam's city on swift feet, and all the gods looked on. Among these the father of gods and men was first to speak: "My eyes behold a man I love pursued about the wall, and my heart is grieved for Hector, who burned many thighs of cattle to me on the peak of many-valed Ida and in the high place of his city at other times. Now godlike Achilles pursues him with swift feet round Priam's town. Come, think, ye gods, and consider whether we shall save him from death or shall now subdue him, for all his valor, before Peleus' son Achilles."

Then the bright-eyed goddess Athena said to him: "Father, you of the gleaming thunderbolt, dark-clouded, what have you said? Do you wish to release from Death the bringer of woe a mortal man long doomed by fate? Do it, but by no means shall all we other gods approve."

Zeus the cloud-gatherer answered her and said: "Take

courage, Tritogeneia, dear child. I speak not with serious purpose and I wish to be gentle with you. Do as your purpose runs; hold back no more."

So speaking, he aroused Athena, already eager herself, and she went darting down from the peaks of Olympus.

But swift Achilles followed Hector, driving him relentlessly. As when a dog rouses a deer's fawn from its bed upon the mountains and chases it through vales and glens, and if the fawn elude it, cowering beneath some thicket, the dog runs ever tracking it until he finds it, so Hector could not elude Peleus' swift-footed son. As often as he started to make straight for the Dardanian gates beneath the well-built towers, in the hope that they might perhaps defend him with missiles from above, Achilles would cut him off and drive him back upon the plain, running himself always on the side toward the city. And as when in a dream one cannot overtake someone who flees—neither can he escape nor the dreamer overtake him—so Achilles could not catch him with his running, nor Hector get away. How could Hector have escaped the fate of death if Apollo had not drawn near him for the last and final time and aroused his might and his swift knees? Godlike Achilles shook his head to the soldiers, nor would he let them loose their bitter shafts at Hector, lest someone win glory by hitting him, and he himself take second place. But when they came for the fourth time to the springs, then the Father raised the golden scales and in them laid two lots of death which brings long woe, the one of Achilles and the other of horse-taming Hector, and grasped the center of the scales. The fatal day of Hector sank and dipped toward the house of Death, and Phoebus Apollo left him.

Then the bright-eyed goddess Athena came to Peleus' son and stood close by and spoke winged words: "Now, Zeus-beloved, glorious Achilles, I think that we shall bring great glory to the Achaeans by the ships through slaying Hector, though he is insatiable of battle. No longer now is he fated to escape us, not even though the Warder Apollo endure much, rolling in supplication before aegis-bearing Father Zeus. Stop now, and get your breath, and I will go and persuade him to fight you hand to hand."

So spoke Athena, and he obeyed, and rejoiced at heart and stood leaning on his ashen spear with its point of bronze. She left him there and sought the godlike Hector, likening herself to Deiphobus in form and in unwearying voice. She stood close by and spoke winged words: "Dear brother, swift-footed Achilles is pressing you hard as he pursues you on swift feet round Priam's town. Come, let us stop and stay here and defend ourselves."

Great Hector of the glancing helmet said to her: "Deiphobus, even before this you were to me far dearest of my brothers, the sons whom Hecuba and Priam begot; now I think I honor you in my heart still more, that you dared for my sake, when your eyes beheld me, to issue from the wall, though others stay within."

The bright-eyed goddess Athena said to him: "Dear brother, our father and queenly mother made me many a prayer, beseeching me in turn, and so did my comrades around me, to remain there, for they were all so fearful. But my heart within me was troubled with wretched grief. Now let us go on and fight; let there be no sparing of spears; that we may know whether Achilles shall slay us and bear the bloody spoils to the hollow ships or shall be slain by your spear."

By such words and guile Athena led him on. And when they came close to one another in their onset, great Hector of the glancing helmet first addressed Achilles: "No longer, son of Peleus, will I flee you, as before I fled thrice around the great city of Priam, nor could I bear to abide your onslaught. But now my spirit bids me stand and face you. I would take you or be taken. Come, let us look to the gods, for they will be the best witnesses and guardians of covenants. For I will not mutilate you horribly if Zeus give me to endure to victory and I take away your life. But when I have stripped you of your glorious armor, Achilles, I will give back your corpse to the Achaeans. And do you do the same."

Swift-footed Achilles looked at him scornfully and said: "Hector, it is not to me that you, the unforgivable, may talk of covenants. As between lions and men there are no faithful oaths nor do wolves and lambs have a harmonious spirit but ever devise evil for one another, so it is not possible for me and you to be friends, nor shall there be oaths between us until one of us sate with his blood the warrior Ares with the bull's-hide shield. Remember all your skill, for now indeed must you be a spearman and a valiant warrior. There is no more escape for you, and Pallas Athena shall at once subdue you by my spear. Now you shall pay back all at once for the woes of my companions, whom you slew as you raged with your spear."

So speaking, he drew back his long-shadowed spear and cast it, but glorious Hector was watching out and dodged it, for he ducked as he saw it, and the bronze spear flew above him and fixed itself in the earth, but Pallas Athena picked it up and gave it back to Achilles unseen by Hector, shepherd of the people. And Hector said to Peleus' blameless son: "You missed; not even yet, godlike Achilles, have you known my doom from Zeus. You thought so, but you were glib-tongued and wily of words, that hearing you I might forget my strength and valor. You shall not plunge your spear into my back as I run away, but drive it through my chest as I rush straight for you, if God grant you that. Now then, dodge my spear of bronze; would that you would take it all in your flesh. The war would be lighter for the Trojans with you slain, for you are their greatest trouble."

So speaking, he drew back his long-shadowed spear and cast it, and struck the shield of Peleus' son in the center, nor did he miss, but the spear rebounded far from the shield. Angry was Hector that his sharp spear had sped from his hand in vain, and he stood confounded, nor had he any other spear of ash. He called in a loud voice to Deiphobus of the white shield and asked him for a long spear, but he was nowhere near him. Then Hector knew in his heart, and said: "The gods have really called me to my death, for I thought brave Deiphobus was here, but he is within the wall and Athena has deceived me. Now evil death is near to me, no longer far away, and there is no deliverance. Such must long ago have been the pleasure of Zeus and Zeus' son, the unerring one, who formerly protected me with zeal. Now my fate has found me out. Let me not perish tamely or without glory, but having done some great deed for the ears of generations who are yet to be."

So speaking, he drew the sharp sword that hung great and mighty at his side, and he crouched and darted like a high-soaring eagle that swoops earthward through dark clouds to seize a tender lamb or cowering hare. So Hector darted, brandishing his sharp sword. Achilles rushed forward, and his heart was filled with a wild fury. He held his fair and subtly fashioned shield before his breast and his helmet nodded with its shining, four-ridged crest, and around it waved the fair golden plumes which Hephaestus had set thick upon it. As the evening star moves among the other stars in the darkness of the night—it is the fairest star that stands in heaven—such was the radiance from the sharp spear point which Achilles brandished in his right hand with evil purpose against godlike Hector as he looked at his fair flesh, to see where it would be most yielding. All the rest of Hector's flesh was covered by the fair bronze armor he had taken when he slew mighty Patroclus, but it showed through where the collarbones separate the neck from the shoulder, the hollow of the throat, where life's destruction is swiftest. There godlike Achilles struck him with his spear as he rushed forward, and the point pierced straight through his soft neck. But the bronze-weighted ash did not sever his windpipe, so that he might speak to him and answer him with words. He fell in the dust, and godlike Achilles boasted: "Hector, you thought to be safe in despoiling Patroclus and took no heed of me, who was far away, fool that you were. I, his far mightier comrade, was left behind, far off by the hollow ships, I who have loosed your knees. You the dogs and birds shall rend shamefully, but him the Achaeans shall give burial."

Weakly, Hector of the glancing helmet said to him: "I beg you by your life, by your knees and by your parents, do not let the dogs of the Achaeans devour me beside the ships but accept ample bronze and gold, the gifts my father and my queenly mother will give to you, and give my body back home, that the Trojans and the Trojans' wives may give to me in death the meed of fire."

Swift-footed Achilles looked at him scornfully and said: "Dog, beseech me neither by my knees nor by my parents. Would that my angry heart would let me cut off your raw flesh and eat it, for what you have done to me. There is none who could ward the dogs off from your head, not though they bring ten and twenty times your ransom and weigh it out here and promise yet more besides; not even though Dardanian Priam should bid them buy you for your weight in gold, not even so shall your queenly mother lay you in your bed and weep for you she bore herself, but the dogs and birds shall devour you entirely."

Then, as he died, Hector of the glancing helmet said to him: "Well do I know you as I look upon you; there was no hope that I could move you, for surely your heart is iron in your breast. Take care now lest I be cause of anger of the gods against you on that day when Paris and Phoebus

Apollo shall slay you for all your valor at the Scaean gates."

As he said this, the end of death enwrapped him. His soul fled from his limbs and passed into the house of Death, bewailing its fate and forsaking manliness and youth. Even when he had died, godlike Achilles said to him: "Die, and my fate I will accept whenever Zeus and the other immortal gods desire to fulfill it."

He spoke, and dragged the bronze spear from the body and set it down apart. He stripped the bloody armor from Hector's shoulders, and the rest of the sons of the Achaeans ran about him and gazed at Hector's stature and surpassing beauty, nor did any stand beside him without giving him a wound. And thus would one speak, glancing at his neighbor: "Hector is much softer to touch than when he burned the ships with blazing fire."

So one would say, and deal him a wound as he stood beside him. But when swift-footed, godlike Achilles had stripped him, he stood among the Achaeans and spoke winged words: "My friends, leaders and counselors of the Argives, since the gods have given to death this man who did much harm, more than all the others, come, let us make trial with our arms about the city, that we may know what purpose the Trojans have, whether they will leave the citadel now this man has fallen, or wish to remain even though Hector lives no more. But why did my soul say this to me? Beside the ships, an unwept, unburied corpse, lies Patroclus. Him I will not forget so long as I am among the living and my knees can move. And even if in Death's house they forget the dead, even there will I remember my dear comrade. Come now, youth of the Achaeans, let us sing a paean of victory as we go to the hollow ships, taking this body. We have won great glory; we have slain godlike Hector, to whom the Trojans prayed throughout the city as to a god."

He spoke, and devised foul treatment for godlike Hector. The tendons of both feet he pierced behind from heel to ankle and threaded them with ox-hide thongs and tied them to his chariot and allowed the head to drag. He mounted the chariot, held aloft the glorious armor, and lashed the horses to a gallop, and not unwillingly the pair flew off. A cloud of dust rose from the dragging Hector; his dark hair spread about, and all in the dust lay his head that was so fair before; but now Zeus gave him to his enemies to mutilate in his own native land.

So his head was all befouled with dust, and his mother

tore her hair and cast her shining veil far from her and gave
a great shriek when she saw her son. Then his dear father gave
a piteous groan and the people around him were filled with
cries and lamentations throughout the city. Most like this it
was: as though all towering Ilium burned from top to bottom. For the people could scarcely hold the old man, who
was beside himself with grief and wished to go out from the
Dardanian gates. He rolled in the dust and begged them all,
calling each man by name: "Stop, my friends, and despite
your care for me let me pass out alone from the city and go
to the ships of the Achaeans. I will beseech that wicked man
of violent deeds, in the hope that perhaps he will respect my
years and have pity on my old age. He has such a father,
Peleus, who begot and reared him to be a trouble to the
Trojans; he has caused me more woe than all the rest, so
many stalwart sons of mine has he slain. Yet I weep not
so much for all, though grieved for them, as for one,
sharp grief for whom will bring me down into the house of
Death, even Hector. Would he had died in my arms; then we
should have had our fill of weeping and mourning, his mother
who bore him, ill-starred woman, and I myself."

So he spoke, weeping, and the citizens wailed in answer.
And Hecuba led the Trojan women in shrill lamentation:
"My child, wretched am I. Why should I live, suffering dreadful grief now you are dead? Night and day you were my
pride throughout the city, the protection of all Trojan men
and women in the town. You were their greatest glory while
you lived, but now death and fate have found you out."

So she spoke, weeping. Now Hector's wife had not yet
heard the news, for no true messenger had gone to tell her
that her husband remained outside the gates. She was weaving at the loom in the inmost corner of her lofty house, a
double web of purple, and was working into its pattern many-
colored flowers. She bade her fair-tressed handmaids in the
house to set a great tripod on the fire, that a warm bath
might be ready for Hector when he returned from battle,
foolish that she was, nor did she realize that very far from
baths bright-eyed Athena had slain him at Achilles' hands.
She heard the wails and lamentation from the tower and her
limbs shook and the shuttle fell from her hand to the floor.
Again she spoke to her fair-tressed handmaids: "Come, two
of you follow me; I will see what has happened. I heard the
voice of my revered mother-in-law, and the heart in my
breast leaps to my throat, and my knees are stiff beneath me.

Some woe is near to Priam's children. But I am dreadfully afraid lest godlike Achilles has cut off my rash Hector alone from the city and is driving him toward the plain and will end his perilous courage, which possessed him, since he would never remain amid the press of warriors but ran far out in front, yielding in his might to none."

So speaking, she rushed through the hall like one beside herself, with throbbing heart, and the handmaidens went with her. When she reached the tower and the throng of men, she stood upon the wall with anxious gaze and saw him being dragged before the city. The swift horses were dragging him ruthlessly to the hollow ships of the Achaeans. Black night enwrapped her eyes and she fell back and breathed out her spirit. Far from her head she let the shining headdress fall, the fillet and the net, the braided headband and the veil which golden Aphrodite gave her on that day when Hector of the glancing helmet wed her from Eëtion's home, after he had given many gifts. Around her stood many of her husband's sisters and her brother's wives, who held her, in her deathly fright, among them. When she had caught her breath and the spirit had returned into her heart, she began to cry in lamentation to the Trojan women: "Hector, wretched am I. For we were born to a single fate, you in Troy in Priam's house and I at Thebe under wooded Placus in Eëtion's house, who reared me when I was a child, unhappy he, unhappy me. Would I had not been born. Now you have gone to Death's house beneath the depths of earth, but me you leave to a hateful grief, a widow in your halls. Your child is still a feeble infant whom you and I, unhappy ones, begot. You will be no protection for him, Hector, since you are dead, nor he to you. For if he escapes the lamentable war of the Achaeans, toil and woe will ever be his hereafter, for others will remove the boundaries of his fields. The day of orphanage robs a child of all his playmates; he is utterly bowed down and his cheeks are wet with tears. In his want the lad goes up to his father's comrades, pulling one by the cloak and another by the tunic, and when they have pity on him, one holds up his cup a moment to his mouth and wets his lips but does not wet his palate, and some child from the feast, with both his parents living, abuses him, striking him with his hands and upbraiding him with words: 'Get out, there; your father is not feasting with us.' And to his widowed mother the lad goes back in tears—Astyanax, who formerly upon his father's lap ate only marrow and the rich fat of sheep, and when sleep took him and he ceased his play, he slept in his bed within his nurse's arms, in a soft bed, his heart full of good cheer. Now he will suffer much for want of his dear father. Astyanax the Trojans call him, for you alone protected their gates and their long walls. Now as you lie naked beside the curved ships, far from your parents, writhing worms shall eat you when the dogs have had their fill. Fine, fair garments made by women's hands lie in your halls, but all these I will burn with blazing fire, not as any help to you, since you shall not lie in them, but as an honor from the Trojans and the Trojan women."

So she spoke, weeping, and the women wailed in answer.

BOOK XXIII

So THEY LAMENTED throughout the city, and the Achaeans, when they had reached the ships and the Hellespont, scattered each to his ship. Yet Achilles would not allow the Myrmidons to scatter, but said to his war-loving comrades: "Myrmidons, you of the swift steeds, my trusty companions, let us not yet loose the single-hoofed horses from the chariots but let us approach with horses and chariots, and weep for Patroclus, for that is the meed of the dead. Then, when we have had our fill of bitter weeping, let us loose the horses and all of us dine here."

So he spoke, and they all began to wail, led by Achilles. Thrice they weeping drove the fair-maned steeds about the corpse, and Thetis roused in them a desire for lamentation. Wet were the sands and wet was the men's armor with their tears, such a deviser of rout was he they mourned. The son of Peleus led them in their shrill lament, laying his man-slaying hands upon his comrade's breast: "My greetings to you, Patroclus, even in Death's house. I now fulfill all I once promised you—that I would drag Hector hither to give to the dogs to devour raw, and before your pyre would cut the throats of twelve glorious children of the Trojans in my anger at your slaying."

So he spoke, and devised foul treatment for godlike Hector, stretching him prone in the dust beside the bier of Menoetius' son. Then the Myrmidons laid off, each one of them, their glittering armor of bronze and loosed the high-neighing horses and sat down in countless numbers beside the ship of Aeacus' swift-footed son. He set for them a heart-easing funeral banquet. Many sleek cattle bellowed upon the iron as they were slain, many sheep and bleating goats; and many white-toothed swine, teeming with fat, were stretched singeing in Hephaestus' flame. On all sides around the corpse blood ran in streams.

But the kings of the Achaeans escorted the lordly, swift-footed son of Peleus to godlike Agamemnon, having hardly persuaded him in his anger of heart for his comrade. When they had reached the tent of Agamemnon, they at once bade the clear-voiced heralds set a great tripod on the fire, in the hope that they might persuade the son of Peleus to wash away the bloody gore. But he stubbornly refused and swore a mighty oath: "No, by Zeus, who is highest and mightiest of the gods, it is not right that baths come near this head until I lay Patroclus in the fire and raise a funeral mound and cut my hair, since grief shall never come thus upon my heart a second time as long as I dwell among the living. But let us now turn to this hateful dinner. Do you, Agamemnon, king of men, bid them bring and provide at dawn such quantity of wood as it is fitting for a corpse to have on its departure to the misty darkness, so that the unwearying fire may consume him the more quickly from before our eyes, and the soldiers may turn to their duties."

So he spoke, and they readily listened and obeyed him. Each quickly prepared the meal and ate, and no heart lacked due portion of the feast. When they had set aside the desire for food and drink, each went to his tent to lie down, but the son of Peleus lay groaning heavily amid many Myrmidons upon the shore of the resounding sea, in the open space where the waves splashed on the beach. When sleep overtook him, pouring painless around him and loosing the cares of his heart—for his glorious limbs were very weary from his pursuit of Hector toward wind-swept Ilium—there came to him the soul of wretched Patroclus, in all things very like the man in stature and in eyes and voice, and clad in like raiment. It stood above his head and spoke to him: "You sleep, and you have forgotten me, Achilles. It is not in life that you neglect me but in death. Bury me with all speed that I may pass the gates of Death. The souls drive me away, the wraiths of those who have done with their suffering, nor will they yet allow me to join with them across the river, but I wander forlorn through Death's wide-gated house. Give me your hand; my grief overcomes me. I shall not again come back from Death's house when you have given me my meed of fire. We shall not, living, sit apart from our dear companions and make our plans, but a hateful fate devoured me, which was mine even at my birth. And it is your own fate, too, godlike Achilles, to perish beneath the wealthy Trojan's wall. Another thing I will tell and bid you, if you will obey. Bury not my bones apart from yours, Achilles, but together with them, as we were brought up in your home, when Menoetius brought me as a lad from Opoeis to your land, on account of a ruinous murder on the day when, poor fool, I slew Amphidamas' son, not with intent, but in anger over dice. Then the horse-man Peleus took me into his house and reared me properly and named me your squire. So may the same urn hold our bones, the urn of gold, two-handled, which your queenly mother gave you."

Swift-footed Achilles answered him and said: "Why did you come hither to me, dear head, and give me each of these commands? I will fulfill them all for you with care and obey even as you bid me. But stand closer to me; though it be for only a little while, let us embrace and take our fill of cruel lamentation."

So speaking, he stretched out his arms but could not grasp him. The spirit, like smoke, sank gibbering beneath the earth. Achilles started up astonished, and smote his hands together and spoke a sorrowful word: "There is a soul and wraith even in Death's house, but it has no heart at all. For all through the night the soul of wretched Patroclus stood beside me, moaning and weeping, and told me its every wish and seemed wondrously like him."

So he spoke, and aroused in them all a longing for lamenta-tion, and to them as they wept about the piteous corpse appeared the rosy-fingered Dawn. Then mighty Agamemnon sent mules and men from the tents on every side to bring the wood. A good man was in charge, Meriones, squire of manly Idomeneus. The men set out with woodcutters' axes in their hands and with well-twisted cords, and ahead of them went the mules. Long they marched, upward and downward, side-ward and aslant, but when they reached the vales of many-fountained Ida, then they cut in haste with the long-edged bronze the oaks with their lofty foliage, and there these fell with a mighty crash. Then the Achaeans split them up and tied them to the mules, and these tore up the earth with their feet, eager to reach the plain through the dense thickets. All the woodcutters carried logs, for such was the order of Meri-ones, squire of manly Idomeneus. They threw the wood down in a heap upon the shore, where Achilles planned a great funeral mound for Patroclus and himself.

Then, when they had thrown down an inexhaustible store of wood on every side, they remained there and sat down all together, and Achilles ordered the war-loving Myrmidons at once to gird their armor on and each to yoke the horses to his chariot. They arose and clad them in their armor, and into their chariots mounted the fighters and the charioteers. Those in the chariots went before, and a great crowd of foot soldiers followed after, in boundless numbers. In their midst, Patroclus' comrades bore him. They had covered the whole body with the locks they had shorn and cast upon it. Last of all, godlike Achilles supported the head, weeping. For he was sending his blameless comrade to the house of Death.

When they came to the place Achilles had appointed, they set the body down and at once piled up ample wood. Then swift-footed, godlike Achilles took other counsel. He stood apart from the pyre and cut off his golden hair, which he had raised in its abundance for the river Spercheius. In grief he spoke, gazing upon the wine-dark sea: "Spercheius, it was in vain my father Peleus vowed to you that if I returned there to my dear native land, I would cut my hair for you and make a sacred offering and sacrifice fifty ungelded rams beside the springs where stand your shrine and fragrant altar. So vowed the old man, but you did not fulfill his purpose. Now, since I shall not go to my dear native land, may I offer my hair to the heroic Patroclus to take with him."

So speaking, he put his hair in the hands of his dear comrade and aroused in all the desire for lamentation. And now the sun's light would have gone down upon their weeping, had not Achilles stood by Agamemnon and said quickly: "Son of Atreus—for the host of the Achaeans will best obey your words—it is possible to have enough of weeping, so now dismiss them from the funeral pyre and bid them make their supper. We who most mourn the dead will care for these things, and let the chiefs stay with us."

When Agamemnon, king of men, heard this, he at once dismissed the soldiers to the fair-lined ships, but the mourners stayed there and piled up the wood and made a pyre a hundred feet this way and that, and, grieving at heart, they set the body on the topmost part of it. Many fat sheep and crooked-horned cattle of shambling gait they flayed and dressed before the pyre. Great-hearted Achilles took the fat from all and covered the corpse from head to foot and piled the flayed bodies around it. He placed two-handled jars of honey and unguents leaning against the bier, and he quickly cast four proud-necked horses on the pyre as he groaned aloud. Nine dogs had fed from the master's table; the throats of two of them he cut and cast them upon the pyre. Twelve noble sons of the great-hearted Trojans he slew with the bronze, and he devised evil deeds in his heart. Into the fire he cast the might of iron, that it might consume it. Then he groaned and called by name upon his dear companion: "My greetings to you,

Patroclus, even in the house of Death. For I am now fulfilling for you all that I promised before. Twelve noble sons of the great-hearted Trojans—all these the fire devours along with you, but Hector, Priam's son, I will not give to the fire to consume, but to the dogs."

So he spoke, threatening, but the dogs did not molest Hector, for Zeus' daughter Aphrodite kept them off him day and night and anointed him with an ambrosial oil, fragrant with roses, so that Achilles might not tear his flesh off as he dragged him. And over him Phoebus Apollo drew a dark cloud from sky to plain and covered all the spot whereon the body lay, lest the might of the sun should too soon parch the flesh on limbs and sinews.

Nor would the pyre of dead Patroclus burn. Then again swift-footed, godlike Achilles took other counsel. He stood apart from the pyre and prayed to the two winds, Boreas and Zephyr, and promised them fair offerings, and he poured many libations from a golden cup in supplication, that they would come so that the bodies might with all speed be burned by fire and the wood be swift to kindle. Quickly Iris heard his prayers and went as messenger to the winds, who were all dining at a banquet in the home of stormy Zephyr. Iris ran and stood upon the stony threshold. When they saw her, they all sprang up and each called her to himself. But she refused to seat herself and said: "No seat for me, for I am going back to Ocean's streams to the Aethiopians' country, where they make offerings to the gods, so that I may take my share in the sacrifices. But Achilles prays Boreas and rushing Zephyr to come and promises you fair offerings, that you may blow into flame the pyre upon which lies Patroclus, whom all the Achaeans mourn."

So speaking, she departed, and they rushed out with a wondrous din, driving the clouds before them. At once they came to the sea, to blow, and the billows arose before their shrill blast; and they came to fertile Troy and fell upon the pyre, and the portentous fire roared aloud. All night they smote the flame together, blowing shrilly, and all night swift Achilles took a double cup and drew wine from a golden bowl and poured it on the ground and wet the earth, calling upon the soul of unhappy Patroclus. As a father weeps when he burns the bones of his son, just newly wed, who, dying, grieved his parents' heart, so Achilles mourned as he burned his comrade's bones, dragging himself about the fire and sobbing heavily.

But when the morning star arose, heralding light upon the earth—and after it the saffron-mantled Dawn spread over the sea—then the fire died down, and the flame ceased. And the winds started to return home again over the Thracian sea, and the sea roared with a surging billow. The son of Peleus drew back away from the pyre and lay down in weariness, and sweet sleep came upon him. But the others all gathered around Atreus' son, and the noise and din of their coming aroused Achilles, and he sat up and said to them: "Son of Atreus, and you others who are best of all the Achaeans, first quench all the pyre with gleaming wine, whatever the might of the flame still holds. Then let us gather the bones of Patroclus, Menoetius' son, picking them out carefully—they are easy to discover, for he lay in the pyre's midst and the others were burned on the outermost edge, horses and men together. Let us put them in a golden urn, in double folds of fat, until I myself descend to Hades. I do not bid you to labor at any great funeral monument, but only such as is seemly, and then do you Achaeans make it broad and high, you who are left behind me in the many-oared ships."

So he spoke, and they obeyed the swift-footed son of Peleus. First they quenched the pyre with gleaming wine, so far as the flame had reached and the ashes had fallen deeply. Weeping, they gathered the white bones of their gentle comrade in a golden urn, in double folds of fat, and setting the urn within the tent they covered it with fine linen. They marked out the circle for a funeral mound and laid the foundation stones about the pyre. At once they piled up the heaped earth, and when they had piled the mound, they started to go back. But Achilles checked the men there and made them sit down in a broad assembly, and he brought from the ships prizes—caldrons and tripods, horses and mules and mighty heads of cattle, and fair-girdled women, and gray iron.

For swift charioteers first he set out glorious prizes—a woman to take, skilled in faultless work, and an eared tripod holding two and twenty measures, for the first; then for the second a mare of six years, unbroken, big with a mule foal; then, for the third, he set out a fair caldron, untouched by fire, holding four measures, white as at first, and for the fourth he set two talents of gold. Then he stood erect and said to the Argives: "Son of Atreus and you other well-greaved Achaeans, these prizes lie in our midst awaiting the horsemen. If now we Achaeans were holding games in honor of any other, I would take first prize and carry it to my tent. For you know how far my horses are superior in excellence; indeed, they are immortal, and Poseidon gave them to my father Peleus, and he gave them to me in turn. But now I shall remain here, I and my single-hoofed horses, so brave and glorious a charioteer have they lost, a gentle one, who often poured olive oil upon their manes when he had washed them with shining water. They stand and weep for him, and their manes sweep the earth as they stand grieved at heart. You others make yourselves ready throughout the camp, whoever of the Argives trusts in his horses and his well-joined chariot."

So spoke the son of Peleus, and the charioteers gathered swiftly. By far the first to arise was Eumelus, king of men, Admetus' dear son, who was skilled in horsemanship. After him rose Tydeus' son, the mighty Diomedes, and led beneath the yoke the horses of Tros which he once took from Aeneas when Apollo saved the man himself. After him rose Atreus' son the fair-haired Menelaus, Zeus-begotten, and he led swift horses underneath the yoke—Agamemnon's Aethe and his own Podargus. The mare was given to Agamemnon by Anchises' son Echepolus as a gift, that he might not follow him to wind-swept Ilium but might remain at home and rejoice, for Zeus gave him great wealth and he dwelt in Sicyon of the wide dancing-floors; her Menelaus led beneath the yoke, greatly eager for the race. Fourth to harness his fair-maned horses was Antilochus, the glorious son of Nestor the high-hearted king, Neleus' son. The swift-footed horses that drew his chariot were born at Pylos. His father stood close to him and gave good counsel, in his wisdom, to one wise himself: "Antilochus, Zeus and Poseidon loved you, for all your youth, and taught you every sort of horsemanship. Therefore there is not much need for me to teach you, for you know well how to turn the post. But your horses are the slowest runners; therefore I think there will be trouble. Their horses are faster, but the men themselves cannot devise more skills than you yourself. Come now, dear son, store in your heart skill of all sorts, so that the prizes may not escape you. By skill a woodcutter is far better than by strength; by skill a helmsman on the wine-dark sea steers a swift ship, tossed by the winds; by skill one charioteer gets the better of another. He who trusting in his horses and his chariot foolishly drives with wide swerves here and there, that man's horses wander about the track, nor does he keep them in hand. But he who knows cunning arts, though driving inferior horses, always keeps his eye on the post and hugs it close, nor does he fail to guide the horses with the ox-hide reins, but holds his horses in hand and keeps watch on the man ahead. I will tell you a plain sign you will not forget. A dry stump of an oak or pine stands about a fathom above the ground. It is not rotted by rain, and two white stones are set against it, one on either side, where the out and home stretch meet, and the track is smooth about them. It is either the monument of some mortal who died long ago or was made a turning post in the time of men of old, and now swift-footed Achilles has appointed it the post. Rounding it, hold chariot and horses very close, and you yourself in your well-plaited chariot lean quickly to the left. Then lash the right horse with a shout and give him a free rein. Let your left horse hug the post, so that the hub of your wheel may seem to touch the stump's edge, but avoid touching the stone lest you harm the steeds and smash the chariot—that will be a joy to the others and a disgrace to you. No, my dear son, be wisely on your guard. For if you overtake and pass at the turning post, there is none who can come after and overtake or pass you, not even though he should drive after you godlike Arion, the swift horse of Adrastus, which was sprung from the gods, or those of Laomedon, the noble steeds which were raised here."

So speaking, Nestor, Neleus' son, sat down again in his place, when he had told his son the chief points of each matter.

Meriones was the fifth to harness his fair-maned horses. Then they mounted the chariots and threw in their lots. Achilles shook these, and out leaped the lot of Nestor's son Antilochus, and after him came mighty Eumelus. Next to him was Atreus' son Menelaus, and next him it was Meriones' lot to drive. Last of all, the lot to drive his horses fell to Tydeus' son, who was by far the best. They stood in a row, and Achilles pointed out the turning post, far out on the level plain. He sent out godlike Phoenix as an umpire, his father's squire, that he might watch the race and tell the truth.

They all together raised their whips above their horses and slapped them with the reins and called to them quickly; and at once the horses sped swiftly over the plain away from the ships. Beneath their chests the dust arose, mounting like a cloud or a tempest. Their manes flew in the rushing wind and the chariots now rolled along the fertile earth, now leaped into the air. The drivers stood in their chariots, and each one's heart beat loudly in his eagerness for victory. Each called to his horses, and they sped in a cloud of dust across the plain.

But when the swift horses reached the furthest stretch and

turned back toward the gray sea, then the skill of each was
plain and the horses suddenly reached out in their course.
Quickly then the swift mares of Pheres' son drew out ahead,
and after them raced Diomedes' stallions, the Trojan horses,
nor were they far behind Eumelus, but very close. For they
seemed ever about to mount his chariot and they warmed his
back and his broad shoulders with their breath and flew with
their heads reaching toward him. And now they would have
passed him or made his victory doubtful, had not Apollo
grown angry at the son of Tydeus and thrown the shining
whip from his hands. Tears poured from Diomedes' eyes in his
anger, because he saw Eumelus' horses running much faster
yet, whereas his own were being worsted as they ran without
the lash.

But Apollo did not escape Athena's notice when he cheated
Tydeus' son, and she rushed very quickly after the shepherd
of the people and gave him the whip and aroused might in his
horses. Then the goddess went in anger after Admetus' son
and broke his horses' yoke. The mares ran to either side of the
course and the pole fell loosened to the ground. Eumelus
rolled out of the chariot beside the wheel and skinned his el-
bows, mouth and nose, and his forehead above his brows was
bruised. His eyes were filled with tears and his mighty voice
was choked. The son of Tydeus swerved his single-hoofed
horses and drove on, darting far ahead of the others, for
Athena aroused might in his horses and gave him glory. After
him came Atreus' son, fair-haired Menelaus. And Antilochus
cried to his father's horses: "You too step out; stretch yourselves out with all your speed. I do not bid you rival those
steeds, the horses of Tydeus' prudent son, to which Athena has
now given speed and to him granted glory, but overtake the
horses of the son of Atreus; do not be left behind. Quickly, lest
Aethe, who is but a mare, put you to shame. Why are you
left behind, you who are best? This I will say, and so it shall
come to pass. You shall have no care from Nestor, shepherd
of the people, but he will slay you at once with the sharp
bronze if through carelessness we take a lesser prize. Follow
them close, and hasten with all your speed, and I myself will
arrange and plan for our passing them at the course's narrow-
est point, nor shall I miss it."

So he spoke, and they, fearing their master's charge, ran
faster for a little while; then suddenly steadfast Antilochus
saw the narrow point of the hollow road. There was a gully in
the earth where water had settled in the winter and had car-

ried off part of the road and hollowed the whole spot. Toward
this narrow way drove Menelaus, seeking to avoid collision.
But Antilochus drove his single-hoofed horses to the side, outside the track, and came after him just a little to the side. The
son of Atreus was afraid, and called out to Antilochus: "Antilochus, you are driving like a fool. Hold back your horses, for
the road is narrow, but it will soon be broader to allow for
passing. Do not harm us both by causing a collision."

So he spoke, and Antilochus drove even faster yet, lashing
on his horses as though he had not heard. As far as a discus is
thrown from the shoulder by a robust young man trying his
youthful strength, so far they ran, and Menelaus' mares fell
back, for he himself willingly let them slacken pace, lest the
single-hoofed horses collide in the road and upset the well-
plaited chariots, and the men themselves fall in the dust, in
their eagerness for victory. Then fair-haired Menelaus spoke
to him with reproach: "Antilochus, there is no other mortal
more wicked than you. Off with you—since we Achaeans
were wrong in calling you prudent. Yet even so you shall not
take the prize without an oath."

So speaking, he called out and said to his horses: "Do not
slow down, nor stop in grief of heart. Their feet and knees
shall tire before yours, for they both lack youth."

So he spoke, and they, fearing their master's charge, ran on
faster and quickly drew near the others.

The Argives, seated at the scene of the games, were watching the horses as they flew across the plain in a cloud of dust.
Idomeneus, the Cretans' leader, was first to glimpse the horses,
for he sat on the edge of the crowd and above it, on a lookout.
He heard the sound of someone shouting far away and recognized him and caught sight of the splendid stallion leading,
all bay, save that on its forehead was a white mark, round as
the moon. He stood up and cried to the Argives: "Friends,
leaders and counselors of the Argives, do I alone see the
horses, or can you too? A different pair of horses seems to be
ahead and the charioteer seems to be another. That man's
mares must have been injured on the plain, who on the outer
lap were leading. Surely I saw them ahead in turning the post,
but now I cannot see them, though my searching eyes scan
closely the Trojan plain—or else the reins slipped from the
hands of the driver and he could not guide them well around
the post and did not make the turn. I think he fell out there
and smashed his chariot and the mares have run away when
madness seized their heart. But do you stand up and look, for

I cannot make out plainly. It seems to me to be a man Aetolian by birth and one who rules over the Argives, the son of horse-taming Tydeus, mighty Diomedes."

Swift Ajax, Oileus' son, insultingly rebuked him: "Idomeneus, why do you talk rashly and too soon? The high-stepping horses are still far off, with much of the plain to cover. You are not so much the youngest among the Argives, nor do the eyes in your head see the most sharply. But you are always talking rashly. You must not be rash of speech, for there are others, better men, close by. The same mares as before are in the lead, those of Eumelus; and he himself stands in the chariot, holding the reins."

Angered, the Cretans' leader answered him: "Ajax, best at strife, but bad in council, you are inferior to the Argives in all other things because your mind is crude. Come here now, let us bet a tripod or a caldron, and let us both choose Agamemnon, Atreus' son, to be the judge as to which horses are ahead, so that you may know—and pay."

So he spoke, and swift Ajax, Oileus' son, arose at once in anger to answer him with bitter words. And now the quarrel between the two would have gone farther had not Achilles himself stood up and spoken: "No longer now, Ajax and Idomeneus, exchange harsh words, evil since they are unseemly. You look with anger on another who would do such things. Sit down among the throng and watch the horses. They will soon be here as they press on for victory. Then you shall each know the horses of the Argives, which are second and which first."

So he spoke, and Tydeus' son came racing in, his whip lashing ever from his shoulder as he drove. His horses lifted high their hoofs as they swiftly covered the ground. The grains of sand continually struck the driver, and the chariot, adorned with gold and tin, rolled after the swift-hoofed horses. There was no deep wheelprint of the tires in the fine dust behind it as the horses eagerly flew on. Diomedes stopped in the midst of the throng, and much sweat poured from the heads and chests of the horses to the ground. He himself leaped from the gleaming chariot to the ground and leaned his whip against the yoke. Nor did mighty Sthenelus linger, but hastened to take the prize and gave the woman and the eared tripod to his high-hearted companions to take away while he unharnessed the horses.

Next, Antilochus, Neleus' son, drove in his horses, having passed Menelaus by cunning, not by swiftness. Yet even so

Menelaus drove his swift horses close behind. As far as a horse is from the wheel as he draws his master in a chariot and stretches out across the plain, and the long hairs of his tail brush the tires and he runs close to it, nor is there much space between as he runs over a wide plain, so far was Menelaus behind blameless Antilochus. At first he had been a discus' throw behind, but quickly overtook him, for he was helped by the great strength of Agamemnon's mare, the fair-maned Aethe. If the race between the two had been longer, he would have passed him and placed his victory beyond dispute. Meriones, Idomeneus' brave squire, was a spear's cast behind glorious Menelaus, for his fair-maned horses were the slowest and he was himself the worst at driving a chariot in a race. Admetus' son came last of all, dragging his fair chariot and driving his steeds before him. When swift-footed, godlike Achilles saw him, he pitied him and stood among the Argives and spoke winged words: "The best man drives his single-hoofed horses last. Come, let us give him the second prize, as is fitting, but let Tydeus' son take the first."

So he spoke, and they all approved his order. And now he would have given him the mare, for the Achaeans approved, had not Antilochus, great-hearted Nestor's son, stood up and answered Achilles with his claim: "Achilles, I shall be very angry with you if you do as you propose. For you are going to take away my prize, thinking that his chariot and swift horses and his excellent self were injured. But he should have prayed to the immortals; then he would not have come in last. If you pity him and he is dear to your heart, there is much gold in your tent, much bronze and many cattle, and there are hand-maidens and single-hoofed horses. Take some of them and give him afterwards a still greater prize, or even now, at once, that the Achaeans may praise you. The mare I will not give up. Let any man who wishes strive in battle with me for her, hand to hand."

So he spoke, and swift-footed, godlike Achilles smiled, pleased with Antilochus because he was his dear companion. And answering him he spoke winged words: "Antilochus, if you bid me to give Eumelus something else from my dwelling, I will do that very thing. I will give him the bronze breastplate that I took from Asteropaeus, with a casting of shining tin running around it. It will be worth much to him."

He spoke and bade Automedon, his dear companion, to bring it from his tent, and he went and brought it and put it in Eumelus' hands and he received it with delight.

Then Menelaus arose before them, grieved at heart, furiously angry with Antilochus. The herald put the staff in his hands and bade the Argives be silent, and then the godlike mortal spoke: "Antilochus, formerly so prudent, what a thing you have done. You have put my skill to shame and hindered my horses, pushing yours ahead, which were much worse. Come, leaders and counselors of the Argives, judge fairly between the two and show no favor, lest some one of the bronze-clad Achaeans say: 'Antilochus has overcome Menelaus by trickery and gone off with the mare, because, though his horses were far worse, he was better in skill and strength.' Come, let me be the judge myself, and I think no other of the Danaans will reproach me, for it shall be fair. Antilochus, come here, Zeus-born, as is proper, and stand before your horses and your chariot; hold in your hands the slender whip with which you drove before, and, touching your horses, swear by him who holds and shakes the earth that you did not with intent delay my chariot by guile."

Prudent Antilochus replied to him in turn: "Wait now, for I am much younger than you, lord Menelaus, and you are older and superior. You know how a young man's transgressions come to pass. For his mind is quicker but his judgment weak. Therefore let your heart be patient. I will myself give to you the mare I won. Even if now you should demand some other larger prize from my own home I should at once wish to give it to you straight away rather than all my days be fallen from your favor, Zeus-born, and be a sinner against the gods."

The son of great-hearted Nestor spoke thus, and took the mare and gave her into the hands of Menelaus, whose spirit was cheered, as dew upon the ears of grain, when the crop is growing and the fields are rippling. So then your spirit was cheered within your heart, Menelaus. And addressing Antilochus, he spoke winged words: "Antilochus, now I myself will yield to you, though I am angry, since formerly you were neither flighty nor thoughtless, but now your youth has overcome your good sense. Another time avoid tricking your betters. No other man among the Achaeans could have won me over easily. But you have indeed suffered much and endured much, you and your brave father and your brother, for my sake. Therefore I will give way to your request and will give you the mare, though she is mine, so that these men too may know that my spirit is never proud nor stubborn."

He spoke, and gave the horse to Antilochus' comrade Noëmon to lead away, and he himself then took the gleaming caldron. Meriones picked up the two talents of gold, in fourth place, as he had driven. The fifth prize remained, the double cup. This Achilles gave to Nestor, carrying it to him through the throng of Argives, and said as he stood beside him: "Here, father, let this be a treasure for you, also, to be a remembrance of the burial of Patroclus, for you shall never again see him among the Argives. I give you this prize freely, for you will not box or wrestle, nor will you enter the javelin throw nor run a race, for already grievous age besets you."

So speaking, he put it in Nestor's hands, and he received it gladly, and spoke addressing him with winged words: "You are right in all these things you said, my son, for my limbs are no longer sound, nor my feet, nor do my arms move swiftly from both shoulders. Would I were as young and my strength as sound as when the Epeians buried mighty King Amarynceus at Bouprasius, and his sons held games in his honor. Then no man could match me, neither of the Epeians nor of the Pylians themselves nor of the great-hearted Aetolians. At boxing I beat Clytomedes, Enops' son; in wrestling, Ancaeus the Pleuronian, who stood up against me. I outran Iphiclus, though he was a good man, and with the javelin I outthrew Phyleus and Polydorus. Only with the horses Actor's sons drove past me, passing me by their number, jealous of the victory since the greatest prizes remained in the lists. They were twins; one drove with double mastery, and the other plied the lash, Such once I was, but now younger men share in such doings and I must heed wretched age, whereas then I stood out among the heroes. But go and bury your comrade with funeral games. I accept this gladly, and my heart rejoices that you still remember me in my gentleness and that I am not forgotten by you in respect to the honor in which I should be held among the Achaeans. May the gods give you proper recompense for this."

So he spoke, and Peleus' son went through the great throng of the Achaeans when he had heard all the praises of the son of Neleus. Then he set out the prizes for the painful art of boxing. He led out a patient mule and tethered it in the throng, a six-year-old, unbroken mule, which is the hardest to break. For the loser he set out a double cup, and he stood up and addressed the Argives: "Son of Atreus and you other well-greaved Achaeans, we bid two men, whoever are the best, to put up their fists and fight for these prizes. Let him to whom Apollo gives endurance recognized by all the Achaeans take the patient mule and go to his tent, but the loser shall carry off the double cup."

So he spoke, and at once a brave and mighty man arose, one skilled in boxing, Panopeus' son, Epeius. He put his hand upon the patient mule and cried: "Let him step up who is to carry off the double cup; for I say no other of the Achaeans shall lead away the mule after winning in the boxing, since I boast to be the best. Is it not enough that I fall short in battle? For a man could not be fated to be skilled in every work. For thus I prophesy and thus it shall come to pass—I shall rend his flesh and crush his bones. Let all who care for him stay on the spot to carry him off when he falls beneath my hands."

So he spoke, and all were hushed in silence. Euryalus alone stood up, a godlike mortal, son of lord Mecisteus, Talaus' son, who once came to Thebes to the funeral of the fallen Oedipus and there bested all the sons of Cadmus. Tydeus' son was his second, cheering him with his words, and he warmly wished him victory. First he put a belt upon him, and then gave him thongs well cut from some pastured ox. When the two had girded on their belts, they stepped out into the center of the ring and, facing off, fell upon one another with mighty fists, and their heavy hands mixed it up. Dreadful was the grinding of their jaws, and sweat poured from all their limbs. Then the godlike Epeius sprang upon the other and struck him on the cheek while he was looking for an opening, and not for long thereafter did Euryalus stand up, for his glorious limbs collapsed upon the ground. As when from a sea ruffled by Boreas a fish leaps up, just off the weedy shore, and then the dark wave covers him, so had he leaped up when hit. But greathearted Epeius seized him with his hands and drew him up, and his dear companions gathered round him and bore him across the ring with dragging feet, spitting thick blood and rolling his head from side to side. They took him and sat him senseless in their midst, and went themselves and took the double cup.

The son of Peleus at once set out a third group of prizes, displaying them to the Danaans, prizes for painful wrestling —for the victor a great tripod, to stand over the fire, which the Achaeans among themselves valued at twelve oxen's worth. For the loser he set forth a woman; she knew many skills, and her they valued at four oxen's worth. Achilles stood up and addressed the Argives: "Step forth, those of you who will try for this prize." So he spoke, and then great Telamonian Ajax started up, and many-wiled Odysseus arose, skilled in tricks, and the two girded on their belts and stepped into the center of the ring and grasped with their mighty hands each other's arms, like the rafters which a famed carpenter had fitted together in a lofty house, to ward off the winds' might. Their backs cracked beneath their mighty hands, as they dragged hard at one another. The gleaming sweat ran down, and many a welt, all red with blood, arose upon their sides and shoulders. But they still strove eagerly to win the well-wrought tripod. Odysseus could not throw Ajax and bring him to the ground, nor could Ajax throw him; Odysseus' strength held firm. But when they began to bore the well-greaved Achaeans, then great Telamonian Ajax said to him: "Zeus-born son of Laertes, Odysseus of many wiles, either lift me up, or I will you; all else shall rest with Zeus."

So speaking, he raised him up, but Odysseus did not forget his tricks. He kicked from behind and hit the hollow of his knee and loosed his limbs, and he fell backward and Odysseus fell on his chest. The soldiers watched and marveled. Then next much-enduring, godlike Odysseus lifted him, but moved him only a little from the earth, and did not, indeed, quite lift him, but crooked his own knee, and both fell close together on the ground, and were fouled with dust. And now they would have risen and wrestled a third time, had not Achilles himself stood up and checked them. "Strive no longer; do not wear yourselves out with the harsh struggle. Victory belongs to both. Take equal prizes and depart, that still other Achaeans may contend."

So he spoke, and they readily listened and obeyed him and wiped the dust off and put on their shirts.

Then the son of Peleus set out another set of prizes, those for swiftness—a silver mixing bowl, carefully fashioned. It held six measures and in beauty far surpassed any other upon earth, since Sidonians, with their great skill, had wrought it well. Phoenicians brought it over the misty deep and moored in a harbor and gave it as a gift to Thoas. Jason's son Euneus gave it to heroic Patroclus as a purchase price for Lycaon, Priam's son. Achilles set it out as a prize, in honor of his comrade, for whoever was speediest with swift feet. For the second he set out a bull, large and rich with fat, and he set out a half-talent of gold as a prize for the last. He stood up and addressed the Argives: "Step forward, those of you who will try for this prize." So he spoke, and immediately swift Ajax, Oileus' son, started up, and many-wiled Odysseus, and then Nestor's son Antilochus, for he was wont to beat all the young men in the race. They stood in a row, and Achilles marked out the lines. Their course started from the post. Then Oileus' son quickly pulled out ahead, and godlike Odysseus pressed very close behind him, as a shuttle is close to the bosom of a fair-girdled woman as she pulls it carefully in her hands, drawing the woof's thread through the warp, and holds it close to her breast, so close Odysseus ran, and his feet struck Ajax's tracks behind him before the dust could settle, and godlike Odysseus' breath fell on his head as he ran ever swiftly. All the Achaeans cheered Odysseus as he strove for victory and urged him on in his great haste. But when they passed the outermost stretch, Odysseus prayed at once in his heart to bright-eyed Athena: "Hear me, goddess, and come as a goodly helper to my feet." So he spoke, praying, and Pallas Athena heard him and made his limbs light, his feet and his hands above. But when they were about to rush swiftly toward the prize, then Ajax slipped as he ran, for Athena tripped him—just where the dung was scattered of the loud-lowing sacrificial bulls, which swift-footed Achilles slew in honor of Patroclus—and Ajax's mouth and nose were filled with bull dung. So, much-enduring, god-like Odysseus took the mixing bowl, as he came in first, and glorious Ajax took the bull. He stood holding the horn of the pastured bull in his hand, spitting out the dung, and said to the Argives: "The goddess tripped my feet, she who always stands like a mother at Odysseus' side and helps him."

So he spoke, and they all laughed gaily at him. Antilochus then took the last prize, smiling, and said to the Argives: "I will tell you all what you know, my friends, that the immortals even now still honor the older men. Ajax is a little my elder, and Odysseus is of an earlier generation and earlier men. They say he is a tough old man, and he is hard for the Achaeans to rival in swiftness, except for Achilles."

So he spoke, and glorified the swift-footed son of Peleus. Achilles, answering, addressed him: "Antilochus, your praise shall not go unrewarded; I will add a half-talent of gold for you."

So he spoke, and put it in his hands, and he received it gladly. Then Peleus' son brought a long-shadowed spear and set it down in the throng, and a shield and helmet as well, Sarpedon's arms, which Patroclus took from him. He stood up and addressed the Argives: "We bid two men, whoever are best, to put on their armor, seize the flesh-biting bronze, and try out one another for this armor before the gathering. Whoever first reaches the fair flesh and touches the entrails through the armor and the dark blood, to him will I give this fair, silver-studded sword from Thrace, which I took from Asteropaeus. Both shall take these weapons as a common prize, and we shall set a goodly meal before them in the tents."

So he spoke, and then great Telamonian Ajax stepped forth, and Tydeus' son arose, mighty Diomedes. When they had armed themselves on opposite sides of the throng, they both stepped into the center, eager to fight, with dreadful glances. Wonder fell on all the Achaeans. But when they came close to one another in their onset, they made three rushes and three times charged close to one another. Then Ajax struck Diomedes' balanced shield but did not pierce his skin, for the breastplate protected it within. But Tydeus' son constantly aimed with the point of his shining spear at Ajax' neck above the mighty shield. At this the Achaeans, in fear for Ajax, bade them stop and take equal prizes. But the hero brought the great sword with its scabbard and well-cut belt, and gave it to Tydeus' son.

The son of Peleus then set out a massive piece of iron, which once Eëtion's mighty strength had hurled. But swift-footed, godlike Achilles slew him and brought it away in the ships with the other booty. He stood up and addressed the Argives: "Step forward, whichever of you will try for this prize. Even though his rich fields are very far away, he will be able to keep and use this for five revolving years. His herdsmen or plowmen shall not go to the city for lack of iron, but he shall provide it."

So he spoke, and then steadfast Polypoetes stepped forward and godlike Leonteus, with his mighty strength, and Telamonian Ajax, and godlike Epeius. They stood in a row, and Epeius seized the lump of iron and whirled about and threw it, and all the Achaeans laughed at him. Next Leonteus, scion of Ares, threw it, and thirdly great Telamonian Ajax from his mighty hand, and cast it beyond the marks of all. But when steadfast Polypoetes seized the lump of iron, as far as a cowherd throws a staff, and it flies twisting through the herded cattle, so far did Polypoetes throw beyond the whole assembly. The soldiers cheered, and the comrades of mighty Polypoetes arose and carried the king's prize to the hollow ships.

Then Achilles set out blue iron for the bowmen, and put down ten double axes and ten single, and erected the mast of a dark-prowed ship far out upon the sand, and tied to it a trembling dove by a slender cord bound to her foot, and bade them shoot at her. "Whoever hits the trembling dove shall pick up all the double axes and take them home with him;

whoever hits the cord, missing the bird, that man is inferior,
and shall carry off the single axes."

So he spoke, and mighty lord Teucer stepped out, and
Meriones, Idomeneus' brave squire, and they took lots and
shook them in a brazen helmet, and Teucer won first place by
lot. He at once shot an arrow forcefully, but did not vow to
sacrifice to lord Apollo a glorious offering of first-born lambs.
He missed the bird, for Apollo begrudged him the shot, but he
hit the cord near the bird's foot, where she was tied, and the
bitter arrow cut the cord straight through. Then the bird flew
up into the sky, but the cord hung down to the earth, whereat
the Achaeans shouted. Hastily Meriones snatched the bow
from Teucer's hand—he had long had an arrow ready while
Teucer was still aiming. Then at once he vowed to unerring
Apollo that he would sacrifice a glorious offering of first-born
lambs. He saw the trembling dove high up beneath the clouds,
and as she circled there he shot her squarely beneath the wing,
and the shaft pierced her and fell back and fixed itself in the
ground before Meriones' feet. But the bird settled on the mast
of the dark-prowed ship, and let fall its neck, and its thick
feathers drooped. Quickly the life fled from its limbs, and it
fell far away from him, and the soldiers looked on and were
amazed. Meriones then picked up all ten double axes, and
Teucer took the single axes to the hollow ships.

Then Peleus' son brought and set down in the throng a long-
shadowed spear, and a caldron untouched by fire, embossed
with flowers, and worth an ox. The javelin throwers stepped
out—Atreus' son, wide-ruling Agamemnon, and Meriones, the
brave squire of Idomeneus. But swift-footed, godlike Achilles
said to them: "Son of Atreus, we know how much you surpass
all and how far superior you are in strength and in javelin
throwing. Come, take this prize and go to the hollow ships; the
spear we shall give to heroic Meriones, if you would be willing, for so I urge."

So he spoke, nor did Agamemnon king of men refuse to
heed him. Achilles gave Meriones the spear of bronze and
heroic Agamemnon gave his handsome prize to Talthybius the
herald.

BOOK XXIV

THE THRONG BROKE UP, and the soldiers scattered, each to go to his swift ship. These made ready to take their fill of food and of sweet sleep, but Achilles wept as he remembered his dear comrade, nor did all-conquering sleep overcome him, but he tossed this way and that, longing for Patroclus' manliness and goodly strength and for all he had achieved with him and all the hardships he had borne, passing through the wars of men and the harsh seas. Remembering these things, he would shed swelling tears, now lying on his side, now on his back, and now upon his face. Then he would arise and wander distraught along the sea, nor did he fail to see the dawn when it appeared above the sea and strand. Then, when he had yoked his swift horses to his chariot, he would tie Hector behind the chariot to drag him, and having drawn him thrice around the tomb of the dead son of Menoetius, he would rest again in his tent and leave him to lie as he had stretched him in the dust upon his face. But Apollo kept all unseemliness from Hector's flesh, in pity for the man even in death. He covered him wholly with the golden aegis, that Achilles might not strip his flesh off when he dragged him.

So Achilles maltreated godlike Hector in his anger, but the blessed gods felt pity as they saw it and urged the far-seeing slayer of Argus to steal away the corpse. Now this pleased all the others, but not Hera nor Poseidon nor the bright-eyed Maiden, but they continued as when at first they hated holy Ilium and Priam and his people because of Alexander's fatal folly—he who slighted the other goddesses when they came to his sheepfold, and praised her who furthered his grievous lust. But when the twelfth dawn after this had come, then Phoebus Apollo said to the immortals: "You are merciless, you gods, and cruel. Did Hector then never burn to you the thighs of bulls and of unblemished goats? Now you have not dared to save him, though he be a corpse, for his wife to see and his mother and his child and his father Priam and his people, who would quickly burn him with fire and give him proper burial. But it is Achilles whom you gods wish to help, he whose heart is not just, nor is the mind placable within his breast, but he is set on cruelty like a lion that sets upon men's flocks in its great strength and proud spirit to get its meat. So Achilles has murdered pity, and he has no sense of shame, which both harms and helps men greatly. Surely someone must have lost another dearer still—an own brother or a son—but he has ceased to weep and mourn; for the fates give an enduring heart to man. But Achilles, when he has taken godlike Hector's life, ties him to his chariot and drags him around his dear companion's tomb. No honor nor glory will this bring him. Let him beware lest we grow angry with him, brave though he be, for it is senseless earth he is maltreating in his wrath."

White-armed Hera said to him in anger: "Your words would hold, lord of the silver bow, if you will give equal honor to Achilles and to Hector. Hector is mortal and sucked a woman's breast, but Achilles is the offspring of a goddess whom I myself nurtured and reared and gave as wife to a warrior, Peleus, who was very dear to the immortals' hearts. You were all present at the marriage, gods, and you, Apollo, dined among them with your lyre, you comrade of evil men, forever faithless."

Cloud-gathering Zeus answered her and said: "Hera, do not be utterly indignant at the gods, for the two men shall not have one honor. But Hector too was to the gods the dearest of those mortals who are in Ilium; so he was to me at least, since he never failed in pleasant gifts. Never did my altar lack proper food, libation, or incense, which are assigned us as our due. Let us renounce stealing bold Hector without Achilles' knowledge; it is in no way possible— for his mother is ever at his side to help him, night and day. But I would that one of the gods would call Thetis to me, that I might speak a prudent word to her, so that Achilles would accept gifts from Priam and let Hector go."

So he spoke, and storm-swift Iris started with the message, and midway between Samos and rocky Imbros leaped into the black sea, and the waters roared as they closed above her. She dropped to the depths like a lead sinker, which, on a bit of horn from a pastured ox, goes bringing death to the ravenous fish. She found Thetis in a hollow cave; around her were gathered the other sea goddesses, and she in their midst was bewailing the fate of her blameless son, who was to perish in fertile Troy, far from his native land. Swift-footed Iris stood close by and addressed her: "Arise, Thetis; Zeus of the everlasting counsels calls you." Then the silver-footed goddess Thetis answered her: "Why did that great god summon me? I am afraid to mingle with the immortals, and I have endless sorrows in my heart. Yet will I go, nor shall any word he speaks be vain."

So speaking, the goddess of goddesses took her dark veil, and no robe was any blacker. She set out, and wind-footed swift Iris led the way before her, and about them the waves of the sea withdrew. They climbed the shore and rose quickly into the sky and found the far-thundering son of Cronus, and around him sat assembled all the other blessed gods who live forever.

Thetis sat down beside Father Zeus, and Athena made room for her. Hera put a fair golden cup in her hand and gladdened her with her words, and Thetis drank and handed back the cup. Then the Father of gods and men began to speak to them: "You have come to Olympus, goddess Thetis, although grieved, bearing dreadful sorrow in your heart. I know it too myself. Yet even so I will say for what cause I called you hither. For nine days strife has raged among the immortals about Hector's corpse and Achilles the sacker of cities. They urge the clear-seeing slayer of Argus to steal the body, but I accord this honor to Achilles, seeking to keep your reverence and love hereafter. Go at once to the camp and give your son our bidding. Tell him the gods are angry with him and that I am angered above all the immortals, because in his madness of heart, he keeps Hector beside the curved ships and has not released him—in the hope that he may fear me and release Hector. Meanwhile, I shall send Iris to great-hearted Priam, bidding him to ransom his dear son—to go to the ships of the Achaeans to take Achilles gifts which shall please his heart."

So he spoke, and the silver-footed goddess Thetis did not disobey him, but went darting down from the peaks of Olympus and came to her son's tent. There she found him weeping loudly, and his dear comrades about him were preparing breakfast in busy haste; for them a great woolly sheep lay slaughtered in the tent. Achilles' queenly mother sat down very close to him and caressed him with her hand and spoke and said to him: "My child, how long will you eat your heart out with weeping and grief, thinking neither of food nor bed? It is a good thing to lie with a woman in love.

Not long will you live; already death and mighty fate are close upon you. Hear me quickly; I am Zeus' messenger to you. He says that the gods are angry with you, and he is angered above all the immortals because in your madness of heart you keep Hector beside the curved ships and have not released him. Come, give him up and accept a ransom for his corpse."

Swift-footed Achilles answered her and said: "So may there be someone to bring a ransom and take away the body, if the Olympian himself bids thus with earnest heart."

So, amid the fleet of ships, mother and son spoke winged words to one another. But the son of Cronus sent Iris to holy Ilium: "Go, swift Iris, leaving the seat of Olympus, and tell great-hearted Priam in Troy to go to the ships of the Achaeans and ransom his son, taking gifts to Achilles which please his heart, but to go alone, and let no other man among the Trojans follow. An aged herald might attend him to drive the mules and the fair-wheeled cart and bring back to the city the dead, him whom godlike Achilles slew. Let him not fear death in his heart, nor be afraid, for such an escort shall we send with him in the slayer of Argus, who will lead him until he can take him and present him to Achilles. And when he takes him into Achilles' tent, the latter shall not slay him, and shall keep all others from him, for he is neither senseless nor thoughtless nor sinful, but will very properly spare a suppliant."

So he spoke, and storm-swift Iris arose to take the message. She came to Priam and found cries and lamentations. His sons were seated around their father within the courtyard and were wetting their garb with tears, while the aged man was in their midst, closely wrapped in his mantle. Much dirt was on the old man's head and neck, which he had heaped upon himself with his own hands as he rolled on the ground. His daughters and daughters-in-law were weeping throughout the house, remembering the many brave men who lay dead, having lost their lives at the Argives' hands. The messenger of Zeus stood beside Priam and said to him, speaking softly—and a trembling seized Priam's limbs: "Take heart, Dardanian Priam, and do not fear; for not to foretell evil am I come here, but with kindly purpose. I am Zeus' messenger to you, for he, though far away, yet has great care and pity for you. The Olympian bids you ransom godlike Hector, taking gifts to Achilles which shall please his heart. But you must go alone, and let no other man among the Trojans follow. An aged herald might attend you to drive the mules and the fair-wheeled cart and bring back to the city the dead whom godlike Achilles slew. Fear not death in your heart, nor be afraid, for such an escort shall go with you in the slayer of Argus, who will lead you to Achilles. And when he takes you into Achilles' tent, the latter will not slay you and will keep all others from you, for he is neither senseless nor thoughtless nor sinful, but will very properly spare a suppliant."

So speaking, swift-footed Iris went away, whereas Priam bade his sons make ready the fair-wheeled mule cart and tie a wagon-box upon it. He himself went down into the vaulted cedar chamber with its lofty roof, which held many jewels. He called in his wife Hecuba and said: "An Olympian messenger has come to me from Zeus, bidding me go to the ships of the Achaeans and ransom my dear son and take to Achilles gifts which shall please his heart. Come, tell me how this seems to your mind. For my might and spirit urge me dreadfully to go there to the ships within the broad camp of the Achaeans."

So he spoke, and his wife wailed and answered him: "Where have your senses gone, for which you once were famous among the men of other lands and with which you rule? How can you wish to go alone to the ships of the Achaeans, before the eyes of a man who slew many of your noble sons? Surely your heart is of iron. For if he catch you and behold you with his eyes—for savage and faithless is the man—he will have no pity on you, nor show you any reverence. Let us now sit apart within our halls and weep. Mighty Fate spun thus for him the thread as he was born, when I myself gave him birth, that he should sate swift-footed dogs, far from his parents, in the presence of a mighty man, on whose very liver I wish I could fasten, to devour it. Then would there be vengeance for my son, since Achilles did not slay him as he played the coward but as he stood before the Trojans and deep-bosomed Trojan women, thinking of neither fear nor flight."

Then godlike, aged Priam said to her in turn: "Strive not to hold me back when I desire to go; be not yourself a bird of evil omen in my house; you shall not persuade me. For if some other among men on earth so ordered me, or if those did so who are prophets, readers of omens, or priests, we would call it a lie and would disregard it the more, but now, since I myself heard the goddess and looked upon her face, I am going, and her word shall not be spoken in vain. If it be my fate to die beside the ships of the bronze-clad Achaeans, I so desire; for let Achilles slay me once I have taken my son into my arms and have had my fill of weeping."

He spoke, and opened the fair lids of the boxes. Thence he took out twelve robes, exceedingly fair, and twelve single cloaks, and as many white mantles and as many shirts beside these. He weighed and took ten full talents of gold, and took two shining tripods and four caldrons. He took out an exceedingly fair cup, which Thracians had given him when he went on an embassy, a great possession. Not even this did the old man spare in his halls, but was above all eager in his heart to ransom his dear son. Then he drove all the Trojans from the porch, scolding them with harsh commands: "Away, vile scoundrels. Is there no mourning in your homes that you have come to trouble me? Or do you scorn me because Zeus has sent me woes, in the loss of my bravest son? You too shall realize this, for you will be all the easier for the Achaeans to destroy, now he is dead. But before I behold with my own eyes the city stormed and sacked, may I go down into the house of Death."

He spoke, and with his scepter drove the men away. They went forth before the old man in his haste. Then he called to his sons, rebuking Helenus and Paris, godlike Agathon, Pammon and Antiphonus and clear-voiced Polites, Deiphobus and Hippothous and famous Dius. Nine the old man called, and gave his orders: "Hurry, wicked children, a disgrace to me. Would you all had died by the swift ships in Hector's stead. I am completely luckless, since I begot the best sons within broad Troy, yet none of them, I think, is left—godlike Mestor and Troilus the chariot fighter, and Hector, who was a god among men, nor did he seem to be the son of a mortal man but of a god. Ares slew them, and all these cowards are left—the liars and the dancers, masters of choral dancing, thieves of rams and kids at home. Could you not at once harness a cart for me and put all these things upon it, that we may go our journey?"

So he spoke, and they, fearing their father's command, lifted out the fair-wheeled mule cart, fair and newly made, and tied the wagon-box to it and took down from its hook the knobbed, boxwood mule yoke, well fitted with its rings. They brought out the yoke band, with the nine-cubit yoke, and they placed them carefully upon the well-polished pole, on the first cap, and put the ring on the yoke pin and bound it thrice on both sides to the knob, and then tied the thong and bent its ends beneath. They brought from the chamber and placed on the well-polished cart a boundless ransom for the head of Hector, and they yoked the strong-hoofed mules that worked in harness, which the Mysians once gave as glorious gifts to Priam. And Priam led beneath his chariot yoke the horses which he in his old age kept himself and reared at the polished manger.

The herald and Priam were harnessing their teams within the lofty house, with clever counsels in their hearts, when Hecuba approached them with a troubled mind, bearing honey-sweet wine in a golden cup in her right hand, that they might pour a libation before going. She stood in front of the horses and called to the men and said: "Here, pour a libation to Father Zeus and pray to come back home from among the foe, since your spirit drives you to the ships against my will. Pray then to the dark-clouded son of Cronus, who dwells on Ida and looks down upon all Troy, and ask of him a bird of omen, even the swift messenger who is dearest to him of all the birds and whose might is greatest, to come upon the right, that you may see it with your eyes and, trusting in it, go to the ships of the Danaans with their swift steeds. But if far-thundering Zeus will not give you his messenger, then would I not urge or bid you to go to the Argives' ships, however eager."

Godlike Priam answered her and said: "Woman, I shall not fail to heed this, your proposal. It is well to raise one's hands to Zeus, in hope he may have pity."

So the old man spoke, and ordered the handmaid who kept their house to pour pure water on his hands, and she stood beside him, holding a basin and pitcher in her hands. When he had washed, he took a cup from his wife. Then he stood in the courtyard's center and, looking up to heaven, poured the wine, and spoke and said: "Father Zeus, who dost rule from Ida, most glorious, most great, grant that I come into Achilles' house as a friend and worthy of pity, and send a bird of omen, even the swift messenger who is dearest to thee of all the birds and whose might is greatest, to come upon the right, that I may see it with my eyes and, trusting in it, go to the ships of the Danaans of swift steeds."

So he spoke, praying, and Zeus the counselor heard him and at once sent an eagle, most perfect of winged creatures, a dark-colored hunter, which they also call dappled. As wide as is the door of a rich man's lofty chamber, well closed with bolts, so wide were its wings on either side. It appeared to them on the right, swooping through the city. When they saw it, they rejoiced, and the hearts of all were cheered within their breasts.

Hastily the old man mounted his chariot and drove forth from porch and echoing portico. Ahead was the four-wheeled cart, drawn by mules, which prudent Idaeus drove; then, behind it, were the horses which the old man, plying the whip, drove quickly through the city. All his friends followed him with many a groan, as though he went to death. Now when they had gone down through the city and had reached the plain, the others came back to Ilium, his sons and sons-in-law; but the two did not escape the notice of far-thundering Zeus as they appeared upon the plain. Seeing them, he pitied the old man, and at once said to Hermes, his dear son: "Hermes, since it is your dearest task to be a man's companion and you give ear to whom you will, go now, and so lead Priam to the hollow ships of the Achaeans that none of the Danaans may see or notice him before he reach the son of Peleus."

So he spoke, nor did the Guide, the slayer of Argus, disobey him. At once he bound upon his feet fair sandals, immortal, golden, which bear him over the sea or over the boundless earth, swift as the blasts of the wind. He took the staff, with which he charms the eyes of those men whom he will, or again wakes them from sleep. With this in hand, the mighty slayer of Argus rose in flight. At once he came to Troy and to the Hellespont, and set out in the guise of a princely lad, with the first down on his cheek, in youth's most charming hour.

When Priam and Idaeus had driven past the great tomb of Ilus, they stopped the mules and horses for a drink; indeed, the dusk had come upon the earth. The herald saw and noticed Hermes close at hand, and spoke, and said to Priam: "Look, son of Dardanus. This calls for a cool head. I see a man and I think we shall soon be slain. Come, let us flee in the chariot, or else let us clasp his knees in supplication, in the hope he may have pity."

So he spoke, and the old man was confused in mind and dreadfully afraid, and the hair upon his bent limbs stood straight up, and he was amazed. The Guide himself drew near, and took the old man's hand and spoke and asked him: "Whither, father, are you driving mules and horses through the sacred night when other mortals sleep? Have you no fear

of the Achaeans, who breathe valor, your foes and enemies
who are near by? If any of them should see you bearing so
many treasures through the swift, black night, how would
you feel then? You are not young yourself, and this man who
follows you is old for warding off a man if any start a
quarrel. But I will do you no harm, and would ward off any
other from you, for I find you are like my own dear father."

Then godlike, aged Priam answered him: "It is as you
say, dear son. Yet there is some one of the gods who held
his hand above me and sent such a wayfarer to meet me at
the lucky moment, handsome as you in stature and in face,
and you are wise of mind and blessed are they from whom
you are sprung."

Then the Guide, the slayer of Argus, said to him: "All you
have said is right, father, but come, tell me this and report it
truthfully, are you taking these many glorious treasures to
men of another land, that these at least may remain in
safety, or are you already all abandoning holy Ilium in fear?
For such a man, the bravest hero, has perished in your own
son, for he fell not short at all in battle with the Achaeans."

Then godlike, aged Priam answered him: "Who are you,
good man, and of what parents? So well have you described
to me the lot of my ill-fated son."

Then the Guide, the slayer of Argus, said to him: "Try me,
father, and ask about godlike Hector. Very often have I beheld him with my own eyes in man-ennobling battle, and
when he drove the Argives to the ships and slew them, cleav-
ing them with the sharp bronze while we stood and marveled.
For Achilles would not let us fight, being very angry with the
son of Atreus. His squire am I, and one well-made vessel
brought us. I am one of the Myrmidons, and my father is
Polyctor. He is rich, but an old man just as you are here. He
has six sons, and I am his seventh. I shook the lots with them
and drew that to come hither. Now I have come out from the
ships upon the plain, for at dawn the bright-eyed Achaeans
will begin a battle around the city, for they are tired of sitting,
and the kings of the Achaeans cannot check them in their
eagerness for war."

Then godlike, aged Priam answered him: "If you are the
squire of Peleus' son Achilles, come, tell me the whole truth,
whether my son still lies beside the ships or Achilles has hewn
him limb from limb and thrown him to the dogs."

Then the Guide, the slayer of Argus, said to him, "Father,
not yet have dogs or birds devoured him; unaltered still he

lies beside Achilles' ship among the tents. This is the twelfth dawn that he has lain there, yet his skin is not rotted nor do worms devour him, which consume men slain in war. Achilles drags him pitilessly around the tomb of his dear comrade, when the bright dawn appears, yet mars him not. You could go yourself and see him, how dewy-fresh he lies, and the blood has been washed from him, nor bears he any stain. Every wound that he was dealt has closed—for many drove their bronze into him. So, you see, the blessed gods care for your son, even in death, since he was dear to their hearts."

So he spoke, and the old man rejoiced and answered him: "My son, it is good also to give fitting gifts to the immortals, since never did my son—if ever he really lived—forget within his halls the gods who dwell upon Olympus. Therefore they have remembered him in turn, even in death's doom. But come, accept this fair goblet from me, and save me myself and escort me with the gods' help until I reach the tent of Peleus' son."

The Guide, the slayer of Argus, said to him: "You are trying me out, old man, because I am younger, but you will not persuade me, you who bid me accept your gifts without Achilles' knowledge. I fear him and honor him in my heart too much to cheat him, lest some ill befall me afterwards. But I would go as your escort even to famous Argos, properly, in a swift ship or accompanying you on foot. Nor would anyone attack you in scorn of your companion."

So speaking, the Guide hastened to mount the horse-drawn chariot, and grasped in his hands the reins and whip, and inspired great strength in the mules and horses. When they reached the walls about the ships, and the trench, the guards were just beginning to prepare their meal, and the Guide, the slayer of Argus, poured sleep upon them all and immediately opened the gates and pushed back the bolts and led in Priam and the glorious gifts upon the cart. When they reached the lofty lodge of Peleus' son—the Myrmidons had made it for their lord, cutting beams of pine, and overhead they raised a thatch of rough reeds which they had mowed in the meadows, and they made with close-set stakes around it a wide court for their lord; one bar of pine held the gate; three Achaeans pushed it home, and three of the rest opened the great bolt of the gates, but Achilles himself could push it home alone—then Hermes the Guide opened it for the old man and brought in the glorious gifts for the swift-footed son of Peleus. He leaped down from the chariot to the ground and cried: "Father, I am an immortal god who am come, Hermes; for my father sent me to be your escort. Now I shall go back, nor shall I go before the eyes of Achilles, for it would be unseemly for an immortal god thus openly to champion mortals. Do you go in and clasp the knees of Peleus' son and beseech him in the name of his father and his fair-haired mother and his child, that you may move his heart."

So speaking, Hermes departed to high Olympus. Priam leaped from the chariot to the ground and left Idaeus there, and he remained holding the horses and mules. The old man went straight into the lodge where sat Achilles, dear to Zeus. He found him within, and his companions sat apart; two only, the heroic Automedon and Alcimus, scion of Ares, waited busily upon him. Achilles had just ceased from eating and drinking, and the table still stood beside him. Great Priam came in unnoticed, and, standing close by, seized in his hands Achilles' knees and kissed the hands, dreadful and murderous, that had slain many of his sons. As when a sore folly overtakes a man who slays some fellow in his native land and comes to the country of others, to a rich man's house, and wonder falls on those who see him, so Achilles wondered as he saw the godlike Priam, and the rest wondered and looked at one another. Priam addressed him then in supplication: "Remember your father, godlike Achilles, as old as I am, on the cruel threshold of old age. It may be that the dwellers round about mistreat him evilly and there is no one to ward off war and ruin. But he, hearing of you alive, rejoices in his heart and hopes all his days to see his dear son coming back from Troy. But I am utterly forlorn, since I begot the best sons in broad Troy, yet none of them, I think, is left. Fifty I had, when the sons of the Achaeans came. Nineteen were from one womb, and the rest the women in my halls bore to me. Impetuous Ares loosed the knees of many, but he who was my very own, who defended the city and its men, him you lately slew as he fought for his native land—Hector. For his sake I now come to the ships of the Achaeans, to ransom him from you, and I bring boundless gifts. Come, Achilles, revere the gods and have pity upon me, remembering your father. I am even more to be pitied, who have borne what no other mortal upon earth has borne, to lift my hand to the lips of the man who slew my son."

So Priam spoke, and he aroused in Achilles a longing to weep for his father. He took the old man by the hand and gently put him aside. The two of them, with their memories, wept—the one lay bent before Achilles' feet, mourning loudly for man-slaying Hector, while Achilles mourned for his father, and again for Patroclus, and the sound of their weeping rose throughout the house. But when godlike Achilles had had his fill of weeping, and the longing had passed from his heart and limbs, he arose at once from his chair and drew the old man up by his hand, pitying his gray head and gray beard, and he spoke and addressed to him winged words: "Unhappy man, you have indeed borne many sorrows in your heart. How did you dare to come alone to the ships of the Achaeans, before the eyes of the man who slew so many of your noble sons? Your heart is of iron. But come, sit down upon a chair and let us allow our woes to rest in our hearts, however grieved we are. There is no gain in chilling grief. For the gods so spun the fate of wretched mortals that they should live in sorrow, whereas the gods themselves are sorrowless. For two jars stand upon Zeus' threshold, full of the gifts he gives—one of evil, one of good. He to whom Zeus, that rejoices in the thunder, gives a mixture, meets sometimes evil, sometimes good; him to whom he gives hateful gifts he makes contemptible, and an evil, ravenous hunger pursues him upon the glorious earth, and he wanders about, honored by neither gods nor mortals. So the gods gave glorious gifts to Peleus from his birth, for he surpassed all men in wealth and plenty and ruled the Myrmidons, and the gods gave him, though a mortal, a goddess for his wife. But evil, too, God sent him, that no brood of mighty children was born to him in his halls, but he begot one short-lived son. Not even now do I protect him in his age, but very far from my native land I sit in Troy, vexing you and your children. You too, old man, were once blest, so we hear. All that Lesbos above, the seat of Macar, encloses, all that Phrygia inland and the boundless Hellespont—all these peoples you surpassed, old man, they say, in wealth and sons. But from the time that they who dwell in heaven brought this woe, ever about your city are battles and slayings of men. Bear up, nor weep unceasingly in your heart, for you will accomplish nothing by grieving for your son, nor shall you bring him back to life; sooner will you endure some other woe."

Then godlike, aged Priam answered him: "Seat me not yet upon the chair, Zeus-nurtured one, while Hector lies untended among the tents, but release him quickly, that I may see him with my eyes; and do you receive the abundant ransom which we bring you. May you have joy of it and reach your native land, when once you have let me live and see the sun's light."

Swift-footed Achilles looked at him askance and said: "Anger me no more, óld man. I myself intend to release Hector to you; a messenger came to me from Zeus, my mother who bore me, the daughter of the old man of the sea. And I know you in my heart, Priam, nor does it escape me that some one of the gods led you to the swift ships of the Achaeans. For no mortal would dare come, not even though very young, into our camp, for he could not slip past the guards nor could he easily push back the fastening of our gates. Therefore, arouse my spirit in my grief no further, lest I spare not even you yourself, old man, in the tents, though you are a suppliant, and lest I transgress the commands of Zeus."

So he spoke, and the old man was afraid and obeyed his words. Peleus' son leaped from the door of the house like a lion; not alone, but two squires went with him, the hero Automedon and Alcimus, they whom Achilles honored most of his companions after the dead Patroclus. They then loosed the horses and mules from the yoke and brought in the herald, the old man's crier, and seated him in a chair, and from the well-polished wagon they took the boundless ransom for the head of Hector. But they left two cloaks and a well-woven shirt, so that Achilles might dress the body and give it to be carried home. He summoned the handmaids and bade them wash the body and anoint it, taking it away, so that Priam might not see his son, lest in his distress of heart he might not control his anger on seeing his son, and Achilles' heart be stirred to anger and he slay him and transgress the commands of Zeus. When, therefore, the handmaids had washed Hector and anointed him with oil, they threw a fair mantle and a shirt about him, and Achilles himself raised him and placed him on a bier, and his comrades with him lifted it to the well-polished cart. Then Achilles groaned and called his dear companion's name: "But not angry with me, Patroclus, if even in Hades you learn that I have released Hector to his dear father, when he gave me no unseemly ransom. To you in turn I shall give a fitting share of these things too."

So spoke godlike Achilles, and went back into the lodge and sat down by the further wall in the richly fashioned chair from which he had arisen. He said to Priam: "Your són has been released to you, father, as you asked, and he lies on a bier. When dawn appears, you shall see and take him. Now let us remember food. For even fair-haired Niobe remembered food, she whose twelve children perished in her halls, six daughters and six youthful sons. The sons Apollo slew with shafts from his silver bow, in his anger at Niobe, and Artemis the huntress slew the daughters, because Niobe matched herself with fair-cheeked Leto. She said Leto had borne two, whereas she herself bore many. Therefore they, though only two, slew all. Nine days these lay in their blood, and there was none to bury them, for Cronus' son had turned her people into stone; then, on the tenth day, the gods who dwell in heaven buried them. But Niobe remembered food when she grew tired of shedding tears. Now somewhere among the rocks on the lonely mountains in Sipylus, where, they say, are the beds of the divine nymphs who dance beside Achelous, there she, though a stone, broods on the woes sent by the gods. Come then, let us too consider food, glorious father. Then you may mourn again for your dear son, taking him to Ilium, and he shall be much wept by you."

Swift Achilles spoke, and starting up he slew a sheep of dazzling whiteness. His comrades flayed it and dressed it properly, cut it up skillfully, and spitted it and roasted it carefully and drew it all off the spits. Automedon took bread and set it on the table in fair baskets, while Achilles served the meat. Then they reached their hands out to the food which lay prepared before them. But when they had set aside desire for food and drink, Dardanian Priam wondered at Achilles, how great and fair he was, for he was like the gods to see. And Achilles wondered at Dardanian Priam, as he beheld his goodly appearance and heard his words. Then, when they had had their fill of gazing at one another, godlike, aged Priam was first to speak: "Show me now quickly to my bed, Zeusborn, that we may both take our fill of lying in soft slumber, for the lids have not closed upon my eyes since my son lost his life beneath your hands, but I have mourned continually and brooded upon my woes, rolling in the dust within my courtyard walls. Now I have tasted food and down my throat poured the shining wine; before this I had tasted nothing."

He spoke, and Achilles bade his comrades and the handmaids place bedding on the porch, and throw fair, purple blankets over it, and spread rugs over that, and pull woolly robes together over him. They left the hall with torches in their hands, and at once in haste made up two beds. Swiftfooted Achilles said to him ironically: "Lie down outside, dear father, lest any of the Achaeans' counselors come hither, they who ever sit by me holding council, as is right. If any one of them should see you in the swift, black night, he would at once report it to Agamemnon, shepherd of the people, and

there would be postponement of the surrender of the body.
Come, tell me this and report it truthfully—how many days
you wish for Hector's funeral, that I may stay here and hold
the soldiers back that long."

Then godlike, aged Priam answered him: "If you are willing
for me to finish the funeral of godlike Hector, you would do
me great favor, Achilles. For you know that we are penned up
within the city and the wood is far away to bring from the
mountains, and the Trojans are very fearful. Nine days we
would mourn him in my halls, and on the tenth we would
hold his funeral and the people would feast, and on the eleventh we would heap a barrow above him, and on the twelfth
we will give battle, if we must."

Then swift-footed, godlike Achilles said to him: "This too
shall be as you request, aged Priam. For I will stop the war as
long as you command."

So speaking, he took the old man's right arm at the wrist,
lest he be fearful in his heart. So the two of them slept there
in the porch of the house—the herald and Priam—with clever
counsels in their hearts, but Achilles slept in a corner of the
well-built lodge, and beside him slept fair-cheeked Briseis.

The others, gods and warrior charioteers, slept all the night,
overcome by soft slumber. But sleep did not seize upon
Hermes the guide as he pondered in his mind how he might
guide King Priam from the ships unnoticed by the mighty
watchers at the gates. He stood at Priam's head and addressed
him: "Old man, you have no thought of evil, that you sleep
thus among the foe, since Achilles let you be. Now you have
won your son's release and given much. But your sons you left
behind would give three times that ransom for yourself alive,
if Agamemnon, Atreus' son, shall recognize you and all the
Achaeans see you."

So he spoke, and the old man was afraid and roused the
herald. Hermes yoked the horses and mules for them and himself drove swiftly through the camp, and no one knew them.

But when they reached the ford of the fair-flowing river,
eddying Xanthus, which immortal Zeus begot, then Hermes
departed to high Olympus, and Dawn, in saffron mantle,
spread over all the earth, and they drove into the city with
wailing and lamentation, and the mules bore the body. No
other of men and fair-girdled women recognized them before
Cassandra, like to golden Aphrodite, who mounted Pergamus
and caught sight of her dear father standing in the chariot,
and of the herald, who was wont to call through the city.

And she saw him who lay upon the bier upon the mule cart, and then she shrieked and cried to the whole city: "Come and see Hector, men and women of Troy, if ever you rejoiced in him when he returned from battle, since he was a great joy to the city and to all the people."

So she spoke, and no man or woman was left there in the city, for overpowering grief came upon them all. Near the gates they met Priam as he brought the body. First Hector's dear wife and queenly mother tore their hair as they rushed upon the fair-wheeled wagon, clasping his head, and a weeping throng stood round them. And now they would have mourned Hector with flowing tears before the gates all the day long until the setting sun, had not the old man addressed the people from his chariot: "Make way for the mules to pass. Then you shall have your fill of weeping, when I have brought him home."

So he spoke, and they parted and made way for the cart. When they had brought Hector into the glorious house, they laid him on his corded bedstead and set bards beside him as leaders of the dirge, and they raised a mournful song, while the women wailed in answer. White-armed Andromache led their lament, holding in her arms the head of man-slaying Hector: "My husband, you are lost from life, though young, and have left me a widow in your halls, and your son is still a mere infant, he whom you and I, ill-fated ones, begot, nor do I think that he will come to manhood, for sooner shall this city fall from its height. For you, its watcher, have perished, you who alone protected it and saved its excellent wives and infant children, who will soon be borne off in the hollow ships, and I among them. And you, child, will either follow me where you may do unseemly tasks, striving for some implacable lord, or one of the Achaeans will seize you by the arm and hurl you from the tower to a pitiable death, in his anger because Hector slew his brother or father or son, for very many of the Achaeans at Hector's hands bit the vast earth with their teeth. Your father was not gentle in dreadful combat; wherefor the people too mourn him throughout the city. Hector, you have brought unspeakable grief and woe to your parents, but to me above all will pitiable grief be left. For in dying you did not stretch your arms out to me from your bed, nor did you speak some understanding word which I should forever have remembered as I wept by night and day."

So she spoke, weeping, and the women wailed in answer. Then Hecuba in turn led them in shrill lament: "Hector, far dearest to my heart of all my children, in life you were beloved of the gods, and they cared for you even in death's doom. For swift-footed Achilles used to sell my other sons, whomever he took, beyond the barren sea, to Samos or Imbros or misty Lemnos, but when he had taken away your life with the long-edged bronze, he dragged you many times around his comrade's tomb, Patroclus', whom you slew. But not even so could he make him rise again. Now, fresh and unmarred, you lie within my halls, like him whom Apollo of the silver bow has come upon and slain with his gentle shafts."

So she spoke, weeping, and roused unceasing wails. Then Helen was third to lead them in their lamentations: "Hector, far dearest to my heart of all my husband's brothers—for my husband is godlike Alexander, who brought me to Troy—and how I wish I had sooner perished. For this is now the twentieth year since I came thence and left my native land. But never to this day have I heard from you a harsh or spiteful word. Even if in our halls I had harsh words from any of your brothers or your fair-robed sisters or your mother—my father-in-law was ever gentle, like a father—you would check and appease them with your words, with your gentle spirit and your gentle speech. Therefore, grieved at heart, I weep both for you and for luckless me. For there is no other gentle or friendly to me in broad Troy, but all who look upon me shudder."

So she spoke, weeping, and a boundless throng groaned in reply. But aged Priam addressed the people, saying: "Bring wood now to the city, Trojans, and fear not in heart any clever ambush of the Argives. For Achilles, when he sent me hither from the black ships, assured me that he would not trouble us before the tenth dawn comes."

So he spoke, and they yoked oxen and mules to the wagons and gathered at once before the city. Nine days they brought in endless stores of wood, but when there rose the tenth dawn that brings light to mortals, then, weeping, they bore brave Hector forth and set his body on the pyre's top and cast fire upon it.

When the early born, rosy-fingered Dawn appeared, then the people gathered about the pyre of famous Hector. When they had gathered and were assembled, first they quenched all the burning with bright wine, wherever the fire's might still held. Then his brothers and comrades sadly gathered the white bones, as swelling tears rolled down their cheeks, and they took the bones and placed them in a golden chest and covered them with a soft purple cloth. This at once they laid within a hollow grave and piled many great stones above it. Quickly they raised the mound, and watchers sat about on every side, lest the well-greaved Achaeans make an attack before they finish. When they had raised the barrow, they went back, and then they gathered and feasted well on a splendid banquet in the house of Priam, the Zeus-nurtured king.

So they held the funeral of Hector, tamer of horses.

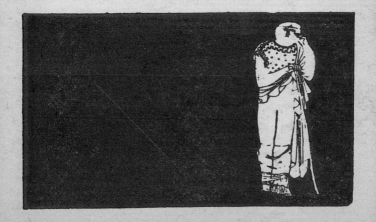

GLOSSARY OF THE MORE IMPORTANT NAMES, PLACES AND EPITHETS

This Glossary is not exhaustive. It includes the principal place names and the names and epithets of the principal gods and mortal characters as well as the names of all characters who bear the same name.

Note on the spelling of proper names. There has never been a universally accepted system for the transliteration of Greek proper names into English. Because some erroneous forms have become sanctified by tradition, it is neither possible nor desirable to attain complete consistency in any one method. We have, however, in general followed the most common system, that of the Latin writers. To this we have made two exceptions in most cases — we have kept the dipthong *ei* instead of replacing it by *i*, and we have retained the Attic *e* instead of replacing it by *a*, particularly in terminations.

Abydus — a city on the Hellespont

Acamas — (1) son of Antenor, leader of the Dardanians; (2) son of Eussorus, leader of the Thracians

Achaeans — a term used generally to refer to the Greeks

Achelous — (1) a river or river god in Aetolia; (2) a river or river god in Phrygia

Achilles — son of Peleus and Thetis, greatest of Greek warriors, hero of the *Iliad*

Actor — (1) father of Echecles; (2) son of Azeus of Orchomenus; (3) father of Menoetius; (4) son of Phorbas, putative father of Cteatus and Eurytus

Adrastus — (1) father of Aegialeia, wife of Diomedes; (2) a leader of Trojan allies from Adrasteia; (3) Trojan slain by Menelaus; (4) Trojan slain by Patroclus

Aeacus — father of Peleus, grandfather of Achilles, who is often called "son of Aeacus"

Aegae — town in Achaea loved by Poseidon

Aegaeon — epithet of the giant Briareus

Aegeus — king of Athens, father of Thesus

Aegialus — (1) region in the Peloponnesus; (2) town in Paphlagonia in Asia Minor

Aegina — island off Attica, home of Ajax and Teucer

Aeneas — son of Anchises and Aphrodite, one of the great Trojan heroes, in later legend founder of the Latin race

Aeolus — father of Sisyphus

Aesepus — (1) son of Bucolion and Abarbarea; (2) river on Mount Ida

Aesyetes — (1) father of Antenor; (2) father of Alcathous

Aethe — mare belonging to Agamemnon

Aethon — horse belonging to Hector

Agamemnon — son of Atreus, brother of Menelaus, commander of the Greek forces

Agenor — Trojan, son of Antenor

Aidoneus — another name for Hades

Ajax — (1) son of Telamon, half brother of Teucer, one of the chief Greek warriors; (2) son of Oileus, the lesser Ajax, another Greek hero

Alalcomenae — city in Boeotia favored by Athena

Alastor — (1) Lycian slain by Odysseus; (2) leader of the Pylians; (3) father of Tros

Alcestis — wife of Admetus, mother of Eumelus

Alcimedon — a leader of the Myrmidons

Alcimus — charioteer of Achilles

Alcmena — wife of Amphitryon, mother of Heracles

Alcyone — another name of Cleopatra, wife of Meleager

Alexander — another name of Paris, lover of Helen

Alpheus — a river or river god in Elis in the Peloponnesus

Althaea — wife of Oeneus, mother of Meleager

Amazons — a legendary tribe of warlike women living in Pontus in Asia Minor

Amphidamas — (1) a Greek of Cythera; (2) father of a child slain by Patroclus

Amphimachus — (1) son of Cteatus, leader of the Epeians, slain by Hector; (2) son of Nomion, leader of the Carians

Amphitryon — husband of Alcmena

Ancaeus — (1) father of Agapenor the Arcadian; (2) wrestler from Pleuron, worsted by Nestor

Anchises — father of Aeneas and Echepolus

Andromache — daughter of Eëtion, wife of Hector, mother of Astyanax

Antenor — Trojan leader, husband of Theano, father of Helicaon, Polybus, Agenor, Acamas, Iphidamas and Coön

Antilochus — son of Nestor, a Greek hero

Antiphus — (1) Greek leader of islanders; (2) son of Talaemenes, Trojan ally, leader of the Maeonians; (3) son of Priam, captured and released by Achilles, slain by Agamemnon

Antron — town in Thessaly

Aphrodite — goddess of beauty, wife of Hephaestus, mistress of Ares, favoring Trojans

Apisaon — (1) son of Phausius, Trojan slain by Eurypylus; (2) son of Hippasus, Trojan slain by Lycomedes

Apollo — god of light, music and medicine, son of Zeus and Leto, brother of Artemis, favoring the Trojans

Arcadia — mountainous region in the Peloponnesus

Areithous — (1) father of the Boeotian Menesthesus; (2) squire of the Thracian Rhigmus, slain by Achilles

Ares — god of war, son of Zeus and Hera, lover of Aphrodite, favoring the Trojans

Argives — properly, men of Argos, but used as a general name for the Greeks

Argos — (1) city in the Peloponnesus ruled by Diomedes; (2) kingdom of Agamemnon, with capitol at Mycenae in the Peloponnesus; (3) Pelasgic Argos on the river Peneius in Thessaly, ruled by Achilles

Ariadne — daughter of Minos, mistress of Theseus, wife of Bacchus

Arisbe — Trojan town

Artemis — goddess of the moon, the hunt, and of childbirth; daughter of Zeus and Leto, sister of Apollo; takes little part in war, favoring the Trojans

Ascalaphus — son of Ares, leader of the Boeotians

Ascanius — (1) leader of the Phrygian allies of Troy; (2) son of Hippotion, a Bithynian ally of Troy

Asclepius — god of medicine, son of Apollo, father of the Greek physicians Machaon and Podaleirius

Asia — a district in Lydia, hence the "Asian meadow." From it the name was extended to the continent

Asius — (1) son of Hyrtacus from Arisbe, a Trojan ally; (2) father of Adamas; (3) son of Dymas, brother of Hecuba, from Phrygia; (4) father of Phaenops from Abydus, a Trojan ally

Assaracus — son of Tros, an ancestor of Priam

Asteropaeus — son of Pelagon, leader of the Lycian allies of Troy

Astyanax — son of Hector and Andromache

Astynous — (1) Trojan slain by Diomedes (2) son of Protiaon, a Trojan

Athena — goddess of wisdom, champion of the Greeks

Athos — the celebrated mountainous promontory in northern Greece

Atreus — father of Agamemnon and Menelaus. Both the latter are called "son of Atreus"

Atrytone — epithet of Athena

Atymnius — (1) father of Mydon; (2) Trojan slain by Antilochus

Augeiae — (1) town in Laconia in the Peloponnesus; (2) town in Locris north of the Corinthian Gulf

Augeias — (1) father of Agasthenes, grandfather of Polyxenus; (2) father of Agamede

Aulis — Boeotian harbor from which the Greeks sailed for Troy

Automedon — principal charioteer of Achilles

Autonous — (1) Greek slain by Hector; (2) Trojan slain by Patroclus

Axius — river in Paeonia in Thrace

Balius — one of the horses of Achilles

Bellerophon — slayer of the Chimaera

Bias — (1) Greek from Pylos; (2) leader of the Athenians; (3) father of Laogonus and Dardanus

Boeotia — region in central Greece

Boreas — the North Wind

Borus — (1) father of the Maeonian Phaestus; (2) husband of Peleus' daughter Polydora, putative father of Menesthius

Bouprasius — place in Elis in the Peloponnesus

Briareus — a hundred-handed sea giant, also called Aegaeon

Bright-eyed — epithet of Athena

Briseis — mistress of Achilles, captured in war

Briseus — king and priest of Lyrnessus, father of Achilles' mistress Briseis

Bryseiae — town in Laconia in the Peloponnesus

Cadmeians — Thebans, descendants of Cadmus, founder of the city

Calchas — Greek prophet and seer

Callicolone — hill near Troy

Calydon — city in Aetolia north of the Corinthian Gulf

Cassandra — daughter of Priam, a prophetess fated always to be disbelieved. She was taken home captive by Agamemnon and slain with him by Clytemnestra

Castor — son of Zeus and Leda, brother of Polydeuces (Pollux) and Helen

Cebriones — bastard son of Priam, Hector's charioteer, slain by Patroclus

Centaurs — a wild Thessalian tribe, reputedly half man and half horse, famous for their battle with the Lapiths

Chimaera — mythical monster, part lion, part goat, and part serpent, slain by Bellerophon

Cheiron — the centaur who instructed Achilles. He was skilled in medicine and prophecy

Chromius — (1) son of Priam, slain by Diomedes; (2) Lycian, slain by Odysseus; (3) Trojan, slain by Teucer; (4) Trojan ally, leader of the Mysians

Chryse — harbor town in Troad with a temple of Apollo

Chryseis — daughter of Chryses, priest of Apollo, given to Agamemnon as a prize of war

Chryses — father of Chryseis, priest of Apollo

Chrysothemis — daughter of Agamemnon and Clytemnestra, sister of Iphigenia, Electra and Orestes

Cilla — Trojan town

Cleopatra — Alcyone, wife of Meleager

Clytemnestra — wife and murderess of Agamemnon, mistress of Aegistheus

Corinth — wealthy commercial city on the isthmus connecting the Peloponnesus with the mainland of Greece

Cos — island in the Icarian Sea, off southern Asia Minor

Cronus — father of Zeus, who is often called "son of Cronus" or "son of crooked-counseled Cronus"

Curetes — Aetolian tribe which besieged Calydon

Cypris — another name of Aphrodite, from the island of Cyprus, which she loved

Daedalus — legendary craftsman, architect of the Labyrinth in Crete and the first man to fly

Danaans — general term for the Greeks

Danaë — daughter of Acrisius, mother of Perseus

Dardania — city founded by Dardanus at the foot of Mount Ida

Dardanians — inhabitants of Dardania; sometimes used for Trojans

Dardanus — ancestor of Priam; the latter is called "son of Dardanus" or "Dardanian." Also ancestor of Ilus, who is similarly called

Dares — Trojan priest of Hephaestus, father of Phegeus and Idaeus. Identified by the Middle Ages with the author of a history of the Trojan War

Dark-clouded — epithet of Zeus

Dark-haired — epithet of Poseidon

Daughter of the mighty sire — epithet of Athena

Deiphobus — son of Priam, brother of Hector

Demeter — goddess of agriculture, sister of Hera, Zeus and Poseidon, mother of Persephone

Deucalion — father of Idomeneus

Diomede — woman from Lesbos, slave of Achilles

Diomedes — son of Tydeus, a Greek hero second only to Achilles in skill and valor

Dione — mother of Aphrodite

Dionysus — god of wine and revelry, son of Zeus and Semele

Diores — (1) son of Amarynceus, leader of the Epeians, slain by Trojan ally Peiros; (2) father of Automedon

Dodona — oracle of Zeus in Epirus on the western coast of Greece. Its replies were supposed to be heard in the rustling of the leaves of an ancient oak

Dodonian — epithet of Zeus, from Dodona

Dolon — Trojan spy slain by Odysseus and Diomedes

Dolopians — tribe from Thessaly

Driver of spoil — epithet of Athena

Dryas — (1) king of the Lapiths; (2) father of Lycurgus

Dymas — father of Hecuba and Asius

Earth-shaker — epithet of Poseidon

Echeclus — (1) Agenor's son, slain by Achilles; (2) Trojan slain by Patroclus; (3) husband of Polymele

Echepolus — (1) descendant of Anchises, living in Sicyon in the Peloponnesus; (2) son of Thalysius, a Trojan slain by Antilochus

Echius — (1) father of Mecisteus; (2) Lycian slain by Patroclus; (3) Lycian slain by Polites

Eëtion — (1) father of Andromache; (2) of Imbros, friend of Priam; (3) Trojan, father of Podes

Eileithyia — goddess of childbirth

Eioneus — (1) father of Rhesus; (2) Greek slain by Hector

Elis — district in western Peloponnesus

Ennomus — (1) Trojan ally, chief of the Mysians, a seer, slain by Achilles; (2) Trojan slain by Odysseus

Enops — (1) father of Satnius; (2) father of Clytomedes the Aetolian; (3) father of Thestor of Troy

Enyalius — epithet of Ares, "the warlike"

Enyo — personification of the tumult of battle

Eos — goddess of the dawn, mother of Memnon

Epeians — a Greek people in Elis in northwestern Peloponnesus

Epeius — Greek boxer and athlete

Ephialtes — a giant

Ephyra — (1) ancient name for Corinth; (2) city in northern Elis in northwestern Peloponnesus; (3) town in Thessaly

Epidaurus — Argive town in northeastern Peloponnesus

Epistrophus — (1) leader of the Halizonians, Trojan allies; (2) son of Evenus, slain by Achilles; (3) Greek, son of Iphitus, leader of the Phocians

Erebus — the lower world

Erechtheus — legendary Athenian hero

Eretria — town in Euboea

Erichthonius — son of Dardanus

Eridanus — legendary river identified as the Po

Eris — goddess of discord

Erymas — (1) Trojan slain by Idomeneus; (2) Trojan slain by Patroclus

Eteocles — son of Oedipus of Thebes, defender of the city against the Seven

Euboea — large island off the eastern coast of Attica and Boeotia

Eumelus — son of Admetus. Took part in chariot race in games at Patroclus' funeral

Eurus — the East Wind

Euryalus — son of Mecisteus, comrade of Diomedes

Eurybates — Greek herald

Eurymedon — (1) squire of Agamemnon; (2) servant of Nestor

Eurypylus — (1) son of Euaemon of Thessaly, wounded by Paris; (2) son of Poseidon, a Greek from Cos

Eurystheus — king of Mycenae who imposed labors upon Heracles

Eurytus — (1) son of Actor, father of Thalpius; (2) an Oechalian from Thessaly

Evenus — (1) son of Selepius, father of Mynes and Epistrophus; (2) father of Marpessa

Far-thundering — epithet of Zeus
Father of gods and men — epithet of Zeus

Ganymede — son of Tros, so beautiful that Zeus bore him off to be his cup bearer
Gargarus — a peak of Mount Ida
Gerenian — epithet of Nestor, from Gerenus, a town in Elis
Glaucus — (1) son of Hippolochus, leader of Lycians, ally of the Trojans; (2) father of Bellerophon
Gorgon — one of three monstrous sisters whose heads were covered with serpents instead of hair. Medusa, slain by Perseus, is the best known. Her head adorned the Aegis
Granicus — river rising on Mount Ida
Guide — epithet of Hermes from his function as guide of departed spirits to the underworld

Hades — the god of the underworld or his abode
Hapmonides — (1) father of Laerces, grandfather of Alcimedon; (2) father of Maeon, a Theban
Halizones — Pontic allies of the Trojans from northern Asia Minor
Hebe — daughter of Zeus and Hera, wife of Heracles, a kind of maidservant among the gods
Hector — son of Priam and Hecuba, husband of Andromache, father of Astyanax; the heroic leader of the Trojans
Hecuba — wife of Priam, mother of Hector
Helen — daughter of Zeus and Leda, sister of Castor and Polydeuces, wife of Menelaus, mistress of Paris
Helenus — (1) son of Priam, best of the Trojan seers; (2) Greek, slain by Hector and Ares
Helice — town in Achaea in the northern Peloponnesus, with a shrine of Poseidon. "Lord of Helice" is an epithet of Poseidon
Hellas — originally a district in Thessaly, later a name for all Greece
Hellenes — inhabitants of Hellas in Thessaly. Never in Homer a name for all Greeks
Hellespont — the narrow channel between Europe and Asia through which the Black Sea empties into the Mediterranean
Helus — (1) town in Laconia in the Peloponnesus; (2) town in Pylos in the Peloponnesus
Hephaestus — god of smiths, son of Zeus and Hera, husband of Aphrodite
Hera — sister and wife of Zeus, sister of Poseidon, queen of the gods, a supporter of the Greeks
Heracles — son of Zeus and Alcmena, performer of the famous labors, father of Tlepolemus and Thessalus
Hermes — god of commerce and travel, escort of the dead, escort of Priam to Achilles
High-throned — epithet of Zeus

Hippolochus — (1) son of Bellerophon, father of Glaucus; (2) Trojan slain by Agamemnon

Holder of the earth — epithet of Poseidon

Hyades — seven stars in Taurus whose rising marks the beginning of the rainy season

Hypereia — a spring in Pelasgian Argos in northern Greece

Hypeiron — epithet of Helios the sun god

Hypsenor — (1) Trojan slain by Eurypylus; (2) Greeek slain by Deiphobus

Iapetus — a Titan

Iardanus — (1) river in Crete; (2) river in Elis in the Peloponnesus

Iasus — (1) father of Amphion; (2) father of Dmetor; (3) Athenian slain by Aeneas

Icarian Sea — part of Mediterranean southwest of Asia Minor

Ida — mountain range near Troy

Idaeus — (1) son of Dares, a Trojan; (2) Trojan herald, charioteer of Priam

Idomeneus — leader of the Cretans, a Greek hero

Ilium — Troy

Ilus — son of Tros, father of Laomedon, an ancestor of Priam

Imbros — island off the coast of Thrace

Iris — goddess of the rainbow, messenger of the gods

Ithaca — island home of Odysseus, off western Greece

Jason — leader of the Argonauts, father of Euneus

Lacedaemon — district in the Peloponnesus of which Sparta was the capital

Laertes — father of Odysseus, the latter being often called "son of Laertes"

Lame god — epithet of Hephaestus

Lampus — (1) son of Laomedon, father of Dolops; (2) horse of Hector

Laodice — (1) daughter of Agamemnon; (2) daughter of Priam, wife of Helicaon

Laodocus — (1) Antenor's son, a Trojan; (2) Greek, comrade of Antilochus

Laomedon — father of Priam

Lapiths — a tribe in Thessaly famous for their battle with the centaurs

Lectus — promontory on the Trojan coast opposite Lesbos

Leleges — piratical tribe in southern Asia Minor

Lemnos — island west of Troad

Lesbos — island off Troad, home of Sappho and Alcaeus

Leto — mistress of Zeus, mother of Apollo and Artemis

Lord of the gleaming lightning — epithet of Zeus

Lord of lightning — epithet of Zeus

Lord of the silver bow — epithet of Apollo

Lycaon — (1) father of Pandarus; (2) son of Priam, slain by Achilles

Lycia — (1) region in the southwest corner of Asia Minor; (2) district on river Aesepus on Mount Ida

Lycurgus — (1) son of Dryas, who banished the worship of Dionysus from his country; (2) Arcadian warrior

Machaon — son of Asclepius, a Greek physician, wounded by Hector

Maeander — a river in Asia Minor famous for its winding course, hence "to meander"

Maeonia — another name for Lydia in Asia Minor

Mecisteus — (1) a Greek, son of Talaus, brother of Adrastus, father of Euryalus; (2) a Greek, companion of Antilochus, slain by Polydamas

Medon — (1) son of Oileus, stepbrother of the lesser Ajax, leader of Methonians, slain by Aeneas; (2) Lycian warrior

Meges — great-nephew of Odysseus, leader of the men of Dulichium

Meleager — son of Oeneus and Althaea, husband of Cleopatra, slayer of the Calydonian boar

Menelaus — son of Atreus, brother of Agamemnon, husband of Helen, king of Sparta

Menoetius — father of Patroclus, often called "son of Menoetius"

Meriones — son of Molus, Cretan, squire of Idomeneus

Minos — famous king of Crete, son of Zeus and Europa, father of Deucalion, Ariadne, and Phaedra, judge of the dead

Mycenae — city in Peloponnesus, home of Agamemnon

Myrmidons — people living in Phthia in Thessaly, ruled over by Achilles; hence, his followers at Troy

Mysians — (1) a tribe on the Danube; (2) their kindred living in Asia Minor, allies of the Trojans

Neleus — father of Nestor, who is often called "son of Neleus"

Neoptolemus — son of Achilles

Nereids — the fifty daughters of Nereus

Nereus — a minor sea divinity, father of Thetis and of forty-nine other daughters

Nestor — son of Neleus, king of Pylos, father of Antilochus and Thrasymedes, a wise but garrulous old warrior whose counsel was much respected by the Greeks

Niobe — daughter of Tantalus, wife of Amphion, king of Thebes. She boasted that she had six sons and six daughters whereas Leto had but one of each. Accordingly, Apollo and Artemis slew all her children. In her grief, she was changed to stone

Notus — the South Wind

Ocean or Oceanus — a Titan, personified god of the sea, husband of Tethys

Odius — (1) Trojan ally slain by Agamemnon; (2) Greek herald

Odysseus — son of Laertes and Ctimene, husband of Penelope, father of Telemachus, king of the Cephallenians, living in Ithaca. The wiliest of the Greek leaders, hero of the *Odyssey*

Oeneus — father of Tydeus, grandfather of Diomedes

Oileus — (1) king of Locris, father of the lesser Ajax and of Medon; (2) Trojan charioteer of Bienor, slain by Agamemnon

Old man of the sea — epithet of Nereus

Olympian, the — epithet of Zeus

Olympus — mountain in Thessaly, supposedly the home of the gods

Ophelestes — (1) Trojan slain by Teucer; (2) Paeonian slain by Achilles

Opheltius — (1) Greek slain by Hector; (2) Trojan slain by Euryalus

Orchomenus — (1) city in Boeotia; (2) city in Arcadia

Orestes — (1) Trojan slain by Leonteus; (2) Greek slain by Hector; (3) son of Agamemnon and Clytemnestra who avenged his mother's murder of his father by slaying her and her lover Aegistheus

Orion — mythical mighty hunter and the constellation named for him

Orsilochus — (1) variant name for Ortilochus, a Thessalian; (2) grandson of (1); (3) Trojan slain by Teucer

Otus — (1) a giant, son of Poseidon and Iphidameia; (2) Greek slain by Polydamas

Paeon — (1) physician of the gods; (2) father of Agastrophus

Paeones or Paeonians — Trojan allies from Thrace and Macedonia

Pallas — epithet of Athena

Pandarus — son of Lycaon, Trojan ally, leader of Lycians, a faithless archer slain by Diomedes

Panopeus — (1) father of Greek Epeius; (2) city in Phocis in northern Greece

Panthous — father of Euphorbus and Polydamas, Trojan counselor and priest of Apollo

Paphlagonia — region in northern Asia Minor south of the Black Sea

Paris — son of Priam, paramour of Helen, also called Alexander

Patroclus — son of Menoetius, foster brother and close friend of Achilles, slain by Hector

Pedasus — (1) town in Troad destroyed by Achilles; (2) town subject to Agamemnon; (3) Trojan slain by Euryalus; (4) horse of Achilles

Peirithous — king of the Lapiths, friend of Theseus

Peisander — (1) son of Antimachus, slain by Agamemnon; (2) Trojan slain by Menelaus; (3) a leader of the Myrmidons

Pelagon — (1) leader of the Pylians; (2) squire of Sarpedon

Pelasgian — epithet of Zeus

Pelasgians — (1) early inhabitants of Greece; (2) Trojan allies from Cyme; (3) Cretan tribe

Pelasgic — epithet of Zeus

Peleus — son of Aeacus, husband of Thetis, father of Achilles, who is often called "son of Peleus"

Pelian — from Mount Pelion, epithet of spear given by Cheiron to Peleus and by the latter to Achilles

Pelion — mountain in Thessaly

Pelops — son of Tantalus, father of Atreus and Thyestes, grandfather of Agamemnon, Menelaus and Aegistheus

Peneius — river in Thessaly

Peneleos — leader of the Boeotians

Percote — town in Troad

Pergamus — citadel of Troy

Periphas — (1) Aetolian slain by Ares; (2) Trojan herald

Periphetes — (1) Mysian slain by Teucer; (2) Mycenaean slain by Hector

Persephone — daughter of Demeter, carried off and wedded by Hades or Pluto, with whom she ruled the underworld

Perseus —son of Zeus and Danaë, slayer of the Gorgon Medusa, father of Sthenelus

Phaestus — (1) Trojan ally slain by Idomeneus; (2) city in Crete

Pherae — (1) town in Thessaly; (2) town in the Peloponnesus

Pheres — grandfather of Eumelus, who is called "son of Pheres"

Philoctetes — possessor of the bow and arrows of Heracles, he was abandoned by the Greeks on Lemnos because of a noisome wound. He had to be brought to Troy to ensure its capture

Phoebus — epithet of Apollo

Phoenix — (1) tutor and companion of Achilles; (2) father of Europa

Phorbas — (1) king of Lesbos; (2) rich Trojan, father of Ilioneus

Phrygia — region in Asia Minor on the south shore of the Hellespont

Phthia — city and region where Peleus and Achilles ruled in Thessaly

Phylacus — (1) father of Iphicles; (2) Trojan slain by Leitus

Phyleus — father of Meges

Podaleirius — son of Asclepius, brother of Machaon, Greek physician

Podarge — a storm wind, dam of the horses of Achilles

Podargus — (1) horse of Hector; (2) horse of Menelaus

Polydamas — son of Panthous, a Trojan

Polydeuces — Pollux, son of Zeus and Leda, brother of Castor and Helen

Polydorus — (1) son of Priam slain by Achilles; (2) a Greek

Polyneices — son of Oedipus and Jocasta of Thebes, brother of Eteocles and Antigone, mover of the expedition of the Seven Against Thebes

Polypoetes — son of Peirithous, one of the Lapiths

Poseidon — god of the sea, brother of Zeus and Hera, favoring the Greeks, often called the Earth-shaker

Priam — king of Troy, son of Laomedon, father of Hector, Helenus, Echemmon, Chromius, Lycaon, Paris, Polites, Gorgythion, Democoön, Deiphobus, Isus, Antiphus, Cassandra, Laodice and many others

Protesilaus — husband of Laodameia. The first Greek to step on Trojan soil and the first to fall

Pygmy — literally "thumbkin," member of a fabulous race of dwarfs

Pylaemenes — Paphlagonian ally of Trojans slain by Menelaus in Book V but appearing again in Book XIII

Pylos — city and region in western Peloponnesus ruled by Nestor

Pytho — name of Apollo's oracle on Mount Parnassus; later Delphi

Rhadamanthus — son of Zeus, brother of Minos, judge of the dead

Rhea — daughter of Uranus and Gaea, sister and wife of Cronus, mother of Zeus, Poseidon, Hades, Hera, Demeter and Hestia

Rhesus — Thracian ally of Trojans slain by Diomedes

Rhodes — island southwest of Asia Minor

Salamis — island near Athens, home of Ajax, son of Telamon. Scene of the famous battle between Greek and Persian navies

Samos — (1) island near Ithaca; (2) island off the coast of Asia Minor

Sarpedon — son of Zeus, leader of the Lycian allies of Troy, slain by Patroclus

Scaean gates — apparently the gates of Troy facing the Greek camp

Scamander — river rising on Mount Ida and flowing past Troy

Scamandrius — (1) real name of Astyanax, Hector's son; (2) Trojan slain by Menelaus

Schedius — (1) son of Iphitus, leader of the Phocians; (2) son of Perimedes, Greek slain by Hector

Selleis — (1) river in Elis in Peloponnesus; (2) river in Troad

Selli — priests of Zeus at Dodona

Semele — daughter of Cadmus, mistress of Zeus, mother of Dionysus

Sestos — town on north shore of Hellespont, opposite Abydus

Shaker of the earth — epithet of Poseidon

Sicyon — city on south shore of Corinthian Gulf

Sidon — great Phoenician city

Silver bow, thou of the — Apollo

Simoïs — (1) small stream rising on Mount Ida and flowing across the plain of Troy into the Scamander; (2) god of the above river

Slayer of Argus — epithet of Hermes

Sminthian — epithet of Apollo, said to mean "mouse-killer"

Sparta — capital of Lacedaemon, home of Menelaus

Spercheius — river in Thessaly

Stentor — Greek with a voice of tremendous strength

Sthenelus — (1) son of Capaneus, Nestor's squire; (2) son of Perseus and Andromeda

Styx — river in the underworld by which the gods swore their most sacred oaths

Talthybius — herald of Agamemnon

Tartarus — place of confinement in the underworld

Telamon — king of Salamis, son of Aeacus, brother of Peleus, father of Ajax and Teucer

Telemachus — son of Odysseus and Penelope

Tenedos — small island just off the coast of Troad

Tethys — daughter of Uranus and Gaea, wife of Oceanus

Teucer — bastard son of Telamon, brother of Ajax, best archer among the Greeks

Thamyris—a Thracian bard blinded by the Muses for his presumption in challenging them

Theano—Trojan priestess of Athena

Thebes, Thebe — (1) city in Boeotia; (2) city in Troad; (3) city in Egypt

Themis — personification of Right

Thersites — buffoon and rabble-rouser in the Greek army

Theseus — Aegeus' son, king of Athens, slayer of the Minotaur

Thessaly — region in northeastern Greece

Thestor — (1) father of Calchas; (2) father of Alcmaon; (3) son of Enops, slain by Patroclus

Thetis — daughter of Nereus, wife of Peleus, mother of Achilles

Thoas — (1) son of Andraemon, an Aetolian; (2) son of Dionysus and Ariadne; (3) Trojan slain by Menelaus

Thoön — (1) son of Phoenops, slain by Diomedes; (2) Trojan slain by Odysseus; (3) Trojan, comrade of Asius, slain by Antilochus

Thrace — region directly north of the Aegean Sea

Thrasymedes — son of Nestor

Thyestes — brother of Atreus, father of Aegistheus

Titans — children of Uranus and Gaea, confined in Tartarus by Zeus

Tlepolemus — (1) son of Heracles and Astyochia, king in Rhodes; (2) Trojan slain by Patroclus

Tritogeneia, Trito-born — epithet of Athena

Troad — region about Troy

Troilus — son of Priam and Hecuba

Trojans — people of Troy

Tros — (1) ancestor of Priam; (2) Trojan slain by Achilles

Troy — city in northwestern Asia Minor, enriched by tolls of the Hellespont; scene of the *Iliad*. It is also called *Ilium*

Tydeus — son of Oeneus, father of Diomedes, slain by Melanippus in expedition of the Seven Against Thebes. Diomedes is often called "son of Tydeus"

Typhoeus — a monster representing volcanic forces

Unerring — epithet of Apollo

Warder — epithet of Apollo
Warrior with the bull's-hide shield — epithet of Ares

Xanthus — (1) Trojan slain by Diomedes; (2) one of Achilles' horses; (3) river in Lycia in Asia Minor; (4) another name for the Trojan river Scamander; (5) one of Hector's horses

Zephyr — the West Wind
Zeus — son of Cronus, husband of Hera, king of the gods, father of gods and men, Olympian lord of lightning, far-thundering, cloud-gatherer, dark-clouded, high-thundering, rejoicing in the thunder

THE ILLUSTRATIONS

The photograph on the cover
of this Bantam book
shows details from the photograph
The Pediments of the Temple at Aegina,
Museum of Munich.

Classic Literature

☐	ANNA KARENINA *by Leo Tolstoy*	NM4609	95¢
☐	THE BROTHERS KARAMAZOV		
	by Fyodor Dostoevsky	RC4424	$1.45
☐	CANDIDE *by Voltaire*	HM4833	60¢
☐	CRIME AND PUNISHMENT		
	by Fyodor Dostoevsky	SM4274	75¢
☐	FAR FROM THE MADDING		
	CROWD *by Thomas Hardy*	NM7047	95¢
☐	FATHERS AND SONS		
	by Ivan Turgenev	HM4143	60¢
☐	FOUR SHORT NOVELS		
	by Herman Melville	NM6786	95¢
☐	GULLIVER'S TRAVELS		
	by Jonathan Swift	NM5971	95¢
☐	HEART OF DARKNESS		
	by Joseph Conrad	NM4134	95¢
☐	THE IDIOT *by Fyodor Dostoevsky*	NM4154	95¢
☐	THE ILIAD *by Homer*	SM4002	75¢
☐	LORD JIM *by Joseph Conrad*	HM7109	60¢
☐	MADAME BOVARY		
	by Gustav Flaubert	FM4297	50¢
☐	MOBY DICK *by Herman Melville*	NM5736	95¢
☐	THE OCTOPUS *by Frank Norris*	NM5648	95¢
☐	THE ODYSSEY *by Homer*	SM5303	75¢
☐	PUDD'NHEAD WILSON		
	by Mark Twain	FC4608	50¢
☐	THE RED AND THE BLACK		
	by Henri Stendhal	SC4181	75¢
☐	SISTER CARRIE *by Theodore Dreiser*	SM4220	75¢
☐	TESS OF THE D'URBERVILLES		
	by Thomas Hardy	NM5970	95¢
☐	THREE SHORT NOVELS		
	by Joseph Conrad	SM4617	75¢